The Book of

Cats

Publications International, Ltd.

Contributing Writer: Lisa Brooks

Images from Library of Congress, Shutterstock.com, Wikimedia Commons, and Wikipedia

Louis Weber, CEO
Publications International, Ltd.
8140 Lehigh Avenue
Morton Grove, IL 60053

ISBN: 978-1-64558-756-9

Manufactured in China.

8 7 6 5 4 3 2 1

Let's get social!

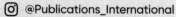 @Publications_International

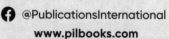 @PublicationsInternational

www.pilbooks.com

Contents

❋ ❋ ❋ ❋

Chapter 1

Mythological Cats
And Wild Cats

Cats and Miacids

What's a miacid?

✳ ✳ ✳ ✳

THE MIACID IS the great-great-granddaddy of all cats. The weasellike creatures with meat-shearing teeth first appeared 61 million years ago and lived in forests. Their retractable claws and agile bodies made them equally at home hunting on the ground or scrambling through the trees. Due to their larger brains, the miacids became expert hunters and outlived other carnivorous mammals.

Miacids eventually evolved into a variety of carnivores, including the civet cat, one of the first members of the cat family. Other evolutions include the *Pseudaelurus*, an ancestor of domestic and great cats. *Smilodon*, a type of saber-tooth cat, evolved from *Pseudaelurus* and first appeared approximately one million years ago. These cats became extinct about 11,000 years ago when the animals they preyed on died out.

Mythological Cats

Cats have captured the human imagination since ancient times. Elegant and aloof, they have played a role in the folklore of any number of cultures. They've been worshipped as gods and goddesses, treated as protectors and threats, and had mysterious powers attributed to them. It's not a surprise, as cats have lived with humans for ages; in fact, scientists today think they lived alongside humans for thousands of years before they were considered domesticated.

✳ ✳ ✳ ✳

FELINES STILL SHOW up today in our folklore—as you'll discover in this essay, feline creatures from ancient times are still pictured in our culture and media today. The figure of Sekhmet, worshipped in ancient Egypt, still pops up in popular culture. Tourists flock to the Sphinx in Egypt and admire the Merlion in Singapore. On a personal level, cat lovers can easily find jewelry and charms to represent their favorite feline with a simple search on Etsy. We may no longer worship cats, but we still honor them with our love, attention, and admiration.

So read on to find out about the role cats have played in mythology throughout the world. If you need to pause to pet or play with your own kitten who's demanded a bit of attention, you can always take a break—the sphinxes, lions, chinthes, and other mysterious figures will be there on your return, waiting patiently for your devotion.

Ammit

Ammit is one of the Egyptian goddesses of death and the underworld, with the head of a crocodile, half the torso of a lion, and half the torso of a hippopotamus. In ancient Egypt, these were the most threatening species. According to their beliefs, Ammit ate the hearts of those deemed unworthy to pass into the afterlife—remember that bodily integrity was vital to how the Egyptians viewed the afterlife, and they preserved all vital organs of those who were mummified. Anubis was the god of death and the weighing of souls, but it was Ammit who carried out the consequences, making her a kind of Grim Reaper figure within the Egyptian pantheon.

Barong

Barong is a mythical wildcat, similar to a panther, central to the mythology of Bali. The western world primarily knows Bali as the setting of "Love" in *Eat, Pray, Love*, and indeed Bali is the most popular tourist destination among the 17,000 different islands  that make up Indonesia. But its history goes back to at least 2,000 B.C., with Hindu culture taking root after that.

Barong is part of a creation myth and pantheon of Balinese deities that predates Hinduism on the island, and the people of Bali brought ideas and figures from their mythology into their burgeoning Hindu beliefs to form a special hybrid unique to Bali. Balinese people have a special ceremonial dance each year where Barong defeats evil in the form of Rangda, the queen of demons.

Bastet

Bastet is an ancient Egyptian goddess with the head of a lioness in some depictions and the head of a domestic cat in later ones. The shift from lioness to domestic cat could reflect changing values within Egyptian society, which considered domestic cats to be sacred and honored them in art. Their lion goddess Sekhmet took on more of the warlike and fierce elements of cat nature, and Bastet grew more nurturing. Cats were mummified and offered as precious gifts to Bastet. She was also the goddess of fertility, often shown with kittens. NASA has used Bastet as the name of part of a comet. There are also dozens of registered show cats named for Bastet.

Cat Sith

The Cat Sith is a mythical black cat, three feet long and with just one white spot on its chest. Like the threatening matagot, the Cat Sith could bring great luck and prosperity, but those who didn't cooperate would be harmed. There's an urban legend that involves a Cat Sith that dates back to British folklore but still appears in horror anthologies. A family man comes home in the evening and tells his wife that he's seen nine cats just like their own cat Tom, who are all black with a white mark on their chests. When he finishes describing the gathering of the cats and how he saw them talk and dance, his cat Tom speaks up and says the event means he's the new King of the Cats. Tom leaves and is never seen again.

Chinthe

The chinthe is a guardian lion, like the shisa in the Ryukyu Islands. They're found all over the Indochinese Peninsula, but may be most associated with Burma. Pairs of chinthe statues are positioned in front of Buddhist viharas, temples, and pagodas to help safeguard what's inside. Like all guardian lions, the chinthe is thought to originally come from ancient China. A special variation on the chinthe is the manussiha, which is specifically found in Burma. Chinthes guard the front entrance of a temple or pagoda, but manussiha figures are usually installed on all four corners. In Buddhism, lions are protectors. Chinthe and manussiha figures have appeared on currency in Burma.

Lamassu

The lamassu is a hybrid human-lion goddess from ancient Sumeria. Some lamassu figures are human-bull hybrids, and the telltale sign is whether a statue has hooves or paws.

The most famous images of the lamassu are public statues, but most were carved into small clay tablets for use in homes. People believed that burying an image of a lamassu near their dwellings would protect them from bad luck and evil. The Iranian secret police used the lion form of lamassu in its insignia. Fantasy literature and games have long drawn on mythologies of the world for their bestiaries, and forms of lamassu appear in games like *Warhammer*, *Dungeons & Dragons*, and many more.

Merlion

The Merlion is the mascot of the tiny but densely populated island nation of Singapore. Singapore's original name is from the Sanskrit term meaning "lion city," and lions are common in Singapore's official documentation. The merlion isn't an ancient piece of mythology—it's a modern construction based on mythical ideas that Singaporeans feel is a worthy emblem of their nation's identity as the lion city on an island. On the island, there are a handful of official, state-sanctioned merlion statues, but the most famous and photographed

merlion is the original: a 30-foot-tall, white figure of a lion with a fish tail. It occupies a major waterfront location that's one of Singapore's biggest tourist draws every year.

Narasimha

Narasimha is one avatar, or earthly form, of the Hindu god Vishnu. Like Sekhmet, Narasimha has the body of a human and the face and head of a lion. Vishnu is said to have ten avatars in a specific sequence, each one with an important task to fulfill. Later ones like Rama and Krishna are themselves major deities within Hinduism.

Narasimha's task is to defeat evildoers and those who persecute religious believers, and Narasimha is often depicted in the middle of an attack. Hindus make up a large part of the tradition of ancient spiritual yoga, and Narasimha is both a popular yoga studio name and a popular iconography in a seated yoga position. The name Narasimha literally means "man-lion."

Nekomata

The nekomata is a cat spirit, or yokai, in Japanese folklore. In Japanese, "neko" means cat, like in the name of the popular game *Neko Atsume*, or "cat collector." Nekomata and yokai in general are Shinto in origin, and each kind of yokai is a form of animism, from a cat with magical powers to a living, breathing umbrella. The legendary beginning of a nekomata is that an everyday domestic cat turns 100 years old and develops magical powers. In an anime called *Mushishi*, a sort of ghost whisperer travels in medieval Japan and puts yokai-like spirit creatures to rest. The Cheshire Cat in *Alice in Wonderland* is also surprisingly similar to a nekomata.

Sekhmet

Sekhmet is the Egyptian goddess of war and protection. Her best, most evocative epithet is "Lady of Slaughter." After Greece first contacted Egypt in ancient times, the Greeks made and circulated knockoffs of Sekhmet figures as an emblem of their cultural interest in Egypt. This time in Egyptian history is associated with metalwork, but the Smithsonian Institution has a glass figure of Sekhmet dating back to the 300s B.C. In the TV show *Sherlock*, a cat named Sekhmet is accused of murder.

Shisa

The Shisa are guardian lions found on the Ryukyu Islands of Japan. Centuries ago, Ryukyu was the center of its own kingdom, and the guardian lions seem culturally linked with Chinese guardian lions from some overlap in history. There is also a flavor of local mythology in how the shisa are designed. Traditionally, the statues come in pairs, one with its mouth open and one with its mouth closed. Locals theorize about which shisa statue is which gender, and what the open and closed mouths mean. If there was ever one true answer, it's lost to history.

Sphinx

Chimeric creatures with some feline parts are found in ruins around the world, but none is more famous than the Sphinx, specifically the Great Sphinx found in the shadow of the Great Pyramids of Giza. This iconic statue is one representative of a tradition of sphinxes in different cultures that dates back at least 12,000 years. Some examples of the sphinx are male and some are female, with personalities and surrounding myths that vary by cultural group.

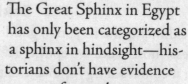

The Great Sphinx in Egypt has only been categorized as a sphinx in hindsight—historians don't have evidence of even the most basic facts about the statue, let alone what creature or legend it's intended to represent. In ancient Greece, sphinx iconography was very common and remains much more transparent: the sphinx was part of the group of proto-gods of the underworld that predated the pantheon at Mt. Olympus. Like many other part-cat mythical creatures, the sphinx was quixotic, destructive, and considered bad luck.

Tefnut

Tefnut is the ancient Egyptian lion goddess of moisture and rainfall. Worship of her was centered in the Nile River delta, perhaps the wettest place in Egypt, in a city the Greeks named Leontopolis—the city of lions. Within the pantheon, Tefnut's brother Shu was also her lover, and he was a humanoid god but the patron god of lions. In many world mythologies, primordial deities make the physical world before a second generation of deities serve the living things in that world. Shu represents the wind, and Tefnut represents moisture, making them two of the foundational elements in Egyptian mythology.

Winged Lion

Winged lions and other big and small cats date back to ancient times in many parts of the world. The most famous winged lion is the Lion of Venice, a bronze statue mounted on a high column in Venice's Piazzetta di San Marco. Parts of this winged lion date back to ancient times, but it has been restored, rebuilt, and reimagined many times over many centuries. Venice is the shared link between St. Mark, author of the Gospel of Mark, and the winged lion. A version of the winged lion holding a Bible is called the Lion of Saint Mark, and this is the official symbol of Venice. Many variations exist, like a winged lion holding a sword instead of a Bible, which is used by the Italian Navy. Outside of Italy, the winged lion is common because of its link with St. Mark. A winged lion image, with or without a sword or Bible, appears on dozens of flags and coats of arms for cities and states around the world.

Wild Cats

Any number of sports teams are named Wildcats, including the team in the High School Musical franchise. But does everyone picture the same image when they hear the term? Some might picture a bobcat, lynx, or mountain lion, others a hissing feral cat. In fact, the term is a bit imprecise.

✻ ✻ ✻ ✻

THERE ARE ACTUALLY two species called wildcats—the European and the African wildcat—and any number of other wild cat species. Wild cat species aren't just domestic cat species that have gone feral; instead, they come from populations that have stayed wild and untamed.

For many, proximity to humans brings danger. Sometimes they are hunted for their pelts or treated as nuisances if they prey on livestock. Sometimes their habitats disappear as humans develop an area. In other cases, a species may dwindle as its members interbreed with domestic cats. Yet they are found in many different countries throughout the world, and protective efforts have been made to help these wild cousins of our domestic friends.

Wild cat species are diverse in their appearance. Usually a little larger than domestic cats, they often have beautiful markings. Some seem like cuter, tinier versions of leopards or panthers, their "big cat" cousins. We examine a diverse array of these cats that are wonderfully adapted as fierce hunters to their environments.

African Wildcat

The African wildcat is the ancestor of all domesticated cats. About 12,000 years ago, people in various places on Earth started to experiment and learn how to take the fruits, vegetables, and grains they gathered and regrow them by planting seeds. As soon as these people began building settlements, they also began storing food, and that food attracts rodents. These lovely, long-legged cats just a little bigger than domestic cats showed up to eat the rodents, and it was there that the working partnership between cats and humans began.

The African wildcat looks very similar to a domestic cat, with longer, thicker limbs and the dark eyeliner and "tear lines" seen on big cats like cheetahs. Most African wildcats are a gray-brown color with a variety of darker stripes and spotty marks, making them the likely progenitor of the domestic tabby cat in particular. The domestic cat descendants of African wildcats date back so far in human history that some modern populations of "wildcats" have turned out to be domestic cat colonies that have been feral for all of recorded history. Especially in the parts of the world where African wildcats are still native, which includes not just Africa but parts of the Middle East and central Asia, feral domestic cats have bred with African wildcats to a point where

their genes can be deeply intermingled. Scientists consider this a major existential threat to the African wildcat as a separate species from the domestic cat.

Black-Footed Cat

Africa is, very broadly, divided into the Sahara Desert across the north, a wide swath of tropical rainforest and other dense vegetation across the center, and then an arid area in the south. The black-footed cat is a wild cat found in the southern tip of Africa, including Botswana, Namibia, and South Africa, in the arid region. Its Latin name, *Felis nigripes*, literally means "cat with black feet."

The black-footed cat only reaches about 5 pounds in adulthood, which makes it the second-smallest wild cat after the rusty-spotted cat and the smallest cat in all of Africa. These tiny cats have thick, sandy-colored fur marked with black and brown swirls to help them blend into the savannas and rocky crags of their home turf. Many domestic cat breeds don't reach maturity until 2 or 3 years old or as late as 4 or 5, but black-footed cat kittens reach maturity in just under a year. Kittens live with their mothers for up to 6 months. It may seem counterintuitive for an animal in a dry, hot climate to have thick fur, but the black-footed cat sleeps all day and is active at night when it's cooler or even cold. They're known to seek out other animals' burrows to sleep in and like to be covered and insulated to help keep out the heat.

Caracal

Caracals are larger wild cats that live all over Africa and into the Middle East. These cats are solid light brown except for a slightly lighter undercarriage and dramatic black markings on their faces and ears. Caracals don't like crowded forest terrain and prefer open areas. They come out to hunt at night and are notoriously difficult to photograph. Most footage of caracals in the wild is from camera traps set up in their favorite locations.

Caracals and servals occupy much of the same habitat, but they pose little threat to each other—the serval is more likely to be hunted by another large mammal than by a caracal. They're also dramatically different in appearance in almost every way other than their similar overall size and weight. The two species are compatible enough to breed, though this seems to only happen in captivity. Serval-caracal hybrids are valued as exotic pets, despite the danger and moral quagmire of keeping a wild animal as a pet.

Many countries outlaw the hunting of caracals, but they're legally considered nuisance animals in some places because they eat livestock. Even where hunting is illegal, farmers may still take the law into their own hands. Overall, the population of caracals is robust and healthy, without danger of extinction in the near future.

Clouded Leopard

The term "clouded leopard" includes two species, the mainland and the Sunda clouded leopards. There are just 10,000 mainland clouded leopards spread across most of southern Asia, which qualifies it as endangered. There are fewer than 10,000 Sunda spotted leopards that live on two large islands that are part of Malaysia and Indonesia. Both species have an all-over pattern of large outlined shapes that gave them their name. They were considered one species with regional variations until the Sunda clouded leopard was separated in 2006. The mainland clouded leopard is the official animal of a state in India called Meghalaya, coincidentally a name meaning "land of clouds." Meghalaya is in the far northeast of India, with overall heavy forest and the most annual rainfall of anywhere in India. The state set aside part of a wildlife sanctuary to dedicate as Clouded Leopard National Park in 2007.

Clouded leopards are rarely observed without camera traps. Both clouded leopard species grow to up to 55 pounds, with heavy bodies and long, thick tails. Their large size, body shape, and large, long faces make them look more like regular leopards than like other medium cats. In turn, leopards are the smallest of the "big cats," and the clouded leopards are thought to be a genetic link between the groups.

European Wildcat

The European wildcat is a shaggy, brown-gray cat that's found across Europe, from Scotland to the south of Spain and all the way east to Caucasus. Local populations in different places have totally different diets, and can even look fairly different, depending on how much the group has interbred with local feral and domestic cats. This is one of the major threats to the rare European wildcat, in fact. The species is protected, but misunderstandings have led to falling numbers. Intermingling with local domestic cats has reduced the population of European wildcats, and because they look so similar to domestic cats to begin with, some are mistaken for feral cats and hunted as a nuisance. They've been hunted to extinction in

England, although they're still found in Scotland.

European wildcats grow longer coats in the winter and shed them for summer, a trait which some domestic cat breeds share. Examples of European wildcats have been found on islands in the Mediterranean Sea, but experts believe these were brought over, not endemic. The cartoon character Sylvester the Cat was named for the Latin name for the European wildcat, *Felis silvestris*, which means "cat of the forest."

Fishing Cat

The fishing cat is the official animal of the Indian state of West Bengal. As its name suggests, it lives along waterfront regions and catches fish as its primary prey. Because of this specialized behavior, there are small pockets of fishing cats found in a huge range along the edges of the Indian Ocean. Adult fishing cats live alone and go fishing or hunting at night—in addition to almost anything that lives in water, the fishing cat will hunt and eat almost anything on land, too, including birds, wild pigs, dogs, snakes, and even carrion.

When fishing, they dive into the water and swim after their prey, which includes fish as well as crustaceans, water snakes, frogs, ducks, mollusks, and snails.

The most interesting part is that the fishing cat doesn't seem to have any special adaptations to help it with fishing or swimming. Its teeth are normal or even small among the wild cats, not large enough to easily grab onto wriggling water creatures. Its fur isn't water resistant like that of a Chartreux domestic cat. Evolutionarily speaking, the fishing cat just seems to be a wild cat that decided to fish, and it's successful despite having no particular advantages. The fishing cat is considered vulnerable and its population is falling due to destruction of wetlands.

Flat-Headed Cat

The flat-headed cat is an unusual, tiny wild cat found in parts of Malaysia and Indonesia. It weighs about 5 pounds and has very large eyes like the rusty-spotted cat. With a compact body and short, delicate limbs, the flat-headed cat looks little like other cats and resembles a mongoose. This cat lives in wetlands, where it preys mostly on fish.

The flat-headed cat is in the same family as the fishing cat, but the flat-headed cat has adaptations that the fishing cat doesn't. It has sharper, longer front teeth to better catch slippery water creatures, and its paws are webbed to help it swim faster. Its specializations make the flat-headed cat a better fisherman, and perhaps as a result, its diet is almost all fish. The fishing cat is "opportunistic," meaning it eats almost anything it can find or catch. The flat-headed cat might be less successful at catching land creatures even if it wanted to.

The major industry in the flat-headed cat's habitat range is palm oil, and huge oil-palm farms have continued to eliminate its habitat. As a result, flat-headed cats are listed as endangered, with fewer than 2,500 thought to live in the entire habitat range. Hunting flat-headed cats is now illegal across most of this range.

Geoffroy's Cat

Geoffroy's cat is a small spotted cat found mostly in Argentina. It's only about the size of a domestic cat, with small features and a small frame. Most Geoffroy's cats have overall light brown fur with a pattern of black spots all over, with variation in size and intensity of spots in different populations, and some solid black Geoffroy's cats. These cats are abundant enough that they're not considered threatened to any extent, but they haven't been studied as much as some other wild cats.

In the past, Geoffroy's cats were hunted in extreme numbers each year—more cats killed per year than the entire populations of some other species. As the fur industry declined and commercial trade died out, the Geoffroy's cat rebounded and is thriving today. Some are still killed by retaliating farmers, but Geoffroy's cats will eat anything they can catch or even find already dead, making it less likely than some wild cats to prey on livestock. Despite its small size, the Geoffroy's cat is the apex predator over much of its habitat. This cat is cute and small, with features like a domestic cat, but it's still a fierce adversary and hunter. Geoffroy's cat is versatile, living in many kinds of biomes without an issue.

Jungle Cat

The jungle cat is an angular, leggy wild cat found all along the southern portion of Asia. It's warm, sandy brown with very few brown markings on its long body and short, blunt tail. And it grows to be quite large, up to 30 or more pounds, resulting in more shared traits with big cats than with some other small wild cats. The jungle cat meows both lower and louder than a domestic cat more quietly than a big cat. It eats a steady diet of small prey.

Some regional groups of European wild-cats will take down goats, and the much larger jungle cat will sometimes hunt gazelles. But the jungle cat primarily sticks with whatever small animals it can find, from fish to birds to rodents, which make up the largest portion  by far. Though generally carnivorous, these unusual cats also eat plants. The jungle cat is solitary by nature and tends to hunt during the day, making it especially vulnerable to hunters.

Overall, the jungle cat is in the "Least Concern" category of global conservation, meaning it is not considered at risk of extinction. But some individual countries within the jungle cat's wide swath of territory have listed it as critically endangered within their borders.

Leopard Cat

The leopard cat is a small, brilliantly marked wild cat that lives through southeast and east Asia, from small portions of India and Bangladesh, through much of China, the Indochinese and Malay Peninsulas, and far into the Koreas and even Japan.

Overall, the leopard cat is not considered endangered, but in a few of the countries where it lives, individual governments have enacted laws to protect it. The leopard cat lives in such differ-ent habitats across such a huge swath of the globe that there are many color variations.

All leopard cats have some overall pattern of spots or spotty marks on a solid-colored background, but they vary from discrete, fully formed rosettes (like a proper leopard) to streaky spots that cover just part of the body like the face, legs, and tail (like fellow small wildcats). The Bengal domestic cat breed began as a hybrid between a leopard cat and a domestic cat, which was then fine-tuned to have a sleeker, silkier coat and more pronounced rosettes than most leopard cats. Northern leopard cat subgroups are shaggier and heavier to protect them from the cold. In China, leopard cats are thought to have been the first domesticated cats about 5,000 years ago, until they were supplanted by established domesticated cats that came from the Middle East.

Ocelot

The ocelot is one of the only small wild cats native to the Americas. Technically the ocelot isn't a small wild cat—it's a medium one. Adults range up to about 35 pounds and can have bodies up to 3 feet long, with another foot and a half of tail. Ocelots live up to 20 years in captivity, and the longer lifespan overall means baby ocelots stay with their mothers until they're up to 2 years old.

Ocelots have brightly patterned coats, with a base color ranging from an orangey tan to nearly white on their undersides. The overlay of spots, stripes, and rosettes is black and darker brown. Their striking fur has made ocelots a target for hunters and fur traders for thousands of years. Like the serval, the ocelot has dramatic white markings on the backs of its ears. They spend most of their time alone and avoid fellow ocelots, so like many other species, they're primarily observed using camera traps.

Though the ocelot's habitat ranges from Brazil and Argentina all the way north to Mexico and Texas, they're heavily concentrated in Brazil but endangered in many of the other countries in their habitat. Rapid deforestation in Brazil has cost the ocelot a lot of its habitat, and many are killed by cars.

Pallas's Cat

The Pallas's cat is one of the most unusual-looking wild cats. It's about the size of a domestic cat, but has the round pupils associated with big cats rather than the vertical slit pupils seen in domestic cats. Pallas's cats weigh just 10 pounds but look far larger because of their very shaggy, sandy brown coats, with wild long guard hairs that stand out even further. Their coats

are often made of many colors, with bands of ticking on individual hairs. The Pallas's cat's ears are also small and quite close to its skull. Together with its shaggy jowls and long, droopy whiskers, these features give the Pallas's cat a lovable, Muppet-like face.

Pallas's cats live in mountainous areas across Asia, comfortably living in elevations up to 16,000 feet. Not much is known about these cats. They live in one of the world's remotest areas and are often only observed because of camera trap technology. Indigenous civilizations within the Pallas's cat's habitat have valued it for its fur, and despite the fact that the species is nearing endangered status, indigenous groups are still allowed to hunt Pallas's cats for personal use. Experts believe this status is exploited to some extent, because Pallas's cat pelts are in demand outside of its direct habitat. Live animals are also desired as exotic pets.

Rusty-Spotted Cat

The rusty-spotted cat is the smallest wild cat in the world, found only in India. As its name suggests, the rusty-spotted cat is an overall rusty brown color with tawny all-over spots. At just 4 pounds, it's smaller than any standard domestic cat, let alone the wild species. Overall, the proportions of the rusty-spotted cat are very like a small domestic cat, with a compact body, short legs, and a short nose.

Relatively little is known about this tiny cat. Limited observation suggests it eats mostly rodents, which is consistent with other small wild cats. The rusty-spotted cat is approaching endangered status, but it's fully protected from hunting in India. The major threat to this species is the march of time in India, where rapid development and adoption of technology mean that the rusty-spotted cat's habitat is cleared to make way for farms. India's world-leading efforts toward sustainability include huge "solar parks" in the country's interior as well. With camera-trap technology, hopefully scientists will be able to study and learn more about rusty-spotted cats. It can be difficult to know a species is threatened if scientists aren't sure where they live to begin with, and before camera traps, most knowledge of the rusty-spotted cat was anecdotal. Firsthand sightings are important, but that's not enough information.

Sand Cat

The black-footed cat lives in very dry regions, but the sand cat is the only desert-dwelling wild cat. Its habitat stretches from Morocco, across Saharan African, and into the Middle East, with sightings as far northeast as Kazakhstan. Sand cats grow to be about 6 pounds, standing 10–12 inches high at the shoulder and with a body about 1.5 feet long. For desert creatures, being very small can be a huge advantage. Small, compact animals can require and lose less moisture. Many desert animals spend the long, hot days burrowing underground or beneath the shelter of rocks and plants, and a smaller animal can more easily find a safe, cool spot. The sand cat's relatively small paws

have fluffy tufts of hair that cover their undersides, letting the cats safely run around on the hot sand. Cats who live in snowy climates have developed fluffy paws for their opposite problem with cold!

Like many other wild cats, the sand cat has a large enough population that it isn't in danger of extinction, but extreme weather caused by climate change will make their habitats much harder to live in.

Serval

The serval is a larger wild cat, weighing up to 40 pounds and ranging up to 2 feet high at the shoulder. Because they're so large, they take longer to reach maturity and also have longer gestation than many other wild cats. Servals live in almost the entire center of Africa between the Sahara Desert in the north and the arid territory of the black-footed cat in the south. Like a house on stilts, the serval has long legs that help protect it from watery conditions below. Its native and preferred habitat is in watery areas like swamps, but the serval doesn't usually eat fish. Instead, it preys mostly on rodents, with rare larger prey like antelopes.

Servals have small heads for the size of their bodies. This exaggerates their large ears, too, which are close together, rounded, and shaped like deep cups for funneling in sounds. Servals have unusual white bands across the backs of their ears. A few species of wild cats have eyespots on the backs of their ears, which are thought to keep predators away. Servals may just have particularly dramatic eyespots, but they also use these ear bands as a show of dominance in order to scare competition out of their territory. They prefer to keep to themselves, though, and they lead solitary lives.

Big Cat Facts

Who or what are the "big cats"?

✳   ✳   ✳   ✳

THE BIG CATS are the cats of legend—felines whose roars may send a shiver down our spine. They are the lions, tigers, leopards, and jaguars.

Where Do Big Cats Roam?

Cheetah, Lion—Africa

Jaguar—Central and South America

Puma—North and South America

Leopard, Tiger—Asia

Big Cats by Weight (Average Weight of Males)

Tiger (350–640 pounds)

Lion (370–500 pounds)

Jaguar (220–350 pounds)

Cougar (77–220 pounds)

Leopard (110–200 pounds)

Snow Leopard (60–120 pounds)

Cheetah (75–119 pounds)

All big cats are spotted, at least for part of their lives—even the tiger, whose stripes may be considered "elongated spots."

The puma is also known as a cougar, mountain lion, panther, catamount, or painted cat.

The record numbers of people killed by single cats are as follows: 84 by a lion, 400 by a leopard, and 436 by a tiger.

The cheetah is the fastest land mammal, with a top speed of 70 miles per hour.

Only the lion, tiger, jaguar, and leopard can roar.

Catcalls

Like bears, cougars also need their space and are starting to show up in areas once thought too civilized for them.

✳ ✳ ✳ ✳

RESIDENTS NEAR MILTON, in Rock County, Wisconsin, began reporting cougar sightings and tracks in January 2008. Over the next several months, other witnesses spied a cougar farther east, in Walworth County.

In April, to the surprise of zoologists everywhere, police sharpshooters shot a cougar in the Roscoe Village neighborhood of Chicago. DNA tests comparing the carcass with blood found in southern Wisconsin confirmed it was the same animal.

Other brushes with cougars include sightings in the Springdale Estates area of Pewaukee in 2004 and numerous other reports that have been made to the state's wildlife officials since 1985.

But not all reports are genuine. So many people have created fake cougar sighting reports that Wisconsin's Department of

Natural Resources devoted a web page to the hoaxes, some of which made the rounds on the Internet before they were detected. A popular chain e-mail in 2008 showed a man holding a large, dead cougar, claiming the man shot the big cat north of Antigo, in Pelican Lake. In truth, the photo was from a wildlife magazine and the dead cougar was actually downed in the state of Washington.

A Wood County taxidermist who was hired to mount a cougar that died in a game farm inspired another round of tall tales. When he stopped at a tavern with the cat carcass in his vehicle in March 2008, a number of bar patrons saw the dead cougar, and soon, people were saying they had seen it doing everything from eating a dead horse to attacking pets.

Tips for Avoiding a Mountain Lion Attack

Mountain lions, also known as cougars, pumas, and panthers, are the largest cats in North America and live in a vast area from the Yukon Territory in Canada to the Pacific Coast, the Rocky Mountains, and even Florida. Mountain lions are more plentiful than most people realize, and, though they generally avoid people, attacks do occur.

❋   ❋   ❋   ❋

❋ Hike in groups. Mountain lions avoid crowds and noise, and the more people on the lookout, the better. If there are children in the group, make sure they are supervised.

❋ Be aware of your surroundings, paying particular attention to what's behind and above you in trees and on rocks and cliffs.

❋ Don't back the animal into a corner—give it a way out. It would much rather run off and survive to hunt again.

* If you encounter a mountain lion, stand still rather than try to run away. Running may cause the animal to chase you, and it's much faster than you are. Stand still while facing the mountain lion, but avoid looking it in the eye, which it takes as a sign of aggression. Watch its feet instead.

* Do things that make you appear larger and bigger than the cat, such as raising your arms over your head or holding up a jacket, a backpack, or even your mountain bike.

* Make loud noises. Growling can make you sound like something the cat would prefer not to mess with.

* Don't crouch down or bend. This makes you appear smaller and, therefore, an easy target. Don't move a lot but don't play dead. To a mountain lion, a perfectly still human looks like an entrée.

* Remain calm and don't act afraid. Like many animals, mountain lions can detect fear.

Chapter 2

All About Cat Breeds

Match Your Cat to Your Lifestyle

*Before you actually get a cat, figure out what kind of cat you
want: kitten or grown-up cat; longhair or shorthair; purebred or
alley cat; male or female; tabby, patched, or solid-color.*

※ ※ ※ ※

IF YOU'VE GOT your heart set on a particular size, age, sex,
breed, or look of cat, do a little extra research before you set
out to find one. You might be surprised to find that the look
you love doesn't fit well with your lifestyle. For example, if you
like a quiet home, a Siamese may not be the cat for you: They're
notorious "talkers." Likewise, a Persian is gorgeous to look at,
but unless you're committed to do almost daily grooming (or
to pay a professional to do it every week or so), a nice shorthair
cat might be a better idea. Do you travel a lot? Then you need
a more mature cat—at least eight months old or more. Two
cats are better still so they can keep each other company while
you're away.

Cat or Kitten?

Everybody loves kittens. They're cute, funny, and cuddly—
there's no doubt about it. But don't make the mistake that
they're "babies." By the time a kitten is ready to be away from
his mother and live in your home, he can walk, run, jump, and
climb like the feline equivalent of a ten-year-old child. What's
more, if you get a kitten today, in just a few short months you'll

have a full-grown cat—a cat who will live an average of 12 to 15 years.

If you have the time, environment, and energy to raise a kitten, by all means do it—it's a wonderful experience. Just remember that kittens are high-maintenance. They demand a lot of attention. They need routine veterinary care consisting of booster shots, worming, and spaying or neutering. Most kittens start off affectionate and passive, but they need some socialization and training to stay that way; and even still, you won't know what their adult personality will be like until they grow up.

Finally, very young children and very young kittens usually don't mix well. It's nice to think that a toddler and a ten-week-old kitten can "grow up together," but it really doesn't happen that way. In six months, that little ball of fur your child could carry around will have grown into ten-pounds-plus of adult cat, and your three-year-old will be . . . three and a half years old!

Finding the Right Cat

"Nobody really owns a cat," a country man once said. "You just make a deal with 'em. You agree to open your home and heart, and he agrees to let you have him sleep in your favorite chair and get fiirst dibs on that big old trout you caught early this fine morning."

Well, it's easier to humor someone when they says things like that, so let's just say for the sake of argument (or to avoid one) that he's right. Maybe you can't really own a cat, but the real question is, what's the best way to go about getting one? There's certainly no danger of a cat shortage—there are plenty of cats to go around and then some. In most parts of the country, you could just open your front door at sunup, and a cat would probably walk in before you finished breakfast. Heck, there are some city neighborhoods where you can't spit without hitting a stray cat. Not that either one of these activities is recommended, mind you.

Getting a cat isn't like getting a lawn mower or a hair dryer; they don't come with guarantees. Each one is going to be different, which means unique joys and problems come with every cat. Still, sources for cats should help you make a decision. Although the source can't promise the cat will never get sick, they can take steps to give the cat the best possible chance of staying well. Sources for finding the right cat for you include:

Friends and neighbors. The odds are somebody you know has a cat or kittens in need of a home. Many times, taking a cat from a neighbor or friend works out best for everyone, especially if it's a kitten from your neighbor's cat's litter or an allergic friend's family pet. Your personal relationship with this source usually means you'll get the straight story on this particular cat, too. A couple of warnings about getting your cat from a friend or neighbor, though: Don't expect the cat to have the extensive veterinary care that a cat from a shelter or breeder has, and be careful about mixing business and friendship.

Animal shelters. Millions of homeless cats end up being euthanized in animal shelters every year. Adopting from a shelter saves a life, makes room for another cat, and is an inexpensive way to obtain a pet with low-cost shots and neutering. Don't expect to find purebreds, and be prepared to go through applications and interviews, some of which might seem a little too personal and pushy. Don't take it personally—they have good reasons for it. Also, be sure to check the facilities and the condition of the adoptable pets. Since the animals live in close company, illness, worms, and fleas can be a problem.

Breeders. If you want a purebred cat, this is the way to go. Good breeders are extremely knowledgeable about cats in general and their breed in particular and are careful about who they sell their cats to. A reputable breeder is interested in maintaining a high-quality animal, keeps careful records, and usually only produces one or two litters per breeding female per year.

Strays. Sometimes you don't even have to worry about finding the right cat, the right cat finds you. Many folks swear that these are the best cats to have. Anyone who has a former alley cat looking over their shoulder as they read this is probably inclined to agree, only because there's a former alley cat looking over their shoulder at this very moment. There's no adoption interviews or fees when you take in a stray, and more than likely you're saving a life. On the other hand, you'll have to cover the cost of shots, worming, neutering, and the like. Many strays have other health problems that may not show up right away and can get expensive to treat. Sometimes local humane societies will help out with initial vet care, or an area animal hospital may offer reduced rates for treating a foundling cat, but don't count on it.

Longhair vs. Shorthair Cats

The magnificent coat of a champion Persian is truly a work of art. But you'd better believe that it took hours of regular grooming to get it—and keep it—that way. It's common sense that the more hair there is to take care of, the more work that goes into it. The fluffier the cat's hair, the more likely it is to form mats, too. These thick tangles of hair can be painful and even tear a cat's skin if the mats get bad enough. Mats get embarrassing for a cat, too, since the only way to get rid of really bad ones is to shave them off. Nothing looks more uncomfortable than a cat who has been shaved.

It's not that shorthair cats don't need regular grooming or never get mats—they do. It's just that their shorter, coarser outer coat requires lower maintenance than a long, silky coat. A shorthair cat who's diligent about her own grooming routine can do a lot to make up for an owner who's a little lazy with the brush and comb. But regular grooming is still a must for both longhair and shorthair cats.

Cats use their tongue and teeth for grooming. Everytime Tabby goes into her contortionist bathing routine, she's swallowing hair. The more hair she has (and the more grooming she does), the more hair she swallows. Hair doesn't digest and can clump up in a cat's stomach and intestines to form hairballs. The least dangerous, but still rather unpleasant, side effect of hairballs is your cat coughing them up—quite often at times or in places you'd much rather she didn't. On a more serious note, a lot of swallowed hair can actually block your cat's intestines, calling for an operation to save her life. The bottom line is to invest a few dollars in a brush and comb—and use them.

Should I Have an Indoor Cat?

Perhaps nothing is as pitiful as the wail of a cat who wants to be on the other side of a door. When it's the front door, many of us take that to mean that our cats won't be truly happy unless they go outdoors. But, then again, most cats make the same kind of racket when they want to come inside (or, for that matter, when they want to get through any door). Do cats really want to go outside? Do they need to? And even if the answer to both questions is "yes," is it really in their best interest?

✳ ✳ ✳ ✳

S AFE AT HOME vs. the great outdoors. "It's more natural for my cat to be outside," argue many cat owners. "Dogs go out every day—why not cats?"

Let's talk about the second point first. The main reason dogs are walked is elimination, followed closely by exercise. Only the smallest dogs can get enough running indoors. Dogs are pack hunters, which means they work cooperatively to run their quarry to exhaustion. That can take all day, which means dogs have a natural instinct to run . . . and run . . . and run. You need a lot of open space for that kind of work. Cats, on the other hand, are "ambush hunters." They rely on relatively short bursts of very fast running. A hallway of any decent length provides plenty of room for that. And since cats instinctively bury wastes (which is why they will use a litter box), there is no pressing reason to take a cat outdoors.

Of course, fresh air and sunshine are good for anyone—human or cat. But is the outdoor life really more "natural" for your cat? Sure, his wild ancestors lived outdoors. But that was a few thousand years and several hundred generations ago. To top it all off, those ancestors lived in the arid regions of the Mideast—a far cry from the climate and surroundings of the United States today. Once cats were domesticated, they stopped being completely "natural;" once they were uprooted from their original habitat, they had to do their best to adapt instincts honed over tens of thousands of years of living in Middle Eastern deserts to their new circumstances. Some of those circumstances—the bitter cold of a Midwestern winter, dogs and wild animals that will turn them from hunter to hunted, and speeding cars and trucks, just to name a few—they can never really adapt to.

The not-so-great outdoors. What's waiting for your cat just outside your front door? Yes, there are trees and grass and all the sights, sounds, smells, and joys of nature—good things for all of us to savor. But there are also vicious animals, cruel people, traffic, disease, and animal-control officers (who may be within their legal right to grab and impound your cat, if he steps off your property). The only reliable way to keep your cat safe from all of these deadly hazards is to keep him indoors.

Truth be told, country cats aren't necessarily safer outdoors than city cats. Sure, there's a lot more chance of being hit by a car or mauled by a stray dog in the city. But out in the country, we've got some predators that run bigger, quicker, and savvier than a feral city dog. We've also got less light on the roads, making strays harder to see—and easier to hit—and usually more kinds of disease-bearing insects, such as ticks.

A whole host of serious and fatal feline diseases need contact with infected cats—or areas where infected cats hang out a lot—to spread. Feline immunodeficiency virus (FIV), which causes a breakdown in the cat's disease-fighting immune system, is mostly passed by bites from infected cats. And feline leukemia virus (FeLV) generally requires prolonged close contact with an infected cat, such as sharing litter boxes or food and water bowls, or mutual grooming. Time and again, the risks for disease are minor or negligible for indoor cats, significantly higher for outdoor or indoor/outdoor cats. Cat owners—especially those with young children—should be particularly aware that outdoor cats are more likely to pick up diseases and parasites that can affect humans, from minor annoyances like fleas to more serious illnesses like Lyme tick disease to extremely dangerous conditions like rabies.

Going outside safely. Just because it's safest for your cat to live indoors and not roam free doesn't mean he can never see the light of day except through the window. A leash and harness (not a collar) is a fairly safe way for both you and your cat to get some fresh air and sunshine. Walking on a leash is an acquired taste that some cats will never acquire, though. Regular experience from kittenhood helps, and some leash-trained cats will even request a walk. Of course, a cat on a leash is still at risk

for picking up fleas—and for encounters with unleashed cats and dogs in the neighborhood.

Building a cat run is actually not as hard as it sounds. Runs must be enclosed on all sides (including the top) and solidly anchored and constructed. Screens should be the heaviest grade of outdoor mesh, and walls should extend a few inches below the ground to prevent cats from digging their way out— or other animals from digging their way in. If the run isn't built attached to your home with a pet door or other door leading indoors, be sure it includes some sort of waterproof shelter where your cat can retreat in the case of inclement weather.

It's especially important for a run or other outdoor enclosure to have a roof. Cats are terrific climbers and leapers, and even an eight- to ten-foot wall may not hold them, especially if there are screens to hook onto. The roof and walls of the run provide another kind of security. They keep other things out. Openings in the roof or walls let unfriendly or dangerous animals, people, and things into an area that your cat may not be able to escape.

Free-roaming cats get into loud, late-night spats with other cats, chew or dig up neighbors' plants, kill local birds (but also may help control the local rodent population), and bury their wastes in other people's gardens. While some folks—and some cat owners—see these as minor annoyances, many other folks see them as much more serious problems. If your cat gets into a fight, it may do more than wake the neighbors because of the yowling and screaming. The superficial scratches you may see on his face or back aren't so bad. But he may also have bite wounds that close up quickly, sealing in dirt and germs and creating a painful abscess several days later. Bites during fights also seem to be the main way to spread feline immunodeficiency virus. Unaltered cats that roam free also contribute to pet overpopulation, a problem that fills animal shelters to capacity and beyond, resulting in millions of dogs and cats being "put to sleep" every year.

Domestic Cats

All domestic cats trace their ancestry back to the African wildcat, which researchers believe domesticated itself after the wildcats realized how many rodents they could find inside and around the food storehouses of humans. Indeed, archaeologists have found ancient human remains with ancient pet cat remains close at hand, showing how humans cared for cats even very long ago. Where domestic dogs were selectively bred for work tasks like herding or hunting, domestic cats were bred for beauty and sometimes for personality.

✳   ✳   ✳   ✳

FROM THE TINY Munchkin cat to the huge Maine Coon cat, there's a size and shape of domestic cat for everyone. Some breeds are naturally occurring, meaning populations of domestic cats developed traits from breeding among their local group—this is especially true for cats on small islands or in other isolated locations, like the bobtailed Manx cat. Other breeds have been developed through human intervention, both before and after the advent of genetic science.

Today, geneticists can help all cat breeds stay healthier and try to avoid inherited health problems, but some breeds are in genetic trouble after decades of close breeding and extreme show breed standards. Cat breeding is also a small silo within the whole population of pet cats around the world: the vast majority of pet cats are mixed breed with no sense of pedigree at all, and they're still charming, special, and varied in personality and looks. One of the best parts of learning about breeds is seeing if you can spot traits your everyday housecat shares with a Cat Fancy kind of cat.

Abyssinian

The Abyssinian cat is a slender, graceful, elegant cat named for the Ethiopian Empire where it's believed to have originated. This cat is distinguished by its unique coat, which appears

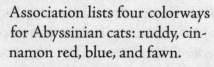

solid-colored overall with some gradients, but is really made of multicolored individual hairs. The Cat Fanciers' Association lists four colorways for Abyssinian cats: ruddy, cinnamon red, blue, and fawn.

Abyssinian cats are active, playful, and curious, with friendly personalities that can bely their subtle, regal beauty. They have long limbs and tails, with coloring that intensifies at the tips and lightens under their bellies. Abyssinian kittens have starker versions of their adult coloring, with fluffier fur that eventually grows into a lush, dense, medium-length adult coat.

These cats make great pets for those who want a cat that is friendly and engaging — more of a "dog" temperament than the stereotype of an elusive cat. These cats need a lot of attention and can get lonely without it. They also thrive in a place with a lot of toys, activities, and vertical spaces where they can explore and play. The rumored first Abyssinian cat is kept alive in illustrated form, a tiny-eared specimen named Zula.

American Bobtail

The American Bobtail cat is big, friendly, and strong. Where the Abyssinian cat has just four colorways that are strictly enforced, American Bobtail cats have many potential colors, including "wild"-appearing ones like tabby, and they aren't penalized for some body markings. They can have point coloring, meaning darker at the ear tips, paws, and tail. This variation extends to their coat length, too. American Bobtail cats may have long, shaggy coats or medium-length coats and are separated into different show categories by the Cat Fanciers' Association based on coat length. Despite the name, the American Bobtail can also have different lengths and shapes of tail. If the Abyssinian cat is a lithe gymnast, the American Bobtail cat might throw a shot put in track and field. These athletic cats are clever and friendly. Some have speculated that the breed is related to a bobcat based on how it looks, but several naturally occurring cat breeds have similar bobtails that have come from a handful of different genetic mutations, so American Bobtails probably have no more "wild" DNA than any other domestic cat. They take longer to mature than some other breeds, which makes sense because of how much their musculature needs to fill out after they're fully grown.

American Curl

The American Curl cat has distinctive round ears that curl backward. The breed can be traced back to a litter of kittens from one specific cat, due to a genetic mutation that was then bred into future litters. Besides their distinctive ears, American Curl cats are pretty average cats, with medium size and body type that are neither slender nor stocky. They can be many colors and have long or short coats, but show cats must have silky fur that lays relatively flat rather than fluffy or dense fur.

When American Curl kittens are born, their ears look straight and traditional. The curl happens quickly and is related to how the cartilage of the ears develops, so the final shape of the ear is stable and healthy for the cat. Kittens have fully curled ears in less than six months. Show cats almost always have a smooth, continuous curve to their ears with a clearly defined angle depending on the organization. Other American Curl cats may have slighter curl or a complete curl to the back of the head. Like Goldilocks, a successful show American Curl must be medium and "just right." The breed is known to be smart and active, with graceful bodies.

American Shorthair

Where the Abyssinian cat has a distinctively African face and body shape, the American Shorthair cat is distinctively European for a cat, with a strong, large build and round, flatter-appearing face. These cats date back to European conquest of the United States, so they come in dozens of colors and patterns and are very populous. They started to be pedigreed in the 20th century, but Americans relied on them as vermin catchers and pets for many, many years before that.

Because the American Shorthair was a successful domestic hunter for such a long time, these cats have powerful and alert senses and strong teeth and jaws. But for those with American Shorthair cats as pets, they are friendly, affectionate, and relaxed cats. Despite being strong and able hunters, they're not especially high energy or active inside the home, preferring to explore and play at a more leisurely pace. They grow to be quite large and have placid, kind facial expressions. In show settings American Shorthair cats are judged heavily on their body and head shape, without much emphasis on any other features, like the remarkable ears of the American Curl.

American Wirehair

The history of the American Wirehair cat is, like the breed itself, a bit unusual. In 1966, two ordinary barn cats, bestowed with the ordinary names Fluffy and Bootsie, produced an extraordinary kitten. This kitten had a springy, dense, coarse coat, that was rougher to the touch than the coats of its parents. The kitten, named Adam, was bought by a breeder, who suspected that Adam wasn't just an unusual cat—he was an entirely new breed. Samples of Adam's hair were sent to a geneticist, who confirmed that the hair didn't match any existing breed. Amazingly, a rare spontaneous mutation had occurred, creating a never-before-seen cat.

In addition to their wiry coat, American Wirehairs possess other unique qualities. Most notable are their high cheekbones and large eyes, which set them apart from their closest cousin, the American Shorthair. Their dense coats, which are similar to some terrier dog breeds, require less grooming than many other cats and come in all colors and patterns. But while their coats may be coarse and hard, their personality is anything but. American Wirehairs are prized for their affectionate, yet independent, nature. They are just as content curled up on the couch purring next to their human companions as they are with entertaining themselves.

The American Wirehair is the rarest of the breeds recognized by the Cat Fanciers' Association, and the mutation that created it has never been seen in another country. Today, all American Wirehairs are descended from Adam—an apt name for the father of the breed.

Balinese

Although they are 100 percent American, Balinese were named after the graceful movement of dancers from the Isle of Bali and the parent Siamese cat. The Balinese is a longhaired version of the Siamese cat, a natural spontaneous mutation. Aside from hair length, the cats are nearly identical. Like the Siamese, these cats love their families and have been known to risk their lives—even fighting off armed burglars—to protect them.

Balinese cats are very intelligent. They can open doors and drawers with ease, but once they are trained, they remember— even if they don't always obey—the words "no" and "come here."

These cats are talkers and alternate between being extremely active and surprisingly sedentary. Balinese cats are also demanding but are so lovable and affectionate that their owners will forgive them for nearly anything.

Balinese are soft and lovely to look at since the longer hair forms an aureole of softness around their limber bodies. According to legend, the aureole was referred to as a veil, and the cat's body was said to move like that of a Balinese dancer surrounded by her swirling, silken veils. Today it's easy to see that every move these cats make is dancelike—they are truly grace in motion.

Bengal

The Bengal cat originates with a southeastern Asian wild cat called the Asian leopard cat, different from a common leopard in almost every way besides the confusing name. A true leopard is large with characteristic enclosed spots called rosettes, compared with the larger, different rosettes on a jaguar or the smaller, solid spots on a cheetah. The Asian leopard cat is the size of a domestic cat (reaching about 8 pounds in adulthood) with a patterned coat that can be rosettes, solid spots, or swirling, streaky spots called "marbling."

These wild Asian leopard cats were bred with domestic cats in order to produce a fully domestic cat with the striking, unique coloration of the Asian leopard cat. For show cats, their last Asian leopard cat ancestor must be at least four generations back, making them a safe domestic cat rather than a direct hybrid cat. This is analogous to the idea of a "wolfdog," which is a hybrid of a wolf and a domestic dog, compared with a handful of domestic dog breeds that began many generations ago with one wolfdog. Bengal cats are beautiful and special, with shiny, soft coats that are uniformly short. Some are glittery, with a sheen unique to Bengal cats because of the careful breeding of Jean Mill, a California activist and breeder.

Birman

Like many other cat breeds, the Birman cat—not to be confused with the Burmese cat—was first brought to Europe and officially recognized during colonial times in a faraway nation. Myanmar, also known as Burma, was occupied by the British when the "sacred cat of Burma," named the Birman cat after the French word for Burmese, was first introduced in the French version of Cat Fanciers' Association. Most of the suggested origin stories seem like romantic myths, featuring Burmese temples and daring smugglers. During World War II, Birman cats were so concentrated in only Europe that the entire breed almost died out. Breeders had to use one surviving pair of cats and continue cross-breeding with similar cats until they had a new line of Birman cats, and the breed was recognized beginning in the 1960s.

The Birman cat's evocative name and mythical origins have given this breed an air of mystery and exoticism, but Birman cats look similar to other colorpoint breeds like Siamese cats. Their special feature is that they have white "gloves" over their dark pointed paws, and they have both solid and tabby colorations. (A tabby-point cat has the same dark face and feet but these areas are also striped.) Their delicate facial features and special coloration can make Birman cats seem dainty, but really,

Birmans are well built and strong. Their frames are large and sturdy, and their fluffy coats resist matting. Besides being beautiful, Birman cats are sweet, healthy, and vigorous. A "perfect" Birman cat has white gloves that match, one pair in front and one pair in back. In reality, almost none are this symmetrical, and their white gloves are charming, no matter their length.

Bombay

The Bombay is our first one-color cat breed. All show-quality Bombay cats are solid black with golden or copper eyes, and even having green eyes will disqualify a Bombay cat from competition. The breed is the result of careful crossing of Burmese cats and American Shorthair cats, resulting in a sweet, affectionate, strong cat that looks like a "miniature panther" by design. Their faces are a pleasing blend of the roundness of American Shorthair cats and the narrower faces of Burmese cats. Bombay cats are medium in size with glossy, sleek, short-hair black coats. Body and eye color are highly prized, with eye color in particular often mentioned in terms like those used for fine gemstones: "the greater the depth and brilliance the better," according to the Cat Fanciers' Association guidelines. The shining black coat means Bombay cats shed less than many other cat breeds, and the coat must be solid, near-perfect black, including individual hairs all the way to the roots. The black panthers that Bombay cats aspire to be are also a black color variant on their species. Some black panthers are jaguars, and some are leopards. The same name "black panther" is given to the solid black members of both groups. Like real black panthers, Bombay cats are athletic and graceful, and their short, reflective coat is striking when they stretch and jump.
These are the cats who seem invisible in dim light.

British Shorthair

The American Shorthair cat resulted when British colonists brought cats with them to the burgeoning United States, which means the original British Shorthair cat dates back to at least then. In fact, the British Shorthair is one of the oldest known cat breeds in the world, likely coming to the United Kingdom when the Romans invaded. Julius Caesar first arrived in 55 B.C., and Rome held parts of Britain for the next 400 years. This means the British Shorthair cat could be anywhere from 1,600 to 2,000 years old.

British Shorthair cats are the most popular cat breed in Great Britain, including the distinctive "British blue" colorway with dark, blue-gray fur and bright golden or copper eyes. But there are dozens of accepted colors for British Shorthair cats, including a rarely seen "none of the above" category in the official breed standard. Each official color has an accepted eye color range as well. British Shorthair cats can have an interesting "crinkle" effect in their fur, especially the British blues. Several colors aren't allowed in competition because they reflect generic hybridity. British Shorthair cats are also pretty large, with thick, strong bodies.

Burmese

The Burmese cat is the subject of an ongoing turf war between British and American cat associations, giving it more melodrama than many other breeds. The Burmese breed dates back to a cat brought from southeastern Asia in the early 20th century, bred in America for a time, and then bred in Great Britain using some American Burmese cats and some other cats. The two groups were kept separate, and their body types diverged over time, with British Burmese cats keeping more of the angular, slender look of a Siamese cat. American Burmese cats developed rounder heads, more snubbed noses, and rounder ears.

Even their paws are rounder. The two groups disagree about what a general "Burmese cat" should be, and as a result, each county has delisted the other's breed standard. In Britain, there's only the British style of Burmese cat. In
America, there is only the American style. Most of the rest of the world accepts both under the heading of Burmese cat. Only recently have there been inroads made between the two groups.

There are only four true colors of the Burmese cat. Almost all Burmese cats have mild shading, which gives their coats a shimmery, dynamic look. Their coats are short and sleek, not fluffy or dense. All colors of Burmese cat must have golden eyes. Their bodies are strong but not stocky—breed standards often call this quality "heavier than they look," and it's a compliment. Burmese cats are notoriously friendly and sociable, building bonds with humans in a way considered rare for cats.

Burmilla

In 1981, an Englishwoman named Miranda Bickford-Smith purchased a male Chinchilla Persian cat named Sanquist as a gift for her husband. Since they already had a female Burmese named Faberge in the house, the two cats were kept in separate rooms until Sanquist could be neutered. But one night, a cleaner accidentally left Faberge's door open, and the two cats found each other. The rest, as they say, is history. This feline *Romeo and Juliet* story resulted in four kittens, all shorthaired, shaded silver females. Bickford-Smith thought the kittens were so attractive that she decided to use them as the foundation of a new breed, and the Burmilla—a cross between "Burmese" and "Chinchilla"—was born.

The Burmilla's distinguishing feature is its coat, which can be either short or long and has a distinctive silvery color. This soft, silky coat generally follows two major patterns, known as tipped and shaded. Tipped Burmillas have a dusting of darker color over about $1/8$ of their hair length, whereas shaded Burmillas have color over $1/3$ of the hair length. The cats are also known for the coloring around their nose, lips, and luminous green eyes, often described as "makeup."

Thanks to the laid-back personality of the Chinchilla and the playful nature of the Burmese, the Burmilla is an easy-going, fun-loving breed, often described as "kitten-like" throughout its entire life. Intelligent, mischievous, and good with children, the Burmilla has won the hearts of fans worldwide.

Chartreux

Like the British Shorthair cat, the Chartreux cat is a distinctly European breed that was almost wiped out during World War II. It was saved by careful people who bred it back from almost nothing following the war. All true Chartreux cats are gray, whether light or dark. The breed dates back hundreds of years at least, appearing in painted portraits at a time when having cherished pets of that kind was much more rare. No one knows for sure where the breed originated, with mythical explanations dating back to the Crusades. The breed was and remains uncommon. Purebred Chartreux cats are stocky (called "husky" by the Cat Fanciers' Association) and their dense fur repels water. Although these cats are large and somewhat thick, they're grace-ful and smart.

Chartreux cats are both talented at hunting and very agreeable family pets. All domestic cats were wild cats at some point, but some speculate that the Chartreux cat is directly descended from a wild cat brought back to France from far afield. This would explain the breed's tough, hardy temperament and body type, with short limbs and athletic grace. A cat with dense, water-resistant fur could dry faster, resist more injuries, and generally get less dirty.

Chausie

The Chausie (pronounced *chow-see*) has probably been around for several thousand years, dating back to ancient Egypt. Egyptians were known to keep cats as pets, forming such strong bonds with their feline friends that they often chose to mummify them after death. It is likely that the domestic cats kept by the Egyptians eventually mated with a species of wild cat found in the Nile Delta known as *Felis chausz*, or jungle cat. From this pairing, the Chausie was created. But it wasn't until 1990 that breeders became serious about preserving and developing the breed, and in 1995, the Chausie was officially recognized as a domestic breed by The International Cat Association (TICA).

Although Chausies come in a variety of colors, only three – brown-ticked tabby, solid black, and grizzled tabby – are accepted at cat shows. Their angular cheekbones, large, tufted ears, and gold or green eyes give them a striking appearance and hint at their "wild" origins.

Since the Chausie is a hybrid between the jungle cat and domestic cats, several different breeds, including Abyssinian and Oriental Shorthair, have been used to produce Chausies. To be eligible for competition, TICA requires that the cats be fourth generation Chausies, and they must be several generations removed from their jungle cat ancestors. As descendants of these wild cats, it might be assumed that Chausies are stand-offish with their human companions, but nothing is further from the truth. This intelligent, playful breed loves the company of humans and other animals, preferring not to be alone and displaying loyalty to its owners.

Cornish Rex

The Cornish Rex cat is named for its origin in the southwestern-most county in the United Kingdom, Cornwall, where it appeared as a mutation in one kitten from a litter. The kitten had very fine, short, wavy hair that turned out to be only the cat's downy undercoat. Most cats have multiple layers of types of hair, the same as many other furry animals, but Cornish Rex cats are missing two other traditional layers of hair. Their body shape is very like that of a Siamese cat, with a small, quite pointy head and a long, almost gangly body. Their appearance is exaggerated by having so little volume of hair, like a fully furred cat fresh from a bathtub compared with its fluffy dry state.

Because the true breed marker of the Cornish Rex is the texture of its coat, there are dozens of accepted colorations, and no colors are specifically outlawed from competition. There are Cornish Rex cats in solid colors, chinchilla, colorpoint, tabby, calico, and more, including "other." The breed is prone to hair thinning or loss because its coat is so delicate, but even thinning hair or hairless spots aren't grounds for disqualification.

Cymric

Legend has it that when Noah called all the animals into the ark, one cat, the Manx, was napping. Waking just in time, it ran for the boat as Noah was closing the door, which he slammed on the Manx's tail, chopping it off. And so the tailless Manx, the short-haired version of the Cymric, was created.

Of course, the real story is a bit less graphic: The Manx is believed to have originated on the Isle of Man, where the tailless trait was a result of genetic mutation. Due to the isolated nature of the island, it was easy for this mutation to replicate, producing generations of tailless cats. While long-haired cats were occasionally also born on the island, breeders were at first disinterested in this mutation. It wasn't until Canadian breeders began intentionally breeding long-haired Manx cats in the 1960s that the Cymric breed began taking hold.

Identical to the Manx in every way except hair length, the Cymric is a compact, sturdy cat, with a short, arched back that gives it an overall rounded appearance. The medium-long coat, which can be any color, has a silky texture and is well padded due to an undercoat. While only completely tailless Cymrics can be show cats, some have very short tails, and others have tails almost as long as a regular cat. Occasionally, the gene that causes the unusual tails can cause problems including spina bifida or fused vertebrae, so responsible breeding is a must. These gentle, loyal cats are right at home in families with children and other pets.

Devon Rex

The Devon Rex cat looks very similar to the Cornish Rex cat, but their curly coats are, improbably, from discrete genetic mutations. Like the Cornish Rex, the Devon Rex began with one kitten with a curly coat. Instead of only having the downy layer of hair, the Devon Rex has the downy layer and an additional layer of short "guard" hairs. (Typical cat breeds have longer guard hairs and a third layer of hair as well.)

Devon Rex cats also differ from Cornish Rex cats in facial features and general head shape. The Cornish Rex cat has a small, pointy head, but its features are closer to the proportions of a traditional cat face, besides its very large ears. The Devon Rex has a long, thin neck, much wider head, and beautiful huge ears. Its appearance overall is more like a sweet cartoon alien or the fuzzy "before" creatures in the movie *Gremlins*.

Devon Rex cats can appear in any color, with no restrictions on show cats. The Devon Rex is notoriously playful and mischievous, maybe enhanced by its elfin face. These cats are eager to play and bond, and they like to snuggle and be carried. They are smart, curious, and interested in other animals and their surroundings.

Donskoy

The Donskoy's startling, hairless appearance may look worrisome at first glance, but the distinctive feature is simply the result of a mutant gene. This mutation was first observed in Russia in 1987, when a woman named Elena Kovaleva rescued a kitten with tortoiseshell fur. Within a few months, the kitten began to lose its hair, despite any treatment Kovaleva attempted. A few years later, the hairless cat mated with a tomcat in the neighborhood, producing a litter of kittens who eventually lost all their hair, as well. Intrigued, Irina Nemikina, a breeder, adopted one of the hairless kittens and continued the genetic line, producing more litters of hairless kittens.

Nemikina called the breed "Don Sphynx," in honor of the Don River in Russia and the cat's sphynx-like appearance, and it was later called the Donskoy. Despite its obvious similarities to the

Sphynx breed, the two are not related. But they do share the rare feature of hairlessness. This characteristic gives Donskoys unique grooming needs compared to other cats. Although they can't be brushed, they do need regular baths and must be wiped down every day to distribute the oils produced by the skin. In addition to their bald appearance, this medium-sized breed has large ears, almond-shaped eyes, and long, webbed toes.

Their lack of fur means that Donskoys are much more sensitive to hot and cold temperatures, and even sunburn, than other cats. For this reason, it is best that they remain indoor cats; but their friendly, affectionate, and loyal temperaments make them perfect companions.

Egyptian Mau

The Egyptian Mau cat has a striking spotted coat, making it one of only a few cat breeds marked in such a way. Egyptian Maus are also one of the rarest cat breeds in the world. Besides their rare spots and shiny, glittery coat, Egyptian Mau cats look very average, in the mathematical sense. They're medium size and weight, strong but not stocky, with head shape neither too angled nor too round. On their foreheads, they have the random streaky marks often seen on the foreheads of tabby cats. In Egyptian Maus, these marks are shaped vaguely like an "M" or, thematically, like a scarab beetle. Egyptian Mau cats all have green eyes, and there are just three colors: silver, bronze, and smoke. Smoke-colored Egyptian Mau cats even have black whiskers. The spots in all colors of Egyptian Maus are made by ticking, which are the bands of color along individual hairs that also give Abyssinians their special glowing color. It's also rumored that an Egyptian Mau cat was used in the breeding process that created the Bengal cat.

To go with their medium size and average shape, Egyptian Mau cats have moderate temperaments. In fact, their averageness may not be a coincidence, because experts believe them to be an ancient breed that helped to originate the modern domestic cat in the first place. Their spots may therefore be a preserved holdover from a truly wild ancestor many centuries ago. Egyptian Mau cats are curious, clever, and acrobatic, perhaps having helped define these as traits so many other domestic cats have as well.

European Burmese

Believed to have been created in 1930, the Burmese is a cross between a Siamese and a type of domestic cat that originated in Burma (now known as Myanmar). Although the first Burmese was born in America, British breeders soon began developing the cats, as well. But the breeding stock was lacking in Europe, so their development followed a different path than their American counterparts. Today, two distinct breeds have emerged: Burmese, and European Burmese.

The main difference seen in the European Burmese is coloring. The original standard color for a Burmese is a dark brown, also known as sable or seal. But the introduction of redpoint Siamese and British Shorthairs in breeding programs in Great Britain resulted in an array of colors for the European Burmese. Colors range from brown, blue, and lilac, to red, cream, and tortoiseshell, and can also be found in combinations, such as the brown tortie and lilac tortie.

European Burmese also differ from American Burmese in head and body shape. While the American breed is a bit stocky and broad, the European breed has an elegant, slender, long-legged appearance, with a wedge-shaped head and slightly almond-shaped eyes. The European Burmese is known for its curious, playful, and people-oriented personality, with some describing it as "dog-like." In fact, these cats will often learn to play games like "fetch" and love sharing a couch or bed with their owners. This breed genuinely enjoys the company of humans and is likely to win over even those who swear they're not "cat people."

Exotic Shorthair

The Exotic Shorthair cat is a carefully bred variation on a Persian cat, with short, dense fur instead of the fluffy and lofty long hair of the Persian cat. The two breeds are still so closely linked that some organizations consider that an Exotic Shorthair born with long hair (odds are fairly good of this happening once in any given litter) can compete as a Persian cat. Exotic Shorthair cats come in a dazzling arsenal of colors, and although the Cat Fanciers' Association lists dozens and dozens of colorations, each one has specific eye, nose, and toe pad colors, with listed disqualifications like white spots or white feet. The Exotic Shorthair cat can look a hundred different ways, but those ways must be exact. Exotic Shorthair cats have sweet, round faces that are flat.

As with pugs and other animals bred with very short snouts, this means Exotic Shorthair cats can have infections and other specific health complaints related to their breeding. They're also more likely to develop a potentially fatal condition called polycystic kidney disease. Otherwise, Exotic Shorthair cats are fairly robust and healthy, with short, stocky bodies and lush fur. They can be reserved and standoffish.

Havana Brown

With a chocolate coat and striking green eyes, the Havana Brown is easily recognizable by cat enthusiasts. This attractive breed is believed to have originated in the 1950s, when a group of English cat fanciers calling themselves "The Havana Group" and later "The Chestnut Brown Group" set out to develop a chestnut brown cat. They crossed a Siamese cat, which carried the chocolate brown gene, to a black cat, which also carried the gene. The result was a litter of chestnut kittens. While the breed's coat colors varied over the next decade, the Havana Brown was soon introduced to America, where the coat evolved into a consistently rich mahogany color.

The medium-sized Havana Brown is quite muscular, feeling surprisingly heavy for its size. Large, rounded ears give it an appearance of alertness, and its head is a bit longer than it is wide, with a unique rounded muzzle that is often compared to a lightbulb. But the breed's distinctive feature is, of course, its short, chocolate brown hair,  which is soft, lustrous, and feels as luxurious as a mink coat. Even the nose and whiskers of the Havana Brown are chocolate colored, complimenting the cat's uniform appearance, and only its bright, oval green eyes stand out in contrast.

The Havana Brown is intelligent, curious, and affectionate, preferring not to be left alone for long periods of time. In fact, many Havana Browns are excellent travelers, enjoying the time with their human companions much more than independence.

Himalayan

Very similar to the Persian, but with the pointed coloration of a Siamese, the Himalayan was first developed in the 1920s by cat lovers who wished for a uniquely colored, long-haired cat. The breed gained popularity in the 40s and 50s both in the United States and the United Kingdom, where it was dubbed the Longhaired Colorpoint, and by 1961, it was recognized by all major U.S. cat associations.

While they may sound like they were named after the mountain range, Himalayans are actually named for their color, which resembles that of a Himalayan rabbit. Their long, fluffy coat comes in all colors, with a strong contrast between body and point colors. Usually the body is a white or cream color, while the points can be anything from black to lilac to tortoiseshell. Large, round eyes give the Himalayan a sweet look, and can be found in all shades of blue.

Himalayans come in two different types that determine facial shape. The traditional, or doll-face type has a classic look, whereas an ultra-typed or "peke-faced" Himalayan has a flatter, "squished" look, not unlike the Pekinese dog it was named after.

Because of their long fur, Himalayans need to be brushed regularly. Fortunately, their gentle, sweet natures make it easy to settle them down for a grooming session, and many of them enjoy the attention. Docile and not at all aggressive, Himalayans are dependent upon their human companions, making them wonderful indoor pets.

Japanese Bobtail

The Japanese Bobtail cat is totally unrelated to the American Bobtail cat, and its tail is much shorter, generally referred to as a "bunny tail." The breed existed in Japan for hundreds of years, thought to have come from the Asian mainland as many as 1,000 years ago.

Like most things in Japan, the Japanese Bobtail cat was largely unknown to the rest of the world until relatively recently, when a western cat breeder brought one back from Japan in the 1960s.

The breed's popularity within Japan is almost ubiquitous, though. The Japanese Bobtail cat is the unofficial street cat of Japan, and because of existing anti-cat laws at the time these cats were released into the streets to catch silkworms, most feral cats in Japan today are purebred Japanese Bobtail cats. They're also featured prominently in historic Japanese art and folklore. Because the Japanese Bobtail has almost no tail, the rest of its body type and musculature must make up for this difference in balance compared with cats with normal tails. Overall, the Japanese Bobtail cat is surprisingly graceful.

Javanese

The name "Javanese" may sound exotic, but surprisingly, this breed's name was chosen by simply pointing at a map. At the time, in the late 1970s, breeders were interested in creating Siamese-type cats with different coats and colors, and they adopted the habit of naming these breeds, such as the Balinese and Tonkinese, after countries and islands in Southeast Asia. When the Javanese was selected for registration by the Cat Fanciers' Association in 1979, it was arbitrarily named after the island of Java, even though it has no connection to the region.

The Javanese shares much of its ancestry with the Balinese, which was developed in both the U.S. and the U.K. in the mid-1800s. It is believed that a Balinese was crossed with a Colorpoint Shorthair to create a Siamese-type cat with longer hair and a unique color, and this became the foundation of the new Javanese breed.

The Javanese has a long, silky coat, but lacks the double coat that many long-haired breeds have, giving it a sleek, slender look. It has point coloration, like a Siamese, but with 24 acceptable color combinations, the Javanese comes in many colors not found in its cousins. Their walnut-shaped, wide-set eyes are always a shade of blue and give the cat an alert appearance.

Like the Siamese, Javanese are talkers, and will attempt to communicate with their enthusiastic meows. These curious felines crave regular attention, as well as food—owners should be careful to monitor their intake, otherwise these sleek cats can pack on unwanted pounds.

Korat

The Korat cat is a beautiful silver-tipped gray cat that originated in Thailand. Like the Chartreux cat, this breed only has one color, but unlike the Chartreux, all Korat show cats are the exact same shade of silver-gray. Their special, luminous gray color is the result of ticking on individual hairs, from silver to gray back to silver. Fully mature adults have striking green eyes, but the cats mature fairly late and are allowed, in competition, to have the amber-tinted eyes associated with kittenhood.

No one is certain when the Korat cat came to be, but it's a cherished part of Thai culture, considered lucky and a good auspice. The Korat cat's external beauty might be enough to explain it, but this cat is also sweet and smart, with a pleasant, open face and striking large eyes. The Korat cat is still found as an outdoor or feral cat in Thailand, where it's an able hunter and good provider for kittens. In its first appearance in a centuries-old book of poems, the Korat appears as a lovingly drawn illustration and is presented as a lucky cat. People describe its face as being composed of heart shapes. The Korat cat was brought to western cat breeders for the first recorded time in the late 1800s. Like most distinctive blue-gray cat breeds, the Korat has kept its striking appearance for decades, even centuries. But the Korat also has the same unique head shape and other features that have been bred out of many other unusual or rare breeds over time.

Kurilian Bobtail

The Kurilian Bobtail is known by many slightly different names in English, probably because of its origins. This fluffy, stocky, bobtail cat originated on a chain of islands that begins in Russian territory and ends near Japan's Hokkaido island. Translating from either language involves transliteration, meaning turning a different alphabet or symbol into its best English soundalike. And because of its isolated home in the far northeast of Russia, the breed has only recently come to the world's attention. Some groups consider it too new to compete, and others, like Cat Fanciers' Association, don't recognize it at all yet. Kurilian Bobtail cats seem related to Japanese Bobtail cats, and with their shared small area of the world, this makes sense. But the Kurilian Bobtail has much warmer fur, thicker and stockier limbs, and an overall disposition for playing and hunting outdoors in a more rugged way than the urbane pest-hunting of the Japanese Bobtail.

The Kurilian Bobtail resembles a wild bobcat or lynx almost as much as it resembles its fellow domestic cat breeds, including fluffy jowls and "lynx tufts" on its ears. Much like Charles Darwin's studies in the Galapagos Islands, the Kurilian Bobtail and other island breeds show how an isolated place can lead to more rapid mutation and new characteristics. Living in a small place with only other cats of the same kind is almost a naturally occurring breeding program. Like the water-resistant Chartreux, the Kurilian Bobtail cat loves to fish. The most distinctive Kurilian Bobtails are longhairs, but their home islands are full of shorthair examples as well, and some organizations recognize these as separate breeds.

LaPerm

The LaPerm is a new breed founded in the Pacific Northwest when a talented mouse-catcher had a litter that included one curly kitten. This cat has been officially bred for less than

30 years. There are longhair and shorthair LaPerm cats, and all have the slightly coarse, curly hair that gives the breed its name. The longhair LaPems look fluffy because of their curls, but their coats are light, airy, and fine rather than plush. These cats usually have no under- coat. Some purebreed LaPerms are born with straight hair, and some have curlier hair than average. The LaPerm cat's progenitor had been selectively bred for a job rather than its appearance, so resulting LaPerm cats come in every coloration possible, with dozens that are defined by show guidelines and a category for "none of the above." The body type of the LaPerm is more standard, with a medium size and build and long, fine limbs.

Because the breed is so new, guidelines often allow it to be "out- crossed," or crossbred, with classic shorthair or longhair cats, at least until 2020. Doing this for as long as possible allows the breed to diversify its genes and helps to prevent any future health problems. LaPerm cats are bright, agile, and light on their feet. Some believe them to be hypoallergenic as a result of their special coat and reduced layers of undercoat.

Lykoi

A cat that looks like a werewolf may sound scary, but the unusual, unique Lykoi is anything but. This rare breed—some experts estimate there are less than 200 in the world—was not created, but rather is the result of a natural genetic mutation that can occur in housecats. The mutation causes patchy, or sometimes complete, hair loss, and a roan color pat- tern, which is a mix of normal-colored hair and white hair.

The ears, nose, and much of the face are almost always hairless, which is what gives the cat a "werewolf" appearance.

The first Lykois were discovered at animal shelters, presumably abandoned by people who may have assumed the cats were sickly due to their hair loss. Fortunately, in 2010 and 2011 breeders in both Virginia and Tennessee came across the abandoned Lykois and realized they had found something special. Eventually, they acquired five cats, found in shelters or as strays, and they were used to create a foundation for the breed. By 2017, the Lykoi was officially recognized by The International Cat Association and was eligible for competition.

While some find the "werewolf" cats ugly, Lykoi enthusiasts insist that they're beautiful. The patchy coat, which looks coarse but is actually soft and silky, is occasionally entirely shed before growing back. Some Lykois are almost bald, similar to the Sphynx, while others retain much more of their coat.

Although "Lykoi" is Greek for "wolves," there is nothing to fear with this cat's temperament. They love interacting with people, and in a home, they will often display "guarding" behavior, watching over children and other pets with a sense of duty, dispelling any concerns about their wild appearance.

Maine Coon

Maine Coon cats are one of the most famous breeds of the internet era, probably because of photos of people holding improbably huge and fluffy examples of this already large breed. The cats in these photos usually look docile and happy to be carried around despite their size. In fact, the Maine Coon is the largest breed. In body type and coat, the Maine Coon cat looks similar to the Kurilian Bobtail cat, with long, shaggy hair in a variety of colors. Both breeds originated in snowy climates, but the Maine Coon cat is thought to be the result of local breeding between American Shorthair cats and longhair cats brought from northern Europe.

Maine Coon cats have been recorded for at least 150 years, and it was a Maine Coon cat named Cosey who won the first cat show held in North America in the late 1800s. For a time, Maine Coon cats were displaced by longhair cat breeds brought from overseas, and the breed was depleted nearly to extinction. It was preserved by dedicated breeders, and kept a low profile for several decades during which it wasn't even formally recognized as a breed by the Cat Fanciers' Association. Today, the Maine Coon cat is one of the most popular breeds again. Maine Coons are prone to a couple of genetic conditions like heart disease and hip dysplasia, but overall they're healthier than some of the longhair cats who, at one time, threatened to replace them altogether.

Manx

The Manx cat and its longhair counterpart the Cymric cat are tailless cats native to the Isle of Man, an independent island midway between England and Northern Ireland in the Irish Sea. Despite its location, the Isle of Man has been relatively isolated, keeping its eccentric local customs and culture and with an entire body of its own folklore dating back to ancient times. The Manx cat is a hunter and mouser prized by the island's farmers since the 1800s.

Like the bobtail cats, the Manx cat's mutation was probably encouraged by its small territory and lack of outside crossbreeding. Unlike the bobtail cats, the mutation is the result of a gene that can endanger the cat's health, even when it's still in utero. The wrong genetic combination is fatal, and depending on how the gene expresses itself in growing cats, they can develop severe arthritis or have debilitating shortened spines. Healthy Manx cats can have anything from a "rumpy" with no visible tail at all to a "longy" with a nearly normal-length tail. Manx cats are compact and rounded. They have short necks and limbs and are strong and muscular without being stocky. Manx cats in shows can be almost any color or combination of colors considered "genetically possible," and their rounded hindquarters give them an appearance of a cat always ready to pounce. Their skill as hunters helped them spread to nearby countries, when they were beloved as ship's cats.

Minuet

Originally known as the "Napoleon," the Minuet, like the French military leader, is known for its short stature. A cross between the fluffy, doll-like Persian and the short, sweet Munchkin, the breed was created relatively recently, in 1995. An American Kennel Club judge and Basset Hound breeder named Joe Smith was intrigued by the Munchkin cat breed, as the feline's short legs are similar to those of the hound. He began breeding Munchkins with Persians, to develop a short and sweet, yet sturdy and substantial, breed that would appeal to cat lovers everywhere.

The result was the adorable Napoleon, whose name was officially changed to Minuet in 2015 by The International Cat Association. Resembling a feline version of a dachshund, the Minuet has short legs but a solid, strong body. A round head, muzzle, cheeks, and eyes give it a cherubic look, and its dense, lush coat, which can be long or short, comes in every color and pattern. While the short-legged Minuet is the standard, occasionally long-legged Minuets are born, with the same characteristics and personality of their smaller counterparts.

The Minuet's personality is just as sweet as its appearance, and it loves to show its human companions plenty of affection.

Unlike some standoffish breeds, the Minuet loves being cuddled and held, making it an excellent pet for families with children. But it also has no qualms about finding solo entertainment, and enjoys playing, running, and jumping, using its low center of gravity to navigate tight corners.

Munchkin Cat

Munchkin cats are a newer breed, with normal-size bodies and very short legs. Their overall dimensions are much like those of a dachshund dog. The munchkin cat dates back to the 1980s, but controversy over its breeding and overall health has kept it from competing in most major cat show organizations, including Cat Fanciers' Association. Despite this, breeders and proponents of the breed insist Munchkin cats are healthy, and claim these cats show no signs of the spinal conditions or mobility problems that similarly short-legged dogs like dachshunds and corgi dogs experience. One important difference is that these dog breeds began with much longer legs and more "natural" proportions, and their status as both working dogs and show dogs was established during that time. It's only since then that selective breeding has taken their characteristics to the extremes seen today. On the other hand, the munchkin cat has been bred from the beginning to have very short legs.

Responsible breeders have sought to keep these cats healthy by outcrossing, meaning crossbreeding, them with general domestic shorthair or longhair cats. The International Cat Association, one of the few organizations that shows munchkin cats, specifies that any cats bred with munchkins must not be purebred. The next champion munchkin could be related to the cats next door.

Norwegian Forest Cat

From the small munchkin to the big kahuna: the Norwegian Forest cat is similar in size to the slightly larger Maine Coon cat. Males range up to 20 pounds or more, and overall the species has a slightly longer lifespan than the Maine Coon. These large cats also have lush, dense fur that helps keep water out and insulates them from the cold in their native Norway.

Norwegian Forest cats are a naturally occurring breed, meaning someone discovered one someday and had it certified as a breed. They come in almost all colors, often with fluffy jowls, lynx-tip ears, and bright eyes that give them the overall look of a more wild cat. Their paws are big and generously padded, with hair tufts between the pads. Norwegian Forest cats also have a fluffy "bib" in front and fluffy "britches" in back. Because it's so large, the Norwegian Forest cat doesn't fully mature into an adult cat until as late as five years old.

Surprisingly, the Cat Fanciers' Association awards the most points to the Norwegian Forest cat's head shape and qualities, including a distinctive profile with no "break," meaning the forehead slopes smoothly into the nose without a bend or dip where the bridge of the nose would be. The next-most valuable qualities are judged from their body shape and features. Norwegian Forest cats evolved to hunt and fish outdoors in extreme cold.

Ocicat

Like the Bengal domestic cat, the Ocicat is seen by many as a way for people to be more familiar with and protective of similar endangered wild cats. At first glance, the Ocicat resembles an Egyptian Mau cat, with similar coloration and spots, but its body shape is much more like the American Shorthair cat. This makes sense, because the first Ocicat was the result of the cross between an Abyssinian and a Siamese cat, but the resulting spotted kittens were crossbred with American Shorthair cats to ensure they were strong and healthy. The Egyptian Mau is an elegant, leggy cat occurring naturally in Egypt, and the Ocicat is a gentle, friendly indoor cat created while someone tried to breed something else.

There are relatively few show colorations for Ocicats, including colors like chocolate that reflect the breed's origins as part Siamese. The Cat Fanciers' Association defines specific markings on the head and body, including where the spots converge and blend into "necklace" markings or rings around the tail. If not for its distinctive spotted coat, the Ocicat looks like an average neighborhood cat, with a medium size and body type and strong but not stocky. The combination of friendly Abyssinian, chatty Siamese, and overall good natured American Shorthair makes for an Ocicat that is sociable, curious, and playful.

These cats make loyal pets and often bond with one person or other animal in particular. They love to be included in what's going on and are known to follow people from room to room.

Oriental Shorthair

The Oriental Shorthair cat is a western spin on the Siamese cat, taking the Siamese body type and crossbreeding it to produce a large variety of other colorations. Because of the inclusion of Siamese, these colors include chocolate and lavender, which are excluded in cats that don't contain any Siamese or other Himalayan-type descendants.

The Oriental Shorthair is a medium size overall, but it is slender and narrow in all features except for its beautiful large ears. These cats have long, thin limbs and one of the narrowest bodies of any cat breed, with angular heads and long faces with no "break" in the profile. Still, they're well muscled and athletic, and their long legs and flexible bodies make them good acrobats. These cats are curious and sociable, and they like to be in groups. Since the Oriental Shorthair was bred for color and pattern variety, it's not surprising that there are hundreds of colorations accepted for competition. All have the same texture of coat, though, which is sleek and smooth, almost more like a seal than the dense, plush coat of some other shorthair cats. The Oriental Shorthair is often combined with its longhair variety in shows.

Persian

The Persian cat is thought to originate in Persia, modern-day Iran, hence its name. Records of fluffy cats resembling modern Persian cats date back hundreds of years, although modern Persian cats don't share genetic markers of cats from the Middle East or Asia. That could be because the brand was adopted by breeders in the western world, which is where modern "championship" cat shows began.

Over time, Persian cats have been bred closely to the point that their facial features are an extreme version of the original competition cats in the late 1800s. Like the modern bulldog, these cats have massive heads that make it difficult for kittens to be born, and their extremely shortened facial features lead to increased respiratory and other problems of the kinds experienced by bulldogs, pugs, and other "smush-faced" types.

One very famous Persian cat, the rotating "Fancy Feast" spokescat, has come from the same breeder for over half a century. These Persian cats have a traditional look, meaning their noses are not excessively shortened. This type is also called a "doll face" Persian and experiences far fewer health problems while still being both very cute and very distinctively Persian. In fact, many show guidelines favor the extreme type of Persian cat, but the public seems to like the sweet and relatable doll face better.

Peterbald

Like the closely related Oriental Shorthair cat, the Peterbald cat is lanky and slender, with long limbs and tail. The breed resulted from a cross between a Russian Hairless cat, also called a Donskoy Sphynx, and an Oriental Shorthair cat.

The Peterbald breed is relatively new. The Donskoy Spyhnx is a hairless cat, but the Peterbald is more of a variety pack. One litter of Peterbald kittens may contain completely bald kittens, charmois kittens with a suede-like feel, velour kittens with a very short coat, and wire kittens with a special coat of short, wiry hairs. Not only that, but the kittens' coats can also change for up to two years after birth, and as adults, Peterbald cats may lose some of or all of their hair. All of these different kinds of hair and hair loss are caused by the same dominant hair-loss gene. The ancestor Donskoy Sphynx cat is controversial because its hairlessness gene can be dangerous to the health of the cat if the cat has two copies, meaning one from each parent.

Because the Peterbald results from a crossbreed and has subsequently continued to be crossbred, it's thought to have less risk of the health problems associated with the Donskoy Sphynx. Both breeds are too new and spottily accepted by official organizations for many conclusions to be drawn.

Pixie-bob

In Washington State in 1986, a litter of kittens was born from the pairing of a brown-spotted female cat and a 17-pound male cat. The male cat, which had been adopted by Carol Ann Brewer, was rumored to have been sired by a bobcat. When the kittens were born, Brewer kept one of the females and later started a breeding program, using her as the foundation cat. The cat was named "Pixie," and she was the first cat used to create the Pixie-bob breed.

Although there is no proof that a bobcat is in the Pixie-bob lineage, breeders insist that such is the case. Brewer eventually introduced 23 cats into her breeding program that she believed to be the result of matings between bobcats and domestic cats, which she called "Legend Cats." With the help of the Legend Cats, the Pixie-bob was accepted by The International Cat Association in 1993.

Bobcat ancestry or not, the Pixie-bob has an unmistakably "wild" appearance. Slightly larger than an average domestic cat, which weighs about 8 pounds, the Pixie-bob averages 11 pounds. Some males, however, have topped out at 25 pounds! They have a thick double coat that requires regular brushing, featuring a striped or rosette pattern. This pattern, coupled with their tawny, light gray, or reddish coloring, gives them their bobcat-like look.

While they may look wild, their personality is quite sociable. Pixie-bobs love being near humans and other animals, and are known for their vocal "chirps" and "chatters." Some will even willingly walk on a leash, proving that while they may look like bobcats, they are perfectly content to be domestic pets.

Ragamuffin

How could a cat breed with the adorable name of Ragamuffin be anything other than a sweet-natured ball of fluff? Like the better-known Ragdoll breed, the Ragamuffin is known for its cuddly, docile nature and its tendency to go limp when held. In fact, although it is lesser known, the Ragamuffin has been around as long as the Ragdoll, and the two breeds share a history.

In the 1960s in Riverside, California, an Angora or Persian cat named Josephine had a litter of usually docile kittens. Intrigued by the sweet natures of these kittens, a breeder named Ann Baker purchased several of them and began to develop a new breed, which she later trademarked as a "Ragdoll." Disinterested in traditional breeding associations, Baker created her own registry in 1975, and called it the International Ragdoll Cat Association (IRCA). But in 1994, several people decided to leave the IRCA and continue developing Ragdolls on their own. Since Baker had trademarked the name, they could no longer call their cats Ragdolls; thus, the Ragamuffin was born!

While the two breeds are similar, decades of separation have resulted in differences. The Ragamuffin comes in a wider variety of colors, with almost any color or pattern being acceptable. They have thick, plush, medium-long fur and large, expressive eyes that give them a sweet look. Their personality is just as delightful, and often described as lovable and cuddly. Since the Ragamuffin is less active than many other breeds, it makes a perfect indoor companion.

Ragdoll

The Ragdoll cat has the dubious distinction of being one of the only trademarked cat breed names, at least until the mark expired in 2005. If breeders wanted to call their purebred kittens Ragdolls, they had to conform to strict rules set out by the trademark holder, including exactly with whom and how their cats could be bred. Eventually, a subset of aspiring Ragdoll breeders split off and formed a new breed they called Ragamuffin. Even the Ragdoll breed itself was liberated: its creator chose to exclude Ragdoll cats from existing organizations and tried to form a parallel shadow organization only for Ragdoll cats, and as a result, her cats and their closely bred offspring are neither part of the breed standard nor eligible for major shows.

The breed standards were created in the image of a rogue group of Ragdoll cats whose breeders wanted their cats to be more widely known and able to compete. Both Ragdoll and Ragamuffin cats are large with voluminous, longhair coats. Ragamuffin cats may be almost any color and pattern, because they've been crossbred with a few more varieties than Ragdoll cats are permitted to be. All Ragdoll cats have point coloration.

Russian Blue

The Russian Blue is one of a handful of naturally occurring blue cat breeds like the Chartreux and Korat cat. And like the Chartreux in particular, the Russian Blue cat was nearly wiped out during World War II, leading to some crossbreeding with Siamese cats that introduced more color variety.

Today, breeders have carefully bred most of these alternate colorations out of litters of purebred Russian Blue cats, and the Cat Fanciers' Association defines a Russian Blue as only the single coloration of dark gray blue, black nose, and bright green eyes. All Russian Blue cats have short, very dense coats that are so thick and soft they can sometimes hold the shape of a handprint.

These cats are well built and dense, with wide-set, round eyes and slightly round faces that are emphasized by their thick fur. But they're fine boned, with quite dainty paws and graceful bodies that can make jumps and other acrobatic moves.

Russian Blue cats are smart and sweet, with calm, peaceful natures that can bely their equal interest in play and exploration. Their striking green eyes and attitude of calm make them a major beauty among cats. Russian Blue cats are believed to come from an area of Russia called Arkhangelsk, or Archangel.

Savannah

The Savannah cat is an example of a hybrid breed, like a wolf-dog, mule, or liger. In the case of a Savannah cat, the cross occurs between a wild African cat called a serval and a domestic cat. Breeding Savannah cats is difficult and controversial because, like wolfdogs, they are illegal to own in many places and can exhibit aggressive behavior naturally associated with wild animals.

The first generation of Savannah cat is called F1, and after that, subsequent generations are named F2, F3, and so forth based on their percentage of wild serval DNA. Servals and domestic cats have different reproductive cycles, which means many of the potential offspring from these hybrid pairings aren't viable, including kittens born very prematurely. Savannah cats are big, since servals are up to 2 feet high at the shoulder and weigh up to 40 pounds. The further out from the original serval ancestor, the more the Savannah cat is likely to be smaller and more domesticated in personality. This hybrid has only existed in quantity since the 1990s, and in that time, breeders have pushed to include it in major cat associations.

Scottish Fold

The Scottish Fold cat has captured the public imagination in the internet era, but this controversial breed dates back to the 1960s, when an owner noticed an outdoor cat with the characteristic folded ears had a litter of kittens that included two with folded ears. In the same way breeders have made flattened noses more extreme, Scottish Fold breeders have gone from original stock with one ear fold to modern stock with two or three ear folds, leading to ears that are totally flat rather than partially flat. The ears aren't the problem, though. The dominant genetic mutation that leads to folded ears in turn causes changes in all the cartilage in these cats, causing most to develop problems at some point in their lives. At first, breeders thought heterozygous folds, meaning one parent with the gene and one without, weren't affected by the genetic condition, and they avoided making homozygous pairs, meaning both parents with the gene. Over time, geneticists questioned how much heterozygous folds were really safe from these problems, and today the evidence points to all folds developing this condition to some extent.

Selkirk Rex

The Selkirk Rex cat has a distinctive curly coat, unique among the Rex, or curly-haired, cats because its coat has all the expected layers with no alterations or losses. The LaPerm cat has an all-over curly coat but without the undercoat that gives cat fur its density and feeling of plushness; the Selkirk Rex has a traditionally soft and lush cat coat that happens to be curly.

The Selkirk Rex originated in the 1980s with one kitten from an otherwise unremarkable litter. Since then, breeding and study have revealed that the nature of the Selkirk Rex's curly gene means there are a few different types of Selkirk Rex curls that come from different combinations of gene pairs. Because the breed is relatively new and the curly gene is not homozygous, breed organizations also allow Selkirk Rex cats to be crossbred with a handful of other breeds, which helps with overall diversity and health within the breed. Some organizations have already begun to restrict these crossbreeds now that the breed has a good foothold, and the Cat Fanciers' Association will phase out the remaining outside breeds beginning in 2020.

Siamese

The Siamese cat may be the most recognizable cat in the world, or at least the most recognizable purebred cat. It can have short or long hair, but the Cat Fanciers' Association and many other organizations only judge the shorthair variety. Like the native Thai cat the Korat, the Siamese cat was first written about and illustrated centuries ago in a well known Thai collection of cat poems and information. And like the Persian cat, there are two major forms of what originated as the Siamese cat.

The earliest Siamese cats brought from Thailand to eventually compete in the west were medium in size and body type, with rounder heads, shorter necks, and more moderate appearances overall. Siamese cats stayed quite conservative in appearance until the 1950s, after which breeding accelerated to produce much more extreme forms of Siamese cats. Their heads grew much more triangular and pointed, with long necks, narrower bodies, and an overall appearance much more like modern Oriental Shorthair cats—not a coincidence, since the Oriental Shorthair was bred from modern Siamese cats. Its close breeding means the Siamese cat is prone to many genetically linked conditions that can contribute to a shortened life expectancy.

Siberian

The first mention of a Siberian cat was in 1871, when Harrison Weir, the organizer of the first cat show in England, wrote about the breed in a book. But the breed is believed to have originated much earlier, perhaps as early as the 11th century, in what is now Russia. Russian immigrants brought their cats to Siberia, and over time, the cats developed longer hair and sturdier bodies to withstand the extreme cold. In fact, Russian stories of the time claimed that their Siberian cats weighed 45 pounds and helped to protect families and property from predators. But despite their long history, it wasn't until the 1980s, after the Soviet Union lifted restrictions on house pets, that breeders began refining the breed and creating standards for the Siberian.

While they no longer tip the scales at 45 pounds, Siberians are a medium to large breed, weighing up to 17 pounds. Well-muscled and powerful, their hind legs are slightly longer than their front legs, making them agile jumpers. They have large, round eyes, which can be shades of blue, green, gold, or copper. But their most striking feature may be their long, triple coat, which adapted to protect Siberians from the bitter cold of their native land. Found in all color combinations, the coat consists of guard hair, awn hair, and down hair, and can vary from coarse to soft, depending on color.

Siberians are an affectionate, intelligent, people-oriented breed who love spending time with their humans. As a bonus, there is evidence that Siberians produce lower levels of dander than other breeds, making them more allergy friendly.

Singapura

The beautiful Singapura cat has an intriguing origin story. Two American breeders brought three cats back from Singapore in the 1970s, claiming they'd found the cats there as representatives of local street cats. These three were bred to form the Singapura breed, named for the Malay word for "Singapore."

Singapura cats are distinguished by their Abyssinian-like ticked brown coat, and in fact only one specific coloration is recognized for show Singapuras. In Singapore, the city copes with massive monsoons each year by having a huge system of sewers and drainage beneath the city, and the feral cats that live there are also called "drain cats." Another breeder later visited Singapore and discovered that the three original Singapura cats had, in turn, been brought to Singapore from the United States. Rather than being true local drain cats, the original Singapuras are believed to be Abyssinian mixes bred by the people who "found" them in Singapore.

Snowshoe

In the 1960s, a Siamese cat in Philadelphia produced three unusual kittens that all had snowy-white paws. Their breeder, Dorothy Hinds-Daugherty, loved the look of these "mittens" and began developing a new breed by crossing them with American Shorthairs. The eventual result was a sealpoint Siamese-patterned cat with four white paws, which Hinds-Daugherty dubbed a Snowshoe.

The Snowshoe exhibits the best characteristics of its Siamese and American Shorthair lineage, starting with its beautiful appearance. The short, smooth coat clearly reflects its Siamese background, and can be mitted or bicolor. In a mitted Snowshoe, the white coat is limited to paws, back legs, chest, and chin, whereas a bicolor requires a white facial pattern, as well. Either pattern gives the Snowshoe a striking appearance, especially coupled with its oval eyes, which are always a shade of blue.

Thanks to its American Shorthair ancestors, the Snowshoe has an easygoing, friendly attitude, and prefers the company of people to being alone. In fact, some Snowshoe owners claim their cats act more like people than animals! One of this breed's more unusual traits is a fascination with water, and it's not uncommon for the Snowshoe to stick a white paw under a running faucet or to even jump straight into a tub. Intelligent and affectionate, the Snowshoe will often choose one member of a family to be their "person," following them from room to room, not unlike a loyal dog. It is this loyalty and sociability that makes the Snowshoe a great fit for a feline friend.

Somali

The history of the Somali breed, which is considered a longhaired version of the Abyssinian, is a bit murky. Some believe that the cat's long hair was a natural mutation of the Abyssinian breed, but others think the lack of breeding stock in the early 1900s led English breeders to introduce long-haired cats into their breeding programs in order to keep bloodlines going. Either way, the longhaired cats began gaining popularity in North America in the 1960s, when a breeder named Evelyn Mague dubbed them "Somalis." This was a nod to Somalia's shared border with Ethiopia, the birthplace of the Abyssinian.

With its large ears and eyes and soft, bushy tail, the Somali is sometimes called the "fox cat." It has a ticked coat, meaning that each individual hair has bands of different colors, with darker colors contrasting with lighter shades. The coat comes in 28 different color combinations, and is usually darker along the spine and the tip of the tail. The fine texture of the hairs makes the Somali softer than other breeds.

Its appearance isn't the only "fox-like" characteristic of the Somali. Like a wily fox, the Somali is clever and mischievous, much to the chagrin of its human companions. It is energetic and requires plenty of time to play, and while it is friendly and affectionate, prefers to simply be near its humans rather than on a lap or cuddled in a pair of arms. But this "fox cat" will bring kitten-like energy to a home until old age.

Sphynx

The Sphynx, or Canadian Sphynx, cat is a hairless cat that can have a layer of very short, fuzzy down hairs or be completely bald. As with other hairless cats, Sphynx cats are said to be less allergenic than cats with traditional coats. Two of the original Sphynx cats were born to a barn cat in Minnesota, and these were cheekily named Dermis and Epidermis, which are terms for different layers of skin.

At first glance, the Sphynx appears very like the loosely related Selkirk Rex and Devon Rex cats, but this resemblance is limited to the face and head, because the Sphynx has a distinctive body type that includes a wider frame and a sweet little protruding abdomen sometimes called a "pot belly." Although it doesn't have a traditional coat, the Sphynx cat still comes in dozens of color varieties, and the colors and patterns show on its skin the same as they would on a full coat of hair. Sphynx cats are sweet, sociable, and devoted, and their lack of body hair makes them seek heat, meaning they love to snuggle up to human owners or other animals.

Thai

As its name suggests, the Thai cat breed originated in Thailand, where it is also known as the *Wichien Maat*, meaning "moon diamond" or "diamond gold." The Thai is an old breed, and is actually considered to be a classical, or traditional, Siamese. These traditional Siamese cats were imported to Western countries in the late 19th century. But by World War II, different breeding practices were producing Siamese cats that were slenderer and more angular than the traditional breed, and an effort began to reintroduce the classical characteristics of the Siamese. Over the next few decades, breeders painstakingly preserved the qualities of the original breed, and in 1990 renamed it the Thai to differentiate it from the Westernized Siamese.

The Siamese and Thai share many similarities since they come from the same ancestry, with the main differences being seen in the body and head shape. The medium-sized Thai is slightly larger and has a rounder head than its Westernized counterpart. But both breeds share a pointed coloration, which means they have a pale-colored body with darker extremities and head. The Thai's silky, short coat comes in every point color, and its bright blue eyes compliment the darker colors of its face.

Like the Siamese, the Thai is outgoing and vocal, enjoying "conversations" with its human companions and requiring a good amount of attention and interaction. It does well in homes with children or other pets, but some daily one-on-one time will keep it purring in happy contentment.

Tonkinese

A cross between Siamese and Burmese, the first Tonkinese cat is believed to have been imported to England in the 1800s, where it was called a "Chocolate Siamese." But the breed we know today is more likely thanks to the work of two breeders—Margaret Conroy in Canada and Jane Barletta in the United States. Conroy and Barletta worked to develop a perfect crossbreed between the Siamese and Burmese, hoping to achieve a balance between the extremes of each breed. And the Tonkinese, named for the Tonkin region of Indochina (now northern Vietnam), was the result of their work.

Tonkinese are medium-sized cats, falling in between the long, slender form of the Siamese and the stocky, broad Burmese. Like the Burmese, they are muscular, feeling heavier than they appear. Their short, silky fur comes in 12 different color and pattern varieties, and like the Siamese, many Tonkinese have a pointed coloration, or darker fur on the extremities and head. Some have "solid" coloring, where the contrast between the body and point color is less noticeable, and others have "mink" coloring, which is a medium contrast between body and point color. Their almond shaped eyes can be blue, green, yellow, or even aqua.

Like its Siamese ancestors, the Tonkinese is a talkative, vocal breed. But its Burmese lineage lends to its intelligent, playful nature, and it will often greet guests at the door or play games like fetch or hide and seek. Trusting of humans and friendly to all, the Tonkinese thrives as an indoor cat.

Toyger

Many cat owners look at their feline friends and can't help but compare them to their giant lion and tiger cousins in the wild. But in the case of the tiger-striped Toyger, it doesn't take much imagination! This striking breed combines the classic look of the wild jungle cat with the domestication of a house cat, resulting in a tiny, family-friendly tiger look-alike.

This wild-looking breed was developed in 1980 by Bengal breeder Judy Sugden, who noticed that one of her cats had a circular pattern on its head, not unlike the pattern found on tigers. She began a breeding program to refine the tiger-like look, using a shorthair tabby and a Bengal, and later added a tiger-striped stray cat from Kashmir, India, to round out the foundation stock. By 1993, the Toyger was accepted by The International Cat Association as a registered breed.

The Toyger—its name is a combination of "toy" and "tiger"—is slightly larger and longer than an average cat, so its bold striping is on full display. Its plush, soft, orange coat is striped with black or dark brown fur, giving it a look that resembles the Sumatran tiger. The comparison is even stronger when the Toyger walks, with a slinking, powerful stride reminiscent of jungle cats.

But, topping out at 15 pounds, the Toyger is nothing to fear. In fact, it is one of the most intelligent cat breeds, and can even be trained to walk on a leash. Playful, friendly, and affectionate, the Toyger may look wild, but it's really a sweet ball of fluff.

Turkish Angora

The striking Turkish Angora cat is thought to be one of the oldest breeds in the world, named for its origin in the Ankara region of modern-day Turkey, which for centuries was the heart of the Ottoman Empire. The Ottoman Empire pushed west and Europe pushed east with the Crusades, leading to the mingling of cultures and previously unseen "exotic" animals like the Turkish Angora and Persian cats. Interestingly, Angora rabbits and Angora goats, responsible for angora wool and mohair, respectively, are both densely woolly white animal varieties that sprang up at the same time in the same region.

Persian cats and Angora cats are sometimes indistinguishable, both in the historical record and as more modern breeders combined them, most often to boost the looks of the Persian cat. Today, the Persian cat has been bred to have an extremely flat face, while the Turkish Angora has been left largely untouched by extreme breed preferences. The more traditional "doll face" Persian cat looks more like a Turkish Angora cat but still has a much shorter profile. The quintessential Turkish Angora cat is white, but there have always been different colors alongside the preferred all-white Turkish Angoras, and these have been allowed in shows for a long time.

Turkish Van

It's common knowledge that most cats hate water; but the Turkish Van isn't like most cats. Known for its fascination with pools, bathtubs, sinks, and occasionally even toilets, this feline swimmer hails from the Lake Van region of Turkey, where summer temperatures can reach 100 degrees Fahrenheit. The "swimmer cat," as it's sometimes known, may have developed its love of water in an effort to cool off. The breed was first brought to Europe in the 11th century, and later imported to the United States in the 1980s, but evidence of the Turkish Van dates back to 5000 B.C., making it one of the oldest cat breeds in the world.

Some believe that the reason most cats hate getting wet is because of the time it takes them to groom their fur back into order. But the Turkish Van has no such worry, as the the breed possesses a cashmere-like coat that repels water and dries quickly, which may explain its love of the wet stuff. It is a large, muscular breed, weighing up to 16 pounds and measuring up to three feet long from nose to tail. This large stature makes them excellent jumpers, and with their energetic nature, owners must be careful to keep them out of trouble.

While not all Turkish Vans enjoy a dip in the pool or bathtub, most do love looking and playing with water, whether it be staring at a running fountain or dropping a toy in a water dish. This intelligent breed has even been known to turn on water faucets, making life with a Turkish Van anything but boring.

The Cat Who Came in From the Cold

Ed Lowe's innovation led to a new kind of pet—the indoor cat.

✳ ✳ ✳ ✳

CATS HAVE BEEN beloved pets for thousands of years. For much of that time, though, felines were considered outdoor animals. They would often spend time in the house, but owners usually put them out at night. Staunch cat lovers who kept their pets indoors paid a rather smelly price, as commonly used cat box fillers such as sand, sawdust, or ashes did little to combat the notoriously rank odors that little Fluffy left behind.

In 1947, Kay Draper of Cassopolis, Michigan, found herself short of cat box filler and went to a neighbor's to see if he might have something she could use. Lucky for Kay and for cat lovers everywhere, her neighbor Ed Lowe was in the business of selling industrial absorbents, and he suggested she try some Fuller's earth—small granules of dried clay used for soaking up oil spills and such. After trying the clay, Draper raved that it was not only cleaner than other fillers she had used, but it also helped keep odors down, thanks to its tendency to chemically bind with the offending ammonia.

Smelling an opportunity, Lowe filled several paper bags with the stuff, scrawled the name "Kitty Litter" on the side, and headed to a local pet store. The owner was skeptical of the idea. Who would pay 65 cents for a bag of dirt when sand and sawdust were virtually free? Undaunted, Lowe told him to give the bags away to any customer willing to try it. Within a short time, those customers came back saying they would gladly pay for more.

Lowe spent the next few years driving around to pet stores and cat shows to promote his new product, and his diligence paid off. Today, Americans spend nearly $800 million a year on clay cat box filler—much of which goes to Lowe's company—and millions of pampered felines enjoy the luxury of indoor living.

The First Cat Name

Nedjem (meaning "sweet" or "pleasant") is the first documented cat name. It dates from the reign of Thutmose III (1479 B.C.–1425 B.C.) in Egypt.

✳   ✳   ✳   ✳

To teach kitty her name, avoid using abbreviations and instead use the same name each time you address her. Reward kitty with a treat when she looks at you when you say her name.

Snowball or Fluffy? Cats respond best to names ending in the "ee" sound.

Chapter 3

Cat Anatomy and Behavior

Speaking Feline

Obviously, cats don't have a spoken language like we do. But they do have a voice, and they make sounds that have different meanings. This is their means of communication.

✳   ✳   ✳   ✳

S PEAKING FELINE NOT only means understanding cats' vocalizations but also understanding the more complex language of cats—body language.

Cat "speech." Cats make a variety of sounds that have been given colorful and descriptive names. Their purpose can range from expressing contentment to a call for help, from solicitation of food or companionship to a bloodcurdling expression of stark terror.

The classic cat sound (or vocalization) is the meow. Newborn kittens will meow with surprising volume. These vocalizations are probably to indicate hunger or cold and to help the mother cat locate them. As the cat gets older, the meow is still used largely to solicit or attract attention (for example, if your cat wants to signal you that he feels it's time for dinner).

An angry, frightened, or aggressive cat may hiss, which is a clear warning that whoever or whatever is approaching should come no closer. Hissing is often accompanied by a yowl, a throaty warning sound that rises and falls. An extremely frightened or angry cat will scream—a sound that needs no further explanation.

Calling or yodeling is that mournful, slightly spooky sound your cat makes (usually in the middle of the night) while wandering around the house. New cat owners (and even some veteran ones) sometimes mistake this normal vocalization for pain, confusion, or loneliness, assuming that their cat is in distress. Female cats in heat (estrus) yodel to signal their readiness to mate. The tomcat calls to the female to advertise his availability in a loud voice called caterwauling. This call also serves the purpose of warning rival males of his amorous intentions.

Three sounds are unique to cats. The chortle, a happy greeting sound, sounds a lot like a quick, high-pitched chuckle. There's also that strange chirping or chattering noise cats make that's usually reserved for when they see birds outside the window. This is the elusive wacka-wacka, a term coined by famed cat cartoonist B. Kliban. Finally, the purr is, of course, the most sublime of all feline sounds. It's also one of the most hotly debated. While a supremely contented cat will purr loudly, so will an extremely nervous or stressed one. This leads some researchers to think cats do it to reassure themselves. It's not even completely clear how cats purr. Most of the wild members of the cat family purr, but the household variety of cat is about the only one that can make the sound on both the exhale and the inhale.

Read my hips. The lithe, often silent movements of a cat actually speak volumes. Every inch of your cat, from the nose to the tip of the tail, communicates something.

We can think of the cat's state of mind as being more inward, more outward, or somewhere in between. A cat that is being defensive is more inward and will usually only attack if pursued. On the other hand, a cat that is ready to launch an offensive attack is more outward. The ears are a good marker of how inward or outward a cat is feeling: The farther back the ears are laid, the more inward the cat's state of mind. This also means a curious or friendly cat will have his ears pricked (forward and erect), since those are both outward states of mind.

Wide-open eyes are an outward sign. Other body and vocal signals will tell you if it's a good kind of outward, meaning that a happy or playful cat will have wide-open eyes but so will a terrified cat. Relaxed, open eyes reflect a more neutral internal state; relaxed, narrowed eyes usually means the cat's submissive, but it could also indicate a contented cat.

The size of the cat's pupils also offer a clue to his feelings: Dilated pupils may indicate fear, while constricted pupils suggest aggressive feelings. A direct stare is an outward sign, meaning, "Back off, buster!"

Even the position of a cat's mouth says something about his feelings. The more open the mouth, usually the more outward the cat's state of mind. Again, this can be rage (lips drawn back, tense) or play (lips not drawn back, relaxed). Of course, if a cat also opens his mouth wide to hiss, spit, and show sharp teeth, it is definitely an indication of anger.

A cat's tail serves many purposes, with one of them being an indicator of what a cat is saying. An erect tail is an outward sign, usually part of a friendly greeting or a "follow-me" message—watch a mother cat leading her kittens, or check out your cat the next time he tries to lure you toward where the cat food is stored. A lashing tail shows agitation, which may mean anger, excitement, or anticipation, especially just before pouncing in play or hunting. A bristled tail indicates fear, while a relaxed, gently swishing tail suggests contentment.

Body orientation is another indicator of inward or outward behavior. A straight-on approach is friendly, confident, or aggressive. When a cat makes himself bigger, by standing taller over another cat, climbing higher, or "puffing up" his hair, it's usually a display of dominance or aggression or an outright threat. This strategy is played out in the familiar "Halloween cat" posture (sometimes called spidering or arching), in which the cat turns sideways, arches his back, puffs up his hair, and hisses. This posture combines defensive elements (such as turning sideways) with clear threats (such as making himself look larger). On the other hand, when a cat makes himself smaller, by scrunching down, rolling to his side, or leaning away, he's trying to show that he's not a threat.

Do Real Cats Hate Water?

One of humankind's most beloved creatures is mysterious in many ways, and a popular feline myth is that cats hate water.

✳ ✳ ✳ ✳

SOME CATS MAY fear water because of how we use it around them: Many a noisy tomcat has had a bucket of water thrown its way, and mischievous kids might tease Mittens with a spray from the garden hose. Forcing a bath on a cat is a sure way to get it to loathe water, but that's no different for any other animal. There's actually a lot of evidence that cats love water. Many cats don't hesitate to jump into a filled sink or running shower and actually seem amused as water from a faucet drips over their heads. One reason for the positive reaction is that cats are attracted to the motion and sound of water.

Among the larger cats, climate makes a difference. Tigers, lions, jaguars, and ocelots from the hot savannas are likely to fancy a plunge into cool, refreshing streams and ponds to get a break from the heat. Logically, cats that live in cold environments—

including snow leopards, lynx, bobcats, and cougars—show little interest in getting wet.

Cats are, of course, creatures of habit, so a pet that has been exposed to water since it was young will tolerate a bath much better than one whose human companion shielded it from water out of fear for its safety.

Milk for Cats

It's an image straight out of a Norman Rockwell painting: a kitty lapping up a saucer of milk as happy children look on. But now we know better—cats and milk don't mix.

✳ ✳ ✳ ✳

✳ Cats may like milk—chances are they even crave it. But just as people should avoid certain things that we enjoy, cats are better off without milk (especially cow's milk).

✳ The notion that Fluffy favors dairy products could have originated on farms, where cats roam freely and help themselves to a quick lap out of the pails when cows are being milked. The question is, are the cats coveting a special source of moo juice or just quenching their thirst when water isn't readily available? Hard to say. But because it's a common behavior, people assume that cats prefer, and perhaps even need, milk.

✳ Once kittens are weaned, they no longer need milk in their diets. What's more, most grown cats are lactose intolerant. In the same way humans do, cats can experience stomach pain and diarrhea when they drink milk. Because cats don't know to stop drinking something that actually tastes good,

they can have continuous diarrhea, which leads to a loss of fluids and nutrients and can endanger their health.

✳ Can you ever give your cat milk? As always, your veterinarian can tell you what's best for your particular pet. To be on the safe side, consider one of the latest products at pet-supply stores: milk-free milk—for cats! At the same time, though, remember that milk and milk substitutes are really a form of food rather than a beverage. The best way to quench your cat's thirst is with a handy source of fresh, cool water.

Why Do Cats Purr?

Devoted cat owners know that no sound is quite as pleasant as the purr of a happy cat. That deep, throaty rumble seems to be the essence of contentment. How do cats do it? Well, it's a purr-fect mystery.

✳   ✳   ✳   ✳

THE PROBLEM, OF course, is that you can't see inside a purring cat. To get an idea of what's going on, scientists turned to electromyography, a process that uses electrodes to measure how and when nerves make muscles contract. Purring cats expand and contract the muscles around the larynx, or "voice box," which contains the vocal cords. This rapid muscle motion causes the air in the box to vibrate as it is pushed in and out of the glottis, a small, narrow space between the vocal cords. Cats aren't about to tell us how they do it.

Animal behaviorists do know a little more about *why* cats purr, though. Kittens initially learn to purr from their mothers on their second day of life. Because kittens are born blind and deaf, the vibrations of the momma cat's purr act as an all-safe signal, letting her kittens know she's home and ready to nurse them. You may have noticed your cat making kneading motions with its paws when it purrs. Kittens do this when they nurse because kneading promotes milk flow. By kneading, a kitten is saying, "I'm feeling safe and warm and good, just like I did when Momma was taking care of me." Cats can't purr with their mouths open, but they can purr while nursing. If your cat is kneading you, it may also mean, "I'm hungry. When's dinner?"

But cats don't purr only when they're happy. They've been known to purr when they're injured, in pain, and when they're stressed, perhaps to comfort themselves. Before you panic, however, be aware that the "pain" purr is usually deeper than a regular purr and is accompanied by other distress signs, such as sensitivity to touch, refusal to eat, and constant licking or scratching of an injured or irritated limb.

Why would an injured cat purr? Again, no one is quite sure, although there's a theory that cats may purr due to a release of endorphins. It may also be an instinctive way of calling for help quietly, without drawing the attention of creatures that might want to prey on an injured cat. If you think your cat is asking for your help, make him as comfortable as you can and then call a vet to find out what your next step should be.

Otherwise, if your cat is purring with his normal blissed-out expression, you can kick back, relax, and enjoy it. Just like him.

Out of Sight, Out of Mind

If you think a cat isn't smart, consider that it's the only animal with enough sense to bury its waste.

✳   ✳   ✳   ✳

Don't Forget About Humans

TECHNICALLY, CATS AREN'T the only animals that bury their waste. We humans have been burying our bodily waste for thousands of years, and all signs point toward the continuance of this habit. We would be overrun by stink if we didn't.

But in terms of "lower" animals, cats are indeed the only animals that have the courtesy to dispose of their droppings.

The only other animal that possesses an inclination to do something special with its feces is the chimpanzee, which will sometimes chuck turds at rival chimps in fits of anger. Every other animal just lets the turds fall where they will.

Uncovering the Origins

The house cat's habit of covering its feces probably goes back to its ancestors in the wild. In nature, cats sometimes bury their waste in an effort to hide it from predators and rival cats. It's the opposite of using urine to mark territory; to remain incognito, cats do their best to hide any trace of their presence.

By the same token, a dominant cat will leave its poop anywhere it pleases within its territory in order to scare off trespassing felines. A pile of fly-covered waste, and the distinctive smell that wafts from that pile, functions like a BEWARE OF CAT sign. For another cat to ignore this warning would be to invite trouble in the form of teeth and claws.

Your house cat's tendency to bury its feces in a litter box may be a sign that it recognizes your dominance in the house. And if it uses the litter box but neglects to cover its leavings—as some cats do—it may be your tabby's way of acknowledging a kind of shared dominance over the abode.

You needn't worry about your place in the pecking order until you come home and find urine stains in the corners of the room and feces in the middle of the floor. At that point, you are trespassing on your cat's territory—sitting on *its* couch, watching *its* television, popping *its* popcorn—and you'd better start paying rent . . . or prepare to face the terrible wrath of the tabby cat.

How Do Cats Always Find Their Way Home?

You can count on two things from your local television news during sweeps week: a story about a household appliance that is a death trap and another about a cat that was lost but somehow trekked thirty miles through a forest, across a river, and over an eight-lane highway to find its way home. You think, "No, I don't think my electric mixer is going to give me cancer, but, oh, that cat . . . "

❋ ❋ ❋ ❋

WHAT'S THE DEAL with felines? How do they always seem to be able to make it home, regardless of how far away home might be? No one knows for sure, but researchers have their theories. One study speculates that cats use the position of the sun as a navigational aid. Another posits that cats have a sort of built-in compass; this is based on magnetic particles that scientists have discovered on the "wrists" of their paws. While these are merely hypotheses, scientists know that cats have an advanced ability to store mental maps of their environments.

Exhibit A is Sooty, one of the felines chronicled on the PBS program *Extraordinary Cats*. Sooty traveled more than a hundred miles in England to return to his original home after his family moved. Sooty's feat, however, was nothing compared to that of Ninja, another cat featured on the program. A year after disappearing following his family's move, Ninja showed up at his old house, 850 miles away in a different state; he went from Utah back to Washington.

But there are limits to what a cat can do—that's why odysseys of felines like Sooty and Ninja are extraordinary. In other words, the odds aren't good that Snowball will reach your loving arms in Boston if you leave her in Pittsburgh.

Holiday Pet Dangers!

The Christmas holidays can pose a variety of hazards to our pets. Don't let this joyous time be ruined by a tragedy that could have been easily prevented.

✳   ✳   ✳   ✳

W ITH THE HUSTLE and bustle that typically takes place over the Christmas holidays, it's easy to overlook the various dangers this special time of year can pose to our four-legged family members.

✳ Tinsel can cause potentially fatal intestinal blockage if ingested by a dog or cat. If you must use tinsel, place it out of your pet's reach.

✳ Glass ornaments are another often-overlooked concern. If your pet sees all ornaments as toys, use only unbreakable plastic decorations.

✳ Never place lit candles wher a cat can reach them. Animals are often attracted to flickering flames, and it takes only one accidentally overturned candle to cause a disastrous fire.

✳ Don't let your pet drink from the Christmas tree stand, especially if you add chemicals to extend the tree's life. If your pet is insistent, place a piece of mesh screen over the stand to keep out thirsty tongues.

✳ Don't feed holiday "people food" to your pet, no matter how much it begs. A lot of holiday dishes are rich in fat and other ingredients that can cause an animal intestinal distress, especially when consumed in large quantities. Bones, especially from poultry, are another no-no; they can splinter in your pet's mouth.

✳ Avoid giving your pet holiday candy—especially chocolate, which can be lethal to dogs.

* Tack down all electrical cords so your pet can't chew on them. Even a gentle gnaw can result in a trip to the veterinarian—and really curly hair for your cat!

* Place all decorative holiday plants where your pet can't reach them. Many plants, such as mistletoe, can be toxic if ingested.

Did You Know . . .

Here are some more cat facts to digest.

✳   ✳   ✳   ✳

* Cats touch each other as a means of bonding and establishing their hierarchy. A nose-to-nose greeting between friendly cats is a sign of affection.

* The rough center of a cat's tongue has no taste buds. It's used primarily as a grooming tool and food grater.

* Cats don't have receptors to taste sweet things. Instead, they react most strongly to sour, salty, and bitter tastes.

* Dr. Samuel Johnson, poet and essayist, used to go out and purchase oysters for his beloved cat Hodge. He could have sent servants but feared they might dislike the cat if asked to perform the task.

* Cats have no specific blood type and can donate across breeds.

* Cats lack a true collarbone. That's how felines end up in odd places. Generally, cats can squeeze into any space they can fit their heads into.

* Adult cats have 32 teeth.

* Cats have right and left "hands" just like people. Forty percent are right-pawed, 20 percent are left-pawed, and a lucky 40 percent of cats are ambidextrous.

* Human bites are more dangerous than cat bites because people have more bacteria in their mouths.

* There are 245 bones in a cat's body compared to 206 in an adult human's.

* Cats are digitigrades. That means they walk on their toes—a great skill for sneaking up on prey!

* Traditional clay litters such as Lowe first produced (see page 87) still account for 40 percent of the cat litter market today.

* Clumping litter accounts for 60 percent of the cat litter sold in the United States.

* Five percent of cat owners have thrown their cat a birthday party.

* Sixty-three percent of cat owners purchase gifts for their feline friends on birthdays, holidays, and just for the fun of it.

* The cost of the average cat gift? $17.

* Regular gifts include catnip toys, cotton mice, jingle bells, a new collar, a water foundation, oat grass, and anything *Garfield*.

* Just like snowflakes or human fingerprints, no two cat nose prints are exactly the same.

* A breeding female is called a queen.

* A castrated male is a gib.

* A "head bonk" is what happens when an affectionate cat nudges you with the front part of its head.

* Cats have about 100 different vocalization sounds. In comparison, dogs have about 10.

* A group of cats is called a clowder.

* The giraffe, camel, and cat are the only animals that step with both left legs then both right legs when they walk (as opposed to alternating left and right).

* A cat uses its whiskers to "feel" its environment.

* A cat's heart beats twice as fast as a human heart: 110–140 beats per minute.

* Presenting an unprotected tummy indicates trust.

Let's "Hear It" for the Cat

Kitty's ears swivel like radar detectors as she takes note of what's going on around her.

✳ ✳ ✳ ✳

THE CAT'S HEARING is among the sharpest in the animal kingdom—they can recognize their owner's footsteps from hundreds of feet away! Cats don't even have to move their heads to know which direction a sound is coming from. Instead, they just maneuver their ears.

People can detect lower tones than cats but felines far outhear us in the high ranges. For example, high-pitched mouse squeaks come in at 40,000 cycles per second. No problem for the feline, who can hear sounds up to the 65,000-cycle range (but problematic for the human, who can hear only up to the 23,000-cycle range). For the most accurate indication of a cat's mood, look at the position of his ears. Confident, curious cats turn their ears forward so they won't miss a thing.

The More You Know...

Because you can never know too much of a good thing, right?

✳ ✳ ✳ ✳

✳ Ever notice a kitty walking around the house, rubbing his cheek against the wall corners and the couch? He's leaving behind a scent mark saying, in effect, "This is mine." Scent glands are found in kitty's cheeks, temple, chin, and even his tail and paws. So when you're the recipient of a face rub or a tail curling around your legs, that's kitty's affectionate way of claiming you as his own.

✳ Newborn kittens smell their mother and literally follow their noses to find her. By the age of three weeks, kittens will have the same highly developed sense of smell as an adult cat.

✳ People tend to carry the most interesting smells on their purses, briefcases, and hands. By smelling those items thoroughly, your cat gets a good idea of where you've been, what you've done, and even if you've petted another cat.

* Cats dislike the smell of chlorine and are adept at detecting even minute amounts of it in tap water. This is why kitty might turn her nose up at a fresh bowl of water and instead lap from a less-than-clean looking pond or puddle.

* Cats drink by curling their tongue into a spoon-shape scoop. They lap the liquid, flicking each scoop to the back of their mouth and swallowing after every four or five laps. The rough center surface of their tongue acts like a sponge to retain water.

* Cats can't see in total darkness, but they need only one-sixth as much light as we do.

* Cats can see blue, green, and yellow hues (but prefer mousy-gray shades!).

* Relative to body size, cats have the largest eyes of any mammal.

* Feline eyes were designed for the hunt; they give a cat nearly 285 degrees of dimensional sight.

* The reflectors in the middle of the road that bounce your headlights back to you at night are called "cat's eyes" and were designed to mimic the way a real cat's eyes reflect light.

* Cats' eyes may be large, medium, or small, but all cats have round eyes.

* The color of a cat's eyes are determined genetically and can range from copper to blue.

* A telltale clue to a cat's mood is the position of his tail. A mere flick of the tail can relay a message worth a thousand words.

* A vertical tail indicates a friendly welcome.

* An upright tail bent forward displays dominance.

* A wagging tail can signal ambivalence, anger, or annoyance.

* When the tail curves down and up, kitty is calm and content.

* FACT: Ten percent of a cat's bones are in its tail.

Something Smells Fishy

A feline's sense of smell is 14 times stronger than a human's. Compared to our cats, we are blind, deaf, and scent-dumb.

✳ ✳ ✳ ✳

CATS USE SMELL not only to reject the dinner you've set out for them (although that does seem to be their favorite use) but also for identification, communication, and navigation.

Cats can even smell with their mouth! "Flehming" involves two extra scent organs found between the hard palate of the mouth and the septum of the cat's nose. The grimacing, lip-curling behavior transfers scent particles with the tongue to tiny ducts behind the upper front teeth where they connect to the special scent organs. Flehming actually falls somewhere between smelling and tasting.

That's a Sunburn

Did you know cats can get sunburned, even if they're not outdoors?

✳ ✳ ✳ ✳

ULTRAVIOLET RADIATION TRAVELS through windows and can damage the delicate nose and ear tips of our feline friends. White cats are especially vulnerable. If your cat spends a great deal of time in the sun (is there a cat that doesn't?) consider applying small amounts of sunblock to the susceptible areas of skin, such as the bridge of the nose and the ear tips. You can also apply a line of sunblock along any part in the fur along the head or back. Add a pair of shades and a boogie board and your cat will be ready for summer fun.

Cats and Babies

So why do cats approach babies?

✳   ✳   ✳   ✳

ONE THOUGHT IS cats are attracted to the smell of a baby's milky breath. Also, cats are so intensely alert to change that some bump noses with a baby if they notice something different. Numerous cats are on record for alerting parents when a baby has a high fever or has stopped breathing. For those who need additional reassurance, nose bumps from felines are a sign of affection, not breath stealing!

The Cat Toss

Cats are curious creatures: Many people believe that a dropped kitty will right itself and land safely on it feet, only to step away aloof and unaffected.

✳   ✳   ✳   ✳

A BELGIAN LEGEND HAS it that in A.D. 962, Baldwin III, Count of Ypres, threw several cats from a tower. It must have been a slow news year, because the residents of Ypres named the last day of their annual town fair "Cat Wednesday" and commemorated it by having the village jester throw live cats from a belfry tower—a height of almost 230 feet. But there's no need to call PETA: The last time live cats were used for this ceremony was in 1817, and since then stuffed animals have been thrown in their place.

As cruel as this custom was, it is unclear whether the cat toss was meant to kill cats or to demonstrate their resilience. After that last live toss in 1817, the village record keeper wrote the following: "In spite of the height of the fall, the animal ran off quickly so that it might never be caught again in a similar ceremony." How could the cat have survived such a tumble?

Twist and Meow

Cats have an uncanny knack for righting themselves in midair. Even if a cat starts falling head first, it almost always hits the ground on its paws. The people of Ypres weren't the only ones amazed and amused by this feline feat. In 1894, French physiologist Etienne-Jules Marey decided to get to the bottom of the mechanics of cat-righting by taking a series of rapid photographs of a cat in midfall. Marey held a cat upside down by its paws and then dropped it several feet onto a cushion.

The resulting 60 sequential photos demonstrated that as the cat fell, it initiated a complex maneuver, rotating the front of its body clockwise and then the rear part counterclockwise. This motion conserved energy and prevented the cat from spinning in the air. It then pulled in its legs, reversed the twist again, and extended its legs slightly to land with minimal impact.

High-Rise Syndrome

The story gets even more interesting. In 1987, two New York City veterinarians examined 132 cases involving cats that had fallen out of the windows of high-rise buildings (the average fall was five and a half stories). Ninety percent of the cats survived, though some sustained serious injuries. When the vets analyzed the data, they found that, predictably, the cats suffered progressively greater injuries as the height from which they fell increased. But this pattern continued only up to seven stories; above that, the farther the cat fell, the greater chance it had of surviving relatively unharmed.

The researchers named this peculiar phenomenon High-Rise Syndrome and explained it this way: A cat that fell about five stories reached its terminal velocity—that is, maximum downward speed—of 60 miles per hour. If it fell any distance beyond that, it had the time not only to right itself in midair but also to relax and spread itself out to slow down its fall, much like a flying squirrel or a parachute.

Chapter 4

Cat Care

Cats and the Law: Is Your Cat a Stray?

Most of us think of "leash laws" in terms of dogs. But many cities, towns, and even counties have revamped these animal control laws to include all kinds of pets.

✳   ✳   ✳   ✳

S OME CAT OWNERS have resisted leash and licensing laws for cats, but the trend seems to be headed that way.

You may be surprised to find out that anytime your cat leaves your property by himself, he's technically considered a stray. That means local animal-control authorities can pick him up, hold him for the required time (which can range from as long as a week or two to as short as 24 hours), then dispose of him however the law allows (this includes euthanasia).

Check with your town, county, and state animal-control agencies to see what the laws are in your area. The odds are, a free-roaming feline is breaking the law.

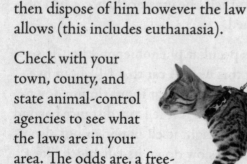

Finding the Right Vet

Choosing a veterinarian for your cat is a lot like choosing a doctor for yourself. You want someone with a good bedside manner and someone you like and trust. If you have special needs, you also want a doctor who understands and keeps those needs in mind.

✳ ✳ ✳ ✳

I F YOU'RE A first-time cat owner, have recently moved to a new area, or need to find a new veterinarian, you can just try opening the Yellow Pages to "Animal Hospitals." All veterinarians go to school for as many years as medical doctors and have to meet strict standards for licensing, so you're bound to find a competent and professional vet that way. But the relationship among you, your pet, and your vet is going to last for many years, and if you took the time to find just the right cat, it makes sense to find the right vet. This might be the one area where city folk have it over country folk. A small town may just have one vet, while a big city has dozens within several miles.

Contact professional organizations. The American Veterinary Medical Association (AVMA) can refer you to affiliated veterinarians in your area, and the American Animal Hospital Association (AAHA) can direct you to clinics that meet its standards. The AVMA can also help you find feline specialists, behavior experts, veterinary eye doctors, and other professionals. Like any specialist, though, expect to pay heftier fees.

Get recommendations from other "cat people." Friends, family, and neighbors who have cats usually also have veterinarians. Take advantage of their experience, and get recommendations from them.

Look Before You Leap

Once you get a referral for a veterinarian, call up, introduce yourself, and find out when you can drop by to see the facilities and meet the doctors. Make your visit brief but thorough.

Be discriminating, but don't be put off if the vet and the clinic staff can't spend a long time with you—they do have a hospital to run and patients to take care of. If you have a lot of questions and need the vet's undivided attention, the most polite thing to do is make an appointment—and offer to pay for it.

Before you meet with the vet, determine what your needs and wants are in a vet and a veterinary hospital. Whether those needs and wants are affordable prices, the latest medical techniques and equipment, or the vet's "table-side" manner, determining your priorities ahead of time will help build a better client-veterinarian relationship.

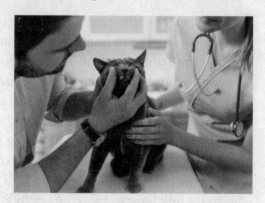

If you are going to drop by the facility and meet with the vet, here are some items to consider:

* Ask about the practice's hours, the availability of after-hour services, and whether 24-hour-a-day emergency care is provided.

* Ask about the type of services offered, from routine physical exams to surgeries to boarding capabilities, and check the hospital's fees for each service.

* Make sure you feel comfortable with the support staff as well. A friendly, attentive staff reassures you that your pet will get the best care possible.

Care and Maintenance

Imagine you had one of those really fine cars. You know—one that costs more than some folks' houses. You'd do your darndest to keep it in top condition.

Well, a cat is a finer machine than humans can ever hope to build—and one that thinks and feels, besides. It just doesn't make sense to talk about your cat's health without the topic of proper care and maintenance coming at the top of the list.

Some folks think that because you don't have to take a cat for a walk three times a day that they're low-maintenance. But keeping your cat happy and fit does require a good amount of time and effort.

Litter Box Accidents

Of all cat behavior problems, these are the ones owners complain about the most—and with good reason.

✳ ✳ ✳ ✳

BESIDES THE MESS and damage, inappropriate elimination is unsanitary and creates an unpleasant (and often malodorous) atmosphere in the home. Cats have an instinct to dig in loose materials and bury their urine and feces, and many of them adapt this instinct to the litter box with few problems. But it's still something they have to learn, and they often need help to get the lesson right.

Boxes, boxes everywhere. Litter boxes and litter should be the first things you buy when you decide to get a cat. Get them set up before the cat sets a single paw in your home. Make sure they are clean, easy to find, and numerous enough. Many cats dislike using a box that another cat has recently used (even if that other cat is herself), so the rule of thumb is: The number of litter boxes in the house should equal the number of cats in the house plus one. Thus, if you have two cats, you should have at least three litter boxes; even households with just one cat should have at least two boxes.

Keep it simple. Deodorizing litters, antibacterial litters, high-tech litters—all of these gimmicks used to sell various kinds of cat box fillers are aimed at the creatures that buy the litter, not necessarily the ones that use it. There's nothing wrong with using a litter that makes your job of tending to the litter box a little easier or a little less unpleasant, but some cats may be put off by the additives, perfumes, and chemical deodorizers used in some of these products. And that means they'll choose to do their business elsewhere. A plain cat box filler like ground clay (unscented) usually works fine.

Stop the madness. Once a cat starts eliminating outside of the litter box, do not assume she'll learn to use the box on her own. Cats habitually return to the same places to eliminate, a habit that's reinforced by the lingering odor of urine or feces. Since a cat's sense of smell is far superior to ours, cleaning up a litter box accident so that you can no longer detect the odor may not be enough to deter the cat from doing it again. Enzyme-based pet odor neutralizers actually break down the chemical structure of urine and feces residue so that your cat can no longer smell it. Pet supply stores usually carry at least one brand.

Block the favorite spots. Deny your cat access to places where she's eliminated outside the litter box. Physical barriers work well, but if that's not possible, try covering the spots with tinfoil or double-sided tape. This provides a barrier to the odor and a texture the cat won't want to walk on. If possible, consider placing a litter box directly on top of the inappropriate spot, and then gradually move the box an inch or so every few days, until it's where you want it to be.

Be your cat's personal trainer. When your cat first comes home, keep her in one room with a litter box. Once she's using that box consistently, give her the run of more rooms. Usually, this is enough to lock in the habit. However, a cat who doesn't completely get the hang of the litter box—or backslides and starts eliminating in other places—needs some training.

The best method is to use a large, portable dog kennel. Set the cat up in the kennel with litter and water and give her meals in there, too. When you see her use the litter box, let her out for a recess. Keep an eye on her, and return her to her private quarters after an hour or two. The next time you see her use the litter box, let her out again. The idea is, she only gets free run of the house when she uses the litter box. This strategy can train (or retrain) a cat to use the litter box in as little as two or three weeks—but longer isn't uncommon, either.

What's the cause? A cat who suddenly begins eliminating in inappropriate places could be announcing that she doesn't feel well. You'll never make any progress on getting her to use the litter box consistently if there's a physical cause for the unwanted behavior, so get her to the vet as soon as possible.

Location, location, location. Sometimes, there's something about the location of the litter box that the cat objects to. Maybe it's too far out of the way (down in a basement or up in an attic, for example) or too hard to get into or out of (especially for small kittens or elderly cats). Sometimes, air fresheners or other odors in the room will keep the cat away. Pine and citrus, for example, are pleasing smells to us but may be offensive to cats. Also, loud noises, such as a nearby stereo, may disturb your cat when she's doing her business.

When should you call the vet? Before you try to treat inappropriate elimination as a behavior problem, take your cat to the vet for a thorough exam. If your vet rules out a physical cause, you know it's probably a straight behavior problem. However, even if there is a physical problem and your vet treats it successfully, your cat still has developed the habit of eliminating someplace other than litter box; you'll still need to follow the steps for correcting the behavior problem.

Feline Fuel: Feeding Your Cat Right

"You are what you eat" is a solid piece of common sense that city and country folk alike understand. And it's just as true for your cat as it is for you. Feed your cat a quality diet, and you're more likely to have a healthy cat.

❋   ❋   ❋   ❋

THE PET FOOD industry is big business—and with good reason. There are well over 100 million dogs and cats living in American homes, plus who-knows-how-many more in shelters, catteries, and kennels across the country. To top it all off, you have thousands of people feeding strays. If you figure a single cat can go through some 90 pounds or more of cat food in a year, we're talking about hundreds of millions of dollars being spent annually, just to feed the kitty.

Just like human food, there are some tasty feline treats that are good for cats and some things that are basically junk food. An occasional snack of the not-so-healthy stuff shouldn't do any permanent harm, but don't make it a part of your cat's diet.

Cats Are Carnivores, But . . .

The wild ancestors of the modern house cat were hunters—an instinct your cat still has. Whether Tabby is bringing you gifts of demised birds and mice or pouncing on a piece of lint, she's expressing a powerful natural drive to stalk and kill prey. If you doubt that your cat is a natural-born meat eater (and preda-

tor), just take a good look at her teeth the next time she yawns. Those fangs are not designed for eating alfalfa sprouts.

The fact is your cat is so much of a carnivore, she can't survive as a vegetarian.

There are certain nutrients found only in animal proteins that your cat needs. One of these nutrients is an amino acid called taurine. Without taurine, cats can go blind and develop enlarged hearts, which will likely give out on them well before their time. And unlike dogs, cats require a dietary source of vitamin A and a fatty acid called arachidonic acid found only in animal tissue. That's why you should never feed dog food to your cat. Dog food just doesn't have enough of the right kinds of nutrients for cats. By the pound it may be cheaper to feed dog food to your cat, but it could cost your cat her health, her sight, or even her life.

Of course, that doesn't mean you should feed your cat raw meat or let her depend on hunting as her only source of food. It's been hundreds of years since cats lived in the wild, so their hunting skills are more than a little rusty. Plus, cats that hunt or eat raw or undercooked meat can pick up several kinds of diseases—including some that might get passed on to you.

Home Cooking or Store-Bought Food?

The best thing about a home-cooked meal is you're the one who gets to decide what's in it. If you're a steak-and-potatoes type, then you'll broil up a nice lean Porterhouse and a batch of new reds. On the other hand, if you go for a green salad, you can pick your dinner fresh from the garden. Trying to cut down on cholesterol and salt? When you're the cook, you make the call.

❋ ❋ ❋ ❋

UNLESS YOU ARE a nutritionist or dietitian, however, you should let the experts—the major pet food manufacturers—prepare the major portion of kitty's diet. Working out the right amounts and balance of foods is a difficult task. Most all food can get lumped into one or more of three categories of nutrients: protein, fat, and carbohydrate.

Different kinds of animals (including people) need different proportions of protein, fat, and carbohydrate in their diets. (That's another reason why dog food isn't good for cats—dogs and cats need different percentages of fat and protein to stay healthy.) What's more, those needs change during an animal's life. A kitten has different nutritional needs than an adult cat, and they both have different needs than an old codger cat. Most pet food companies have special formulas for different levels of age and activity, and there's a whole line of prescription diets for cats with various health problems.

We've all seen a cat come running at the sound of a can opener—there's no doubt that kitty loves getting canned food. But is canned food better for cats than dry food? Not necessarily. Each type of food has its advantages and disadvantages. The most important factor is whether the food meets your cat's nutritional needs. Of course, your budget and your cat's preference also play a role in which type of food you should choose. Store-bought cat food comes in three general forms:

* Dry cat food is also called "kibble." It's just what it sounds like: crunchy nuggets or kernels of food. Dry pet food can be stored for a long time (in a rodent-proof bin, if you have problems with mice), has no smell, and packages can be kept at room temperature for weeks without spoiling.

* Canned or "wet" cat food has a fairly long shelf life as long as it's unopened. Once you open the can, though, it doesn't hold up very well. Wet cat food usually has a pungent smell and tends to be a little bit messy to handle. If you feed your cat wet food, any uneaten food should be picked up and discarded after 15 to 20 minutes—it's a breeding ground for bacteria that can make your cat sick. Unused portions of newly opened cans can be refrigerated in an airtight container for up to a day or two.

* Semimoist cat food also consists of individual nuggets but without the crunch of dry food. It's usually packaged in

sealed canisters or individual meal-size foil pouches and is highly processed. Some semimoist cat foods are formed into interesting shapes or dyed different colors. Semimoist foods in resealable containers keep well at room temperature.

Each of these types of foods has its strong points and weak points. For instance, dry food is convenient, economical, and can be left out all day. On the other hand, the way some dry foods are formulated seems to encourage the formation of bladder stones. The rich aromas of canned food will tempt even the pickiest eater, but the crunchiness of dry food helps prevent dental plaque. Semimoist combines the convenience of dry food with the tastiness of canned food but may contain the most nonfood fillers and dyes.

All brand-name cat food covers the basic nutritional needs of your average cat. But if you're worried about the overall quality of the boxes, bags, and cans of feline food in the pet supplies aisle of your local market, you might want to consider one of the premium-brand foods, usually found only in pet stores or through veterinarians.

Feeding your cat store-bought food ensures that she is getting the nutrients she needs. At the same time, a home-cooked supplement to your cat's regular diet is okay if you make sure the foods you select are appropriate for cats. There's nothing wrong with getting the most out of a whole fryer by cooking up the gizzards for the cat, unless they become the major part of Tabby's diet. You see, organ meats (kidney, stomach, and even liver) are all right for your cat in moderation, but they've been linked to health problems if your cat eats too much of them. Likewise, every cat on the planet loves milk and cheese, but most cats have trouble digesting them well.

What's In My Cat Food?

Careful consumers are label readers—and that's a good place to start in figuring out just what you're feeding your cat when you buy cat food.

* * * *

MANY PET OWNERS compare the nutrition information on different brands of pet food and notice that a less-expensive brand has the same nutrients as a premium cat food. What that really means is that those two foods match up in the laboratory.

For example, old shoe leather might rate as high as lean chicken breasts in protein content; of course, you and your cat would both rather eat chicken. So, what you need to know is how the various nutrients match up in your cat.

You see, it's not how much of a particular nutrient there is in a can of cat food that matters but how much your cat's digestive system can take up. Cheap foods are usually made from cheap ingredients, which your cat may not digest well. Just because your cat gobbles it up and yowls for more doesn't mean a food is good for her. (Think about kids and junk food.)

The moral of the story is brand-name and specialty pet foods are made by companies that do a lot of research into pet nutrition. They're always improving their foods to keep pace with the latest information, and they use quality ingredients that have nutrients your cat can use. Brand-name cat food may cost a little more, but it's worth it.

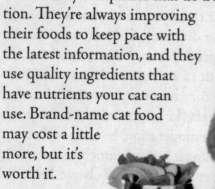

Please Eat the Daisies

If it's green and it grows from the ground, the odds are some cat will try to eat it. This vegetarian quirk in the carnivorous cat's personality is particularly worrisome if the plants are your prized houseplants—or worse, if they're poisonous to your cat.

❋ ❋ ❋ ❋

MANY CAT OWNERS look at plant eating as a behavior problem—and it is if the cat is eating plants you don't want her to. Some folks assume that a cat who eats plants isn't getting enough of the right kinds of food in her diet. They're right, too—but only in the sense that what the cat needs more of in her diet is . . . plants.

The experts have a few ideas why cats eat plants. It could be to get some trace nutrients, to help with digestion, or as an emetic to help bring up swallowed hair and other nonfood items. Whatever the reason, eating vegetation is an instinctive behavior in cats; you can't stop it. So the best thing to do is point the behavior in a direction you can both live with.

Plant a "cat garden." You can find ready-made kits in pet shops and catalogs, but a more economical choice is to just do it yourself. If you're handy, you might build a fancy container out of wood or you can just use something on hand. Whatever you do, make sure you plant your cat garden in a container that doesn't tip or move easily. All you need is just a couple of inches of good potting soil and some seeds. Oat grass or catnip are good choices. You might want to keep the garden out of reach from your cats while your "crop" is coming up, but once the greens are a few inches tall, set it out and let your cat munch.

Get your plants out of reach. Cats are incredibly good climbers and leapers, so putting your houseplants on stands or shelves probably won't help much. Mantels, windowsills, and the like are easy landing pads for feline acrobats. Hang plants from the ceiling, put them behind cat-proof barriers (on a sun porch closed off by glass doors, for example), or set them in locations that your cat absolutely can't jump, climb, or crawl to.

Shield your plants. If you can't get your plants out of kitty's reach, try forming a protective shield around your plants. Placing chicken wire, plant markers, or even mothballs in the soil around your plant may safeguard it from prying paws, but these barriers aren't so pretty to look at. Try adding some Spanish moss around the base of your plant to keep your cat away. Sometimes, spraying bitters on the leaves will discourage a cat from chewing. Other times, though, putting some bad-tasting substance on a plant does more harm to the plant than the cat's teeth would.

Kitty Snacks and "People Food"

A well-fed cat doesn't need to snack between meals any more than you do. Too-frequent snacks will have the same effect on your cat that it can have on you: unhealthy weight gain and an imbalanced diet.

✳ ✳ ✳ ✳

O F COURSE, IT'S hard to resist the temptation to give your feline pal a treat now and then—and it's perfectly all right to give in to that temptation, assuming there's a long enough stretch of time between now and then. How long of a time depends on your cat and the kinds of treats you give her. If your cat is still eating the recommended amount of quality cat food every day and isn't overweight, then you're probably not giving her too many treats. If, on the other hand, your cat is chowing down on tasty but not-so-nutritious snacks and is either getting plumper or turning her nose up at dinner, it's time to change your strategy.

Store-bought cat treats tend not to be packed with good nutrition. Their main purpose is the same as human treats: to taste good—real good—and that's about it. "Gourmet" cat snacks usually have fewer artificial colors and fillers in them but still aren't meant to be fed as a regular part of Tabby's diet. The good thing about "gourmet" treats is the cost: They're usually so expensive that cat owners won't overfeed them to their cats!

A question vets hear all the time is, "Can I feed my cat people food?" There's very little that people eat that cats shouldn't (or won't), so that's not really so much of a problem. The question once again is nutritional balance. Just like with home cooking, feeding your cat leftovers or using people food for snacks may not be providing her with the right nutrients in the correct amounts.

Still, people food might provide some of the healthiest snacks for cats. If you give your cat some scrambled eggs or a couple of pieces of pasta, at least you know what's in it. And you might be surprised what your cat will eat. Cat owners report their pets begging for predictable tidbits such as fish and chicken as well as unexpected ones, including tomatoes and cantaloupe.

Water, Water Everywhere

Your cat needs about an ounce of water per pound of body weight every day. That doesn't sound like much, but it adds up: An average-size cat would need more than a gallon of water every week.

Of course, cats get water by drinking. But there's another important source of water for your cat: the food she eats. The more water there is in her food, the less she needs to drink. Canned cat food is more expensive because you're buying water along with the food (up to 75 percent of wet cat food is water) and paying a little more for the container. Dry cat food has much less water (perhaps 10 percent by weight), which means a cat whose diet consists of only dry food has to drink a lot more.

Dehydration (not enough water in the body) is a serious problem for any living creature, and cats are especially prone to it.

A cat can go without food for days, losing up to 40 percent of her body weight, and still survive. But a loss of body water of only 10 to 15 percent can kill her. Other liquids—like milk, if it doesn't make your cat sick—are a good source of water, but nothing beats the real thing. Be sure your cat has plenty of clean, fresh water available at all times.

Cat Grooming

Because longhair cats need regular grooming (with daily grooming really being the best), you might want to consult your budget before answering this question. But even if you have the means to bring your longhair cat to a professional groomer weekly, you should still have grooming tools on hand at home—and know how to use them.

✳   ✳   ✳   ✳

YOU NEVER KNOW when your cat might get into something that needs to be combed out right away or when she might need a touch-up between trips to the groomer.

Do I Need a Professional Groomer?

The main advantages of a professional groomer are training, skill, and experience. A good groomer can get your cat's coat looking spiffy quickly and humanely, with a minimal amount of trauma. Really bad mats and tangles can be dealt with at home, but if you've never done that sort of thing before, you run the risk of injuring your cat—an injury that will probably need veterinary attention. Such grooming problems are probably best left to the professionals, too.

Even folks who learn to wield a slicker brush and metal comb with a good amount of expertise will turn to a professional groomer from time to time. It could be for a bad mat or tangle, during a particularly heavy period of shedding, or just to get the full treatment so that Tabby looks her best.

Tools and Tips for At-Home Grooming

Every cat owner needs some grooming supplies. A metal comb is the most essential basic grooming tool. Sturdy stainless-steel combs with wide-set, round teeth are widely available and reasonably priced. A slicker brush has bristles that look like dozens of tiny bent nails. They resemble the rasps on a cat's tongue and serve the same purpose in grooming. Most cats enjoy the sensation of the slicker brush and the metal comb—unless, of course, you hit a tangle or mat.

You may also want to invest in a flea comb, particularly if you let your cat outdoors, live in a year-round flea climate (like southern Florida or Louisiana), or have other pets who go outdoors. Flea combs look like metal combs but with very fine teeth set close together. Flea combs can be used for regular grooming, as a "touch-up" after the slicker brush or metal comb. Grooming mitts fit over your whole hand and let you work a larger surface while petting your cat.

Here are a few tips for home grooming:

Make it fun. Most cats love being stroked and enjoy the feeling of light grooming. It's good social behavior—cats who get along well will blissfully groom each other for long periods of time. When it's time to do some grooming, approach your cat in a friendly way, and intersperse the grooming strokes with some regular petting.

Use restraint. It's okay to restrain your cat (gently!) as long as she doesn't start to panic, but be sure to restrain yourself, too. Don't try to force your cat to sit still or stay in an awkward or uncomfortable position for too long. And be careful not to get too exuberant in your grooming strokes. Think about how much you don't like having your hair pulled, then imagine what it's like to have hair getting pulled all over your body.

Know when to quit. You may not be able to groom your cat completely in one session. That's okay. If you get her back and tail, and then she starts to fight you, give up and try finishing in a day or two. It's better to have a half-dozen five-minute grooming sessions spread out over a week and a happy cat than one 25-minute battle and a cat who runs and hides at the sight of the brush.

Get professional help. If your cat has a bad mat or tangle—or gets something nasty on her fur—put a call in to your veterinarian or professional groomer. If your cat just doesn't seem to be cooperating with home grooming, schedule an appointment with a professional. While you're there, ask for some tips and a demonstration of basic techniques. Groomers are usually happy to do this for clients; there's nothing more annoying for a groomer than having to constantly shave out and untangle bad mats. The cat suffers, and the groomer is more likely to get bitten or scratched.

Cat Baths and Haircuts

Except for removing a mat or performing a medical procedure, there is almost no reason to shave a cat's hair. Cats are built to have a full coat of hair—taking it away can throw off regulation of their body temperature and expose the usually protected skin underneath. Trimming a longhair cat's coat for appearances and to prevent tangles is fine, but it should be done by a professional groomer.

✻　✻　✻　✻

I T'S USUALLY NOT necessary to bathe a cat, either, since they do so well keeping themselves clean. Sometimes, though, a bath is called for to treat or control fleas, to clean up an adventurous feline explorer, to treat a skin condition, or to remove a noxious or dangerous mess from your cat's fur. The squeamish, the inexperienced, and the uncertain should probably let a veterinarian or groomer take care of these mandatory baths. For those who want to try it at home, here are several bath basics.

Be prepared. Lay out your bathing supplies ahead of time. You'll need a good pet shampoo (get medicated shampoos for fleas or skin conditions from your vet, not over-the-counter), a large fluffy towel, a brush and comb, and either a handheld shower head or plastic tumbler for wetting and rinsing. It's a good idea to comb out your cat's hair before bathing, if possible, especially for longhairs. If you know how, now is the time to trim your cat's nails. (Note: You can protect your cat's eyes during a bath with a neutral ophthalmic ointment available from your veterinarian.)

Ready your bathing stations. Use a large sink with a dish sprayer attachment or the bathtub. Start the water before you put the cat in, and make sure it's not too hot or too cold. A comfortable temperature for your hands should work fine. You're going to get wet, splattered with suds, and possibly jumped on by an upset, sopping cat, so dress appropriately in clothes that can get soiled yet protect you from scratches.

Before you add the cat. Bathing a cat is often a two-person job—one to restrain and one to bathe—but you can do it yourself. Either way, practice restraint techniques on dry land before the bath. With one hand, grasp your cat firmly but gently at the base of the neck or on the scruff, pressing down slightly. See how well you can reach the various parts of your cat's body with the other hand. Figure out when and how you'll have to change grips during the bath. Get your bathing routine down step-by-step before the cat is in the tub or sink; otherwise, Tabby will be able to make a break for it in your moment of hesitation or confusion.

Start the suds. Wet down your cat, starting from the head and working your way to the tail. Apply the shampoo the same way, lather, and rinse thoroughly. (Read the label directions on medicated shampoos carefully. Some require 5 to 15 minutes before rinsing in order to be effective.) Thorough rinsing is important. Leftover soap residue can irritate your cat's skin or be swallowed when your cat licks her fur. Rinsing also gets rid of fleas and other parasites that are immobilized—but not killed—by the bath.

Dry and fluff. Gently squeeze excess water out of your cat's fur, wrap her up in a large fluffy towel, and dry her off. If she'll stand for it, you can comb out any tangles right away; otherwise, wait until she's dried off and settled down. If you're lucky, your cat may tolerate the sound and feel of a blow-dryer. Don't count on it, though—many cats are terrified of them. This is not something to discover right after a bath. See how your cat reacts to the blow-dryer on a nonbath day. If she's scared witless, stick with a towel. You might be able to gradually get her used to the sound and feel (especially if you begin regular baths in kittenhood)—and then again, you might not!

Cat-Proofing: Making Your Home Safe

We all know to keep dangerous substances away from children, and it's important to remember that we should be even more careful with cats. We all know the old saying about what curiosity did to the cat. Because they are smaller, more mobile, and have more sensitive noses than children, cats are more likely to investigate, getting into things that can be dangerous. To prevent your cat's curiosity from becoming fatal, there are a few household dangers to look out for.

❋ ❋ ❋ ❋

DRAPERY, BLIND, AND **electrical cords.** To your cat's eye, the dangling end of a drapery or blind cord is an open invitation to play—and possibly to disaster. Even just crawling between drapes or blinds and the window (an all-time favorite feline pastime) can land Tabby in a tangle. Cats who get caught in the loops of pull-cords panic. At the very least, the blinds or drapery rod will come down with a crash. At worst, a cat can strangle, do fatal internal damage, or actually get so worked up that his heart gives out. For maximum safety, tie or wrap all window cords well out of feline reach.

Electrical and telephone cords pose something of a tangling threat but more often are dangerous on account of chewing. It might be the taste or texture of the plastic coating, but for some reason, a lot of cats can't resist nibbling. There's not much direct danger in chewing phone cords (except when you try to make a call on a line that's been put out of commission by your cat) since there's very little current running through them.

Electrical cords are another story altogether, of course. Wherever possible, run the cords under rugs and carpets or behind furniture that sits flush to the floor and wall. If a cord has to be run where a cat can reach it, buy some inexpensive plastic conduit, which is available at most hardware and building supply stores. For a larger investment, you can get strips of heavy-duty vinyl that not only protect the electrical cords, but also keep the cords flush to the floor to prevent tripping.

Occasionally, a very determined cat will make his way through all the physical barriers. Treating the cords with a bad-tasting substance like bitter apple might do the trick.

Cleaning fluids, antifreeze, and other poisons. We don't just buy cleaners to get our house clean; we want it disinfected and smelling nice, too. Unfortunately, some of the very products we buy to sanitize and deodorize pet areas are outright dangerous for your cat.

Pine-based cleaners and those containing phenol (the most popular being Lysol disinfectant) are particularly toxic to cats and shouldn't be used on food bowls or in pet areas, sleeping quarters, or litter boxes. Of course, any cleaning compound can be poisonous if taken internally, so keep everything secured in a locking cabinet. (A simple spring latch won't keep a determinedly curious cat out.)

Ethylene glycol is the stuff that makes antifreeze work. It just so happens that it also smells and tastes very sweet. A significant number of cats and dogs—and even small children—suffer from ethylene glycol poisoning every winter. Because it's present in large amounts in almost every home and is often very fatal if swallowed, antifreeze and other products containing ethylene glycol should be considered dangerous and never left where pets or children can get to them.

Cats who go outdoors run the added risk of lapping up antifreeze spills and drips, an especially tempting thing for a thirsty cat to do since those puddles of tasty liquid don't freeze on cold days. You can protect your own cat (and other outdoor cats and strays) by immediately cleaning up and washing down any of your own spills or drips, or you can purchase one of the new nontoxic brands of antifreeze that contain propylene glycol rather than ethylene glycol. It's important to also keep in mind that once your cat leaves your property, there's no guarantee that everyone else in the area is going to be equally careful.

In general, anything that's toxic to you will be poisonous to your cat as well. The rule of thumb is: If you'd keep it out of reach of a child, keep it out of reach of your cat.

Poisonous plants. A cat chewing on your houseplants is more than an annoyance, it can be dangerous or even fatal to the cat.

Technically, any plant that makes your cat sick when eaten is a "poisonous" plant. (Nearly all cats will eat grass or plants to purge themselves, however, so vomiting alone may not be a reliable sign of poisoning.) Still, some plants have particularly serious effects. The list of potentially poisonous plants includes: apricot (pits), azalea, buttercup, caladium, calla lily, castorbean, cherry (twigs, leaves, bark, fruit, and stones), chrysanthemums, crocus, daffodil (bulbs), daphne (berries), holly, hydrangea, iris (leaves, roots, and fleshy parts), ivy, lily of the valley (leaves, flowers, roots), mistletoe (especially the berries), mushrooms, narcissus (bulbs), oak (acorns, young shoots, and leaves), oleander, peach (pits), philodendron, poison ivy, potatoes ("eyes" and sprouts from the eyes; the edible part of the potato is safe), privet, rhubarb (leaves), rosary pea (shiny red and black seeds), star of Bethlehem (bulb), string-of-pearls, sumac, and sweet pea (seeds and pods).

Dieffenbachia is a fairly common houseplant that also goes by the name of "dumb cane." The dumb cane is aptly named. Chewing dieffenbachia can actually paralyze your cat's mouth, making it impossible for him to eat and drink. The name "dumb cane" comes from the most noticeable effect of this paralysis on people: They can't talk.

Poinsettias (Christmas flowers) belong to the nightshade family—flowers notorious in fact and literature for their deadly properties. A study a few years back seemed to show that poinsettias—long believed to be dangerously toxic to cats and dogs—don't make cats any sicker than many plants considered nonpoisonous. Still, it's always safest to keep cats away from any houseplant, just to be sure.

Windows, balconies, and screens. "High-rise syndrome" might sound like some sort of pop psychology explanation for violent crime, but it actually describes an epidemic that hits a number of cats every year, especially in warmer weather. "High-rise syndrome" is a collection of various injuries that are the result of a fall from a high window.

Amazingly, there are many stories of cats surviving falls from several flights up. But there are far more who fell and didn't make it. The saddest part of it is nearly all of those falls could have been prevented.

Every window that you plan to open needs to have a screen. And not just any screen. A cat-proof screen has to fit the window frame securely enough to stay firmly in place when confronted by ten or more pounds of cat. When ordering or replacing screens, use a heavy-duty grade of hardware cloth since ordinary screens can be easily torn by claws or teeth. Even a fall from a second- or third-story window can cause serious injury or death, so inspect all screens regularly, especially toward the end of winter in cold-weather areas of the country. Screens can warp, tear, or fatigue in the off-season.

Some city cat owners think letting Tabby out on the balcony of their apartment is a safe way to give him some fresh air and sunshine. Actually, a good number of "high-rise syndrome" cats were stalking moths, birds, or other irresistible things on an upper-floor balcony, when an ill-timed pounce or missed step sent them over the railing. Even a leash or tether on an open balcony doesn't ensure your cat's safety. A panicked cat dangling by his collar or harness can be strangled, seriously injured, or squirm loose and fall anyway.

Fix It: The Case for Neutering and Spaying

Neutering and spaying (otherwise known as "altering" or "fixing" your cat) are routine operations that a skilled vet can usually do in 30 minutes or less.

* * * *

BOTH NEUTERING A male cat (also called orchiectomy or castration) and spaying a female cat (also known as complete hysterectomy or ovariohysterectomy) make the cats sterile (incapable of producing offspring). Neutering and spaying are usually done around the ages of five to seven months, when pet cats are raised from kittens. Adults can be altered at any age, unless they're too weak or ill or have some health problem that makes surgery too risky.

In recent years, so-called "early" neutering and spaying has become popular, especially among animal shelters. Kittens as young as seven weeks undergo surgical sterilization. In the past, the prevailing wisdom said that anesthesia and surgery on kittens that young were dangerous and probably foolhardy. Further, neutering and spaying that young would be expected to have serious long-range effects on the cat's health. As it turns out, that doesn't seem to be the case. Seven-week-old kittens are up and playing within a few hours after surgery and don't seem to have any significantly different side effects than cats neutered or spayed at seven months—the more typical age for altering.

Neutering and spaying do four good things for your cat:

Your cat will live longer. On average, cats who are neutered and spayed have double the life expectancy of unaltered cats.

Your cat will be happier. You only have to see (and hear) a cat in heat once to know that she isn't having a good time. Male cats who haven't been neutered can detect a female cat in heat from great distances and will escape and roam (and get into fights) to find her.

Your cat will be healthier. Believe it or not, intact cats (cats that haven't been neutered or spayed) run a higher risk of certain diseases, including some kinds of cancer. This is especially true for female cats. Pyometra is an infection of the cat's uterus that can be fatal if not caught and treated in time. Since the treatment includes spaying the cat anyway, that should be reason enough to spay your female cat while she's still healthy. If that doesn't convince you, try this: Having even one heat cycle dramatically increases a female cat's risk of mammary tumors, which is the feline equivalent of breast cancer. The longer your cat goes without being spayed, the greater the danger.

You'll prevent homelessness and save lives. We really don't know how many stray and homeless cats there are in the United States, but estimates range from a few million to tens of millions. What we do know is that several million cats are put to sleep in animal shelters every year because there aren't enough homes for them all.

Cats and Pregnancy: The Straight Story

One of the most common—and saddest—bits of misinformation that gets handed out about cats is that cats and pregnancy don't mix.

✳ ✳ ✳ ✳

WHILE IT'S TRUE that toxoplasmosis can cause serious birth defects, that's primarily true for a woman who is infected with toxoplasmosis for the first time during her first trimester. Infection for the first time during the second and third trimester can cause some problems, but they are rare.

A simple blood test can determine if a woman has already been exposed to the toxoplasma organism. If she has, she's immune and it's nearly impossible that toxoplasmosis will be of any concern. If not, she should just take precautions to prevent infection: Never clean the litter box, wear gloves when gardening or working with plants and wash hands thoroughly afterward, and avoid eating raw or undercooked meat. She should also take extreme care handling meat, making sure not to touch her mouth or nose and washing thoroughly immediately afterward

It is not necessary to remove cats from the home of a pregnant woman.

Scaredy Cats

* To calm a frightened cat, place your hands over its eyes or allow him to bury his head in your lap or armpit until he calms down.
* A frightened cat can sprint up to 31 miles per hour.
* Try gently stroking a cat's forehead to relieve stress or anxiety.
* Cats can leap up to six times their body length.

* In martial arts, the "cat stance" allows for quick blocking, attacking, and leaping out of the way of an attack. It is best known for the distance between the front and rear legs.

Notes From a Cat:
How to Keep Your Owner Happy

* Resist the urge to show them your backside every time they enter a room.

* Remind yourself, the suitcase is not for peeing in.

* Hop in their laps while they're watching TV and start purring. Humans need to be reminded that real life is more interesting than sitcoms.

* Do not jump from behind closed doors to attack the dog (or at least restrict yourself to no more than twice a day).

* Twine yourself between your owner's legs no matter what they're doing. Bonus points apply if they are carrying something heavy.

* Allow them to think it's their idea that all the comfy chairs in the house are reserved for you.

* Rub your head on all available surfaces to mark what's yours. Owners will appreciate this clear delineation of who owns what.

* Every once in a while, allow them to pet your belly. It feeds their souls.

Chapter 5

Problem Behaviors

Understanding Cat Behavior

There are so many fascinating ways that cats communicate with each other. Some of their methods are so subtle that we humans are not sensitive enough to understand what they are saying.

✳ ✳ ✳ ✳

CATS OFTEN USE mild and controlled signs of body language. A minor flick of the tail or the slightest movement of the ears send messages that are worth a thousand words to another cat. But since their body language is so restrained, we often find it difficult to comprehend, so we end up making mistakes trying to interpret their messages. It's easier for us to discern what cats are saying when they use their voices. Their range of sounds—from a gentle purr to a seething hiss—let us know if a cat is happy or angry. Once we learn to make sense of the body language and the vocalizations of cats, we are one step closer to understanding cat behavior.

Nature of Nurture?

In the study of behavior, experts talk about nature versus nurture, meaning which behaviors are inbred (or instinct) and which are learned. It's an argument that will probably never be completely settled. Most experts agree, however, that animals like cats and dogs have both kinds of behavior; they just disagree on which ones are which—and which kind is more important.

An example of an instinctual behavior would be what happens when you run your hand down the cat's back, from his head to his tail. That response of sticking his backside up in the air is hardwired into his nervous system. A learned behavior is something like your cat running into the kitchen whenever he hears the can opener. That is, if you've ever given him anything out of a can.

Reflex actions. Animal behavior experts talk about reflexes and have their own nature-versus-nurture debate. Unconditioned reflexes are those the body seems to produce on its own. For example, if you kick your leg up when the doctor taps your knee with a rubber hammer. A conditioned reflex is a learned response. Most of us have heard of Pavlov's dog, who was trained to know that food was coming whenever he heard a bell ring. After awhile, Doc Pavlov could ring the bell and his dog would start salivating—even if there was no food present.

The great debate resolved. Actually, even Pavlov had to admit that his conditioned dog didn't have a completely learned response. If there wasn't an instinctive response of salivating in the presence of food to begin with, Pavlov could never have trained the dog to do it when he heard the bell. What Pavlov really proved was that animals are born with a set of instinctive, natural behaviors, and they learn how to apply and adapt them as needed.

What it all means for your cat. In order to train your cat, you need to understand his behavior. You'll never get him to do anything that's totally outside of his natural behaviors, but you can teach him how to adapt those behaviors so that both of you live happily ever after.

The best example is the litter box: Cats have the instinctive behavior of digging in loose materials and burying their urine and feces. As long as the litter box is the place that appeals to the cat most, that's where he'll consistently eliminate. However, he may be more intrigued by soil in your potted palm, the loose, fluffy pile of your carpeting, or the nice, soft pile of socks left in a corner of the utility room. As long as the behavior is shaped toward the litter box, you've got no problem.

Getting a Cat to Change His Ways

Can a cat be trained? Surprisingly, the answer is a resounding "yes!"—but it has to be done on feline terms.

✳   ✳   ✳   ✳

DON'T EXPECT YOUR cat to jump through hoops or roll over on command. However, you can expect your cat to stay within the boundaries of acceptable behavior in human society.

Emily Post for cats. It's probably best to make your training goal to cultivate good manners in your cat. Manners can be defined as performing normal and natural cat behaviors in the places, at the times, and in the way that satisfies both human and feline needs. This means finding the middle ground—in other words, what you can live with—and sticking to it. For example, it's unrealistic to think you can train your cat to never jump up on the dining room table. It's completely possible, however, to train him that it's bad manners to do so when humans are eating or when food is present.

Avoid bad habits. When it comes to behavior problems, most cat owners don't think in terms of prevention—and more's the pity. It may be cute when your 12-week-old kitten plays with your bare hand, but six months later when the now ten-pound beast sinks his full set of predator's teeth into your wrist, he's really only doing what he was taught to do. So, the best rule of thumb to follow is a common sense one: Never encourage any behavior you don't want to see later on, and always discourage any behavior you never want to see again.

Shape your cat's behavior. It's important to realize that certain cat behaviors can't be discouraged completely; they can only be shaped into a form that is socially acceptable in your household.

This is also known as behavior modification.

A good example is scratching. This is an instinctive behavior for which many cats are declawed, lose their homes, or are even put to sleep each year. A better strategy is shaping the scratching behavior toward an acceptable object, such as a properly constructed scratching post, while simultaneously making other choices unpleasant or difficult.

Accentuate the positive. The most successful, long lasting, humane, and commonsense way to train or shape the behavior of any animal is positive reinforcement. The opposite method, negative reinforcement, punishes the animal for exhibiting a particular behavior in any way other than what the owner or trainer wants. In the example of scratching furniture, this would mean following the cat around the house 24 hours a day and correcting him every time he lays claw to upholstery. Since scratching is instinctive and can't be stopped, this method is doomed to failure anyway. Also, praising and petting the cat when he uses the post and offering minor corrections (not punishments) when he's caught in the act of scratching elsewhere will help modify the behavior.

Cat Stats

* In one study, when asked, "Who listens to you best?" 45 percent of respondents chose their pet, while only 30 percent chose their spouse or significant other.

* The majority of Americans think their pet has humanlike personality traits.

* In case of natural disasters such as floods or earthquakes, 55 percent of Americans have an emergency preparedness plan that includes their pet.

* Studies have shown that stroking a cat can lower your blood pressure. Pet owners agreed!

* A majority of Americans see their pet's veterinarian more often than they see their own physician.

* If away from home during the day, more than 80 percent of Americans think of their pet more than once.

* If marooned on an island and able to choose only one companion, 50 percent of Americans would pick a dog or cat over a human.

* Willing to risk your life for your pet? You're not alone: more than 90 percent of respondents would do the same.

Aggression and Play

When a cat becomes destructive, the owner is often shocked to hear the professional advice: Get a second cat. The owner's understandable concern is that two cats will do twice as much damage, and the destructive cat will now have another cat to shred. Fortunately, the former is rarely true, mostly because the cat's energy is focused on another cat. This also seems to make the latter a valid fear. There must be a period of introduction, and some hissing and minor scuffles are normal. However, many multiple-cat owners witness normal vigorous feline play and are convinced the cats still aren't getting along.

✳   ✳   ✳   ✳

PLAY WE MUST. Play is an instinctive behavior. All mammals—including cats, dogs, and people—play. While play is more frequent and energetic in younger animals, adults play as well. In fact, play persists throughout an animal's lifetime.

We must . . . but why? For decades, animal behaviorists have argued that play—like all instinctive behaviors—must have some deeper reason behind it. Citing the theory of natural selection, they say that if play behavior was completely frivolous, it would be a waste of time and energy and would have been eradicated over time. Clearly, these researchers need to get out and have fun more often.

Play may well serve as practice for important adult behaviors, which is why so much of it looks like aggression. So when one cat hunkers down, twitches his backside, lashes his tail, and then pounces on his feline roommate, landing full on the unsuspecting victim's back and seizing his neck in his jaws, it's definitely play; the real-life use of that sequence of behavior is stalking and killing prey. But researchers are finally, grudgingly admitting that play could have another purpose, one which humans have known about for time immemorial: It's fun!

How do I know when it's for real? Feline play is often no-holds-barred fun: noisy running, hot pursuit, pouncing, stalking, slamming bodies, wrestling, biting, the works. But in terms of vocalization, it's relatively quiet. An out-and-out catfight would include all the same behaviors as a fun bout of play but with lots of loud hissing, yowling, screaming, and flying fur. Play uses the same behaviors as aggression, but they are inhibited: There are smacks to the head, but with claws retracted; bites, but with relaxed jaws and exaggerated movements. Other hallmarks of play include frequent changes in who's the aggressor—who's on top in the wrestling match, who's chasing whom, or whose body language is more inward or outward—and the play face (a relaxed, open jaw and wide-open eyes). If you doubt that humans use the play face, just watch a bunch of schoolchildren heading out the door for recess!

Bring out the best. Now that you can recognize play behavior in your cat, you can make him happier and healthier by encouraging it. If there's only one cat in the home, you have the responsibility of being his playmate. Cat toys are fine as long as they're safe, but your cat also needs you to play with him. Chasing, stalking, and pouncing games are at the top of the feline hit parade. Cats see moving edges better than stationary ones, so toys that wiggle, bounce, roll, or bob are particularly intriguing.

Even in multiple-cat households, the humans need to play with the cats. The more your cats recognize humans as potential playmates, the better socialized to people they will be.

Biting and Scratching (Humans and Other Cats)

You're walking down the hallway in your home, minding your own business, when suddenly your cat flings herself at your ankle, sinking in her teeth and claws, then dashes away. Is it an aggressive attack? An expression of jealousy? Possibly, but it might be neither.

✳ ✳ ✳ ✳

A CAT WHO BITES or scratches when in pain, frightened, or being forced to do something she doesn't want to do doesn't have a behavior problem; she's acting like a normal cat. Problem biting and scratching is usually either a learned habit or miscommunication, both of which can be corrected over time. Sometimes, however, sudden unprovoked biting or scratching can be the result of a nervous system disorder or a serious disease. (Note: Any bite or scratch you get from a cat who does not have a current rabies vaccination should prompt a call to your own doctor; always assume cats have not had rabies shots unless they have a current rabies tag or registration.)

Who taught her the trick? Many kittens learn to use human limbs as toys, climbers, and scratching posts. Many owners are surprised to learn that they are the ones who taught their young cats these bad habits.

Here are some rules to follow:

✳ Never allow or encourage a kitten or cat to play with your bare hand or foot.

✳ Never think you can get around the first rule by wearing protective gloves. There should always be some sort of appropriate cat toy between your limbs and your cat's teeth and claws. A tiny kitten may look cute climbing your pant leg or batting at your thumb, but you'll be singing a different tune when she repeats those behaviors as a full-grown cat.

It's probably play. Pouncing, biting, and smacking are normal parts of cat play behavior. The only way your cat knows how to relate to you is as if you were another cat. It's up to you to explain to her—in ways she'll understand—that she's being too exuberant.

First, make sure your cat has enough outlets for normal feline play. Just leaving some toys around isn't enough; cats need active and interactive play. So play with her. Get her running, jumping, and batting at toys. If she tries to grab at you during a play session, grab her gently by the scruff of the neck, firmly (but not too loudly) say "No," and immediately substitute a proper cat toy for her to play with.

Boredom during the day may encourage your cat to be overly exuberant in playing with you, too. If you have a single cat, consider getting her a feline friend.

A break from the routine. Once your cat has the habit of playing with you by biting and scratching, just changing the rules probably won't be enough to get her to stop. Try to notice when she's most likely to chomp your hand or swat your ankle, then deliberately set up one of those situations. Have a spray bottle or squirt gun full of room temperature water handy, and give her a spritz the moment she digs in with a tooth or claw. Don't yell at her or pursue her with the water; you want her to associate the action with the inconvenience of suddenly getting wet.

Defensive biting and scratching. Teeth and nails are a cat's primary weapons. If other warnings don't work, cats will bite and scratch to protect themselves. Pay attention to your cat's vocal and body language; she'll usually let you know when she's on the brink of defensive biting or scratching. You don't have to show a cat who's boss once she's warned you. The best approach is to back off whatever it is she doesn't like or use a safe method of restraint, if it's something that must be done.

Likewise, look for warning signals when a cat is aggressive with other cats. If your cat is warning another cat that she's ready to bite or scratch, do not try to touch or restrain either of them. The cats have their attention focused on each other, and the "fight or flight" response is in full readiness. Your touch can actually trigger a fight. Instead, try to distract both cats by stamping your foot, clapping your hands, and shouting "No!" in a sharp, loud tone.

Unprovoked aggression. Sudden, unprovoked, and vicious attacks are especially scary. This is not just a cat swatting at your ankles and perhaps causing a little scratch. This is send-someone-to-the-emergency-room kind of stuff.

Sometimes, serious biting and scratching is the result of mis-communication: Something startles the cat, and she has the impression that the person or pet nearest her is responsible. Other times, however, there really is something physically wrong with the cat that causes her to actually attack without cause or warning. If your cat's bites and swats rarely break the skin, they're probably "inhibited" play bites and scratches. A cat who launches a serious attack (with multiple or deep bites, for example) should be examined carefully by a veterinarian.

When should you call the vet? If your cat is launching serious attacks, especially without warning or provocation, get her in for a thorough veterinary exam as soon as possible. Cats often know when there's something going wrong with them, but can't put it into words. The aggression might be a reaction to pain, a hormonal change, or the sign of a problem with her nervous system.

Chewing

Fortunately, cats don't have the strong need for chewing that dogs have. However, they are very prone to gnawing certain objects or materials, particularly telephone and electrical cords—a potentially fatal habit. Less dangerous but equally as annoying is the occasional cat who likes to gnaw the wood on the corners of furniture or chew paper or plastic.

✳ ✳ ✳ ✳

MAKE IT HARD **to swallow.** There are several commercial products that can be applied to whatever the cat is chewing—especially wires and cords—to correct the behavior. Pet stores sell a variety of bitter pet repellents. Basically, these are just liquids that leave a bad-tasting residue when they dry. You might be able to accomplish the same thing by applying bitters to whatever the cat is munching on. Enclosing phone wires and electrical cords in hard conduit or running them under rugs, inside walls, or along moldings may be better long-term solutions, though.

Give her what she wants. It's possible you have a cat who just likes to chew. Sometimes, a hard rubber chew toy or rawhide stick will satisfy the craving. Edible chewies for cats have been marketed from time to time but with only limited success.

Is she telling you something? Chewing can sometimes be a sign of boredom, tooth or mouth discomfort, or something missing from the cat's diet. Usually, though, the message from the cat is, "Don't leave any of this particular item laying around where I can reach it, unless you don't mind tooth holes in it."

When should you call the vet? Chewing behavior rarely has a physical cause. However, your vet can help you determine a course of treatment or refer you to a competent behaviorist.

Climbing

Cats are natural vertical climbers and leapers. In other words, the higher a cat can go, the happier she often is.

✳   ✳   ✳   ✳

IT'S NO BIG deal for a young, healthy cat to make a straight jump from the floor to a flat surface four or five feet off the ground. Panicked searches for "lost" cats frequently turn them up on top of refrigerators, on top of doors, or even inside cabinets that humans need a step stool to reach.

A cat's love of heights probably came about for security while sleeping. If you're at the highest vantage point, nobody can sneak up on you, and any other animal trying to climb up to get you has to use most of its legs and strength just to hang on.

Give her a place of her own. Build or buy one or more cat trees—central posts with perches and enclosed hiding places. You can use a large tree limb as the central post to give the piece a more natural look and make it more inviting for the cat. The base must be wide, sturdy, and well-weighted to prevent tipping over. The perches and hidey-holes are often carpeted to make them more comfortable and help blend in with decor or color schemes.

Make other options less appealing. To discourage your cat from climbing or jumping on something, you need to make that action have a less pleasant outcome. Once again, you can set your cat up with the squirt gun or water bottle. Stake out the place in question, and spritz her once with room temperature water as soon as she makes her move. Using your voice to startle her off can work, too, but she may associate the correction with your presence, which is no help at all when you're not in the room.

When should you call the vet? This type of behavior usually doesn't require any veterinary attention. However, keep an eye on your cat in case she has a fall. While it's true most cats land on their feet, there are still risks of injury—especially internal injury—from the fall.

Escaping

Cat owners sometimes mistake those unexpected dashes for the door as the cat's way of expressing her need to be in the great outdoors. While the wide open spaces with all the interesting sights, smells, and sounds are certainly intriguing to cats, they will just as happily shoot through any forbidden door. It's largely a game, but if what's on the other side of the door is unsafe for the cat, it can be a deadly game.

✳   ✳   ✳   ✳

SHOW HER WHAT'S there. If your cat is intensely curious about what's beyond the door, get a leash and cat harness and take her out under controlled conditions. The fun part is usually getting past the door; once she's done that, the challenge is over, and she'll probably lose interest quickly.

Be sure nothing is driving her out. Cats may try and escape for the same reason people do: There's something they want to get away from. A cat who's stressed—by the arrival of a new baby, the departure of an elderly companion cat, or the merciless teasing of a two- or four-legged member of the household —may simply want to get away from it all. Occasionally, there may be environmental stresses in your home that drive the cat out the door. One example was the family that got an ultrasonic home alarm system—silent to humans but well within a cat's range of hearing. The family would come home, deactivate the alarm, and open the door, and the cat, who'd been subjected to a constant barrage of ultrasonic noise all day, would streak out the door at a dead run.

Make it less fun. If your cat is door-dashing for the fun of it, you want to get the message across that it's no laughing matter. Load a water pistol or spray bottle with room temperature tap water and lure her into thinking you're going through the door. As soon as she makes a break for it, spritz her.

When should you call the vet? Escape behavior usually doesn't require any veterinary attention.

Tales From The Country Vet: Morris and Me

❋ ❋ ❋ ❋

I ONCE GOT A call about the finickiest cat in the world, an orange tabby male called Morris. No, not the Morris, but one who was every bit as persnickety about his eating, and then some. Morris's owner insisted the only things Morris would eat at all were tuna (a particularly expensive name brand, packed in water—never the off-brands and never packed in oil) and chicken liver, panfried in a little olive oil. Now, it seemed, Morris was starting to turn his nose up at the liver, so what else, the owner wanted to know, could I suggest feeding him?

I told the owner to bring Morris in for an exam. He was a reasonably healthy cat, considering his limited diet of late. Everything else checked out normally, so I prescribed the 20-minutes-and-up method, using a good-quality, premium-brand dry food. After several false starts ("Well, yes . . . I did give him a few treats before I went to bed so he'd stop meowing so much"), Morris's owner finally stuck to his guns, and Morris learned to eat like a normal cat—although it took more than four months to get there!

Finicky Eaters

Finickiness is one of the most famous of all feline traits. According to many behaviorists, however, it's a learned behavior and not an inborn one. Cats will happily eat the same food twice a day for their entire lives, provided it's nutritionally complete and tastes good enough.

✳ ✳ ✳ ✳

DON'T TEACH HER the habit. Surprisingly, a lot of feline finickiness is taught to cats by their owners. Thinking the cat will get bored with a single flavor or brand, owners stock up on a variety of foods, trying different ones with each meal to determine a pet's favorites. If a cat walks away from a particular brand or flavor and the owner immediately opens another can, box, or bag, the cat quickly learns that finickness pays. If you feel you must vary the flavors in your cat's diet, adopt the old-fashioned approach of, "Eat what's put in front of you. If you don't like it, you don't have to eat it—but that's all there's going to be until the next meal." Unless a cat eats absolutely nothing for a couple of meals running, there's no danger to her health if she has a few lean meals now and then.

Try the 20-minutes-and-up method. If you find yourself opening six cans at every meal and following your cat around the house, trying to coax her to have a nibble, you've got a serious finickiness problem going. At the next meal, put down a food you know the cat has eaten before. Wait 20 minutes, and then pick up the food and do not give any other food, snacks, or treats until the next meal. Repeat the process at that meal and every subsequent meal. Be prepared for an all-out tantrum by your cat— loud meowing, attempts to steal food, being an incredible pest, the works. Be strong and don't cheat to try to appease her. This method has a remarkable success rate. Many owners see improvement after three days, although some cats may persevere for several weeks.

When should you call the vet? If a previously good eater suddenly becomes finicky or finickiness persists despite the 20-minutes-and-up method, your cat may have a physical problem and need veterinary care. A cat who quits eating completely or has a loss of appetite accompanied by other symptoms of illness should be seen by the veterinarian right away.

Knocking Things Down

Most of the time, cats send things crashing to the floor in the course of vigorous play; a wild run up the front hall culminates in a ricocheting leap from floor to couch to end table, sending the intervening lamp crashing to the floor in the process. Sometimes, though, a cat will deliberately nudge an item over the edge of a shelf or table, then gleefully dash away from the resulting chaos and infuriated humans.

❋ ❋ ❋ ❋

Is it nature or nurture? "Toying" with prey is a common behavior in feline hunters. When your cat nudges a small, stationary object with her paw, she's practicing the same behavior.

Your cat's instincts tell her that paperweight or knickknack could turn out to be a mouse. Her poking paw would send it scurrying, giving her a good game (and possibly a good lunch).

However, once a cat learns that knocking something to the floor will bring humans on the double-quick, she may actually do it on purpose to get your attention, particularly if she feels that a meal is long overdue.

Give her something else to do. A bored cat will find her own ways to amuse herself, and shoving things off high places to watch them drop is often one of them. Ample appropriate toys, climbing and hiding places to call her own, and a playmate—preferably another cat—can provide her with better options.

Take temptation out of her way. Low shelves; countertops; or tables lined with knickknacks, collectibles, or small easel-backed picture frames are an invitation to disaster in a home with cats. Anything that won't survive a trip from whatever surface it's on to the floor should be put somewhere else or surrounded by a cat-proof barrier, such as putting porcelain figurines in a glass-front case rather than on open shelves.

When should you call the vet? This type of behavior usually doesn't require any veterinary attention. However, keep an eye on your cat to make sure she doesn't knock anything down on top of herself.

Pica or Eating Nonfoods

Every kitten has tried to eat kitty litter—and many have succeeded.

✳ ✳ ✳ ✳

FAR FROM BEING a behavior problem, this is part of a cat's natural curiosity, and one of the ways a growing kitten explores her world and learns about what counts as food—and what doesn't. Other cats, however, will get a yen for strange items that don't really qualify as food, some of which may even be unsafe.

Keep temptation out of her way. Rubber bands, paper clips, twist ties, bits of foil, and cellophane wrappers are some of the everyday things that cats love to explore with their mouths. Whether swallowed accidentally or on purpose, these otherwise harmless items can cause potentially deadly blockages in the cat's digestive system. Cat owners should be careful to keep tiny, easily swallowed items safely in drawers.

Is she telling you something? Pica is occasionally a signal that a cat isn't getting enough to eat—or enough of the right nutrients. It can also sometimes be a sign that something is out of balance in the cat's body. Other times, the cat gets into the habit of eating odd things out of boredom—in which case, more play or a playmate often takes care of the problem.

When should you call the vet? It's always a good idea to consult your vet if your cat develops a craving for a nonfood or if you know she's swallowed a potentially dangerous item like a rubber band.

Not On My Watch . . .

A BLACK-AND-WHITE CAT NAMED *Duchess saved a sleeping family in Texas by repeatedly throwing herself against their closed bedroom door. Getting up to see what Duchess needed, the family discovered their mobile home was on fire. The smoke alarm never sounded. They were able to get everyone to safety, thanks to the alarm sent by Duchess.*

Gizmo, a Burmese cat living in Colorado, was given a hero award for awakening his owner from a heavy medication-induced sleep. The cat jumped on his owner, meowing and pawing. The reason for Gizmo's attention? The electric blanket the owner was sleeping under had caught fire.

Scratching (On Furniture and Other Things)

Every kind of cat, from lions and cheetahs to Siamese and alley cats, have an instinctive need to scratch.

✳ ✳ ✳ ✳

SCRATCHING BEHAVIOR SERVES three functions: marking territory, keeping the cat's claws in proper condition, and stretching the muscles and ligaments in the toes and feet. Declawing (the surgical removal of the first joint of the cat's toes, which includes both the nail and the cells from which new nails grow) does not stop scratching behavior, although it tends to reduce the amount of damage the cat can do. Your goal, then, is not to stop your cat from scratching—that can't be done—but rather to limit her scratching to the places you choose.

Give her a good scratching post—or two, or three.
Remember the three reasons for scratching, and get a post that meets all those needs. It should be tall enough for an adult cat to reach up and get a good stretch. It has to be sturdy enough that a 10- to 15-pound cat repeatedly pulling on it near the top won't bring it toppling over on her head. This would be a quick way to train her not to scratch on the post! The post should be covered with a nubby, coarsely woven fabric that shows scratching damage, such as sisal cloth. Cats are attracted to textured surfaces as scratching zones, and the coarse weave lets them hook in and get a good stretch. Being able to see the results of their handiwork reinforces the territory marking part

of scratching. These are the absolute basic requirements for a proper scratching post.

Put it in plain sight. Remember the last time you were looking for a particular address and none of the houses were clearly marked? You probably muttered to yourself, "Why don't they mark these things so people can see them?" Your cat's scratching damage is how she marks her territory—her address, so to speak. If the scratching post can't be seen from cat height (about six or seven inches off the ground) and from many angles in the room, your cat is more likely to ignore it and make her statement on your couch or carpet.

Take temptation out of the way. Try to structure your cat's environment so that the scratching post is the most accessible and attractive thing to scratch on. If you're committed to a lifetime of having cats, it's probably better to outfit your home with washable area rugs and hardwood floors than wall-to-wall deep-pile carpeting in every room. Likewise, furniture upholstered with textured weaves and wicker are almost certain to sustain scratching damage; if you know you'll always have cats, pick another decorating scheme.

Of course, there is an old-fashioned, tried-and-true way to keep cats from scratching expensive draperies, furniture, and carpeting: Put those pieces in one room, shut the door, and allow the cat to roam only in the other rooms.

Pause for claws. Trim your cat's nails regularly to reduce her ability to inflict serious scratching damage. If you're squeamish or your cat is particularly uncooperative, you can have your vet or groomer do it for you.

Hide the damage. If your cat has already done some scratching damage, block it from her view. This means putting stereo speakers on high shelves, covering afflicted pieces of furniture with a sheet, or removing items behind closed doors. The good thing about scratching damage in inappropriate places is your cat has identified the locations she thinks are best for scratching. Once you cover or remove the damaged items, put a proper scratching post next to it or in its place.

Make some corrections, but accentuate the positive. Employ the spray bottle or squirt gun to correct occasional scratching in undesirable locations. Use positive reinforcement techniques to encourage your cat to use the scratching post exclusively: Dangle some toys from the top and encourage her to climb the post or bat at them; scrabble your fingertips on the fabric of the post to get her to start scratching there; physically remove her from scratching in an inappropriate spot and place her paws in scratching position where you want her to go. In all cases, lavish her with praise and petting for doing the right thing.

When should you call the vet? Scratching behavior rarely has a physical cause. However, your vet can help you determine a course of treatment or refer you to a competent behaviorist.

Shyness

More than just the fabled feline aloofness, shy cats can be all but invisible, running and hiding even from their owners.

❋ ❋ ❋ ❋

A T SOME TIME during the day, virtually every cat wants to be alone and will find a secluded place to crawl into. But shy ones and "scaredy-cats" may spend most of their time out of sight. A cat that spends most of her time under the bed isn't having a good time—and may not be getting enough food, water, or exercise.

Why are some cats so shy? Some breeds are more reserved than others, and some cats, usually those who have not been socialized to humans, tend to be people-shy. In certain cases, the cat may be frightened of certain types of people—children or men, for example.

They only come out at night. Cats are naturally nocturnal animals. If your cat rarely comes out during the day, don't assume she's not prowling around the house at night. Since cats can have very quiet footfalls when they want to, you may not hear her—and you won't see her because you're asleep. By the way, just because you find her in the same hiding place in the morning that you left her in the night before also doesn't mean she spent the whole night there!

To try to help a shy cat feel more secure, try waiting until nightfall. Turn off all the lights and pull the shades. Then, wait and see if your scaredy-cat is more willing to venture out.

Try a little tenderness. Give a shy cat attention, but on her own terms. Talk to her in her hiding place—perhaps even feed her there if she doesn't come out to eat. Give her space, but reassure her with your words, tone of voice, and actions, and let her know you mean her no harm. Be patient. Making progress on socializing a shy cat can take weeks or months.

Make it worth her while. Treats, soft talk, and petting can help coax a nervous cat into society. If you find something she particularly likes—a specific food, a rub behind the ear, grooming with the slicker brush—reserve it to give her only on occasions of social interaction.

Don't force the issue. Let a shy cat build her confidence on her own timetable. If you try to drag her out of her safe spot and force attention on her, you may actually make her more shy—or risk being bitten or scratched. There's no law that says your cat must greet your visitors or play with the neighbor children. If she wants to be a recluse on social occasions, let her.

When should you call the vet? If a previously friendly cat starts acting antisocial or hides a lot, she could be signaling the onset of illness. Notify your vet right away.

Spraying

Urine spraying to mark territory is a common behavior in cats.

✳ ✳ ✳ ✳

MATURE UNALTERED MALES do it most typically, but neutered males and even spayed females may also show the behavior. The cat backs up to a vertical surface, standing with its tail erect. Urine is sprayed on the surface with a characteristic jiggling of the tail and treading with the back feet.

What to Do About Spraying

Get to the bottom of it. Urine spraying may be a sign of physical maturity in a male kitten, a signal that there's either a physical problem with the urinary tract, or a behavioral problem that needs prompt attention. Don't assume it's just a behavioral problem though; if a physical problem is the original cause, no amount of behavior modification will help. On the other hand, the longer the physical problem goes untreated, the more ingrained the habit of spraying becomes and the harder it will be to break (if you can at all) once the physical cause is removed. Have your cat thoroughly examined by your veterinarian. If everything checks out normally, it's probably a behavior problem.

"Fix" the problem. When male cats reach sexual maturity, they often announce it by beginning to mark their territory—your home—by spraying urine. Mature tomcat urine is especially pungent, so you'd be well advised to nip this behavior in the bud by neutering male kittens by the age of six months (unless your veterinarian recommends waiting longer). Some humane organizations now promote or practice early neuter or spay, altering kittens as young as seven weeks old. Preliminary studies show no major problems with cats neutered younger than six months of age, and the kittens recover amazingly fast.

Girls will be boys. Sometimes, a spayed female cat will begin spraying, although females aren't especially known for marking territory that way. The reduction in female hormones after spaying is suspected as the culprit, and your vet may recommend hormone therapy as a way of breaking the habit. In fact, female hormones may be used with neutered male cats who spray, for the same reason.

When should you call the vet? Make an appointment with your vet as soon as your cat starts spraying. Remember, the sooner you find or rule out a physical cause, the more likely you are to change the behavior. If your cat shows spraying behavior but produces no urine, watch to see if he urinates in the litter box. If so, consider yourself lucky—he's just going through the motions. However, if he produces no urine in the litter box, produces frequent small amounts, or cries in pain while attempting to urinate or spray, he could have a urinary blockage. This is a life-or-death emergency that needs immediate veterinary attention.

Wool Sucking

There's nothing quite so incongruous as seeing a big old former street cat sitting on top of a pink sweater, blissfully kneading with her front paws and sucking away like a tiny kitten. Although called wool sucking, cats who display this type of behavior may go after other kinds of fabrics as well. At the very least, they can snag it, slobber on it, and shed hair all over it. But wool suckers are also prone to chewing and can destroy items such as expensive clothes, blankets, and comforters faster and more efficiently than moths or small children.

✳   ✳   ✳   ✳

IT'S NOT COMPLETELY clear why cats do it, although some behaviorists suspect it's more common in cats who were weaned too young. Certain breeds, most notably Siamese, are more prone to wool sucking, so it has a strong genetic factor.

If your cat is a wool sucker, don't despair; there are several guidelines you can follow in order to guard your garments from destruction.

Take temptation out of her way. It may be cute to see your cat all cuddled up in your sweater drawer, but if she turns out to be a wool sucker, you may end up having to replace your wardrobe. Get into the habit of putting clothing, blankets, towels, and other textiles away in secure drawers, closets, and cabinets.

Either way, it's fiber. Sometimes, a cat's desire to suck and chew fabric fibers can be curbed by giving her more dietary fiber. A crunchy dry food is higher in fiber than canned food and may provide the oral stimulation that a wool sucker craves. If your wool-sucking cat shows an interest, you can also try tearing up a leaf or two of lettuce for her to munch on instead of your cardigan.

The old switcheroo. When you see your cat heading for your favorite wool sweater, replace the sweater with a chew toy or a wool-covered toy. Providing your cat with plenty of toys to chew on may prevent her from going for your expensive garments.

Age before beauty. As a preventative measure, before you get another pet, consider the cat's age. Since there might be a connection between early weaning and wool sucking, you may want to consider adopting kittens who are at least ten weeks old and have been with their mothers the whole time. Although weaning often occurs around five weeks of age, a ten-week-old kitten is sure to have made the transition completely.

When should you call the vet? Wool sucking usually doesn't require any veterinary attention. However, keep an eye on your cat to make sure she doesn't swallow any loose strings; this can cause intestinal problems, which require immediate attention.

Chapter 6

Cat Tricks and More Fun

Teaching Your Cat Tricks

Can cats be trained? To some people—and perhaps to some cats—the mere idea of training a cat sounds like a joke. But while cats are by nature independent animals, with enough patience and the right reward, they can be taught to do almost anything.

※ ※ ※ ※

Oᴺᴇ ᴏꜰ ᴛʜᴇ most important things to remember in training is to use a calm, gentle voice. Tricks should be taught in an area or in a room that is free of distractions so you and your pet can concentrate on the lesson being taught.

Above all, make sure the training is fun for you and your cat. Cats respond to rewards, not punishment. Keep your training sessions short. Don't expect to spend an hour on learning a trick. Instead, try to spend five or ten minutes a day, and practice each day. If at any point you feel yourself getting frustrated, or if your cat is losing interest, stop the training session.

Patience is key. You may need to spend more time and repetition than originally planned. But keep at it! Once your pet learns a new trick, you'll have a deeper appreciation for him, and he'll be happy to get your affection and a tasty reward.

Clickers

One of the best training tools you can invest in is a small handheld clicker that you can buy at any pet store. You can teach your cat to associate the clicking sound with a treat (food is the usual motivator, but it's not the only one). Each time the cat responds to the clicking sound, reward him with a small treat. Soon he will have a positive association with the sound. You can then click to reward those behaviors you want to encourage.

Touch an Object

One easy, impressive trick you can teach your cat is to touch a specific object on command. Get your handheld clicker and a small object, like a small rubber ball, and you'll be ready to go.

In a room free of distractions, place the object a few inches away from your pet. Whenever she looks at or does anything in connection with the object, click the clicker and reward her with a treat.

Practice at the same time every day, clicking and rewarding each time your cat approaches or touches the object.

After a while, she will realize that pawing the object means food, and she'll begin touching it with the intended purpose of receiving a reward. Start giving the command "Touch the object." Say this the moment before you click as your pet reaches for the object.

With sufficient practice, your pet will automatically touch the object upon your command. You don't have to click and reward every time she performs this trick, but you should do so most of the time to reinforce the desired behavior. If you don't, your bet will grow bored and stop responding to your command.

Sit

In a quiet room, stand in front of your cat with a treat in your hand. Show her the treat so she is aware of it. Raise your hand up and over her head toward her back just a little bit; as she follows your hand with her head, her body will automatically fall into a sitting position. The moment she does this, reward her with the treat and give her some praise.

Once your cat becomes used to sitting by following your hand, start using the "Sit" command.

Say this right before she sits, then reward her with a treat. Practice for 10 minutes a day, every day, until she begins sitting on command. You don't have to reward her every time, but you should do so often enough to reinforce the behavior.

You can also use a handheld clicker as part of the training. Click right before your cat sits and receives a reward as a form of positive reinforcement.

All cats can learn this trick, but younger cats tend to pick it up more quickly than older cats who are more set in their ways.

Come When Called

Teaching your cat to come on command serves two functions: It guarantees feline companionship whenever you want it, and it also ensures your pet's safety during an emergency by making your cat easy to locate.

Cats are extremely intelligent animals and can be taught to do almost anything. However, they need the right motivation. Some cats will come when you call simply because they like to be petted, but others may need more incentive—such as a yummy snack or treat.

To make this trick work, you should start training your cat when he is young. Call him by name every time you play together, and reward him with affection whenever he approaches you.

Before long, he should respond positively every time you call him. If, however, your cat still refuses to come despite your affection, it may be time to try a different approach. Continue to say his name every time you play but now reward him with a snack when he comes to you. Soon your cat will associate his name with a treat and come on command, a phenomenon known as the Paviovian response.

Once the behavior is firmly established, gradually substitute praise for food. To keep him motivated, however, you should still occasionally reward him with a treat.

Keep in mind that kindness goes a long way when training a cat. Never be too forceful or yell in anger or frustration. This will only frighten your cat and make the teaching process more difficult.

Eat On Cue

Dog owners commonly train their pets to wait for a signal before eating their food. In fact, a very well-trained dog will even wait for the right cue before consuming a treat placed on his nose! Cats can also be trained to wait for a signal before eating something, but don't attempt the nose trick; no self-respecting feline will let you go that far!

In a room free of distractions, sit on the floor with your cat in front of you. Place a treat between you and your pet, and hold your hand over it while giving the "Wait" command. Raise your hand. If your cat tries to eat the snack, use your hand to gently block her. Repeat the "Wait" command as you do this. Continue this exercise until your cat waits a few seconds as instructed, then give the "Go" command and allow her to eat the treat.

As training progresses, give the "Go" command at the instant your pet reaches for the treat.

With enough practice, she will hold steady at the "Wait" command and won't reach for her treat until she hears you say "Go." Of course, this is counterintuitive to a cat's natural instincts, so don't give up if your pet doesn't grasp the concept right away. Practice makes perfect.

Hint: If your cat insists on going for the treat despite your best attempts to get her to wait, remove the treat, let her calm down, then try again.

Lie Down

Once your cat has learned to sit, teaching him to lie down is not too much of a stretch.

When your cat is in a sitting position, hold a treat in front of his nose and lower it to the floor. He will likely follow it down, finally resting on his stomach.

Once he is on his stomach, give him the treat and praise him.

After practicing this a few times, start the trick by saying your cat's name along with the command, "Down."

Hint: If the treat in your hand isn't enough to coax your cat down, try gently nudging his shoulder blades to help him along.

The easy method: Wait for your cat to lie down. Say "good cat" and pretend you had something to do with his choice.

Roll Over

Your cat can learn this trick in two parts. To begin, make sure your cat is in the "Down" position. Kneel beside her, take a treat, and put it in front of her nose. Say "Roll over," and move the treat toward your cat's shoulder blade in the direction you'd like her to roll. Once she has rolled onto her side, reward her with a treat.

When your cat is used to rolling onto her side, it's time to take her the rest of the way. Instead of rewarding her after just a side roll, move the treat from her shoulder blade toward her spine so she will follow it and roll over. Once your cat has touched her other side to the floor, reward her with the treat.

It's easier if you try to teach this trick on a carpet or other soft surface. Cats may be uncomfortable rolling over if the surface is too hard.

Shake Hands

Cats tend to come in two types: aloof and extremely affectionate. But regardless of your pet's temperament, she should have little trouble learning how to shake hands. All it takes is a little practice and right incentive.

With your cat sitting in front of you, hold a treat in one hand and touch one paw with your other hand. When she raises the paw, hold it gently while saying "Shake." Reward your pet with the treat and say "Good girl." Repeat two or three more times, always with the proper command and a treat after a shake.

With enough practice, your cat should start raising her paw on her own in anticipation of a treat. When she does, give her your palm for a furry high-five.

Cats learn best through repetition, so try to practice this trick at the same time every day. (Right before mealtime works well because your cat will be more responsive to a food reward.) Keep the training brief, and stop at the first sign that your pet is losing interest.

Hint: Get your cat's attention by saying her name while giving the "Shake" command.

Walk on a Harness and Leash

Not all cats adapt well to wearing a leash, but some love the chance to put one on and explore the great outdoors!

The first step is to buy an adjustable harness and leash. (Don't opt for a collar—even cats that aren't normally escape artists might slip through one.) Let the cat explore the harness, sniffing it and determining that it is safe, before you attempt to put it on for the first time. You may even want to leave the harness and leash in the cat's area for several days, so that the scent and sight of it will become familiar.

When you put the harness on for the first time, do so at a mealtime, and reward the cat with a treat. Make sure that the harness fits comfortably and doesn't impede your cat's movements. Over the course of several days, let your cat become accustomed to wearing the harness by itself for short periods around the house. Praise the cat and reward her with treats and attention each time she does so.

When your cat is accustomed to the harness, attach the leash. Again, let your cat become accustomed to wearing the leash around the house. However, do keep a close eye on your cat during these times—you don't want

the leash to get tangled around something. When your cat is comfortable with the leash, take up the other end. First, follow your cat where she leads. Then begin to direct the walk. You can use treats to guide the cat in the direction you want to go. Take care that it doesn't become a battle of wills.

When you do take your cat outside, take your cat to a quiet area—a fenced-in backyard is ideal.

Hint: If your cat seems reluctant at any stage, go back to the previous stage, and let your cat set the pace for moving to the next one.

Turn the Lights Off

Teaching your cat to turn off the lights is a simple trick that is both entertaining and useful. Begin by holding a feathered cat training toy or your cat's favorite treat against the wall inches above the light switch. (A traditional flip switch works best.) Give the order "Lights" and reward your pet with the treat when he scratches at the switch. Repeat as necessary.

Next, enhance this behavior by holding a treat in your hand above the switch and a few inches away from the wall. Tap the switch with your free hand while repeating the order "Lights." Praise him, and release the treat when he rises upright or jumps and paws the wall two or three times. Once your cat gets the idea, tap the light switch while giving the order "Lights," then lower your handle and let your pet paw the wall by himself.

Reward him every time he successfully paws the switch and turns the lights off. Repeat this exercise until your cat has it figured out.

For the final step, stand across the room and give the order "Lights." Your cat should rise up or jump up and paw at the switch as instructed. Reward him with affection and a treat every time he is successful. Before you know it, your cat will be turning the lights off on command.

Fetch

This trick uses two small balls to get things started. Hold one ball where it can get your cat's attention. Once your cat is interested, toss the ball a few feet away and say, "Fetch."

If your cat gets the ball but doesn't bring it back, use the "Come" command. However, even if she returns, she may not want to give you the ball, which is where the second ball comes in. Present the second ball to her, maybe tossing it from hand to hand or tossing it up and down in one hand—whatever you can do to make it appealing to her. When she drops the first ball and allows you to pick it up, give her a treat, and toss the second ball for her to retrieve.

Although you need to repeat the trick and practice, make sure that you don't practice so long that your cat gets bored by the activity.

You can play fetch with any toy your cat likes, or even something as simple as a ball of paper.

Hint: Different breeds have different levels of interest in fetching. Young cats may be particularly interested in and successful with this trick.

Jump Through A Hoop

Jumping through a hoop is a classic trick, and one of the easiest things to teach your pet.

Begin by purchasing a hula hoop or similar toy if you don't already have one. (If the hoop comes with beads inside, remove them; the noise can be frightening or distracting.) Hold the hoop vertically on the floor with one hand, then give the command "Hoop" and lure your cat through the hoop with a treat or by dangling a feathered cat training toy. If your pet continually tries to go around the hoop instead of through it, position the hoop in a doorway to block his way.

Repeat this a few times until your cat easily walks through the hoop on command. Once he's comfortable, raise the hoop a few inches off the ground and repeat, again use a treat as a reward. Over the course of a few days, gradually raise the hoop higher and higher until your cat must jump through it. Many cats are great jumpers and won't need much encouragement!

Practice until your pet enthusiastically leaps through the hoop on your command.

If your cat trips while going through the hoop, release it immediately to avoid injury. Continue training as if nothing happened; if you react negatively to such an incident, your pet may pick up on your emotions and become afraid of the hoop.

Make this trick more exciting by decorating the hoop with colored ribbons and other dazzlers. Make sure they don't distract your cat or get in his way.

Run an Obstacle Course

It's easier than you might think to turn your cat into a four-footed Olympian by teaching her how to run an obstacle course. Not only will she have fun, but running a course is also great exercise.

Create a small course in your living room using household objects such as cardboard boxes, plastic tubs, stacked books, wood planks (detachable bookshelves work well), chairs, and pillows. You can also construct platforms on poles, or purchase them pre-made at any pet supply store.

Give your cat a day or two to explore the various items that make up the course, then begin training. After you have your cat's attention, stand in the middle of the course and drag a feathered toy to a string along the various obstacles. Your cat will chase the toy over, through, and across everything in her path in an attempt to catch it. At the end of the course, reward your pet with a treat.

Practice two or three times a day, stopping when your cat begins to lose interest. Once she becomes adept at running the course, put on a show for family and friends.

Hint: Don't expect your cat to run the course without your participation. Unlike other tricks, this one is usually dependent on giving her something to chase.

Good Toy, Bad Toy: Playtime Safety

It's like something right out of a Norman Rockwell painting: a fuzzy little kitten tumbling around with a ball of yarn. Well, old Norman apparently never had to rush his cat to the vet for emergency surgery to get a couple of feet of that yarn unraveled from the poor cat's digestive tract. Yarn and string can turn even the most disinterested cats wide-eyed and playful but should never be left where cats or kittens can get at it on their own. Besides choking and intestinal blockage dangers, a cat who gets tangled up in string or yarn—even during supervised play—can panic and injure himself, possibly fatally. Take special care to keep sewing thread and dental floss out of feline reach; it can become embedded in your cat's mouth, stomach, and intestines.

✳   ✳   ✳   ✳

CATS WILL TURN anything shiny, crinkly, or small enough to bat across the floor into a toy. Since Tabby doesn't have hands, he has to pick up these makeshift toys in his mouth, where they can be easily swallowed (or if not easily swallowed, can cause choking). At best, a foreign object in your cat's digestive system can trigger vomiting or diarrhea, but it can often be much worse. Keep things like paper clips, foil, and rubber bands safely tucked away.

Cellophane candy wrappers are particularly dangerous. Cats can't resist the crinkly texture, and the sugary residue makes them a cinch to get eaten. The wrappers can liquefy in your cat's stomach, coating the lining and blocking the uptake of nutrients from food.

What makes for a good cat toy? Here's what to look for:

Something sturdy. If it can get tossed, thrown, gnawed, clawed, batted, kicked, licked, and repeatedly pounced on without coming apart, it's a good cat toy. Catnip-filled toys encourage play, but most cats like to eat catnip and will try to lick and chew their way to that scrumptious herbal filling. Catnip toys made from light fabric or felt will most likely be in shreds—and the shreds in your cat's tummy—within a week. Ditto for plastic or vinyl toys that can be chewed up, cracked, or shattered.

No (re)movable parts. Catnip mice with yarn tails; crinkly caterpillars with bug eyes; oversized plush "bumblebees" with glued-on felt features, and plastic mesh balls with tantalizing little bells inside are four of the more popular cat toys. But they share a common failing: small and potentially dangerous parts that come off. If you can pull or peel a part or decoration off a cat toy, the odds are your cat can, too. In fact, go ahead and try it with all your cat's toys—it's better to have some catnip mice without tails than make a trip to the vet to get the tails out of your cat's stomach.

Something fun. A toy just isn't a toy if your cat won't play with it. Cat owners are often disappointed—and frequently annoyed—to find that the $100 worth of custom cat toys they bring home get passed over for a piece of crumpled paper or a simple table tennis ball. Cats like games that involve what they do best: climbing, running, leaping, stalking, and pouncing. Pick toys that encourage those behaviors, and your cat is bound to use them. That's the allure of the table-tennis ball—it rolls and hops and skitters away when your cat pounces on it, encouraging batting and chasing. Cats see moving edges better than stationary objects, so toys that wiggle, bob, or weave fascinate them and trigger their stalking and hunting reflexes.

Cheap Cat Tricks

* Tie a string to just about anything, and pull the object along the floor. Watch a kitty stalk and pounce!

* Drop an ice cube on the kitchen floor for an impromptu game of ice hockey.

* Goldish (safely contained) are good for hours of meditative gazing.

* Turn on a faucet so kitty can have some water playtime.

* Hide a feather or cotton mouse underneath pillows, a T-shirt, or a loose pile of newspapers. Cats love hidden prey.

* Place some kibble in a treat ball, and make kitty work for his dinner. He won't even realize he's exercising.

* Table-tennis balls in the bathtub. Does it get any better?

Playing with Your Cat

Are you ready to play?

* * * *

PLAYING WITH YOUR cat is a win-win situation: It's fun for both of you, it's good for your cat's physical and mental well-being, and there's nothing cuter than a playing cat. Here are some tips so you and your cat can get the most of playtime.

* Provide your cat with **a variety of toys**. Rotate out toys so she doesn't get bored.

* When you're playing with a toy that mimics hunting, make sure your cat succeeds in catching the "prey" before you put the toy away. A successful "hunt" will make your cat happy and pleased to play again.

* Playing before mealtime is a natural fit for cats. You can also incorporate food into the play session to satisfy your cat's instincts. Hide a treat in a bottle with a large mouth and let your cat get it out, or hide tidbits around the room and let your cat go on a treasure hunt.

* Hide a feather or cotton mouse underneath pillows, a T-shirt or a loose pile of newspapers. Cats love hidden prey.

Laser Pointers

Letting your cat chase the dot from a laser pointer is an inexpensive, fun, entertaining way to give your cat some exercise. If you add this toy to your repertoire, though, keep a few things in mind for maximum safety and enjoyment:

* Never shine the light in your cat's eyes. Make sure to put away the toy in a place where your cat can't find it and accidentally turn it on.

* Cat's love chasing prey, but ultimately they love catching it most. Some cats find a laser pointer dot frustrating because they can't physically catch it. If your cat seems to get wound up or frustrated, this may not be the toy for him.

* Keep play sessions short. Throughout the session, rest the dot on something your cat can pounce on, another toy or a bit of food. This helps satisfy your cat's need to finish the hunt.

A Playtime Don't

Never allow or encourage a new kitten or cat to play with your bare hand or foot. A tiny kitten may look cute batting at your thumb, but you'll be singing a different tune when she repeats those behaviors as a full-grown cat.

If your cat tries to pounce on, bite, or otherwise capture and conquer your hand or foot, withdraw and say "no" calmly but firmly. Provide other toys that will let your cat fulfill that instinct. However, take care not to give the substitute toy right as the kitten is pouncing on you—that just teaches them that a bad behavior will get a treat.

Some household objects should not be used as toys, as they're dangerous for the cat. Avoid plastic bags, rubber bands, paper clips, and string. Toys—homemade or purchased—that have elements that could be swallowed should only be played with under supervision.

To Costume Or Not

There are some arguments among cat owners over whether or not costumes are a good idea for cats. Some argue that they make cats unhappy and even scare them; others point to specific cats that will happily let you dress them for Halloween, Christmas, and every other occasion.

✳ ✳ ✳ ✳

IF YOU DO want to try costuming your cat, here are some tips:

✳ Let your cat become accustomed to the costume in the days before you want him to wear it. Leave the costume in the cat's area so that it will begin to take on the cat's scent.

✳ Make sure the costume is sturdy and doesn't have any parts, such as string, that can be torn off or swallowed.

✳ Don't put on costumes that are tight or reduce the cat's range of vision or motion. Don't put on costumes that cover your cat's paws or face.

✳ Young cats may respond better to costumes than older cats.

✳ If your cat seems unhappy, take the costume off immediately.

Dressed to the Nines

People dress up their pets for several reasons—some of which are practical, others psychological.

✳ ✳ ✳ ✳

WHY ON EARTH would people dress up their pets? On the practical side, certain breeds of dogs don't have enough meat on their bones or fur in their coats to keep themselves warm in cold weather, so you can buy little coats or wraps to help them stay warm.

Of course, you can also buy your dog a bathing suit, though there's no physiological need for it. Indeed, Web sites sell thousands of doggie Halloween costumes—from pirates to princesses, Superman to Darth Vader. And this brings us to the psychological part of the equation. Many people consider a pet to be a member of the family, which helps explain why Americans spend billions of dollars per year on their animals.

What other reasons might we have for putting capes on our dogs or Santa Claus hats on our cats? One study suggests that it may be because we are lonely. In research conducted at the University of Chicago, 99 people were asked to describe their own pet or the pet of someone they knew. The lonelier the people were in their everyday lives, the more likely they were to use human traits to describe their pets, employing such words as "thoughtful" and "sympathetic."

The lesson? We are social creatures, and when the need to connect with other humans is not fulfilled, we seek out ways to fill the void. For some of us, Mr. Fluffy clad in a woolly sweater fits the bill.

Say Cheese! How to Take a Photo of Your Cat

✻ Let kitty pose herself.

✻ Use props to catch kitty in an action pose.

✻ "I'm ready for my close-up." Fill 70 percent of the shot with kitty's face.

✻ Get on your cat's level. Kneel, squat, or lie on the rug. Photos are more interesting if you're at the same level as kitty.

✻ Move fast and take lots of shots. Most won't turn out but the more you take the better you'll get and the more gems you'll find. Worry less about getting the "purr-fect" shot and instead just have fun.

✻ Leave your camera out for impromptu shots.

※ **Chapter 7**

Cats and Other Animals (In Fiction and In Real Life)

What's the Difference Between a Cat Person and a Dog Person?

"Dogs have owners; cats have staff." There's truth to this clever saying. In fact, the contrasts between the two animals can help to explain the differences between "cat people" and "dog people."

※　※　※　※

FOLKS SEE A bit of themselves in their pets—that's the conclusion of a Ball State University study released in 2008, anyway. In this research, cat people described themselves as distant and independent, like their feline companions; dog people saw themselves as friendly and outgoing, like their canine companions.

Dog people tend to be sociable sorts who thrive on teamwork. This shouldn't be a surprise—dogs are social animals. A dog seeks out a pack in order to help keep it fed, safe, and warm. Canines need to be in a group setting to survive and thrive.

Cat people, meanwhile, aren't overly concerned with regular social interaction. This shouldn't be a surprise, either—cats are independent animals. They don't interact with their fellow felines as much as they simply share space with them. Cats are all about "me" time.

There you have it. We'll conclude with another little saying that homes in on what cats and dogs mean to humans: "Everyone needs a dog to adore him and a cat to bring him back to reality."

"The Cat and the Two Sparrows" (A Poem)

This seventeenth century poem depicts the relationship between a cat and two birds.

✳ ✳ ✳ ✳

To Monseigneur The Duke De Bourgogne.

Contemporary with a sparrow tame
There lived a cat; from tenderest age,
Of both, the basket and the cage
Had household gods the same.
The bird's sharp beak full oft provoked the cat,
Who play'd in turn, but with a gentle pat,
His wee friend sparing with a merry laugh,
Not punishing his faults by half.
In short, he scrupled much the harm,
Should he with points his ferule arm.

The sparrow, less discreet than he,
With dagger beak made very free.
Sir Cat, a person wise and staid,
Excused the warmth with which he play'd:
For 'tis full half of friendship's art
To take no joke in serious part.
Familiar since they saw the light,
Mere habit kept their friendship good;
Fair play had never turn'd to fight,
Till, of their neighbourhood,
Another sparrow came to greet
Old Ratto grave and saucy Pete.
Between the birds a quarrel rose,
And Ratto took his side.
'A pretty stranger, with such blows
To beat our friend!' he cried.
'A neighbour's sparrow eating ours!
Not so, by all the feline powers.'
And quick the stranger he devours.
'Now, truly,' saith Sir Cat,
I know how sparrows taste by that.
Exquisite, tender, delicate!'
This thought soon seal'd the other's fate.
But hence what moral can I bring?
For, lacking that important thing,
A fable lacks its finishing:
I seem to see of one some trace,
But still its shadow mocks my chase.
Yours, prince, it will not thus abuse:
For you such sports, and not my muse.
In wit, she and her sisters eight
Would fail to match you with a mate.
(Jean de La Fontaine)

"The Cat and the Old Rat" (A Poem)

What happens when a wise rat sees through a cat's disguise? This poem seeks to answer that question.

✳   ✳   ✳   ✳

A story-writer of our sort
Historifies, in short,
Of one that may be reckon'd
A Rodilard the Second,
The Alexander of the cats,
The Attila, the scourge of rats,
Whose fierce and whisker'd head
Among the latter spread,
A league around, its dread;
Who seem'd, indeed, determined
The world should be unvermined.
The planks with props more false than slim,
The tempting heaps of poison'd meal,
The traps of wire and traps of steel,
Were only play compared with him.
At length, so sadly were they scared.
The rats and mice no longer dared
To show their thievish faces
Outside their hiding-places,
Thus shunning all pursuit; whereat
Our crafty General Cat
Contrived to hang himself, as dead,
Beside the wall with downward head,
Resisting gravitation's laws
By clinging with his hinder claws
To some small bit of string.
The rats esteem'd the thing

A judgment for some naughty deed,
Some thievish snatch,
Or ugly scratch;
And thought their foe had got his meed
By being hung indeed.
With hope elated all
Of laughing at his funeral,
They thrust their noses out in air;
And now to show their heads they dare;
Now dodging back, now venturing more;
At last upon the larder's store
They fall to filching, as of yore.
A scanty feast enjoy'd these shallows;
Down dropp'd the hung one from his gallows,
And of the hindmost caught.
'Some other tricks to me are known,'
Said he, while tearing bone from bone,
'By long experience taught;
The point is settled, free from doubt,
That from your holes you shall come out.'
His threat as good as prophecy
Was proved by Mr. Mildandsly;
For, putting on a mealy robe,
He squatted in an open tub,
And held his purring and his breath;
Out came the vermin to their death.
On this occasion, one old stager,
A rat as grey as any badger,
Who had in battle lost his tail,
Abstained from smelling at the meal;
And cried, far off, 'Ah! General Cat,
I much suspect a heap like that;
Your meal is not the thing, perhaps,
For one who knows somewhat of traps;

Should you a sack of meal become,
I'd let you be, and stay at home.'

Well said, I think, and prudently,
By one who knew distrust to be
The parent of security.
(Jean de La Fontaine)

Something to Crow About . . .

CASSIE, A BLACK-AND-WHITE *kitten, was abandoned in the Massachusetts backyard of Ann and Wally Collito. As the Collitos set about caring for the kitten, they noticed someone else taking an interest—a wild crow they nicknamed Moses. "Moe the Crow" would take the food the Collitos set out for Cassie and place it in her mouth. "She trusted no one but the bird," says Ann. If Cassie wandered too near the street, Moe did everything possible to turn her back. The two also played together, rough-housing, tumbling, and exploring the yard. Eventually, Cassie came to trust the Collitos as well. But no one was as special to her as her adopted dad Moe. "They make a beautiful team," states Ann. "I think they'll always be the best of friends."*

"Cat-Pie" (A Poem)

Fortunately, this cook's meal is more hare than cat.

✳   ✳   ✳   ✳

While he is mark'd by vision clear
Who fathoms Nature's treasures,
The man may follow, void of fear,
Who her proportions measures.

Though for one mortal, it is true,
These trades may both be fitted,
Yet, that the things themselves are two
Must always be admitted.

Once on a time there lived a cook
Whose skill was past disputing,
Who in his head a fancy took
To try his luck at shooting.

So, gun in hand, he sought a spot
Where stores of game were breeding,
And there ere long a cat he shot
That on young birds was feeding.

This cat he fancied was a hare,
Forming a judgment hasty,
So served it up for people's fare,
Well-spiced and in a pasty.

Yet many a guest with wrath was fill'd
(All who had noses tender):
The cat that's by the sportsman kill'd
No cook a hare can render.

(*Johann Wolfgang von Goethe*)

"The Cat, The Weasel, and the Young Rabbit" (A Poem)

La Fontaine wrote this poem sometime in the sixteenth century.

✳ ✳ ✳ ✳

John Rabbit's palace under ground
Was once by Goody Weasel found.
She, sly of heart, resolved to seize
The place, and did so at her ease.
She took possession while its lord
Was absent on the dewy sward,
Intent upon his usual sport,—
A courtier at Aurora's court.
When he had browsed his fill of clover
And cut his pranks all nicely over,
Home Johnny came to take his drowse,
All snug within his cellar-house.
The weasel's nose he came to see,
Outsticking through the open door.
"Ye gods of hospitality!"
Exclaim'd the creature, vexèd sore,
"Must I give up my father's lodge?
Ho! Madam Weasel, please to budge,
Or, quicker than a weasel's dodge,
I'll call the rats to pay their grudge!"
The sharp-nosed lady made reply,
That she was first to occupy.

"The cause of war was surely small—
A house where one could only crawl!
And though it were a vast domain,"
Said she, "I'd like to know what will
Could grant to John perpetual reign,—
The son of Peter or of Bill.—

More than to Paul, or even me."
John Rabbit spoke—great lawyer he—
Of custom, usage, as the law,
Whereby the house, from sire to son,
As well as all its store of straw,
From Peter came at length to John.
Who could present a claim, so good
As he, the first possessor, could?
"Now," said the dame, "let's drop dispute,
And go before Raminagrobis,
Who'll judge, not only in this suit,
But tell us truly whose the globe is."

This person was a hermit cat,
A cat that play'd the hypocrite,
A saintly mouser, sleek and fat,
An arbiter of keenest wit.
John Rabbit in the judge concurr'd,
And off went both their case to broach
Before his majesty, the furr'd.
Said Clapperclaw, "My kits, approach,
And put your noses to my ears:
I'm deaf, almost, by weight of years."
And so they did, not fearing aught.
The good apostle, Clapperclaw,
Then laid on each a well-arm'd paw,
And both to an agreement brought,
By virtue of his tuskèd jaw.
This brings to mind the fate
Of little kings before the great.
(*Jean de La Fontaine*)

A Leopard in India

WHO KNOWS WHERE *the heart will lead? A leopard from a village in India decided to start paying nightly visits to a cow. According to wildlife warden Rohit Vyas, "It was unbelievable. They approached each other at very close proximity and the fearless cow would lick the leopard on its head and neck."*

The leopard showed no interest in harming or befriending other animals in the village, and the villagers actually welcomed the nightly visits from the leopard, which kept other crop-damaging animals at bay.

The forest department decided against trapping the leopard, much to the delight of both cow and cat.

"An Old Cat's Dying Soliloquy" (A Poem)

An old cat imagines heaven in this eighteenth century poem.

✳ ✳ ✳ ✳

Years saw me still Acasto's mansion grace,
The gentlest, fondest of the tabby race;
Before him frisking through the garden glade,
Or at his feet in quiet slumber laid;
Praised for my glossy back of zebra streak,
And wreaths of jet encircling round my neck;
Soft paws that ne'er extend the clawing nail,
The snowy whisker and the sinuous tail;
Now feeble age each glazing eyeball dims,
And pain has stiffened these once supple limbs;
Fate of eight lives the forfeit gasp obtains,
And e'en the ninth creeps languid through my veins.
Much sure of good the future has in store,

When on my master's hearth I bask no more,
In those blest climes, where fishes oft forsake
The winding river and the glassy lake;
There, as our silent-footed race behold
The crimson spots and fins of lucid gold,
Venturing without the shielding waves to play,
They gasp on shelving banks, our easy prey:
While birds unwinged hop careless o'er the ground,
And the plump mouse incessant trots around,
Near wells of cream that mortals never skim,
Warm marum creeping round their shallow brim;
Where green valerian tufts, luxuriant spread,
Cleanse the sleek hide and form the fragrant bed.
Yet, stern dispenser of the final blow,
Before thou lay'st an aged grimalkin low,
Bend to her last request a gracious ear,
Some days, some few short days, to linger here;
So to the guardian of his tabby's weal
Shall softest purrs these tender truths reveal:
'Ne'er shall thy now expiring puss forget
To thy kind care her long-enduring debt,
Nor shall the joys that painless realms decree
Efface the comforts once bestowed by thee;
To countless mice thy chicken-bones preferred,
Thy toast to golden fish and wingless bird;
O'er marum borders and valerian bed
Thy Selima shall bend her moping head,
Sigh that no more she climbs,
with grateful glee,
Thy downy sofa and thy cradling knee;
Nay, e'en at founts of cream shall
sullen swear,
Since thou, her more loved master, art not there.'
(Anna Seward)

"Lisy's Parting with Her Cat" (A Poem)

A girl imagines her cat's sadness as she readies to leave for school.

❋ ❋ ❋ ❋

The dreadful hour with leaden pace approached,
Lashed fiercely on by unrelenting fate,
When Lisy and her bosom Cat must part:
For now to school and pensive needle doomed,
She's banished from her childhood's undashed joy,
And all the pleasing intercourse she kept
With her grey comrade, which has often soothed
Her tender moments, while the world around
Glowed with ambition, business, and vice,
Or lay dissolved in sleep's delicious arms;
And from their dewy orbs the conscious stars
Shed on their friendship influence benign.
But see where mournful Puss, advancing stood
With outstretched tail, casts looks of anxious woe
On melting Lisy, in whose eye the tear
Stood tremulous, and thus would fain have said,
If nature had not tied her struggling tongue:
"Unkind, O! who shall now with fattening milk,
With flesh, with bread, and fish beloved, and meat,
Regale my taste? and at the cheerful fire,
Ah! who shall bask me in their downy lap?
Who shall invite me to the bed, and throw
The bedclothes o'er me in the winter night,
When Eurus roars? Beneath whose soothing hand
Soft shall I purr? But now, when Lisy's gone,
What is the dull officious world to me?
I loathe the thoughts of life:" thus plained the Cat,
While Lisy felt, by sympathetic touch,
These anxious thoughts that in her mind revolved,

And casting on her a desponding look,
She snatched her in her arms with eager grief,
And mewing, thus began—"O Cat beloved!
Thou dear companion of my tender years!
Joy of my youth! that oft hast licked my hands
With velvet tonge ne'er stained by mouse's blood;
Oh, gentle Cat! how shall I part with thee?
How dead and heavy will the moments pass
When you are not in my delighted eye,
With Cubi playing, or your flying tail!
How harshly will the softest muslin feel,
And all the silk of schools, while I no more
Have your sleek skin to soothe my softened sense!
How shall I eat while you are not beside
To share the bit? How shall I ever sleep
While I no more your lulling murmurs hear?
Yet we must part—so rigid fate decress—
But never shall your loved idea, dear,
Part from my soul, and when I first can mark
The embroidered figure on the snowy lawn,
Your image shall my needle keen employ.
Hark! now I'm called away! O direful sound!
I come—I come, but first I charge you all—
You—you—and you, particularly you,
O, Mary, Mary, feed her with the best,
Repose her nightly in the warmest couch,
And be a Lisy to her!"—Having said,
She sat her down, and with her head across,
Rushed to the evil which she could not shun,
While a sad mew went knelling to her heart!

(James Thomson)

Iguana-Cat Therapy

L IZ PALIKA AND her husband, Paul, do reptile rescue in California, taking in unwanted pet reptiles and finding them new homes. Conan, a green iguana, had been a pet-store mascot, well loved and very spoiled, when some teenage burglars broke into the store and stole him. After weeks of abuse, Conan was found by the police. When the Palikas took him in, he was traumatized and scared and wanted nothing to do with the pair of humans. However, Xena, the Palikas' three-year-old tabby (herself a rescue), decided to take Conan on as her special project. Within weeks, the two diverse species, prey and predator, had established a rapport and would bask in the afternoon sun together. Conan observed as Xena allowed herself to be handled and petted by the Palikas. Slowly, the iguana began to allow his new owners to handle him. Within months, thanks to Xena's example, Conan was again the calm, gentle iguana he used to be. Conan was adopted by a new home where he now lives contentedly with several feline friends.

A Snack of Convenience

Mice aren't really a cat's favorite food—they just happen to be easy prey.

✳ ✳ ✳ ✳

T HERE'S NO DENYING that cats have a thing for mice. It begins with the thrill of the chase, and if all goes as planned (for the cat), it ends with the satisfaction of downing a wiggling bundle of fur and bones, squeak and all.

It's feline instinct, but it's not entirely unlike the way you hit the couch, reach for the remote control, turn on the television, enjoy the thrill of a cop-show chase, and stuff your face with those special potato chips—the cheap, greasy ones that you'd never admit to loving. What's the similarity? For both the cat and for you, it's the easiest thing that's available because it's right in front of you. It's low-hanging fruit, so to speak.

If a mouse is so brazen or so foolish as to wander into Tabby's territory, the cat is going to make entertainment and a snack out of it. If that television is just going to sit there and if those chips are simply going to take up cupboard space, your best option is to make entertainment and a snack out of them. You get the general idea, right?

A cat would rather dine on, say, a tuna, but there aren't any flopping around your family rec room. Mice, on the other hand, are plentiful. Remember, cats also dine on bugs—and you don't see bug-flavored cat food at your local pet store, do you?

"The Duel" (A Poem)

It's dog versus cat in this humerous poem.

✳   ✳   ✳   ✳

The gingham dog and the calico cat
Side by side on the table sat;
'T was half-past twelve, and (what do you think!)
Nor one nor t' other had slept a wink!
The old Dutch clock and the Chinese plate
Appeared to know as sure as fate
There was going to be a terrible spat.
(*I wasn't there; I simply state
What was told to me by the Chinese plate!*)

The gingham dog went "Bow-wow-wow!"
And the calico cat replied "Mee-ow!"

The air was littered, an hour or so,
With bits of gingham and calico,
While the old Dutch clock in the chimney-place
Up with its hands before its face,
For it always dreaded a family row!
(*Now mind: I'm only telling you*
What the old Dutch clock declares is true!)

The Chinese plate looked very blue,
And wailed, "Oh, dear! what shall we do!"
But the gingham dog and the calico cat
Wallowed this way and tumbled that,
Employing every tooth and claw
In the awfullest way you ever saw—
And, oh! how the gingham and calico flew!
(*Don't fancy I exaggerate—*
I got my news from the Chinese plate!)

Next morning, where the two had sat
They found no trace of dog or cat;
And some folks think unto this day
That burglars stole that pair away!
But the truth about the cat and pup
Is this: they ate each other up!
Now what do you really think of that!
(*The old Dutch clock it told me so,*
And that is how I came
to know.)
(Eugene Field)

Which Is Smarter, a Dog or a Cat?

Most people—whether they own a cat or a dog—are convinced that their little wookums is the most amazing pet in the world, and no one can tell them otherwise.

✳   ✳   ✳   ✳

U NTIL EITHER A dog or a cat develops a cure for cancer, we can't settle this ongoing debate. The concept of intelligence is too nebulous, and dogs and cats are too different from one another.

The biggest obstacle in crowning an ultimate pet genius is that cats and dogs have contrasting goals. Dogs evolved as pack animals—their ancestors hunted in groups—so they are highly social. Dogs are hardwired to pick up signals and understand commands, and they are driven to please their pack leaders. These days, those pack leaders tend to be humans, which helps explain why canines are so easily trained.

Cats, on the other hand, evolved to hunt alone; consequently, they're motivated to take care of themselves. Most felines exhibit remarkable intelligence when it comes to self-preservation and self-reliance. They're extremely skilled at mapping out their surroundings: They can travel long distances, escape from tight spaces, and pull off spectacular leaping, balancing, and landing maneuvers.

If you define intelligence broadly—as the mastery of complex skills—there's a good case to be made for both dogs and cats. But if you define intelligence the way we do in school—as the ability to absorb information and then utilize this data when tested—dogs appear to be at the head of the class.

In experiments in which animals are rewarded for figuring out complex tasks (like hitting levers or navigating a maze), dogs invariably outperform cats. Dogs have learned to do things that cats can't come close to doing, like distinguishing photos of different dog breeds and even human faces. The evidence suggests that dogs also possess greater language abilities. Some dogs understand well more than two hundred words or signals; this is roughly the equivalent of a two-year-old human's vocabulary. Cats, meanwhile, seem to top out at approximately fifty words, which is about the same comprehension that an eighteen-month-old human displays.

But the evidence might be misleading—dogs are more innately driven to perform in order to earn praise and treats. It's difficult to motivate cats to do anything in experiments because they're so independent. And language is a social ability, so it's more suited to a pack animal like a dog.

The counter argument is that cats could master the same skills as dogs, but they're smart enough not to bother. Why bust your butt if you can lounge around while someone feeds and shelters you? Doesn't this mean that cats are smarter than their owners, too? Most cat owners have long suspected as much.

Chapter 8

Common Cat Illnesses

How Sick Is My Cat?: Evaluating Your Cat's Conditions At Home

Your cat can actually tell you a lot about how he's feeling, if you can understand what he's saying. No, there's no secret code to your cat's meows and purrs. But in many ways you might overlook, your cat is making clear statements about his health. Here's what to look for and what to do.

✳ ✳ ✳ ✳

BEHAVIOR. VETS GET a lot of the same kinds of phone calls. One of the most common is what the staff at one animal hospital has dubbed a "comedian cat" call. That's when the owner calls and says, "My cat is acting funny . . .

Many times a cat will "act funny" at home, but he'll be so nervous at the vet's office, he won't do anything; so the more accurate your report, the better your vet can determine what's going on. And since describing your cat's condition as "funny" or "sick" is a little too vague to pin a solid diagnosis on, you need to specifically describe what your cat is doing. A good idea is to write out a detailed description of what you see. (It's not a good idea to take time to do this in a life-threatening emergency, of course.) Try to think of the way you would try to describe to your doctor an ailment or pain you're experiencing. Some descriptions seem easy, such as "My cat is coughing," but might be a little trickier than you think. What you call coughing, another cat owner might call choking. Use words to paint a picture of what you observe, even imitating the sound, if you can.

Appetite and elimination. As unpleasant as it may seem, keeping a close eye on what goes into and out of your cat's body is a valuable home health care tool. How much food a cat needs will depend a lot on his age, life stage (growth, pregnancy, lactation, or old age, for example), activity level, and the type of food he gets. How much he eats is more a function of how much food is available and his health.

If you notice your cat isn't eating as much as before, you also need to know the context. For example, does he just seem uninterested in food? Or does he come running as usual for his food, but then eat little (if any) of it? In the first case, it would be completely correct to say your cat has no appetite; he isn't hungry. In the second case, he's definitely interested in food; he has an appetite but something is making him feel like he can't eat very much.

It's usually not polite to talk about elimination, and most of us aren't comfortable discussing it in the kind of detail that you need to know to help a sick cat. But it is important in understanding the health of your cat. Are stools well formed, soft, or loose? Is there any trace of blood in urine or feces? Is there mucus in the stool? Even things like color or odor can be important.

Of course, eating and elimination are two sides of the same coin (or two ends of the same digestive system, to be more accurate), so pay attention to how they go together.

For example, if your cat has a ravenous appetite but doesn't seem to put on any weight (or actually seems thinner), that should alert you to a possible problem. He could be the feline equivalent of those people we all envy who can eat anything and never gain an ounce—or there could be something a little more serious going on. Once you've noticed these changes in your cat, take him to the vet to determine the cause of the problem.

Mucous membranes. This is the term for the skin that lines the mouth and nose. It's pretty tough to look up a cat's nose, so that's probably out of the question. You might be able to get your cat to cooperate with you looking in his mouth for a second, but the odds aren't good. Still, how to open a reluctant cat's mouth is something every cat owner should know.

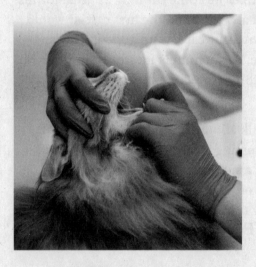

The best way to check your cat's mouth is to grasp the top of your cat's head with your thumb on one side and your fingers on the other. Tip your cat's head back so his nose points upward. Now, using your other hand, put one finger where the front teeth meet and push down gently with steady pressure on the lower jaw. As your cat's mouth opens, you'll have a few seconds to get a good look inside.

The color of the skin in your cat's mouth and on his gums tell an important story. A healthy cat usually has a tinge of pink. Stark white could be a sign of anemia. A yellowish cast (jaundice) is often a sign of liver trouble. A bluish tint may mean your cat isn't taking in enough oxygen, usually as a result of a respiratory problem or poisoning.

If your cat isn't cooperating with having his mouth opened—or you're squeamish about doing it—you can also check the color of his gums. Hold his head the same way you would to open his mouth. Gently pull down on the skin covering the lower teeth at the corner of the mouth, using the thumb and forefinger of your other hand.

A word of warning, though. It's not unusual for a cat's gums—and even the roof of his mouth—to take on some of his coat color, especially as he gets older. For some reason, orange cats are also prone to developing "freckles" on their lips, gums, and inside their mouths. Black gums on a black cat aren't anything to worry about, but pale, yellowish, or bluish gums on any cat should be reported to your veterinarian right away.

Coat condition. A healthy, well-groomed cat has a soft, clean, slightly lustrous coat. A cat whose fur is dull, dry, oily, or unkempt may not be getting groomed well enough or often enough by his owner, or he may be under the weather.

Even with regular grooming by humans, a cat needs to do some of his own grooming to keep his coat looking good. Cats are usually pretty diligent about their personal hygiene, so a cat who's not keeping up his appearance is likely not being lazy, he doesn't feel good.

On the other hand, a cat who's grooming himself raw is also telling you something. Excessive grooming can be a sign of stress, a skin problem, or a reaction to fleas. Look for "hot spots"—patches where your cat licks so much that the fur is gone and the skin is red or raw.

Of course, not all hair loss is from grooming. Take note of any bald patches or areas where the hair is thin or sparse. Most of your cat's body should be covered with a coat of hair thick enough to hide the skin underneath. (About the only place where it's normal for the fur to be thinned out is the area between your cat's eyes and ears.) Whatever the case, your vet's advice will help put your cat back on the path to a healthy coat.

Ears. Make it a point to check your cat's ears periodically. Grooming time is a good time to do this. Look for a change in color inside the ears. Just like the gums and inside of the mouth, a yellowish or bluish cast to the skin on the inside of your cat's ears can be a sign of a major health problem; alert your veterinarian right away.

Cats do a pretty good job of keeping their ears clean. Outside of some normal wax, then, you shouldn't see much in your cat's ears other than . . . well, ear. Any sort of inflammation, raw skin, or crustiness is a tip that something's amiss. Debris in a cat's ear—it usually looks like dirt or coffee grounds—is an indication of ear mites, tiny insects that live and breed in the ear canal. Itchiness is another sign of ear mites, but not all cats with ear mites will scratch or rub at their ears—and not all cats who scratch or rub their ears have ear mites.

Cats who go outdoors need to have their ears inspected from time to time for other reasons. In cold weather, frostbite is a real danger. Those nice, tall, pointy feline ears are made up mostly of skin and cartilage. There isn't a lot of blood flow to the ears. Even being caught outside for an hour when the temperature takes a sudden drop can be enough for the tips of your cat's ears to freeze.

Outdoor (or indoor/outdoor) cats are also more likely to get into scrapes with other cats. The ears are easy targets for scratches and bites during even the mildest of cat fights. A cat's small, sharp teeth can make a puncture wound that seals up immediately, trapping dirt and germs inside, causing infection. The cat may look and act all right when he comes home, but a few days later an abscess—a tender, swollen area of trapped pus—may form, and the cat can run a fever. At this point, you'll need to take your cat to the vet.

Eyes. "The eyes," goes the old saying, "are the windows of the soul." Fortunately for cat owners, the eyes are also a window to how your cat is feeling.

* A cat's pupils can look like anything from vertical slits, to the classic spindle-shaped "cat's eye," to full dilation—big black dots that take up all of the colored part of the eye. Certain diseases,  including trouble in a cat's nervous system, can cause the pupils to be noticeably different sizes. A cloudy, milky, or filmy look to the pupils might be a sign of cataracts, viral ulcers, or other vision problems.

* The iris is the colored part of the eye. Cats usually have some variety of green, yellow, or blue eyes. Occasionally, a cat will be "odd-eyed"; each eye is a different color. If you notice changes in your cat's iris or the appearance of splotches of other colors, contact your vet. (Note: It's not unusual for the iris to change with age. Old cats' irises may take on a "Swiss cheese" look, as if they're falling apart—although they aren't!)

* The "white" of the eye is officially known as the sclera. Obviously, this should be white (perhaps with some small blood vessels visible). Yellow or "bloodshot" sclera, ulcers or splotches of color, and signs of damage (like scrapes or bruises) are indicators of trouble.

* Conjunctiva is the pink, fleshy stuff under the eyelids that helps hold the eye in place. You usually don't notice the conjunctiva unless it swells up, in which case it may protrude from under the eyelid, giving the eye a "meaty" appearance.

* The third eyelid appears when your cat blinks or closes his eyes; this wonderful adaptation moves from the inside corner of the eye to cover the front surface of the eyeball. Again, it's something you rarely notice unless there's a problem. One of the ways cats announce that they don't feel well is when their third eyelids are up—that is, they've moved partially across the eyeball.

Hydration. A cat who hasn't been eating well may also not be drinking enough to meet all of his needs for water, and he may become dehydrated. To check your cat's  hydration, gently grasp the skin between his shoulder blades, pull up slightly, and open your fingers to let go. If the skin snaps back into place immediately, your cat is well hydrated. If not, the odds are the cat is dehydrated and may need to be rehydrated by your veterinarian to prevent serious harm.

Coughing, sneezing, runny nose and eyes. An occasional cough or sneeze—or even an occasional bout of coughing or sneezing—is a normal reaction to the millions of unseen irritants in the air. Even good, clean country air has pollen, dust, and other tiny things floating around in it. So if your cat sneezes or coughs now and then, it's most likely nothing to worry about.

Of course, cats are notorious for coughing up hairballs—another natural part of being a cat (especially a longhair cat). Regular grooming can keep down the number and severity of these clumps of swallowed fur (some well-groomed shorthair cats never seem to get them), but periodic coughing or "throat-clearing" sounds are also pretty normal.

Repeated or frequent bouts of sneezing or coughing are usually a sign of a health problem. Sneezing accompanied by a "runny nose" is a definite symptom of illness, as is swelling or discharge from your cat's eyes.

Temperature. Ever notice that a cat is particularly nice to cuddle up to on a chilly night? That's because the average body temperature for a cat is 101.4 degrees Fahrenheit (a good three degrees warmer than ours), although an individual cat's temperature may range between 100 and 102.5 degrees Fahrenheit and still be considered "normal." Disease—or prolonged exposure to heat or cold—can send a cat's temperature above or below the normal range.

Usually, a mild fever is a normal part of a cat's natural disease-fighting system. But extremely high or persistent fever can do serious—or even fatal—damage, and calls for professional help.

Early Warnings

Whenever something isn't quite right with your cat, there are usually early warning signs. Unfortunately, the signs may be so slight when they first show up, you can easily miss them. Other times, you might notice something a little different about your cat, but it appears harmless—and even cute. Keep in mind, the early warning signs may build up so slowly over such a long time that by the time you notice them they aren't early warnings anymore.

* * * *

WHEN YOUR CAT has a serious illness, nothing is worse than 20/20 hindsight—that terrible feeling of not seeing something coming when all the signals were there. To help spare you all of that, here are some important things to look out for.

Changes in behavior. Has your usually friendly cat become more moody, shy, or touchy about being petted lately? Or has your usually moody or shy cat become noticeably more friendly? Any kind of personality change in a cat could be a signal of a developing health problem. New behaviors or increased frequency of behaviors may also be an early warning, such as a cat that never drank from the faucet suddenly learning the trick or an "itchy" cat scratching or rubbing her ears more often.

Likewise, if your cat seems thirstier (drinks more often or for longer periods of time), she could be telling you she's got a kidney problem, early diabetes, or simply that it's a little too dry in the house.

You see, it's important to stress here that these behavioral early warnings are just that: warnings. They don't necessarily mean there's a serious problem with your cat, that she has something that could develop into a serious problem, or even that there's anything wrong with her at all. If you catch an early warning sign, just keep a closer eye on your cat to see if the warning sign continues or worsens. Make a call to your veterinarian at your earliest convenience and discuss what you've seen. Your vet may suggest making an appointment for an exam or just ask some questions and give you some other clues to keep watch for.

Remember, any sort of behavior change may be significant, no matter how slight or unimportant it might seem. Being a good cat watcher not only helps you catch emerging health problems early—when they have the best chance of being treated successfully—it can give you a deeper appreciation for the beautiful and complex behavior of cats.

Change in appearance. Does there seem to be a little less of your cat around these days? Or perhaps a little more? Assuming her diet and appetite are the same, a gain or loss of weight could be telling you something potentially more serious

is happening inside your cat's body. Does her hair seem thinner? Coarser? Has it lost its healthy shine? A dull coat, excessive hair loss, or fur that feels dry, coarse, or brittle are important signs of possible health problems, too.

Of course, changes in appearance are natural with advancing age, including some loss of body bulk or somewhat scruffier-looking fur. But even these normal changes are important signals; they're saying you now have a senior-citizen cat whose needs will be changing along with her body.

Changes in appetite and elimination. Cats are notorious for being picky eaters. But, in fact, finickness isn't really a normal part of cat behavior. In general, cats will turn up their nose at food for the same three reasons kids will: It doesn't taste good, they're holding out for something better, or they just don't feel that good.

If your cat has been steadily eating the same diet, then suddenly loses enthusiasm, don't assume she's just gotten tired of the same old food. If we can eat the same breakfast cereal or have the same coffee and Danish pastry every morning, there's no reason why your cat can't be satisfied with the same menu every day. Going off her food (or, for that matter, becoming ravenously hungry) is another way your cat lets you know she's not feeling well.

Since cats use the litter box, you may not notice a change in elimination habits right away. As unpleasant as it may seem, it's a good idea to at least be aware of what you're scooping or dumping from the cat's litter. A marked increase or decrease in urine or stool, the presence of blood or mucus, or a particularly pungent smell (when the box has been recently cleaned) are all warnings of possible trouble ahead.

Likewise, a cat who is litter-box trained but suddenly seems to forget is sending you a message. It could be a behavioral, stress-related, or environmental thing, but it could also be triggered by worms, a bladder infection, or other potentially serious problems.

It's often hard to pinpoint if a change is strictly in behavior, appearance, or appetite and elimination. For example, pacing the floor might be considered either a behavioral change or an indication of a hyperactive thyroid gland, and a cat who has scratched off patches of hair has a change in appearance that could come from a change in behavior. What's more, changes can happen over a period of days, weeks, or months—or they can just pop up from one moment to the next.

Sudden or abrupt changes are easier to notice. Long-range changes add up over time, usually so slowly we don't catch them until they've made some significant progress. Let's go back to diabetes as an example. A cat developing diabetes will drink more and will make more frequent trips to the litter box, producing larger volumes of urine. It would be almost impossible to notice your cat making just one extra trip to the water bowl or litter box in the course of a week, and it would still be fairly difficult even when increased to an extra trip every day. And even several extra trips per day can slip past your notice, too, especially since cats are nocturnal and most of the additional water or litter-box breaks could be coming while you're sleep.

By the time you're thinking, "Gee, that cat seems to be spending a lot of time at the water bowl or litter box," she's probably at the several-extra-trips-a-day level. You must work at training yourself to notice your pet's daily habits so you can detect and report any subtle and gradual changes to your vet.

Know When to Call the Vet

Of course, early warnings don't do you any good if you don't do something about them.

✳   ✳   ✳   ✳

YOU SHOULD CHECK out any indicators of potential health problems with your vet as soon as possible, just to be sure. But there are other times when a call to the vet—or a trip straight to the animal hospital—is a right-this-minute priority.

Any emergency situation. The common sense definition of a veterinary emergency is when you would call the doctor for yourself if it happened to you. Emergencies would therefore include:

✳ Profuse bleeding, including any open wound or bleeding from the nose, mouth, ears, or any other body opening.

✳ Fractures or dislocations. If you suspect a broken bone, don't try to find the break or set it yourself. Let a professional handle it.

✳ Loss of consciousness.

✳ Fever of more than 102 degrees Fahrenheit. Cats have a normal body temperature that's a few degrees warmer than ours, but a persistent fever over 102 needs medical attention.

✳ Difficulty breathing, swallowing, standing, or walking, including prolonged or frequent panting (cats will sometimes pant in extremely hot or humid conditions, or when they have overexerted in play), staggering, or an uncoordinated or clumsy gait. (Kittens are always a little clumsy, of course.)

✳ Straining or crying in the litter box, especially during urination. Some cats naturally make a big production out of using the box or even make sounds while digging, eliminating, or burying. You'll have to determine what's normal for your cat, but if you have any doubts, call the vet anyway.

* Convulsion, electrocution, or drowning.

* Blunt trauma, including high falls, being hit by a car, or getting caught in doors or machinery, even if there is no apparent serious injury. These kinds of accidents may cause internal bleeding or injuries only a vet exam can detect.

Any sudden significant change. While slight or gradual changes in appetite, elimination, appearance, or behavior are usually early warnings that call for timely but not necessarily immediate veterinary attention, a big or sudden shift may be cause for alarm. The chowhound cat who won't even get off the couch for breakfast one morning, for example, is showing a strong sign of potentially serious illness and needs to be checked out as soon as possible. Even if the change doesn't seem to be life-threatening, if it's a major departure from what your cat usually does, it's better to invest a little time and money to find out it's nothing rather than take a "wait-and-see" approach and find out it's really something serious—but it's also too late to do anything about it.

Any symptom that persists more than 48 hours or worsens (even a relatively mild one). Let's say you notice your cat has started sneezing a lot. It could be that she just crawled into a dusty nook somewhere, or it could be the start of a feline cold. If the sneezing doesn't go away after several hours, the cold begins to look like the more likely choice. If your cat is still sneezing a lot by the second day, it's pretty clear it's not going away by itself any time soon and it's time to call the vet.

Of course, if any symptom worsens suddenly or interferes with your cat's breathing, eating, drinking, walking, or elimination, don't wait 48 hours. Call the vet immediately.

The Home Veterinary First Aid Kit

You can buy a ready-made kit or put one together yourself. Here are some useful items to have on hand:

* * * *

* Disinfectants/antiseptics: povidone-iodine (0.001 percent to 1 percent dilution) hydrogen peroxide (not stronger than 3 percent solution) dilute Dakin's solution (one part household bleach to 20 parts water)

* Bulb syringe or turkey baster (for flushing wounds)

* Cotton swabs

* Gauze bandages, tape, bandage scissors

* Socks (for bandages and splints)

* Splints

* Cotton balls

* Rectal thermometer, petroleum jelly

* Tweezers and forceps (for removing ticks and foreign bodies)

It's also a good idea to include your vet's phone number, the animal emergency hospital phone number, and a first aid handbook in the kit.

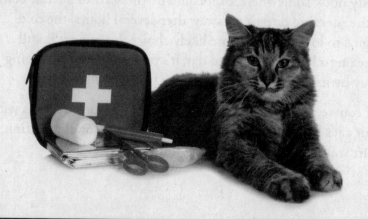

Handling, Restraining, and Moving a Sick or Injured Cat

If you think you know some people who make difficult patients when they're sick, at least those folks aren't likely to bite and scratch you to the point that you need medical attention. A sick or injured cat is scared and in pain, and, therefore, likely to be very touchy and defensive.

❋   ❋   ❋   ❋

Y OU HAVE TO give a cat like that some healthy respect: Those teeth and claws can do serious damage. But it's just as important to know how to handle and hold your cat with confidence in an emergency. In fact, you're less likely to get hurt if you have a good technique and act decisively.

A really sick cat may be fairly easy to handle and move if he's weak or lethargic from his illness. To transport a seriously ill cat—or any cat, for that matter—use a sturdy carrier with enough bedding to keep him warm and comfortable. The carrier shouldn't be too big, or else the cat will get jostled. Be sure you keep checking on a cat who's unconscious or not moving a lot, making sure his breathing and other vital signs are okay.

Moving an injured cat is a lot trickier. Try to splint or otherwise immobilize broken or crushed limbs, and keep the cat reclining as much as possible. Again, a cozy-size carrier with comfortable bedding will help. Even healthy cats will fight going into a carrier headfirst, so try setting the carrier on its back end and lowering the cat tail first. Close the door quickly; then gently tip the carrier down to its regular position.

For a cat who is struggling wildly, don't press the fight—you'll only get hurt, and the cat will get hurt worse than he already is. Pop the cat into a pillowcase and tie an overhand knot in the open end. The weave of the fabric allows air through, and the complete enclosure is actually reassuring for the cat.

There are several occasions where you may have to restrain your cat: for examination, treatment, medication, grooming, or just to carry him. Here are some tried-and-true techniques for restraining cats.

The "Press." With one hand, grasp the scruff of the cat's neck. Place the palm of the other hand over the cat's sacrum (the "lower back," just above the tail), and press down with firm, gentle pressure with both hands. This is a low-level restraint technique, for a relatively calm cat.

Football hold. This is a common one. With the cat's body resting on a solid surface, tuck him under one arm like a football, using your elbow to snuggle his body up against your side. Grasp his forelegs between the fingers of the hand of the restraining arm. Your other hand is free to do whatever has to be done or to grasp the cat's scruff if more secure restraint is needed for someone else to do something to him.

Throw in the towel. If you need to get to the cat's mouth or face (such as to give pills, liquid medicine, eye ointment, or ear mite medication), you can wrap up the rest of the cat in a thick towel. A good swaddling, leaving just the head out, will keep those claws under wraps and probably reduce struggling. Use the football hold on a wrapped-up cat.

Taking Your Cat's Temperature

You can't really rely on touching your cat to tell if he's running a fever, and you most likely can't get him to hold a thermometer under his tongue.

✳ ✳ ✳ ✳

HOWEVER, THERE ARE other options for taking a cat's temperature: under the armpit and in the ear canal. The first of these isn't very reliable, and the second requires an expensive electronic thermometer. Unfortunately, the most accurate and reliable way to take your cat's temperature is the way he's going to like least—rectally.

Obviously, a rectal thermometer is the equipment called for here. Shake the thermometer down below 99 degrees Fahrenheit, and lubricate the end with petroleum jelly or vegetable oil. With his feet firmly planted on a secure surface, tuck your cat under one arm with his tail pointed outward and his nose back by your elbow. With the hand of that same arm, hold the cat's tail up, and gently insert the thermometer in the anus with the other hand (you may have to bear down slightly at first). Slowly insert the thermometer about one inch, and keep it there for up to three minutes, if possible. Gently remove the thermometer, wipe off the glass, and read the temperature.

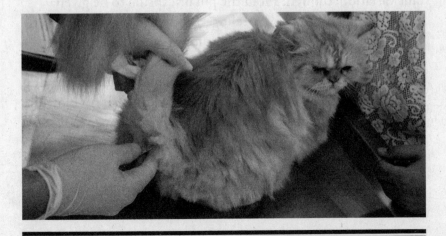

Giving Cats Medications

Mary Poppins can sing about "a spoonful of sugar" until the cows come home, but nothing is going to convince a cat to take his medicine willingly. A notable exception was an old cat named Buddy, who would eat just about anything that didn't eat him first. About one day out of three, you could get him to take his thyroid medicine just by dropping the pill on the floor in front of him—he'd gulp it down before he realized what it was. But not all cats are like Buddy, so here are some ways to get your cat to take his medicine.

* * * *

L IQUID MEDICINES ARE administered with an eyedropper or syringe. Open the cat's mouth and squirt the liquid slowly into the back of his throat. You can also slip the end of the dropper or syringe between the back teeth and squirt the liquid into the back of the throat that way. Hold the cat's head steady and keep his nose pointing up until everything is swallowed, otherwise he might shake his head and send the medication flying around the room instead. Gently rub the cat's throat to stimulate swallowing.

To give your cat a pill, open his mouth using the technique described for checking mucous membranes. There's one important variation, though: Hold the pill or capsule to be given between your thumb and forefinger, and use the middle finger of the same hand to lever open the lower jaw. Place the pill at the back of the cat's mouth, in the groove at the base of the tongue. You may have to nudge the pill slightly with your index finger to trigger the swallowing reflex. You can also try blowing gently on the cat's nose, or running your finger across it. If the cat licks his nose, he's probably swallowed the pill.

For cats who have an especially hard time taking pills, you can try crushing the tablet and mixing it in with his favorite snack.

CPR for Cats

A cat who stops breathing needs mouth-to-mouth resuscitation. A cat whose heart and breathing stop needs cardiopulmonary resuscitation (CPR). If you think your cat needs mouth-to-mouth or CPR, he also needs to get to the vet as soon as possible. Call for help, get a friend to start driving you to the animal hospital, or call a cab—before you do anything else.

✳ ✳ ✳ ✳

B E SURE THE cat really needs resuscitation. Giving mouth-to-mouth or CPR to a cat who doesn't need it (or practicing them on a healthy cat) can do serious harm.

If the cat is:

✳ Breathing; heartbeat present (feel for it by gently grasping the cat's chest, thumb and forefingers on either side of the rib cage just below the armpits): Do not begin mouth-to-mouth or CPR.

✳ Not breathing; heartbeat present: Begin mouth-to-mouth resuscitation. Grasp the cat's muzzle with one hand, cover his nose and mouth with your mouth, blow gently, then remove your mouth to let him exhale; repeat about 12 times per minute.

✳ Not breathing, no heartbeat felt, bluish cast to the tongue or inside of the mouth: Begin CPR immediately.

To begin CPR, grasp the cat's chest as you check for a heartbeat and gently compress the rib cage on a 3-count sequence—squeeze for 2 counts, release on 3—about 90 times a minute. Continue giving mouth-to-mouth. If you have help, your partner should give 1 breath after every 5 compressions, making sure not to give a breath until you have released the last compression. If working alone, give 2 breaths after every 15 compressions.

Dirty Work: Collecting Urine and Stool Samples For the Vet

One of the best ways to check out what's going on inside a cat is to analyze what comes out of him.

✳ ✳ ✳ ✳

PROBLEMS AS ROUTINE as worms or as serious as diabetes and kidney disease can be caught by checking stool or urine samples. A cat can be hospitalized and the animal hospital staff can collect the samples, but it's a lot of stress on the cat, and some cats will just hold it while they're in a strange place. So when a stool or urine sample is called for, it's usually up to you to get it.

Here's an easy trick for collecting either kind of sample. Close your cat in a room with his own litter box. The box should be thoroughly washed first and filled with those plastic foam "peanuts" used for packing. (If those aren't available, you can try cut-up plastic trash bags instead.) Listen for your cat to start scratching in the box and collect samples as quickly as possible. (If a cat urinates and defecates in the box, the urine sample is contaminated and can't be used.)

Collect urine samples in a clean, dry container with a tight-fitting lid. Stool samples can be collected in an ordinary sandwich bag and sealed with a twist-tie. Samples should be taken straight to the vet. If you can't leave immediately, they can be refrigerated for up to three hours.

Life-Threatening Emergencies: Urinary Blockage

It strikes cats of any age, but younger adult males seem to be at the highest risk.

❋ ❋ ❋ ❋

THE CULPRIT IS usually stones or sand that form in the cat's bladder, often as a result of a diet high in ash or mineral content. Once it happens, it's likely to happen again. On the plus side, when the problem occurs, there is usually an uncomplicated—but painful—way to fix it. On the negative side, it can quickly become fatal; even if the blockage is caught early, it can result in permanent damage to the cat's kidneys and other vital organs.

The urinary tract dumps the chemical wastes of everyday life out of your cat's body. If that pathway blocks up, all those wastes back up, poisoning the cat. So when a bladder stone gets lodged in the urinary tract, the clock starts ticking and every minute counts. If you notice your cat squatting in the litter box and straining or crying but not producing anything or producing small amounts of bloody urine, run—don't walk—to the nearest veterinarian.

The vet can fix the problem by "unblocking" a cat. This procedure can be as simple as a little skillful pressure and manipulation to break up the obstruction. More serious cases call for catheterization: The cat is sedated, and a flexible tube is used to clear out the blockage. In extreme cases, emergency surgery may be called for.

Emergency Care For a Blocked Cat

What if your cat blocks up in the middle of the night, while you're away at work, or without any warning signs?

❋ ❋ ❋ ❋

SEVERAL HOURS CAN pass before the blockage can be noticed, and by that time, the cat may be in serious trouble. It's a life-or-death situation, and you may have to try to unblock the cat yourself.

First, be aware of three important points:

❋ Every second counts, so it's best to try unblocking the cat while you're in the process of getting him to the vet;

❋ While urinary blockage is extremely painful, unblocking usually hurts even more; even the nicest cat will bite or scratch when in pain;

❋ Even if you're successful in unblocking the cat, he still needs prompt veterinary care.

To unblock a cat, it's best to have the assistance of another person. Have the other person use one hand to apply pressure over the cat's shoulders, forcing the cat down firmly while using the other hand to hold one or both of the cat's back legs. Now lift the cat's tail to expose its hind end. Grasp the urinary opening between your thumb and forefinger, and gently wiggle back and forth. You can also use a "milking" motion, going from the body outward. Either of these may produce mucus or a white, gritty-looking substance, possibly tinged with blood. If the obstruction breaks loose, urine usually starts to flow.

Occasionally, a blockage can be pushed loose by gently squeezing the bladder. Put your hand around the cat's underbelly, just in front of the back legs. Squeeze with even pressure but not too hard or too long—since the bladder can't empty, it's stretched tight and can rupture.

Vaccinations

Kittens get a series of shots. Adults get annual boosters. But what exactly are vaccinations, and how do they help keep cats healthy?

✳   ✳   ✳   ✳

Here's how most vaccines work. Researchers find the germ causing the disease—for example, the virus that causes feline distemper. Next they produce a harmless, non-contagious version of the virus. This form of the virus is used to vaccinate healthy cats. The vaccine triggers the cat's disease-fighting immune system, which attacks and destroys the virus. This exposure "primes" the immune system so that if the same virus shows up again—even the dangerous, contagious version—it will be destroyed before it can cause illness.

Vaccines protect your cat from common diseases, mostly caused by viruses. When a virus invades an animal's body, no medicine can kill it. You can give a cat with a virus antibiotics from now until doomsday, and it won't cure the disease (although the antibiotics will help treat or control infections that might start as a result of the cat's being sick with the virus). Viral diseases just have to run their course, after which the victim is often immune for life. Vaccines (usually with regular booster shots) provide your cat with the benefits of being immune without actually having to suffer through the disease.

Vaccines can't cure diseases caused by viruses. Going back to feline distemper for a moment, if a cat has already contracted this disease, the vaccine won't stop it. Vaccines also can't prevent every viral disease every time. No vaccine is 100 percent effective, so every once in a while a cat who has all his shots will still get sick with something he's supposed to be protected against. Some diseases, like FIV, are caused by viruses that shut down the immune system when they first enter the cat's body. In those cases, the vaccine can't do its job because its tools (the disease-fighting system of the cat's body) have been taken away.

Get your cat's shots from a veterinarian or animal hospital. At the bare minimum, cats should be up-to-date on their rabies shot and distemper-combination vaccine. The combination shot usually carries protection against feline distemper (panleukopenia) and common upper respiratory diseases that cause cold- or flu-like symptoms in your cat (feline viral rhinotracheitis and calicivirus). Any cat being vaccinated for the first time usually needs a series of shots, spaced a couple of weeks apart. Young kittens don't have full-blown immune systems and need boosters every few weeks until they're three or four months old, and then annually after that. (The exception is rabies vaccinations; a kitten usually receives one shot given at three to four months of age. Rabies boosters are given annually or every three years, depending on the type of vaccine or the requirements of state law.) Most vaccines are given under the cat's skin and don't hurt much at all.

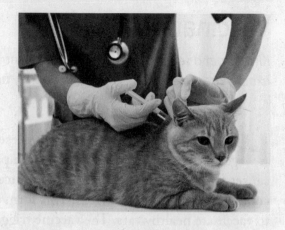

Vaccines for other cat diseases have been around since the mid-1980s, particularly the one for feline leukemia virus (FeLV). FeLV (or FeLeuk, as it's sometimes known) attacks a cat's white blood cells and can produce a kind of cancer. Research shows that most cats exposed to FeLV don't get sick, but even infected cats who appear healthy can still pass the virus on to other cats. Once a cat does get sick from FeLV, the odds are almost 100 percent that it will be a fatal illness.

The FeLV is a funny creature—it doesn't last long outside of a cat's body, unless it stays a little moist. So the most common way FeLV gets passed is prolonged close contact between a healthy cat and infected cat—things like mutual grooming, or sharing food, water, or litter boxes. This also means that the FeLV vaccine may not be necessary for a cat that is never exposed to FeLV-infected cats. A simple blood test can determine if your cat (or any new cat you're thinking of taking into your home) is infected. If not, keeping your FeLV-free cats indoors and away from FeLV-infected cats is probably all the protection they need (outdoor or indoor/outdoor cats are a different story). If your cat tests positive for FeLV, the vaccine won't help, either; vaccines don't kill the virus, they only protect uninfected cats from getting it.

Feline infectious peritonitis (FIP) is also a fatal cat disease caused by a virus. There are blood tests for FIP, but they're not as conclusive as the FeLV tests. There is an FIP vaccine, but the jury is still out on how safe and effective it is. Your veterinarian can help you figure out if your cat is at risk for FIP and if the potential benefits of the FIP vaccine outweigh the added risks.

How to Give a Cat a Pill

It isn't always easy, that's for sure.

✳ ✳ ✳ ✳

SIT ON THE sofa. Pick up the cat and cradle it in the crook of your elbow as though you were going to give a bottle to a baby. Talk softly to it.

With your right hand, stroke the cat's throat until it opens its mouth (be patient). Drop pill into mouth. Let go of the cat, noticing the direction it runs.

Pick the pill up off the floor and go get the cat. Sit on the floor in the kitchen, wrap your arm around the cat as before, and drop the pill in its mouth. Let go of the cat, noticing the direction it runs.

Scoot across the floor to pick up the pill, and go find the cat. Bring it back into the kitchen. Hold cat as before, but hold down its front paws with forearm. Drop pill into its mouth.

Pry claws from back legs out of your arm. Go get the cat, pick up the half-dissolved pill from the floor and drop it into a garbage can.

Get a new pill. Go into the bathroom, and get a fluffy towel. Stay in the bathroom with the cat, and close the door.

Sit on the bathroom floor, wrap the towel around the kitty, leaving only his head exposed. Cradle the kitty in the crook of your arm, and pick up the pill off of the counter.

Retrieve the cat from the top of shower door (you didn't know that cats can jump five feet straight up in the air, did you?), and wrap the towel around it a little tighter, making sure its paws can't come out this time. With fingers at either side of its jaw, pry it open and pop the pill into its mouth. Quickly close mouth (his, not yours).

Sit on the floor with the cat in your lap, stroking it under the chin and talking gently to it for at least a half hour, while the pill dissolves.

Unwrap towel, open bathroom door. Wash scratches in warm soapy water, comb your hair, and go find something to occupy your time for seven hours, then repeat.

Yin and Yang

Yin and Yang, black-and-white feline brothers, consider themselves staff members at the San Francisco SPCA Hearing Dog Program. The program has trained more than 750 dogs to be aides for hearing-impaired individuals, and Yin and Yang take a personal interest in every dog that enters the program.

The cats joined the staff when Training Coordinator Glenn Martyn noticed the dogs became over excited when encountering the downstairs office cats. Martyn asked permission to find a cat to live at the program's training facility, then discovered Yin and Yang on a trip to Montana.

Easygoing and playful, Yang was the more immediately sociable of the two, approaching dogs and even initiating playful wrestling matches with smaller breeds.

Yin was more laid-back, choosing to ignore the dogs until they came close and then batting at them when his personal space was invaded. For a while, Yin's favorite game was to lie underneath the telephone table and wait for a dog to come over so he could swat at it. "Not so great when we're trying to train a dog to respond to the telephone," explains Martyn.

Observing how the staff trained the dogs to use their mouth and paws to open cabinets, Yin and Yang learned to do the same. This proved problematic when the duo figured out the apartment window had a similar latch. "We had to redo the window to keep them from getting out to 'play' with the pigeons they so admire," says Martyn.

The Chinese yin-yang symbol denotes balance and harmony in life. For up, there is down. For black, there is white. And for dogs at The San Francisco Hearing Dog Program, there will always be cats.

Asthma

Asthma is a chronic breathing problem. Both cats and people suffer from it, but it isn't contagious. An asthmatic cat (or person) has bouts of extremely difficult breathing called asthma attacks. An asthma attack is fairly easy to spot; you'll notice rapid, open-mouthed breathing accompanied by wheezing and often by forced exhalations. Because breathing is so severely restricted during an asthma attack, the cat's gums and tongue may take on a bluish color. (Do not try to give mouth-to-mouth resuscitation or CPR to a cat having an asthma attack.)

* * * *

ASTHMA OFTEN DEVELOPS from another breathing problem called allergic bronchitis. This is pretty much what it sounds like: The airways in the cat's lungs get inflamed as the result of an allergic reaction to inhaled germs, dust (including dust from litter), wood smoke, and other irritants. Usually the cat has no other major signs of illness, a normal temperature, and continues to eat well. The only telltale sign is that she just has fits of deep, moist-sounding coughing. If the allergic bronchitis goes untreated or the source of the allergy isn't removed, the lungs can be permanently damaged, resulting in emphysema and asthma. Once the damage is done, even removing the original cause or causes of the allergic bronchitis won't make asthma go away.

Recently, some studies have been done on the effects of secondhand smoke on pets. The news is about what you'd expect: Secondhand smoke isn't particularly good for your cat. Cats with asthma or other breathing problems suffer more from secondhand smoke. Remember, asthma is related to allergies, so anything that irritates the air passages of the lungs—including cigarette smoke—can trigger an asthma attack.

What to Do About Asthma

Reduce stress. Stress makes allergies and asthma worse. Right about now you're saying to yourself, "Stress? What the heck kind of stress does a cat have?" That's a fair question. They certainly don't have to worry about paying bills or where their next meal is coming from. (Those are your stresses, actually.) They don't have job pressures or deadlines to meet. Heck, they don't even have to think about what they're going to wear every day.

Cats have stress that we like to call "domestication stress" or "family stress." You see, cats weren't originally designed and built to live among humans. They've done a superb job of adapting, but no matter how independent and primal your cat seems, she's still having to deal with the human world and human civilization every single day. And that gets tough. Be sure to give her plenty of options to do cat things such as run, climb, stalk (preferably another cat), bat things around, hide, and nap in secluded spots.

If the stress level goes up in your life or in your household, it goes up in your cat's life, too. She can't understand why things are getting tense—she just knows people are moving and sounding anxious. Remember, "stress" doesn't just mean negative things; positive events carry stress, too. In fact, probably the worst kind of stress for a cat is change. A new baby, for instance, is not only a time for great joy but also for great change—and the stresses that go with that. For you, those stresses mean less sleep (or none at all), a change in lifestyle, and an extra mouth to feed. For your cat, it means some strange new animal who makes odd noises, smells funny, and doesn't do much, suddenly takes all the human attention away from her

Clear the air. Secondhand smoke isn't the only thing that can make asthma worse. Even things that we think make our home more pleasant can be a no-no for a cat with bronchitis or asthma. Perfumes, room fresheners, deodorizers, and even scented litters or litter additives can trigger allergy and asthma attacks.

Likewise, the fumes from paints, cleaners, varnishes, and new carpeting are actually chemical irritants that create problems for the asthmatic cat. Use natural objects, such as flowers, eucalyptus sprigs, and fresh floral potpourri, to provide a fresh scent to a room instead of sprays or solids that contain chemicals. Use strong-smelling paints, stains, cleaners, and solvents in well-ventilated rooms, and keep the cat out until the smell goes away. And put out those smokes.

It's a good idea to use plain, natural, unscented litter and to stay away from deodorizers you add to the litter. Also the dust from the litter itself irritates the lungs and can cause attacks in asthmatic cats. Some natural litters—like the ones made of recycled paper—have virtually no dust at all. To cut down on dust from clay litters, pour them slowly, keeping the opening of the bag just a few inches from the litter box.

Wetter is better. Dry air dries out the lining of your cat's air passages, encouraging coughing and making your cat more vulnerable to infection and allergic reactions. Be sure to have a good humidifier going, especially in winter, during heating season, and in arid areas of the country. There's an added bonus to this remedy: You will also be less likely to have as many coughs, stuffy noses, and colds in the air if your home is kept moist.

Moderation in all things. A sedentary cat is more prone to health problems, but a cat who already has asthma can have a severe attack if she exerts herself too much. On the other hand, if she barely exerts at all, her breathing will be more labored because her heart and lungs aren't fit. Plus, she'll probably gain weight, and the heavier the cat, the more trouble she'll have with her asthma. Stick to the right amount of a high-quality, healthy diet; cut out the snacks and treats; and make sure your cat stays active. Get her a feline playmate and a good supply of toys. Be certain to play with her yourself, but keep the play sessions short and low-impact.

When should you call the vet? Any full-blown asthma attack is a medical emergency, which means your cat needs immediate veterinary medical care. Likewise, if your cat gasps for air, collapses, or turns blue in the gums and tongue, take her to the animal hospital immediately. Milder signs (such as noisy breath, occasional and intermittent wheezing or moist coughs, or slightly labored breathing after exertion) aren't emergencies, but you should get your cat to the vet as soon as possible. They could be caused by something other than allergies. And if it is bronchitis or the start of asthma, your vet may be able to give your cat medication that can prevent the danger and fright of a full-blown attack.

Coughing

We all know what coughing is and that it has different sounds: a dry, hacking cough; a moist-sounding cough; a single, gagging cough; a wheezing cough; and that half-cough, half-clearing-the-throat thing.

✳ ✳ ✳ ✳

COUGHING IS A reflex; when something irritates the back of the throat, breathing passages, or lungs, the body responds, expelling whatever is causing the irritation. But coughing is one of those reflexes that is not completely beyond conscious control; when needed, it can be done at will. In other words, coughing is an important mechanism for protecting the lungs and air passages from foreign objects and expelling infectious matter from the body.

What to Do About Coughing

From hairballs to heart trouble there are many reasons why a cat might cough. For a cat with any kind of cough or respiratory trouble, follow the steps for helping a cat with asthma. Other kinds of help depend on why the cat is coughing.

Hairballs are a common problem of cats and can be easily treated. Persistent coughs due to feline colds or flu can sometimes be helped with over-the-counter cough suppressants. (Do not use any cough medicine or other over-the-counter drug without the advice of your veterinarian. And keep in mind that dosages will vary widely.) If your cat is coughing and also pawing at her mouth or shaking her head, there may be something stuck in her throat or mouth. Open your cat's mouth—taking care that you avoid being bitten—and look inside. If you find a foreign body and can remove it easily, go ahead. Then keep a close eye on your cat for the next few days to see if infection develops. If, however, the object is stuck in the roof of the mouth, between the teeth, or you can't locate it, see your vet right away.

A collar can sometimes be the cause of a cough, especially if it's too tight. If your cat wears a collar, check the size. You should be able to slip the tip of your finger between the collar and the cat's neck easily. Since cats like to squeeze into tight places, collars can pose a choking hazard. Many experts recommend you only use cat collars with elastic or breakaway features so that if the cat gets the collar snagged, it comes off easily.

When should you call the vet?

Any cough that persists for more than 24 hours or is accompanied by wheezing, shortness of breath, or bluish gums and tongue means a trip to the vet. Coughs combined with other serious symptoms should prompt a call to the vet, too.

Cystitis (Bladder Inflammation)

A cat's bladder can become inflamed because of infection or irritation. Cystitis most often happens as part of a collection of bladder and urinary problems commonly called feline urological syndrome (FUS) or feline lower urinary tract disease (FLUTD).

✳ ✳ ✳ ✳

ATTACKS OF CYSTITIS or FUS (which includes cystitis, along with inflammation of the urinary tract and the formation of stones or sand in the bladder) are announced by bloody urine, frequent urination of small amounts, litter box accidents, spraying, excessive licking of the urinary opening, straining in the litter box, and possibly tenderness of the lower abdomen.

The pH of a cat's urine—how acidic or alkaline it is—has a lot to do with cystitis and FUS. If the cat's urine is alkaline, it's much easier for urinary crystals to form. These crystals in turn form gritty "sand" or small stones that irritate the lining of the bladder and can plug up the urinary opening in male cats, which is an extremely serious problem.

What to Do About Cystitis

Serious complications of cystitis and FUS show up most often in adult male cats. The first flare-up usually occurs when the cat is fairly young, and repeated bouts can pop up for the rest of his life. That said, don't think that just because you have an older or female cat that you're in the clear: Urinary tract problems can strike any cat.

Food for thought. Although there's still some discussion about this, most experts agree that diet is a major factor in feline bladder problems. Plant-based cat foods tend to make a cat's urine more alkaline (higher pH), which encourages the formation of crystals and stones and is a more hospitable environment for bacteria. Some commercial dry cat foods seem to have the same effect on urinary pH. As a result, cats who develop cystitis or FUS should only eat dry foods recommended by a veterinarian or stick to prescription dry food specially formulated for cats with bladder problems. Your vet may also suggest a urinary acidifier to add to your cat's diet, making sure the pH of his urine stays low enough to prevent bladder stones.

Magnesium is an important trace nutrient that every cat needs. Unfortunately, some commercial cat foods provide it in a form that also encourages crystals to form in the cat's urine, which can lead to bladder stones and, which, in turn, can cause a urinary obstruction. A quality commercial canned food is usually relatively low in magnesium, easy to digest, produces more acidic urine, and provides more fluid intake.

Water, water everywhere. The body is an amazing thing: If it doesn't have enough of something it needs, it finds a way to get it. If a cat isn't drinking enough, his body will find a way to conserve and reclaim water. One way is by reabsorbing water from the urine, making it more concentrated. The urinary tract lining in cats that have already had a bout of cystitis or FUS is particularly sensitive, and concentrated urine can trigger additional attacks.

Make sure your cat has constant access to plenty of clean, fresh water. Watch for your cat's drinking preferences—some favor a water faucet or even the toilet over a water bowl on the floor. It might seem odd or even a little bit disgusting, but it's probably a good idea to cater to his water-drinking whims, especially if the option is a flare-up of bladder disease.

Cats also get water from their food. The higher the moisture content in his diet, the more water he's getting—even without drinking. A cat who eats canned food gets a lot of water with the meal and more as a result of breaking down the higher fat, higher energy ingredients that are in most wet foods.

Less stress. The "body-mind connection" works for cats just as well as it does for people. Country folks know that a healthy attitude toward life makes for a healthy body. Unfortunately, you can't explain that to your cat. Instead, it's up to you to minimize his stress and maximize his health.

Try to anticipate problems. Do you know a major change is coming up in your household? Whether it's a new baby, someone going off to college for the first time,

a family vacation, or remodeling the kitchen, if you know it's coming it's best to either ease the cat into it slowly or expect an attack of urinary problems and take the necessary precautions. (An example of the easing-in-slowly strategy is preparing for a new baby: Set up the nursery ahead of time; if you're going to keep the cat out of that room, start doing it before the baby is born; or bring in a supply of whatever lotions or creams you're going to have so the cat has time to get used to the new smells.)

You should have realistic expectations for your cat. Sure, cats are clever and agile and maybe even a little sneaky, but they're still cats. It's entirely possible that your cat understands everything you say and is just playing dumb or being obstinate.

However, it's equally possible that he's only learned how to get along in human society just well enough to find himself a comfortable situation and doesn't have a clue why you're so bent out of shape that he's been urinating in your beautiful potted plants instead of the convenient litter box you bought him.

If a cat doesn't understand why he's being reprimanded, he stresses out. A stressed cat will announce his unhappiness with a change in behavior, often by elimination. And, to a cat, leaving it where you're sure to notice it—where your personal smell is strongest—is a great way to guarantee you'll get the message.

Finally, to lessen your cat's stress, try to stay cool yourself. Have you ever tried to enjoy a favorite activity with someone who was really, really intense about it right next to you? To cats, life in your home is basically one long stay at a resort hotel: The weather is always fine; everything is already paid for; you don't have to work; and you can eat, sleep, and play whenever you like. If the humans in this little paradise are under stress, though, the vacation is suddenly over. Some of this may be cats' fabled sensitivity to people's emotions, but some of it certainly is a reaction to the changes in the way we humans move and speak when we're agitated.

Check the box. A clean litter box filled with the appropriate kind of litter must be available to the cat at all times. Using the litter box is not an instinctive behavior in cats; the instinct part is the action of digging in loose materials to bury their urine and feces (especially if there is a habit of using that spot or the very faint residual smell of elimination there). If something turns them off to the box (like it's too dirty, too perfumey, or

too much trouble to get to), they'll either hold it too long (increasing bladder irritation and the risk of infection) or find another "toilet." Check your cat's litter box regularly, making sure it is clean and free of irritants.

When should you call the vet? Cats with urinary tract problems will often deliberately urinate outside of the litter box, even if they've been 100 percent accurate all their lives. If your cat suddenly starts having "accidents," spraying urine, or squatting and straining outside of the box, don't punish him. He's probably telling you he's got a problem. Call the vet as soon as you notice one of these signals and schedule an appointment for an exam. If it's a physical problem, the sooner you catch it, the easier it will be to treat. If it's a purely behavioral thing, you can start correcting it before it becomes an ingrained habit.

If your cat is straining in the litter box (or elsewhere) and not producing any urine, produces small amounts of bloody urine, or cries during urination, call the vet immediately. These are the signs of a urinary blockage, an extremely serious—and potentially fatal—problem.

Dandruff/Itchy Skin

Those same little white flakes that sell millions of dollars of medicated shampoo to human consumers can affect cats as well. Since a cat has hair all over her body, dandruff is easy to spot. The flakes are dead, dried-out skin and usually the result of some sort of allergic dermatitis—a reaction to something that makes the cat's skin dry, itchy, or scaly.

✳ ✳ ✳ ✳

THE CAUSES OF allergic dermatitis can be anything from parasites—such as fleas or mites—to sunburn, to a sensitivity to new carpeting, or even to something as simple as the air being too dry during heating season. Don't confuse dandruff—the result of abnormally dry or itchy skin—with dander. Dander refers to normal shedding of dead skin cells, combined with proteins in the cat's saliva that is left on the hair and skin when the cat grooms herself. (This dander isn't the result of an allergic reaction in the cat, but it is the cause of allergies to cats in humans.)

What to Do About Dandruff

What's the humidity? If you feel like the air is dry in your home and your skin feels dry and tight as a result, you can bet your cat is experiencing the same thing. Humidifying will not only lick the dry skin problem, it will cut down on static electricity in your cat's coat and reduce the chance of winter colds.

Look for freeloaders. Check your cat for parasites. Bites from fleas, lice, and mites can all cause allergic dermatitis. Cheyletiella mites have been called "walking dandruff" since they're large enough to see with the naked eye but too small to distinguish detail. All skin parasites can be treated fairly easily, but in order to stamp them out completely, you'll probably have to treat all other animals in the home, the house itself, and sometimes even the people.

Made in the shade. A cat's coat protects the sensitive skin underneath from the burning rays of the sun. But cats that spend a lot of time outdoors can still get sunburnt, especially on the tips of their ears, eyelids, nose, or lips. Any place the hair is sparse—the area on the head above the eye and below the ear or wherever the cat has scars or bald patches—is particularly sensitive. Sunburn kills the top layer of skin, which dries up and flakes off. Repeated sunburn can cause skin cancer—another reason to keep cats indoors. At the very least, cats that have had a sunburn or are especially at risk for it (cats with thin, sparse, or white coats, for example) should be kept indoors during the most intense period of ultraviolet (burning) sun rays.

When should you call the vet? Persistent or worsening itching and flaking or the presence of parasites calls for professional veterinary care. Over-the-counter pet shampoos and parasite treatments usually aren't potent enough to do the trick.

Deafness/Blindness

Cats can lose hearing or vision in accidents, as a result of disease, or because of birth defects. Reactions to some medications or lack of oxygen during birth can also impair hearing and sight.

✳ ✳ ✳ ✳

I F A CAT doesn't get enough of the amino acid taurine in her diet, her retinas (the layer of light-sensitive cells inside the eyeball that send messages about sight to the brain) can deteriorate, causing blindness. All-white cats with blue eyes have a high risk of being deaf, a condition related to Waardenburg syndrome in humans. White cats with yellow eyes or one blue eye have a greater-than-normal chance of being deaf, although not as likely as blue-eyed white cats.

What to Do About Deafness/Blindness

Find the reason. When vision starts going bad because of diet, switching to the right kind of food can often stop—but not reverse—the deterioration. On the other hand, cataracts (cloudy lenses in the eyes) can be corrected surgically, just like in humans. A thorough veterinary exam can determine if a cat's hearing loss is treatable (for example, an obstruction in the ear canal like impacted wax, ear mite debris, or a tumor) or not.

Make adjustments. Incredibly, blind cats can eventually figure out the layout of their home, more or less by the Braille method. You may want to keep a blind cat restricted to certain rooms or levels of the house to avoid accidental tumbles down stairs or exits out external doors. Once a blind cat learns the lay of the land at home, do your utmost not to change anything. If a door is usually open, leave it open. If furniture has to be moved for some reason, put it back where it was. A blind cat relies on landmarks that are at cat level—just a few inches off the floor—so even something as simple as leaving shoes in the hallway can throw her off.

Seeing (and feeling) is believing. Deaf cats process the world through their sense of sight and touch. The feline eye perceives moving objects better than stationary ones, so deaf cats take particular pleasure in making things move—especially downward from high places to shatter below. The thuds, crashes, and smashes that would send a hearing cat running for cover are lost on a deaf cat. Any visually stimulating thing is particularly interesting to deaf cats, so their owners should take note and try to provide visual stimulation—and to prevent cats from creating their own potentially unsafe diversions. For example, owners should remove breakable knick knacks from shelves so ambitious cats can't knock them off.

Sound is felt as vibrations in the deaf world. You may not be able to get your cat's attention by calling her name, or you may not be able to reprimand her with a sharp "No!" However, you can do both by stamping your foot or knocking on whatever surface the cat happens to occupy.

The golden years. All the senses and body functions slow down with advancing age, and hearing and vision are no exceptions. Once a cat passes middle age (anywhere from six to ten years old), expect her to lose a little of her edge. The difference with an elderly cat whose vision or hearing has gone down is that her other faculties have diminished, too, and she can't adapt as well. She also has a lifetime habit of relying on full-functioning eyes and ears. At that point, the most important ingredient for dealing with a blind or deaf cat is patience—she's doing the best she can with what she has.

When should you call the vet? If your cat seems to be less responsive to sound, bumps into things, or her pupils stay dilated even in bright light, contact your vet for an evaluation.

Diabetes

The pancreas is a long gland that lies directly beneath the stomach. A cluster of specialized cells in the pancreas produces insulin, which regulates the body's uptake and breakdown of sugar. Diabetes mellitus (usually just called diabetes or sugar diabetes) is the result of a shortage of insulin. Diabetics have intense thirst, produce large amounts of urine, and have abnormally high levels of sugar in their blood and urine. Other signs of diabetes are increased appetite and slow healing.

✳ ✳ ✳ ✳

LEFT UNTREATED, THE diabetic cat will lose weight (despite eating more) and become lethargic. Later signs of untreated diabetes include vomiting, diarrhea, rapid breathing, weakness, and finally collapse and death.

Your vet's diagnosis of diabetes is based on the cat's clinical signs, physical exam findings, and laboratory test results, primarily a persistent presence of abnormally high levels of sugar in the blood and urine.

Diabetes is a disease of older cats, rarely occurring before the age of seven years. It can be managed through diet and, when necessary, supplementary insulin. With treatment, diabetic cats can live ordinary lives, and a few may return to normal function for reasons that are not well understood.

What to Do About Diabetes

Watch that weight. Obese cats are more likely to develop diabetes. In fact, cats who weigh in at 15 pounds or more have double the risk of diabetes than the under-15-pound crowd. Keeping your cat's weight under control is a simple formula: Feed only the recommended amounts, limit (or eliminate) snacks and treats, and make sure Tabby stays active.

You are what you eat. A high-fiber diet helps control diabetes by regulating the rate at which nutrients are taken into body cells.

This, in turn, keeps blood sugar levels more consistent. Feeding several small meals during the day has a similar effect on blood sugar. A couple of large meals spread several hours apart cause a post-meal blood sugar surge, followed by a below-normal level by the time the next meal comes around. A normal cat's body smoothes out these peaks and valleys, but it's a problem for diabetics. Many diabetic cats can have their blood sugar levels returned to normal through diet and weight loss alone.

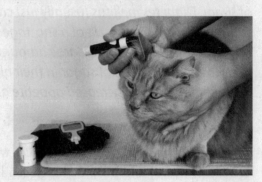

Be prepared. One of the most important aspects of managing the health of a diabetic cat is consistency. Food and medication must come at regular times, so be sure you always have an adequate supply of both and never skip or substitute.

Occasionally, a diabetic cat on insulin will have her blood sugar level suddenly swing dangerously to the low side—a condition known as hypoglycemia. Signs of hypoglycemia include shaking, disorientation, salivating, staggering and falling, and seizures. Keep an emergency sugar source on hand at all times (honey or Karo syrup are the usual recommendations). At the first sign of hypoglycemia, rub some on the cat's gums—and call the vet immediately.

When should you call the vet? If your cat shows signs of diabetes, schedule a veterinary exam as soon as possible. The longer a diabetic cat goes untreated, the more serious her condition gets. The earlier you can catch and control her diabetes, the more likely she is to have a normal life.

A cat who's already being treated for diabetes needs to go to the vet immediately if she shows signs of hypoglycemia or any kind of reaction to her medication.

Diarrhea

When the body needs to get rid of something quickly, it speeds up the action of the intestines and cuts down on water reabsorption from the gut. The end result (no pun intended) of this important defense mechanism is diarrhea. Once the cat's body has expelled the suspect stuff—and no more is taken in—diarrhea usually clears up by itself.

❋ ❋ ❋ ❋

CERTAIN VIRUSES AND diseases, a change in diet, or a food allergy can also trigger diarrhea. In the case of illness or food allergy, the diarrhea may not clear up for several days. Because it also removes fluid from the body, bouts lasting more than 24 hours may cause dehydration, which is a potentially serious condition.

What to Do About Diarrhea

An occasional loose stool or bout of diarrhea is a normal part of life and will pass without you having to do anything. When a cat suffers "the runs" for more than a day, though, you may need to help nature along.

What's the cause? Make a mental checklist of the previous 24 hours. Did your cat rummage through the garbage? Have a snack of "people" food? Eat a new food of any kind? Have a major stress or trauma (such as a plane trip)? Now think about the past week. Has there been an increase in stress for the cat? Did she eat some nonfood item? Has she been showing other symptoms of illness? These are all questions to ask yourself when evaluating your cat's condition.

Try the "quiet diet." The less work your cat's digestive system has to do, the faster it will settle back into its normal functioning.

You'll need to keep dairy products away from your cat. Although cats love dairy products, they don't digest them well.

A saucer of milk or cream may be the storybook feline snack, but the lactose (milk sugar) in dairy products frequently is a cause of diarrhea.

Get rid of cat foods that contain dyes. Cat food that comes in attractive colors, is processed to look like chunks of meat, or stays moist in the container for months includes dyes and other artificial ingredients. These are nonfoods, and the gut has to work harder to process them—just the opposite of what you want for a cat with diarrhea. Although changing foods also can cause diarrhea, switching to a brand with no dyes or additives can help clear up the current trouble and prevent future bouts.

Try to give your cat foods that are easy on the stomach. Cooked white rice mixed with boiled hamburger or chicken meat is

bland and easy to digest. Some cats balk at rice, so you may have to use potatoes or pasta instead. If you don't feel like cooking for your cat, lamb and rice cat foods are available at most pet supply stores.

You can also try fasting your cat. Sometimes fasting your cat for 24 hours is enough to drop the intestines back into low gear. If nothing at all goes in (except water), there's nothing to process; and by the end of the 24 hours, nothing should be coming out. When you resume feeding, begin with the bland rice mixture, then slowly mix in regular food, reducing the amount of the rice mixture until the cat is back on a normal diet.

If Not Nature . . . Although common sense says that adding a stool-softening laxative to your cat's food will keep the bowels moving, a bulk-forming laxative such as Metamucil seems to have a normalizing effect on cats with diarrhea. If your cat's stools are still a little soft during or after a couple of days of the "quiet diet," try adding about a half-teaspoon of the Metamucil laxative to each of her meals for a day or two.

Keep her hydrated. It's important that a cat with diarrhea keeps drinking. In fact, her need for fluids is actually greater, so make sure she has plenty of water available at all times. Besides losing fluids, though, a cat with diarrhea is losing key nutrients called electrolytes. These nutrients, such as sodium and potassium, make the nerves work right. To replenish electrolytes, keep fluid intake at the necessary level and provide some extra energy boost, you can try filling a bowl with a sports drink.

Nature's way. Nature provides its own way to slow down and get back to normal. Relaxation, stress reduction, and gentle exercise (take your cat for a walk on a leash and harness, if she likes it) may be all that are needed to clear up an attack of loose stools. Avoid the temptation to use over-the-counter diarrhea products, unless your vet specifically tells you to.

When should you call the vet? Call the vet immediately if severe (watery or "explosive") diarrhea continues for more than 24 hours or if diarrhea worsens; is bloody; or is accompanied by other symptoms such as vomiting, fever, or difficulty walking. A cat with diarrhea should drink a little more, but intense thirst with diarrhea may be a sign of diabetes.

Ear Mites

Tiny, pinpoint-size ear mites live and breed in the ear canals of cats and dogs. They feed on skin debris and can gnaw on the tissue of the ear canal, using cell fluids and blood for food, too. Ear mite infestations usually itch, so cats with ear mites will scratch excessively at the backs or insides of their ears (sometimes to the point of producing raw patches), shake their heads, or hold their ears at an angle to their heads.

* * * *

EAR MITES PRODUCE a black or brownish waxy debris in the ear canal, which looks very much like coffee grounds. Live mites can be seen in this debris with a magnifying glass or by spreading a small amount on dark paper and watching for tiny, moving white points.

Treatment of ear mites involves removing the debris from the ears and using a topical insecticide in the canal for a period of time to kill off the remaining mites and new mites that hatch out of eggs left behind. Since the mites can crawl out of the ear canal and onto the cat's fur—or the fur of other animals—all animals in the house should be dusted, sprayed, or dipped with an antiflea product. Ear mites are extremely common, and treatment is usually inexpensive and effective.

What to Do About Ear Mites

If your cat has itchy ears and you see the telltale debris in the ear canal, gently remove a little bit of the junk with a cotton ball and examine it under bright light with a magnifier or spread it on a piece of dark paper. Any movement—

including tiny white moving specks—means mites. Sometimes, mite debris is located deep in the ear canal where you can't see it. If you suspect your cat has mites, gently massage the back of the ear at the base between your thumb and forefinger. A cat with no mites usually enjoys it or, at worst, will fuss and try to get away. A cat who has unwanted company living in her ear canal will usually start scratching vigorously, so watch your hand because she won't.

Other ear problems can cause itchiness and debris in the ear canal, too, so don't start home remedies for ear mites until you're fairly certain that's the problem. Seeing live mites is real proof. When you have that proof, try to ease your cat's discomfort.

Clean them out.

The first step toward clearing up an ear mite infestation is to get as many tiny critters (and their belongings) out of the ear canal as possible. Put several drops of mineral oil into the ear canal and  massage gently. If the debris is particularly hard and crusty, you may have to let the oil work in for a few hours to soften things up. The massaging will help bring debris up to the outer part of the ear where it can be wiped away with a cotton ball or tissue. (Do not use cotton swabs, even though you may have seen your vet clean your cat's ears that way—one slip could puncture an eardrum.) If you want to do a thorough cleaning job (and you're courageous enough), you can use lukewarm distilled water in an ear syringe to gently flush out the canal. Repeat the cleaning procedure until the debris is gone.

Hit them while they're down. While the mineral oil immobilizes any mites left behind, it won't kill them all. To do that, you need insecticide eardrops. Reliable products that contain pyrethrins (a natural insecticide found in flowers of the mum family) are widely available at pet supply stores. Follow directions carefully, making sure to massage the drops in well and wipe away any excess.

Where mites might be. By the time you notice your cat has ear mites, there are literally thousands of the itty-bitty things around. Smaller than the period at the end of this sentence, a single ear mite can crawl out of your cat's ear canal and hide out deep in her fur—only to crawl back in after all the excitement of treatment is over and repopulate the colony. Therefore, cats with ear mites need regular treatment with flea products to knock out those adventurous mites that go exploring elsewhere on the cat's body.

Once is not enough. A single cleaning and treatment with eardrops won't do the trick. Just one surviving female mite with eggs can have your cat right back where you started from before you know it. You must be absolutely diligent about cleaning out your cat's ears every day or two and using the medication exactly as directed. It's not enough to kill all the mites in your cat's ears, either. Microscopic mite eggs can hatch days after a treatment, starting the infestation all over again. It usually takes a few weeks of treatment before you can safely assume your cat and home are ear mite free.

When should you call the vet? If your best home remedies don't knock out ear mites within a month, or the skin in or around the ear becomes raw or inflamed, you need professional help. Likewise, if your cat has itchy ears, shakes her head, flattens her ears, and has discharge from the ear canal—but there are no mite debris or live mites to be found—check with your vet. It could be a yeast or bacterial infection or another type of ear problem.

Feline Immunodeficiency Virus (FIV), Feline Infectious Peritonitis (FIP), and Feline Leukemia Virus (FeLV)

FIV, FIP, and FeLV are three extremely serious, incurable, and usually fatal cat diseases caused by viruses. Each is caused by a different kind of virus. However, they are all contagious only between cats, are nearly 100 percent fatal once they cause serious illness, and have the interesting quirk that not all cats exposed to them will get sick.

✳ ✳ ✳ ✳

UNLIKE THE VIRUSES that cause upper respiratory diseases or distemper in cats and can be carried in the air, these three require the physical presence of an infected cat in the same place (although not necessarily at the same time) as the cat who catches it. FIP and FeLV are spread most often by prolonged close contact with an infected cat. Close contact can include mutual grooming or sharing food, water, elimination areas, or sleeping quarters. This means a cat who goes outdoors and urinates or defecates where a cat carrying FIP or FeLV goes can catch the virus without ever having had physical contact with the carrier. FIP and FeLV can also be spread to kittens by a mother with the virus.

The main route of infection for FIV appears to be a bite from an infected cat. Cats who go outdoors—particularly if they fight—are therefore at risk. The most common profile of an FIV-positive cat is an unneutered male who goes outdoors and has sustained bites and scratches from other cats.

Cats who appear otherwise healthy may be carrying these viruses. Reliable blood tests exist for FeLV and FIV. There is a test for FIP; however, a positive FIP test alone—without other symptoms or risk factors—is not absolute proof the cat has the virus.

FIV is sometimes also called feline AIDS (or FAIDS). FIV does have a few general similarities to HIV, the virus associated with AIDS: It belongs to the same class of viruses; can stay in the body for years without causing illness; and when it becomes active, slowly breaks down the disease-fighting immune system. However, AIDS is a human disease, and FIV cannot infect humans.

What to Do About Feline Immunodeficiency Virus (FIV), Feline Infectious Peritonitis (FIP), and Feline Leukemia Virus (FeLV)

There's no question that these three diseases are scary. Once any one of them starts making your cat sick, there's not much that can be done other than to make the cat as comfortable as possible for as long as she has to live. The good news is these diseases can be prevented and, in many cases, with 100 percent success.

Take the test. Since a cat can appear healthy and still carry one of these viruses, a new arrival— even your first cat— should be tested for FeLV. Kittens probably don't need FIV tests unless they were strays, but it's probably a good idea to test adult cats from any source. Your veterinarian may recommend a retest in a few months. This isn't a scam; if your cat was very recently infected, it may not show up on the first test.

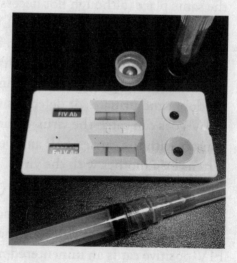

Stop the spread. There's only one surefire way to prevent your cat from contracting FeLV, FIP, or FIV: Keep her away from the sources of the viruses. In other words, keep her away from other cats and the places they frequent. This usually means keeping cats indoors at all times. It definitely means testing any new cat added to your household for FeLV and FIV before she's allowed to meet the resident cat or have run of any of the same areas. Preventative vaccines are available for FeLV and FIP. Schedule an appointment with your vet to talk about whether you should vaccinate your cats for these diseases.

Be positive about positives. If your cat tests positive for FeLV or FIV and a retest confirms it, don't give up hope. With good care, FeLV- and FIV-positive cats can live for years, even after signs of disease appear. New treatments are coming all the time, and there may be a breakthrough that will help your cat long before she gets seriously ill. Be responsible about the news. Keep your cat away from uninfected cats, and don't add any FeLV- or FIV-negative cats to your household. It may be tempting to start taking in other FeLV- and FIV-positive cats who are facing euthanasia, but think it over carefully. Eventually, the disease will catch up with them, and they'll demand a lot of time and resources. It may be best to focus on the special status of your own cat and give her the best possible quality of life.

Treat the symptoms. The best thing you can do for cats who are sick with FeLV, FIP, or FIV is to just make them feel better. This might be as simple as indulging them with their favorite foods when their appetites are poor or coaxing them to eat with petting and hand-feeding. However, each virus has its signature complications that may also need attention, usually from the vet and with follow-up or nursing care at home. FeLV causes lymphosarcoma, a kind of cancerous tumor that may need to be removed. The "wet" (effusive) form of FIP causes fluid to build up in the chest, making breathing difficult, or in the abdomen, giving the cat a bloated appearance. This buildup is a problem your vet can sometimes relieve by suctioning out the fluid with a needle and syringe. Since FIV attacks the immune system, you'll have to stay on top of secondary infections with prevention and medication.

When should you call the vet? These three viral diseases are a strong case for annual veterinary checkups. The early signs of any of the diseases are often too subtle for the average cat owner to notice, but a veterinarian knows what to look for. In between checkups, notify your vet of any sudden abdominal bloating or swelling, low-grade signs of illness that never quite go away (sneezing or diarrhea, for example), any lumps on your cat's body, or bites or scratches from cats not known to be FeLV- and FIV-negative.

Cats who have been diagnosed with FeLV, FIP, or FIV should see the vet regularly.

Fleas

These small, flat-bodied insects are no bigger than a pinhead, yet they have literally conquered the world. Fleas are found just about everywhere, they are tough to kill, and they can leap many times their body length.

✳ ✳ ✳ ✳

FLEAS CAN LIVE off the blood of just about any warm-blooded animal, but they prefer the higher body temperature of dogs and cats over humans. They reproduce quickly, and their eggs can survive in the environment for long periods of time—time enough to hatch and take over the skin of the next host that happens by.

In areas that have cold winters, outdoor fleas die off (although untreated indoor infestations can last year-round). In warm and humid regions like south Florida and Louisiana, however, "flea season" is a year-round event.

Surefire signs of fleas are small, black comma-shaped droppings in the cat's coat and, of course, the presence of live fleas. Both may

be noticeable when the cat is being combed or brushed—
another good reason for regular grooming. To check a cat for
flea dirt, stand her on a white or light-colored surface and ruffle
her fur vigorously. If you see black specks around her, moisten
a cotton ball or tissue and smear the specks. A streak of blood
confirms flea dirt.

What to Do About Fleas

Make no mistake about it, when your cat has fleas, you are
going to war against an enemy that is not about to surrender.
You have to wipe it out or put it into retreat down to the last
man, woman, and child. There's no such thing as peaceful
coexistence.

Kill them on the cat. Forget over-the-counter flea sprays and
powders—they're just not strong enough. You need profes-
sional-strength flea treatment, which means going to your vet
or a groomer. Flea collars are also very little help in the battle
against fleas. A plastic band with time-released insecticide at
your cat's neck isn't going to do much to kill fleas riding on your
cat's tail. Worse, if flea collars get wet, some can release all of
their poison at once.

Kill them in your home. If your cat has fleas, your house has
fleas. Not a pleasant thought, but true. If you just bathe, dip, or
spray the cat, any fleas not killed will immediately abandon ship
(remember their astounding jumping ability) and wait until the
coast is clear to return to your cat. Or, they may switch over to
a human host for a while until the pesticide on your cat is gone.
Actually, treating the cat for fleas is the easy part (although it
may not seem like it at the time). Treating your home is more
complicated.

"Evict" fleas from your home by thoroughly vacuuming
the entire house, including floors, carpets, and upholstery.
Immediately dispose of the vacuum cleaner bag in an outdoor
garbage can. In hot water, wash the bedding and linen from
anywhere the cat sleeps.

The next step is to "bomb" the annoying insects. Cover or securely put away all dishes, eating utensils, baby or pet toys, and other items. Remove all pets and people from the home, and set off the appropriate number of insecticide foggers for the size and number of rooms of your house. Use veterinary-strength foggers, not over-the-counter house or yard products. A good way to coordinate tactics is to take the infested animals for their flea baths or dips while the foggers are doing their work. You'll probably have to stay out of the house for a few hours after the foggers have been set off.

Even if you've been successful in killing every flea on your pets and in your home, there can still be flea eggs left behind. You'll probably have to repeat the treatments again to catch these stragglers as they hatch out. Newer flea products contain growth regulators that prevent eggs and young fleas from maturing, which can make things easier; however, some people may be allergic to these chemicals.

Keep them out. You may have defeated the enemy on the home front, but you've only won the battle—the war goes on. Cats who go outdoors are almost guaranteed to pick up fleas again. Fleas can also be brought back inside to indoor cats by the family dog. Even without a dog to serve as the "flea train," though, the more the door and unscreened windows are open during flea season, the more likely one or more of those hardy little critters are to hop into your home. Regular preventative flea treatment in your home will help prevent a sneak attack.

When should you call the vet? As soon as you see live fleas or flea dirt on your cat, call your vet. The longer you wait, the more fleas you'll have to fight. Your vet can give you the shampoos, foams, dips, sprays, topical treatments, oral medications, and foggers you'll need for your war on fleas, or you can have the vet or groomer do the treatment on the animals.

Hair Loss (Alopecia)

Cats shed constantly, so there's a certain amount of natural hair loss every cat owner should expect. However, bald patches, "hot spots" (areas that are inflamed and red and that the cat may lick or scratch excessively), and hair that gets so sparse you can see the skin underneath are all signs of a problem.

❋   ❋   ❋   ❋

HAIR LOSS HAPPENS for reasons as simple as a scar to more serious causes such as skin fungus, mites or fleas, or hormonal imbalances.

Dermatitis is another word for inflamed skin, and many kinds of dermatitis result in hair loss, too. Stress can also cause hair loss. A stressed cat not only sheds more but an anxious cat may actually tear out her own hair by excessive licking or chewing.

What to Do About Hair Loss

Location, location, location. If the hair loss is someplace you see your cat licking, biting, or scratching regularly (leg, paw, or side, for example), it could be a "hot spot" that is stress-induced or a reaction to bites from fleas or mites. Check your cat's coat for parasites. If it's a flea-bite allergy, you'll have to get rid of the fleas before you can hope to have the hair grow back. If the hair loss is in a hard-to-reach place (between the shoulder blades, for example) or in many places, it's probably not the cat doing it to herself. If the hair loss seems limited to one area of the body

(for example, on the legs from the paws up to the "elbows"), suspect a "contact allergy" or something similar. (Hair loss on the lower legs may be a reaction to new carpeting.)

You are what you eat. Have you been cutting corners on food costs by giving Tabby an off-brand or trying to go with table scraps only? Hair loss can be a sign of improper nutrition, so make sure your cat is getting the nutrients she needs.

Less stress is best. Actually, this advice could be added to every remedy! However, once your cat develops the habit of chewing, licking, or pulling out hair, it might be hard to break even after you cut down on stress. Do not scold or otherwise punish your cat when you see her working on a "hot spot" or pulling out hair. Scolding just adds more stress. Instead, try some behavior modification. Give her something else to do: Engage her in active play, pet her, open a securely screened window and let her sniff the great outdoors. Substituting a happy activity for the bad habit redirects her attention and energy.

When should you call the vet? A cat with hair loss plus other signs of disease—fever, loss of appetite, weight loss, vomiting— needs to be seen by a veterinarian immediately. Certain kinds of alopecia are caused by parasites or fungus that can be passed to people, so the sooner a cat with no other symptoms than hair loss is seen by the vet, the better.

Hairballs

Every time your cat grooms herself, she swallows some loose hairs. The hairs don't digest and then they get passed through the cat's stomach and intestines.

✳ ✳ ✳ ✳

SOMETIMES—ESPECIALLY IN LONGHAIR cats, during periods of heavy shedding, or in cats who groom other cats or groom themselves excessively—the cat swallows enough hair so that it forms a wad in her cat's stomach. These wads of hair are ejected as hairballs.

Virtually all cats have hairballs at some point in their lives. Many are passed through the intestines, but cats who swallow large amounts of fur can develop hairballs that actually clog the digestive system and have to be removed with surgery.

What to Do About Hairballs

Many times, the best thing to do when your cat coughs up a hairball is . . . nothing (except clean it up, of course). Once the hairball is out, everything's usually fine. Still, if your cat is bringing up hairballs regularly or to prevent future hairballs, there are some tried-and-true tricks to take care of this common cat complaint.

Brush up a bit.
Regular grooming, even just a little bit every few days, removes the loose hairs that cause hairballs. Remember, every loose hair you brush or comb off your cat is one less for her to swallow.

Ease the passing. A small amount of intestinal lubrication will help hairballs make their way through the digestive system instead of coming back up. You can buy commercial hairball remedies, use a little bit of melted butter, or give your cat a small dollop of petroleum jelly. The petroleum jelly is probably the cheapest and most effective method, but it's also the one most difficult to convince the cat to swallow. Butter is probably a better bet, since most cats love dairy and fat. Give your cat about a half-teaspoon of melted butter once a day for a few days (and no longer); it should do the trick. Commercial remedies taste good and are very effective, but always read and follow label directions carefully. (Never give any hairball remedy as a daily part of the cat's diet or for more than four or five days in a row, unless specifically recommended by your veterinarian.)

Bulk up your cat's diet. Too many snacks, too little fiber, and not enough exercise. It may sound like what the doctor told you at your last checkup, but it's equally sound advice for your cat. A hairball is a problem because it just sits there. Unless you get your cat's system moving a little more vigorously, hair will continue to collect, form hairballs, and be thrown up on your best rug or next to the bed for you to find with your bare feet in the middle of the night. A higher fiber diet, fewer empty-calorie snacks, and a little more exercise may be all it takes to lick a hairball problem.

When should you call the vet? A hairball once in a while is normal. Hairballs several times a week or even daily is a problem. Hairballs usually come up in one or two tries. If your cat continues retching and trying to bring something up or has diarrhea that won't stop or loses her appetite along with hairballs, call your vet right away. It doesn't happen often, but hairballs can get so bad they block the throat, stomach, or intestines, and that can be fatal.

Kidney Failure

The kidneys' major job is filtering out wastes. Age, injury, or disease can damage and destroy the function of kidney tissue.

✳ ✳ ✳ ✳

THE BODY CAN adjust to minor kidney damage or the early stages of kidney failure, so there may be no noticeable signs at first. As damage or failure worsens, a cat produces more urine and drinks more to compensate. In the later stages of failure, the kidneys can't keep up the pace, and wastes back up in the body, poisoning the cat and causing vomiting, loss of appetite, weight loss, and often telltale "ammonia breath."

Unfortunately, once kidney failure reaches this point, it's usually irreversible. The best way to detect a kidney problem is by a blood test. Mature cats and cats that show any signs of early kidney disease should be screened for kidney function.

What to Do About Kidney Failure

Kidney failure is sneaky. Many times, the symptoms are masked or completely invisible until the damage is critical. The typical cat in kidney failure has already lost about 70 percent of her kidney function by the time she's diagnosed. Veterinarians sometimes talk about what is called "end-stage" kidney disease when things start getting that bad. This diagnosis is just what it sounds like. Treatment for end-stage kidney disease can prolong the cat's life and make her feel better, but the end is inevitable.

This doesn't mean that every cat showing signs of kidney trouble is doomed. Sometimes, an infection can set in and the kidneys will shut down. Quick treatment can stop the infection and get the cat back on her feet with very little long-term damage.

Watch for the signs. Do you notice your cat drinking more? Has she suddenly quit eating? Is she listless or depressed? Does she seem to be urinating a lot more or barely at all? Does she seem sore over the lower part of her back or sit in a hunched-up "pain crouch"? All of these—along with vomiting and diarrhea—are signs of a possible kidney problem or infection.

Get to the vet. Home care for cats with kidney problems is only follow-up care. You need a vet to diagnose the problem, start treatment, and possibly even hospitalize your cat until she's stable.

Do the right thing. You'll probably be given a very strict diet for your cat and possibly some medications. Follow your vet's instructions as if your cat's life depends on it—because it does.

When should you call the vet? You should call the vet immediately if any of the warning signs of kidney failure show up in your cat. Other problems have similar symptoms, and only a thorough exam and blood test can determine for sure that it's a kidney problem. The sooner you can catch it, the better the odds will be.

Liver Disease

The liver plays an important role in metabolism and taking toxins and other unneeded compounds out of the blood. Liver damage or disease can be the result of a birth defect, infections, poisoning, or other conditions such as heart disease.

✳   ✳   ✳   ✳

BECAUSE LIVER PROBLEMS are often part of other illnesses, they usually don't have unique symptoms of their own. The notable exception is jaundice, which is a yellowish cast to the white of the cat's eye and possibly even her skin and under her tongue. Usually, abnormal liver function is only discovered or verified through blood tests.

What to do About Liver Disease

Keep a sharp eye out. Liver problems due to infection and poisoning can often be stopped and much of the damage reversed if caught early enough. Watch for symptoms, and don't wait too long to call the vet if your cat is sick (especially if she's not getting better).

Since the clinical signs of liver disease are the same as several other illnesses it can be difficult to determine what's wrong with your cat. These signs include loss of appetite, vomiting, diarrhea, fever, weight loss, dehydration, seizures, and increased urination (thus increased water consumption). Once you notice these symptoms, check for any signs of jaundice to determine if the problem is liver-related.

Follow directions. Once a cat has been diagnosed with liver disease, her recovery depends on you. Carefully follow all diet and medication instructions your vet gives you. Resist the temptation to cheat in order to make your cat "feel better"; in the long run, you may be shortening her life.

When should you call the vet? Jaundice is a sure sign that something's not normal in the liver, so call the vet immediately.

Obesity

Obesity is usually defined as being 15 percent or more over the average body weight for a particular individual. Since cats usually weigh somewhere between eight and ten pounds, any cat that tips the scales at more than 12 pounds is probably carrying too much weight.

✳ ✳ ✳ ✳

I T'S DIFFICULT TO get an accurate weight on your cat at home, so another way to tell is feeling the cat's ribs. You shouldn't be able to see the cat's ribs, but you should be able to feel each one under the hair and skin. As in people, a belly that protrudes much farther than the ribs is also a sign of weight gain.

Overweight cats are at higher risk for more serious, even life-threatening illnesses, including heart disease and diabetes. They are less active, which may also be an important factor in urinary tract problems like FUS.

What to Do About Obesity

Get 'em going. There's only one way to lose weight safely: Burn more calories than you eat. You're not going to convince your cat to get on the treadmill or the stair machine or to take up jogging, so it's up to you to increase her activity. Sometimes, introducing a young, active cat will get an obese cat moving out of self-defense, but the most reliable method is for you to exercise her with regular daily play sessions.

Less is more. A weight loss diet means cutting your cat's calories by about 30 percent until she hits the target weight, then maintaining the right number of calories to keep her at her lower weight. (This will be fewer calories than she was eating to maintain her weight.)

Cats are particularly notorious for being bad sports when they don't get as much to eat as they want (or have become used to), so be ready for some protests at first. To get your fat cat on the road to fitness, be sure to feed her less. Reducing calories means reducing the amount of food. Period.

You should also cut out snacks and treats. If you feel you absolutely must give your cat a treat, take a few morsels of food out of an already smaller meal and give it to her later. The overall calorie count (amount of food) for the day must stay down, no matter what!

Another guideline to follow is to give her lots of small meals. If your dieting cat gorges on her more humble repast and acts like she's starving three hours later, try splitting her food up into several little meals, gradually reducing the number until she's back to two or so a day.

And finally, don't "free feed" your cat. You can't tell how much your cat is eating if you leave a bowl of food out all day. Keep meals at regular intervals, and pick up what isn't eaten.

Easy does it. Your cat didn't get fat overnight or in one week. It took months or years. Gradual weight loss lets the body adjust to the changes and puts less stress on internal organs. The increase in your cat's activity will help regulate the rate of weight loss and speed things up as your cat gets fitter. Never put a cat on a starvation diet; starvation and rapid weight loss can trigger a fatal liver disease.

What about low-calorie foods? Low-cal cat foods are designed to make your cat feel full while actually giving her less calories than a full meal. In some cases, your vet may prescribe a weight-reducing food or suggest buying one of the low-cal commercial brands. In general, it's better not to change your cat's food—if you can help it—and just feed less of what she usually gets. However, switching to a low-cal food so that your cat successfully loses weight is better than keeping her on the same food—and keeping her fat.

When should you call the vet? It's probably a good idea to talk to your vet before you begin a home weight reduction program for your cat, just to make sure there's nothing you've overlooked. If your weight-loss program doesn't seem to be working after several weeks, you should definitely call the vet for advice. Any cat who begins looking plumper in a very short period of time needs to see the vet as soon as possible; quick weight gain can be a sign of very serious illness.

Ringworm

Ringworm isn't a worm, it's a skin fungus. It gets its name from the round, red, scaly patches that the fungus often causes.

✳ ✳ ✳ ✳

CATS ARE INFAMOUS for getting ringworm and for being carriers. A cat can actually have an active case of ringworm and have no symptoms at all. Ringworm can be spread to other cats, dogs, and even people. Also, spores from the ringworm fungus can stay active in the environment (in other words, your home) for a very long time.

Cats—and people—with weak or undeveloped immune systems are more likely to have cases of ringworm, so very young or very old cats or cats debilitated by other diseases are at the greatest risk.

What to Do About Ringworm

Treat your cat. If you think your cat has ringworm—a safe bet when you see the "classic" round bald patches with red, scaly skin, but a distinct possibility with any kind of rash or scabs on your cat—you've got to knock out the fungus on the cat and in the home (including on other pets). Clip the hair around the scaly patches and scrub with Betadine (povidone-iodine) every day. Then use a cotton ball to apply a dilution of household bleach and water, consisting of one part bleach to 32 parts water. (Be absolutely certain to dilute first!) Over-the-counter products are also effective, with those containing miconazole or clotrimazole being the best.

If you're not sure what you're seeing is ringworm, the lesions get worse, or the outbreak spreads, get help from your vet as soon as possible. Ringworm is usually a self-limiting problem, meaning that it goes only so far and then stops of its own accord; but if it gets out of control, it can be around for a long time and keep coming back.

Treat all your pets. Most likely, all your cats and dogs (if you have them), as well as the infected cat, will need at least an antifungal bath. In some cases, your vet may recommend an oral medication for the affected cat and possibly for other animals as a preventative or to knock out spores on carriers.

Treat the home. Wash all pet bedding, toys, and bowls in hot water. If it can't be washed or disinfected, discard it in an outdoor trash can. Thoroughly vacuum all floors and furniture and discard the vacuum-cleaner bag immediately in an outdoor location. Disinfect uncarpeted floors and other hard surfaces in rooms where the cat goes with the diluted bleach solution.

Cleaning and disinfecting must be repeated at least weekly until the cat is completely free of all signs of ringworm. It's a good idea to do a disinfection from time to time after that, since ringworm spores can survive in your home for years.

An ounce of prevention. Cats who don't go outdoors and aren't exposed to other cats rarely have ringworm. Keep your cat indoors and use in-home pet sitters instead of boarding, and you most likely will not have to deal with a ringworm outbreak.

When should you call the vet? Since ringworm is persistent, it is sometimes hard to diagnose without special equipment, and cats can carry it without symptoms, veterinary assistance is always a good idea. Lesions that don't heal, look infected, get worse, spread rapidly, or don't respond to home treatment are either something other than ringworm or a very hot case of ringworm that's gotten out of control. Either way, call your vet.

Scrapes and Scratches

Abrasions (scrapes and scratches) are damage to the outer layers of skin. The most common cause of scrapes and scratches in cats is other cats. Usually, cats keep their claws retracted during play, and their thick hair protects them from accidental nicks.

✳ ✳ ✳ ✳

VIGOROUS PLAY, A miscalculation, or an unplayful smack can cause an abrasion, usually most noticeable around the ears and face where the hair is more sparse. Unaltered cats and cats who go outdoors are more likely to get into out-and-out fights and suffer bite and scratch wounds.

What to Do About Scrapes and Scratches

Keep it clean. For fresh scratches simple soap-and-water cleanup, using a washcloth or cotton ball, is usually enough first aid. Don't try to prevent your cat from licking a scratch—that's Mother Nature's way of taking care of it, and she knows what she's doing. But do keep an eye on your cat. Occasionally, a cat may overdo it and require some type of restraint to prevent mutilation of the wound.

Look for more. Ruffle through your cat's fur and check for additional scratches. A veterinarian from an animal shelter remarks, "Any time we had to shave a stray cat with visible scratches for surgery, we found more scratches or scars all over her body."

Plumb the depths. How deep is the wound? Anything that bleeds noticeably needs more attention than a simple scratch. First, stop the bleeding with direct pressure, using a cotton ball or gauze. (You may need help restraining the cat.) Trim the hair from around the edge of the wound, and wash thoroughly with soap and water. Bandaging usually isn't necessary, and most scratches, scrapes, and minor wounds heal better and faster in the open air. Just be sure to keep the wound area clean.

When should you call the vet? Any serious wound or a wound that won't stop bleeding needs immediate veterinary attention. If direct pressure doesn't stop bleeding in a couple minutes—or if the wound is spurting blood—your cat is in grave danger. Take your cat directly to the vet, and continue to apply pressure and bandages until you can get her there.

Bite wounds should be treated by a vet, too, since they can become infected easily. Sometimes bites or other wounds will close up with some dirt or germs inside, causing an abscess—a painful, swollen pocket of infection. If the site of a wound swells, leaks pus, or is sensitive to the touch, or if your cat suddenly begins to run a fever, call your vet right away.

Seizure

Seizure, or convulsion, is a catchall word used to describe sudden attacks of changes in behavior that include loss of consciousness, loss of motor control (staggering, falling down, poor coordination), and loss of bladder or bowel control.

✳ ✳ ✳ ✳

SEIZURES CAN BE so mild as to be almost unnoticeable (the cat walks a bit strangely or acts "spacey" for a few minutes and then is fine), but they can also be frighteningly severe (the cat staggers, falls down, voids bladder and bowels, loses consciousness, and goes stiff).

Nervous system disorders, injuries (especially to the head), concussions, poisoning, tumors, stroke, infection, and high fever are just some of the causes of seizures. Epilepsy is a recurring seizure disorder in which a malfunction of the nervous system causes the brain to "misfire" messages to the body. These "misfired" messages result in a seizure.

A frequent myth about seizure victims is that they may swallow their tongue and suffocate. While an unconscious or semiconscious cat should be kept on her side to prevent the tongue from sliding to the back of the throat and partially obstructing the breathing passage, it's physically impossible for a normally attached tongue to be swallowed. Sometimes, an injury or an allergic reaction to a food, medicine, or insect bite (anaphylaxis) can cause the tongue to swell and prevent breathing. This is a dire emergency, and veterinary medical care is needed immediately.

What to Do About Seizures

Keep her in one place. Witnessing a cat having a seizure is frightening. Being the cat is even more frightening. She needs you to stay calm and keep her under gentle restraint so she doesn't injure herself. Unfortunately, she doesn't know she needs you to do that, so put a fluffy towel or light blanket over the cat to restrain her; any cat will bite or scratch, often severely, when in seizure. Don't try to stop the involuntary jerk-

ing movements that go with some seizures since you can hurt the cat. Talk to her in soothing tones; even if she seems to be unresponsive, she may be able to hear you (and it will help to steady your nerves).

Watch the time. The first time it happens, a seizure seems to go on forever. However, most really only last a minute or two before the cat starts coming out of it. If the seizure doesn't show signs of letting up after two minutes (or if it passes but recurs again in less than 24 hours), you have an emergency on your hands—get to the vet.

Get to the root. Even if your cat recovers quickly from a seizure, make an appointment with the vet to try to figure out the cause. Seizure can be the result of tumors, hypoglycemia, nutritional deficiencies, or epilepsy—all of which can usually be treated or controlled.

When should you call the vet? A seizure that doesn't begin to let up after a minute or two, lets up but then comes on again, or recurs in less than 24 hours is a serious symptom and needs immediate veterinary care. Cats who have seizures that let up quickly and from which the cat fully recovers should be seen by the vet as soon as possible.

Ticks

Ticks are small, blood-sucking insects that attach themselves to warm-blooded animals by burying their mouth parts into the skin.

✳ ✳ ✳ ✳

O NCE A TICK begins to feed, its body expands, often to many times its normal size. A gorged tick may look like a small mole or roundish bump of odd-colored flesh. Ticks are usually found on vegetation, several feet off the ground, and drop onto passing animals such as your cat or dog.

Because their mouth parts make contact with the bloodstream of the host, ticks can transmit diseases, most notably Lyme disease. It's important, then, that ticks be removed as soon as possible—and with their entire body intact. The longer the tick is embedded, the greater the risk of spreading anything it might be carrying, and any part of the tick left behind could still contain infectious matter.

What to Do About Ticks

Keep out of the country. Cats that remain indoors almost never get ticks, unless they're carried in by other pets, people, or rodent pests. Even if your cat goes outdoors in a "controlled" way (on a handheld leash, for example), keep her away from tall grass and out from under bushes and shrubs—anywhere ticks could be lurking, waiting to drop.

The best defense is a strong offense. If your cat goes outdoors, regularly dust or spray her with a flea and tick product containing pyrethrins (a natural insecticide found in flowers from the mum family). Rodents often carry ticks, so eliminating rodent populations and nesting sites from your home and property will cut down on the number of ticks, too.

Nice and easy does it. Check your cat for ticks any time she goes outdoors, especially in more suburban and rural settings and during warmer weather. If you find a tick on your cat's body, it's important to remove it quickly. The best way to do this is to grasp the tick at the skin line with a pair of forceps or tweezers. Try to grab the tick as close to its head as possible and pull gently and steadily straight out from the cat's body. Forget what you may have learned about burning ticks out; it doesn't work well, and you run the risk of burning your cat.

It ain't over 'til it's over. Ticks are hardy creatures. When you remove one, don't assume it's dead or that you'll be rid of it by throwing it in the garbage or sending it down the drain or toilet. They can crawl back out from any of these destinations, ready to attach themselves to the next mammal that happens by. Throwing them outdoors gets them out of your house but may just be passing the problem along to someone else. It's best to put the removed tick immediately into a small jar with rubbing alcohol or insecticide, and then seal the jar securely. This method not only ensures the demise of the little pest and seals off any escape, it preserves the insect in case the tick-bite victim develops complications.

Watch for complications. Once you remove a tick from your cat, keep a close eye on her for the next week or so. Ticks can carry some serious diseases, so contact your vet at the first sign of sickness, especially fever, loss of appetite, listlessness, or apparent stiffness or aching in the joints. Sometimes the tick bite itself can cause a progressive weakness in the back legs of the cat, a condition called tick-bite paralysis. This usually clears up on its own, once the tick is removed.

When should you call the vet? Contact your veterinarian if your cat shows any signs of illness within a week or so after you remove a tick, or if any redness or swelling develops at the bite location. Ticks are small and can be easily missed, so be particularly aware of symptoms any time your cat goes outdoors.

Tooth and Gum Problems

Just like people, cats have a set of baby (deciduous) teeth when young, which are replaced by permanent teeth. Similarly, keeping the teeth and gums healthy requires regular preventative care.

✻ ✻ ✻ ✻

FOOD AND SALIVA form plaque, which can mineralize into hard deposits of tartar. Gingivitis (inflammation of the gums) and loss of permanent teeth can result. Actual cavities are relatively rare, but pitting and other tooth damage can result from neglecting oral hygiene. Mouth pain and tooth loss may reduce a cat's interest or ability to eat, causing weight loss and making the cat more prone to illness.

What to Do About Tooth and Gum Problems

Brush regularly. You don't need to have an actual toothbrush and paste, but giving your cat's teeth a good going-over a few times a week is the best way to fight plaque. There are pet toothbrushes available, but you can also just use a piece of gauze or rough cloth that is moistened and wrapped around your index finger. Rub the cloth vigorously over the outside surfaces of the teeth (you don't usually need to get the inner or biting surfaces). This will help keep your cat's teeth clean and gums healthy.

Give Tabby the crunchies. Hard, dry cat food is the best bet to prevent plaque and tartar. If you can convince your cat to chew rawhide or a hard rubber dog toy, that can help, too—although many cats refuse them. There are now some chew-toy products on the market made especially for cats.

Look out for tartar. Plaque is a mushy whitish material that you can easily scrape off the teeth with your fingernail. Tartar, on the other hand, is greyish, white, or brown and does not come off with brushing. Tartar buildup needs to be removed by your vet.

Gums the word. Giving your cat a weekly gum massage helps keep gums healthy and prevents tooth loss. Using a cotton swab, rub the area where the teeth and gums meet. If the gums are red or there's any bleeding, it could be gingivitis, and your cat may need veterinary treatment.

Broken teeth and abscesses. A cracked canine tooth isn't rare in cats, especially outdoor cats and former strays. Broken teeth are usually only a problem if the pulp (the capsule of blood vessels and nerves in the middle of the tooth) is exposed. This can be quite painful, and the tooth may die. In either case, there's a risk of infection in the tooth root—an abscess. Abscesses can also form from bad oral hygiene. Symptoms include swelling around the mouth that may come and go and tenderness. Broken teeth that have exposed pulp, die, or abscess need to be removed by your veterinarian.

When should you call the vet? Make an appointment with your vet if your cat has tartar buildup, shows signs of gingivitis (red or bleeding gums), has a broken tooth with exposed pulp or that has died (it will usually become discolored), has any swelling or tenderness around the mouth, or has any loose permanent teeth. Adult cats often lose teeth as they get older—especially the small front incisors—and veterinary care usually isn't necessary for this.

Upper Respiratory Diseases (Feline "Colds")

Coughing, sneezing, runny eyes and nose, and possibly a fever are all the familiar symptoms of a cold. Unlike in humans, however, most feline "colds" have known (and preventable) causes, usually one of three kinds of viruses. Safe and reliable vaccines are available to prevent them all.

✳ ✳ ✳ ✳

EVEN VACCINATED CATS may have upper respiratory infections, though, and most will resolve within a few days to two weeks. Severe infections or those in cats with weakened immune systems may last several weeks. Although antibiotics won't kill the viruses, they are often prescribed to treat or prevent secondary infections that take hold when the virus damages tissue in the nose, eyes, sinuses, mouth, and possibly even the lungs of an affected cat.

Early signs of upper-respiratory disease include sneezing, watery eyes, and a clear discharge from the nose. The cat usually runs a fever and may salivate. As the infection advances, the lining of the eyes may get inflamed (conjunctivitis), giving the eyes a "meaty" appearance; the nasal discharge contains pus; the tearing from the eyes turns white; and ulcers may appear in the mouth or on the tongue. Advanced symptoms—most commonly seen if the disease is left untreated—include the eyelid being glued shut by pus and discharge with ulceration and destruction of the eyeball, loss of appetite due to obstruction of the nose by mucus and pus, and pneumonia. Viral pneumonia can be fatal and about one in five cats that develop it will die.

What to Do About Upper Respiratory Diseases

Be sure she has her shots. Current vaccinations are the best protection against upper respiratory viruses. Even indoor cats who never have contact with another cat need their shots since the viruses are carried through the air.

Don't wait for it to go away. Even though many upper respiratory infections clear up on their own, don't assume this one will. Notify your vet. The virus can attack the eyeball, causing permanent damage or blindness. Also, a cat with an untreated cold will stop eating or may develop a fatal case of pneumonia.

Don't spread it around. Upper respiratory viruses are highly contagious. A cat with an active case must be kept away from other cats. Wash your hands thoroughly with soap and hot water after petting, medicating, or otherwise working with the sick cat.

When should you call the vet? If you call the vet when you see the early symptoms of a cold, the odds are you can prevent the worst-case scenario. Veterinarians can recommend a vaccine that can prevent feline "colds." This vaccination may not always work, but it can improve your cat's chances for a healthy recovery. At any rate, once any of the later symptoms appear (pus in the discharge from nose or eyes, ulcers in the mouth or on the tongue, loss of appetite), get the cat to the vet immediately.

Vomiting

Vomiting means that the contents of the stomach or intestines are ejected through the mouth.

✳ ✳ ✳ ✳

THIS SHOULD NOT be confused with regurgitation, which is the ejection of the contents of the esophagus (the swallowing tube of the throat) and the pharynx (the space where the back of the mouth meets the top of the esophagus and windpipe). Regurgitation means that the expelled material has not made it all the way to the stomach and could be a sign of a problem in the mouth, pharynx, or esophagus.

Anyone who has a cat knows that vomiting is not that uncommon. When accompanied by other signs of illness, it can be an important early warning or a symptom of serious trouble. A cat that vomits once or twice—without any other symptoms like fever, persistent diarrhea, weakness, or pain in the abdomen—probably just has an upset tummy from what (or how much) she ate and can be safely treated at home.

What to Do About Vomiting

Slow down the chowing down. Reflex vomiting happens when a cat bolts down her food in too much of a hurry. Cats rescued from the outdoors are notorious for "stray syndrome"; they still believe they have to gobble up as much food as they can in as short a time as possible. The result is often the whole thing coming back up again. There are several ways to slow down the pace:

⁎ Reduce competition from other pets. The mere presence of other animals at mealtime encourages a chowhound cat to gobble her food, since she may feel the need to get as much food in while she can. Be sure she has her own food bowl and gets fed at predictable mealtimes. Feed her in a separate room, if possible.

⁎ Feed your cat less but more often. Several small meals during the day will often stay down better than gorging on two or three big ones. Also, consider changing the type of food you feed your cat. The faster the food goes down, the faster a chowhound cat will eat. Soft food can be swallowed as quickly as the cat can get it into her mouth. A good crunchy, dry food has to be chewed up, which slows down her eating.

* Take a look at what's in your cat's food. Pet food or food additives can disagree with cats' tummies. Keep track of when your cat vomits. Is it usually after eating a certain kind, brand, or type of food? She may like fish, for example, but it may not like her. The eye-catching cat food with the bright colors may have dyes she's allergic to. And the stuff that looks like chunks of meat may have additives she can't digest well.

What doesn't go down, can't come up. Fast your cat for at least 12 hours (but no more than 24) to give her stomach time to settle and her system time to clear out whatever is disagreeing with her. Break the fast with a small meal of bland, easy-to-digest food such as turkey or chicken baby food. Look for the pureed—not the chunky—kind and get the "beginner" or "first" baby food. If she keeps that down for a few hours, give her another small meal, continuing with more every few hours as long as the vomiting doesn't start again. The next day, try giving her full-size meals at the regular times, but use bland foods.

Keep her hydrated. It's important to make sure your cat is getting enough water, especially since she's not getting any from her food. If she has loose stools with the vomiting, she's losing even more fluid. However, an upset stomach can be irritated even by being full of water, so limit how much she can drink at a time. Try putting a single ice cube in the water bowl (you can crush it if you prefer) to ensure she only drinks small amounts. Replace the cube when the bowl is empty.

Make the medicine fit the problem. Vomiting isn't a disease in and of itself; it's a signal that something else is wrong. It could be as simple as a cat eating too fast or as serious as liver or kidney disease. You should never continue a home treatment if vomiting persists for more than a day, doesn't improve after 24 hours of home treatment, or is accompanied by other signs of disease. Some over-the-counter stomach remedies are safe and effective for cats, particularly those with magnesium hydroxide or magnesium aluminum (products like Milk of Magnesia or Kaopectate). Be sure to call your vet to get the correct dosage.

Look for a foreign invasion. An alien horde in your cat's stomach or intestines—in other words, worms or other parasites—is a common cause of vomiting. Cats are also curious creatures and will eat things we would find unappetizing or downright disgusting. Although sometimes those strange food items just make Tabby sick, other times the cat can swallow a nonfood item that gets stuck in the esophagus, stomach, or intestine. These "foreign bodies" must be removed by your veterinarian and sometimes require surgery.

When should you call the vet? A cat who vomits repeatedly, retches repeatedly without producing anything substantial, shows blood in the vomit, or has projectile vomiting (the material is expelled with great force) should go to the vet immediately. If your cat has other signs of illness—especially fever, weakness, depression, or a painful or swollen belly—call your vet right away, even if the cat has only vomited once or twice.

Worms

Your cat's stomach and intestines are home to a host of tiny creatures—microscopic critters that are actually normal, natural, and healthy for her. But sometimes the eggs of parasites get into her digestive system, developing into adult worms or other things that feed off the food going through her gut and steal its nutrition. Worms will thrive in the cat's gut, producing more eggs that are shed in the cat's feces and spread to other hosts.

✳ ✳ ✳ ✳

THE MOST COMMON unwanted tenants of your cat's digestive tract are roundworms, tapeworms, and Coccidia. Roundworms (or ascarids) look like short strands of thick white thread, and a cat with a particularly bad case may actually vomit some up.

Adult roundworms lay eggs, which are passed in the cat's stool, and can be seen under a microscope. Tapeworms attach to the lining of the cat's intestine by their heads (called the scolex) and grow by segments. Each segment contains eggs, ripens, and is shed with the cat's stool. Since the eggs are contained in the segments, microscopic examination of a stool sample may not find them. Sometimes, the tapeworm segments—which look like grains of rice—can be found clinging to the cat's rectum. Coccidia aren't actually worms but microscopic one-celled organisms that live and breed in the cat's intestines.

What to Do About Worms

Vanquish the vectors. Your cat has to get worms from somewhere or something else. A vector is the fancy word for the thing she gets it from. Fleas, for example, carry tapeworms. A cat with fleas grooms herself, swallows the flea with the tapeworm eggs, and—voila! Similarly, a cat who shares a litter box (or goes outdoors) where a cat already infected with worms goes is likely to come in contact with eggs or spores shed in the infected cat's stool and—voila! Another common vector is infected birds, mice, or other misfortunes that your cat captures and eats. Cats who hunt or are used as "mousers" are more likely to pick up parasites of many kinds, including toxoplasmosis, which has some health concerns for humans.

No news may not be good news. Kittens with worms may show diarrhea, slow weight gain, and a potbelly, and adult cats may have dark tarry stool, vomiting, diarrhea, and weight loss—or no signs at all. Just because your cat doesn't have any symptoms doesn't mean she doesn't have worms. If your cat has never been checked for worms, it's a good idea to do it and to have a stool sample checked for any new cat brought into your home. Even if your cat has been treated for worms, should she get fleas, go outdoors, or hunt mice or other small creatures regularly, it's almost a sure bet she's got them again.

Only rely on the good stuff. Over-the-counter worming medications don't have enough punch to knock out worms for good. No home or folk remedies have been shown to be both effective and safe enough to get the job done, either. Prevention is the best cure, but if your cat does have worms, get the right medication in the right doses from your veterinarian.

Soothe the symptoms. Even after your cat has been treated for worms—and sometimes as a result of the treatment—she may have some stomach or intestinal distress.

When should you call the vet? All cats should have a stool sample examined for worms—the earlier the better. While many cats who have worms may have no symptoms, an infestation that goes unchecked for months or years has been robbing your cat of nutrients. What's more, she's been shedding the worms' eggs in her stool, passing them along to other animals in the house and in some cases, even to people.

Even if a cat has been wormed in the past, the treatment is not effective for life—it just kills the worms that are in the cat's body at that time. Cats who go outdoors, hunt, are fed (or eat) raw or undercooked meat or meat products (including organs), have fleas, or share quarters with a cat who has been diagnosed with worms have probably been reinfected and should have a stool sample checked.

Alternative Medicine for Cats

More and more people are using acupuncture, acupressure, essential oils, and other kinds of alternative medicine these days. If you've found them working for you, you might wonder, what about your cat?

✳ ✳ ✳ ✳

ALTERNATIVE MEDICINE HAS become more popular in recent history. You might try it, as long as it doesn't hurt the cat, might make her feel better, and doesn't blind you to the obvious (giving herbs to a cat with a broken leg is great, but she also needs a splint and a cast.)

Acupuncture is the use of tiny needles placed in strategic locations to help healing energy flow in the body. There are plenty of studies that show its success on people, and there's no reason to believe animals can't benefit, too. Those who are squeamish about needles can try acupressure, which involves pressing on the points instead of sticking them. Naturopathy is a whole system of helping get the body back to full health by restoring natural balance. Some alternative methods, such as homeopathy and chiropractic, are already used regularly and widely for humans. Other choices include herbs, flower essences, and gemstones.

Caring for the Elderly Cat

Old age catches up with all of us, humans and cats alike. We slow down, get set in our ways, and nothing works quite as well as it used to.

✳   ✳   ✳   ✳

SIGNS OF AGE happen inside and outside a geriatric cat. She'll probably drop some weight and muscle tone, giving her a gaunt "old cat" look. Her coat will probably lose some of its shine and may seem more disheveled, usually because she can't groom as well on account of losing teeth and those rough rasps on her tongue. Loss of flexibility and arthritis will slow down her pace, make jumping and climbing tougher, and make her less interested in play—and possibly more ornery when bothered.

As the internal organs wind down, her appetite and elimination will change along with her physical appearance. Your vet can tell you if these changes are within the normal range for an aging cat.

Your geriatric cat needs more peace and quiet (so don't get her a brand new kitten to "pep her up"), a diet designed for her changing needs (check with your vet or a veterinary nutritionist), and most likely more litter boxes, since the urges come on quicker and are harder to control.

Chapter 9

Cat Grief

When It's Time

Kitty got me through a lot of hard times," says Lauree about the cat she had as a teenager. "He would always know when I was upset or sick and would come and just stick by me. One time I was very upset about something, and I was close to being at the end of my rope. It was summertime, so I went to the edge of our property and just sat and cried. Even though I didn't call him, Kitty came and sat with me as if to reassure me that he was there and that I would be okay."

✳   ✳   ✳   ✳

WHILE IT'S TRUE that we tend to ascribe human emotions to our pets (and they can't say anything to deny it), it's also true that scientists are finding increasing evidence of emotional behavior among animals. Lauree may be not only intuitive but also scientifically accurate when she says Kitty was trying to reassure her. Perhaps you've had similar moments with your pets. Over time, you learn to

read their responses, and they learn to read yours. They know when you're upset, and it only makes sense that they would try to help you, if only to allow you to continue to help them.

The best thing about a pet is that he or she is there for you. Pets usually spend time with their owners (although admittedly, some cats play hard-to-get!). Every time you walked the dog, every time your cat fell asleep on your lap, or you were ringing a bell to entertain your budgie, you were building a relationship. You got to know the rhythms of your pet's life and they got to know yours. Both of those rhythms adapted to the other. You and your pet were sharing your lives together. In light of this, it's no surprise that losing such a companion would be a major jolt.

When It's Time

Georgie was refusing to eat. Jo noticed that the 21-year-old cat was more lethargic than usual, finding a spot on the floor and hardly moving all day. Something was definitely wrong. They'd been to the vet with Georgie's various ailments in recent months, and Jo knew there wasn't much time left.

"Georgie's an old man now," the vet had said, preparing her for the inevitable. "We can do a few things to keep him going a little longer, but eventually you'll have to let him go. You'll know when it's time."

Jo rescued Georgie as a young neighborhood stray; years later, he remained a bit rough around the edges. Though Georgie required some extra patience, Jo was happy to have his company. Always an indoor-outdoor cat, he would take off on a couple of "vacations" for weeks at a time, then would strut back in as if he'd never been gone. Georgie mellowed as the years went on, and he found a home in Jo's heart. At night he would sleep on her shoulder, cuddling his head against her neck.

There was one earlier health scare when 13-year-old Georgie was diagnosed with a thyroid problem. He was already old for a cat, so Jo was prepared for bad news. Luckily, the vet was able to treat the problem; however, the treatment cost over a thousand dollars. It was a challenge for Jo's budget, but she felt the cost was worth it. After all, she gained eight more years with the cat she loved.

But now Georgie—shaky, thin, and delicate—was moving with difficulty, when he was moving at all. It looked like he was in pain. From the kitchen, Jo heard a thump from the living room. Georgie had tried to jump up onto the couch, a move he had effortlessly made thousands of times, but now he couldn't. He was splayed out on the floor and seemed to be in agony.

Jo knew it was time.

Gathering her beloved pet in her arms, she sat on the couch for an hour, reminiscing. She thanked Georgie for all the joy he had brought to her life. She asked God to take Georgie wherever good companions go. She whispered assurances to her beloved cat—he wouldn't have to suffer much longer—and then she took him to the vet.

An examination confirmed her fears. There would be no miracle cure this time. Georgie was given something for the pain, and then something to stop his heart. Jo was able to stay by his side the entire time.

Jo knew there was no second-guessing her decision—there really was nothing else to be done. Georgie had lived a long, full life, and Jo was very grateful, although also very sad. Spend that many years that close to anyone, and you will miss them terribly.

Jo slept in the guest bedroom that night. She couldn't quite manage the old bed without Georgie on her shoulder.

A Lose-Lose Situation

Many people have struggled with this decision to euthanize their pets, and a good many of them later feel guilty, or perhaps second-guess themselves. What if I had more money to spend on treatment? What if we took a chance on an experimental procedure? Maybe my pet would have bounced back on its own.

❋ ❋ ❋ ❋

THERE MAY BE some second-guessing, but more often than not, the difficult decision they made is the right one. Vets generally give thorough, well-informed information to pet owners, who tend to have an intuitive sense of their pets' pain. The factors mentioned above— money, expectations, emotions—might not be quantifiable on a spreadsheet, but they're part of the decision-making process.

"A risk-reward rationale comes into play," says psychologist Thomas Whiteman, who has also been through this difficult situation with a pet. "You have to weigh the benefits and costs of the different options." While it may seem inappropriate to be so mathematical about the life of your treasured companion, you have to acknowledge a 20 percent chance is different from an 80 percent chance. You may want to cling to any hope of your pet's recovery and survival, but you also need to face reality: Is a slim chance of success worth the risk? What's more, would your pet really want to go through that experience, given the long odds against its success?

It may feel like a lose-lose situation. Few congratulate themselves on making a good choice in the matter, but many pet owners—advised by caring veterinarians— get a sense of what they need to do, whether it's taking a chance on a medical procedure, putting the pet to sleep, or waiting a bit longer. You may still second-guess your decision, but as long as you have the pet's best interests in mind, it's hard to make a bad choice.

The Association for Pet Loss and Bereavement notes on its website, "Most people later worry that they finally opted to do this too late—or too soon. Rarely do we meet with a client who feels this was done at the right time . . . they are now experiencing what we commonly refer to as euthanasia remorse. The decision was not theirs anymore. It had been taken away from them by the terrible illness. Actually, there was no longer any decision to make. It simply had to be that way."

"It was extremely difficult," says one woman who had gone through this experience with her dog, an Oriental shorthair. "My vet twice suggested that I needed to let [the dog] go, and I canceled both appointments. In the end, my dog had lost half his body weight and was on all types of meds including appetite stimulants. However, the ulcers in his mouth were so bad it was impossible for him to eat. The day he could not jump and fell was the day I made the hardest decision of my life—to let him go."

A while back, a wise friend told her that when the dog was ready to go, he would let her know. As it happened, she sat in the car outside the vet's office, telling her dog it would be the last time they would ever need to go there. "To my utter shock, he reached out of his carrier and put his paw on my hand, as if he was saying, 'It's okay. I'm ready now.'"

Reality Check

We often like to think of our pets in "people" terms, attributing to them human thoughts and emotions, but, of course, they're not human. It's impossible to know exactly what goes on in their minds, and we can't assume that they approach the end of life the same way we do.

✳   ✳   ✳   ✳

OUR PETS DO not get upset or sentimental at the prospect of their own death, writes counselor Wallace Sife. "That is a projection of our own fear . . . We should not torture ourselves during our grief by agonizing about this and distorting the final memories of our beloved companion animals."

The animal world is, in a word, beastly. Pain and death are part of life. In a way, by domesticating our pets, protecting and providing for them, we remove them from the dangers of the wild. We take responsibility for them, which we exercise in many ways during their lives. That care extends to medical treatment, which of course would not be available to them in the wild. We extend their life by bringing them into our homes, and when it seems that there is nothing left for them but great pain, we ease their death. This is also part of the responsibility we take on as pet owners and caregivers.

Most pets have short lives, compared to our own. It may not be something we want to think about, but the truth is that we take on the responsibility of pet ownership knowing that, at some point, we'll have to say goodbye.

"Pets are with us such a short time," says animal rescue expert Jennifer Wesh, "and yet just long enough to make it through milestones with us—graduations, losses, marriages, babies, breakups, new jobs, etc. They are there to see us through those things, and they are a part of those things."

Even when we're still reeling in shock from the turn of events, we may have to make difficult choices about putting the pet to sleep. The first stage of grief is denial, so it makes sense that of course we want to avoid all discussion of death. Let the vet fix the prob-

lem, make the pet good as new, and then we can all act as if this never happened. It's sobering when we learn this isn't possible.

If you've already been in this situation, you've been through an emotional wringer. As you begin the process of emotional recovery, you might be feeling guilt and regret. If only I had seen it sooner. Did I make the right choice? What should I have done differently?

Although it may be difficult, try to let go of these nagging questions. As we've seen, the choice of putting a pet down or continuing with treatment has many variables, and that includes your emotional state and the pet's well being. There's no perfect answer. Perhaps you had to make a momentous decision in a rather short time, when you were still reeling from the initial news of your pet's problem. You had a lot of issues to weigh; you weighed them, and then you made a choice. Whatever that choice was, it was a loving act of a responsible caretaker.

In the Room

"She didn't mind going to the vet," says Amelia about her 13-year-old cat. "So when we got there, she just went to the exam room. I was crying so hard, I decided I could not stay with her. I don't know to this day if that was the wrong decision, but I can still picture her face looking at me when I walked out of the room."

Of course that moment is a highly emotional one. Vets often give pet owners the opportunity to stay in the room and even cradle the animal while the final injections are given. Some owners choose to do this and some choose not to. Those who don't stay in the room often feel some guilt afterward.

"I'm a coward!" exclaims one woman, who has had several cats over the years. "I can never be with them as they leave this world. It hurts too much."

If you feel bad about leaving your pet before the very end, remember that you are or were dealing with several different factors in making that decision. Amelia was facing a situation where her cat was carefree, but she was a basket case. If she was bawling in the cat's final moments, it might have upset the cat. By leaving, she allowed the cat to remain peaceful in a place it enjoyed, right up to the end.

It's all too easy to second-guess your decisions regarding your pet's health care and euthanasia. The stress involved with making these choices may leave you feeling especially vulnerable, but cut yourself a break. Trust that you made a legitimate choice during a difficult time. Your pet would certainly not blame you.

Euthanasia: Things to Consider

There are many things to consider.

❋   ❋   ❋   ❋

WHAT ARE THE odds? Many people find veterinarians are even more forthcoming than their own physicians when it comes to discussing various treatment options. You'll hear possibilities and percentages. Of course, these are educated guesses—no one can know exactly how your pet would respond, but the information provided can help pet owners weigh the options. Don't be afraid to ask your vet questions.

Current quality of life. Sometimes there's nothing to be done for the ailing pet, and it becomes a matter of time. Consider your pet's quality of life during this time: Is the pet in pain or discomfort now? Is it losing control over its functions? Does this ailment make the pet difficult to live with?

Quality of life during and after treatment. Perhaps there is something that can be done to prolong the life of your pet. Surgery certainly isn't fun for anyone, and a lengthy recuperation period can be frustrating and even painful for your pet. What will your pet's life be like if it can't walk or run, or if it can't do other things it once enjoyed?

Life span with or without treatment. The vet should be able to give you an educated guess, but it's no guarantee. Given the pet's age, how long would you expect it to live even if a treatment were successful?

Your economic situation. There is no shame in recognizing your financial limitations. What is the estimated cost of the treatment and necessary care? If you use the money for surgery or other treatment, what will it mean for your own or your family's financial future? In terms of your financial situation, how would you describe the chance of care for your pet?

* Impossible

* Would set us back financially for many years

* A big stretch, but we could recover

* Affordable

Your family. Consider how the options presented to you will impact the whole household, including children and any other animals you may have. Will you have to focus all your attention on one pet, to the detriment of others in your home? Do you need to confer with other family members to make this decision?

If you do opt for euthanasia . . . Who needs to say goodbye to the pet? How can you give them that opportunity?

Your emotional state. It is certainly emotionally difficult to deal with the death of your pet, but it might also be tough to handle a lengthy period of uncertainty as your pet struggles to recover from an illness.

Some Final Thoughts

Here are some things to consider when making an end-of-life decision for your pet.

✳ ✳ ✳ ✳

Ask questions. Know the choices, the chances, and the vet's recommendation.

Can you be with your pet at the end? Do you want to?

Should you get the whole family involved? Would they want to be involved? How would you do this?

Be realistic about money. How much can you really pay for treatment?

Do you need some final moments with your pet? What will you say or do? . . . and after the decision has been made:

Let it rest. Fight the urge to go back through pro-and-con arguments.

Cry. You're not mourning the decision, but the situation that made the decision necessary.

Comfort one another. Especially if there were several people involved in the decision, you'll need to affirm each other in this difficult choice.

Tell those closest to both you and your pet. Make these calls as a way of honoring their relationship with the pet and mobilizing emotional support for you.

Death at Home

Whether expectedly or not, if your cat passes away at home, it can be difficult to know what to do with the body. You may be able to leave the body with a veterinarian, local shelter, or city sanitation department for disposal; call ahead and ask before making the trip. As the body will not maintain for long, the sooner this is handled, the better.

✳ ✳ ✳ ✳

HOWEVER, THERE ARE times when one must keep the body for a short period of time while a decision or arrangements are being made (or other circumstances). The American Society for the Prevention of Cruelty to Animals (ASPCA) recommends the following:

✳ Place the cat wrapped in plastic in a refrigerator or freezer. The exception to this is if you plan to have a necropsy performed to determine cause of death. Then the body should be refrigerated but not frozen. If you do want a necropsy performed, you must contact your vet as soon as possible after the death.

✳ If your cat cannot fit into a refrigerator or freezer, the body should be placed on a cement floor or concrete slab. Do not cover or wrap the body in this instance, as doing so will trap heat in the body.

✳ If neither of the above are options, then as a last resort you should keep the body (wrapped in plastic) in the coldest part of your home, out of the sun, and packed with bags of ice. The body will not decompose immediately, so there is no need to worry about odor.

Burial and Cremation

If your pet passes away at the animal clinic, you'll have to decide what to do with the body. Most veterinarians will dispose of the body if asked. Be sure to specify your wishes—it would be horrible to assume you had time to decide, but the doctor (unless he or she was told otherwise) went ahead and had the body cremated.

✳ ✳ ✳ ✳

THE MAIN OPTIONS for body disposal available to pet owners are burial and cremation. (Taxidermy and freeze-drying are also choices, but both have inherent difficulties, and we won't discuss them here). Factors such as cost and religious beliefs will come into play in your decision-making.

Your veterinarian should be able to help you make a decision. Even if you haven't euthanized your pet, the vet may be able to put you in touch with local pet cemeteries or give advice on burial options. Your local animal shelter or ASPCA chapter may also be of help. Don't be afraid to ask for advice or recommendations.

Burying Your Pet at Home

In some states and cities, it's legal to bury an animal as long as you own the property. In others, there are regulations that forbid the burial of animals on private property. It's best to check with your local municipality before proceeding. Here are some other things to consider.

✳ There may be municipal regulations about digging, for public safety and for fear that utility lines will be damaged. If you do not own the property or if you want to bury your pet on public property (like a favorite park), it will almost certainly be illegal.

✳ There may also be rules about how to bury your pet, particularly regarding the depth of the grave. Generally, it's a good idea to dig the grave two to three feet deep, so that other animals (or children) don't dig it up.

✳ In the past, it was suggested that the body be wrapped in plastic; nowadays biodegradable materials are preferred. Online vendors even sell eco-friendly pet caskets.

Pet Cemeteries

If you feel you need a location at which to remember your pet, then you might consider burial at a pet cemetery. These places offer beautiful surroundings where you can memorialize your pet with a gravestone or other display. However, such cemeteries can be costly. It will be up to you to determine whether you can afford the cost.

Home Burial

Many people choose a do-it-yourself approach with pet burial. If the pet is small, this can be done rather easily, but there are still questions to consider.

✳ Are there laws in your community regarding the digging of holes or the burial of animals?

✳ Is it important to you to have a nearby site (say, in the backyard) where you can remember your pet?

* What would happen if you move or if you build an addition or put in a pool?

* Would you put up any kind of marker?

* Would the burial occur as part of some sort of ceremony, giving friends and family a chance to say goodbye to the pet?

* Are you ready for the physical process of handling the pet's body in order to bury it?

Cremation

If your vet euthanized your pet, he or she will probably offer to have your pet's body cremated. Cremation is generally the easiest option, and it's often reasonably priced. If you choose this option consider the following: Do you want your pet cremated by itself or with other animals? It's cheaper to cremate several animals at once, but if you want to keep the ashes (or "cremains") in an urn, jewelry, or some other container, your pet should be cremated alone.

Some people have strong feelings about the burning of a human body in cremation, but do the same feelings apply to a pet's body? Essentially, the difference between the methods has to do with the speed of destruction. Whether slowly by burial or suddenly by cremation, the body will be destroyed.

But if you believe that the pet's essence lives on in spirit form, in memories, or in future resurrection, then the body has served its purpose and need not be preserved.

Because of public health concerns, scattering ashes is as legally tricky as home burial. It's best to check your state and local laws regarding the scattering of your pet's ashes.

Memorial Events, Mementos, and Sites

We humans mark out the major transitions of our lives with rituals: marriages, funerals, graduations, birthdays, baby showers, retirement dinners, and so on. These are gatherings that say, in essence, "That was then; this is now." A line is drawn. This couple walked into the room as separate people; they leave as one. This person was a student; now she's a graduate. When there's a big change in our lives, we often use ritual to show its importance.

✳　✳　✳　✳

IF YOU HAVE lost a pet, you are at a transition point. This creature was important in your life, and possibly that of your family. Now that pet will be important in your memory. Some people go further and feel a need to mark this event with a memorial service of some kind—a ritual, if you will, that honors their pet fittingly.

Keep in mind that it's not necessary to hold an event. Many people lose their pets and go on quietly without any official ceremony. But a memorial ceremony may help you find closure along your own grief journey. It can help you connect with supportive people. And it may honor your pet in a way that will close the book on its earthly life in an appropriate manner.

Planning the Event

Is it a little crazy to hold a funeral service for a pet? No, not at all. When we hold a funeral for a person, it's not really for him or her. It's a way for everyone else to say goodbye. A memorial service is not for the dead but for the living, and that holds true whether you're honoring a dearly departed human or animal.

The memorial may be connected to the final disposition of the pet's body, but it doesn't have to be. If you have chosen to bury the body, you may have a memorial event in addition to the burial. But even if there are no remains involved, you can still have a memorial to honor the pet's memory.

You might look into holding a service at a funeral home. Some morticians offer their facilities, normally reserved for humans, for pet funerals. They might be able to help you plan such a service as well. Again, these services will involve a fee.

But let's say you're having a simple memorial service in your own backyard. How will you do it? What's involved? Well, let's look at three ingredients involved in planning a memorial event.

Invite people who care. Your immediate family will likely be in attendance, but you may want to reach out to your friends as well, especially anyone who knew your pet—children who played with it, neighbors who watched your pet for you, and so on. You can always ask. Be gracious if they turn you down, but you may be surprised by who shows up.

Prepare to say a few words. You don't need to be a great orator; just speak from the heart. What did this pet mean to you? It might help to tell a fun story about the pet. You don't need to drag this out—just a few minutes is plenty of time. If you'd like, invite others to contribute with a favorite quote, poem, or a few simple words.

Make it artistic. Display a picture of your pet. Set up some of its favorite toys. You don't need balloons or streamers, but make your yard (or wherever) look a little different than usual. Are certain songs appropriate to the occasion? See what you can do to provide music for the event.

You might have two people at this memorial or you might have ten. It's not really important. Fight the urge to define "success" by attendance numbers. What's important is that those who knew this animal best have the opportunity to share their appreciation and their love. When the pet is sufficiently honored, the pet lovers can move on.

Mementos

Many of our best memories are associated with certain objects, and when we lose a pet, we can savor the memories by saving some mementos. It's not silly at all to distribute the toys or dishes of a departed pet. Some grieving owners put their pet's paw prints, photos, or ashes in key chains or pendants. They want to carry the memory with them. Photos are especially precious because they will help people visualize the pet even after the memories have long faded.

Special Sites

Is there a special place that your pet loved—a sunny spot by the window or perhaps a shelf in the laundry room? Another memorial idea is to make this place special by decorating it with pictures or mementos of your pet. Or use your gardening skills to plant a space in the garden that will remind you of the pet.

Darla was heartbroken when she had to put her 16-year-old Persian cat, Cookie, to sleep. Darla brought Cookie's body home from the clinic, wrapped the cat in a quilt, and buried her in a peaceful spot behind her house. "I planted a bag of pink tulips over her grave and tried to deal with the huge empty spot in my heart her passing had left."

Months later, Darla returned to the grave. "There was a feeling of spring in the air, so I went back to the site. It was covered with beautiful pink tulips! I have since moved from that house, but, 12 years later, every spring I think of Cookie and hope the tulips are still blooming."

Creative Tributes

As children deal with this sort of grief, it's often suggested that they draw pictures of the pet they've lost. Why shouldn't adults do the same thing? Perhaps the memory of your pet will inspire you to

unleash your creative talents. Draw pictures. Don't just gather photos; put them in an album and decorate it appropriately. Make a scrapbook, including memories and stories by different family members. Write a poem. Keep a journal of your memories. Make a tribute video, interviewing everyone who knew the pet. Write a song. Make a playlist of songs that your pet would have loved (or did love) or tracks that remind you of your pet.

Of course, you may not be a professional artist. That doesn't matter. This creative output isn't about you becoming a star—it's about saying thanks to a pet that enriched your life. And it might also be an effective way to turn your mourning into dancing: Take the energy of your grief and transform it into creative expression.

Memorial Websites

You can post on various websites as a memorial for your pet. Simply do a search for "online pet memorial" and you'll see a number of such sites. Some will provide an artistic template to create a page for your pet. Other sites just let you upload pictures and comments. You can often browse other memorials and read their stories as well.

Some online memorial pages are connected with very helpful websites that provide articles, resources, chats, "webinars," and support groups for grieving pet lovers. So check out what the rest of the site has to offer before you post your memorial. If you already have a website or a blog, you may choose to dedicate a page in tribute to your pet.

As always, keep your wits about you when putting out personal information on the Internet. Many of the online pet memorial sites are free to use, but you usually need to register first, and that would put your address on some e-mail sales lists. That might not be such a bad thing, but keep in mind that there are people who seek to take advantage of those who are grieving. Just be smart about it.

Benefiting Others

What would your pet want you to do as a memorial tribute? That's a hard question to answer, but it's worth thinking about. Web pages, shrines, poems, and key chains—they can all be a part of the healing-and-remembering process. But let's think in a completely different direction. Is there some incredibly loving, charitable act you could do in your pet's name that would truly make a difference?

Why not make a donation to an animal charity? The ASPCA, the most well known of these groups, is a long-standing non-profit organization with a good reputation. Or perhaps you'd like to support an organization that helps fund therapy animals for handicapped people or autistic children. If you need other ideas or don't have access to a computer to help in your research, call your local vet or shelter and ask if they can recommend a group.

Don't forget to think locally, too!

There's probably an animal shelter in your county that's operating on a shoestring budget, and they need all the support they can get. They might even be able to use your old pet supplies. Some items, such as kitty litter or cage bedding or even half a bag of chow, would be welcome. Depending on the health of your pet and the circumstances of its death, other, more personal items such as toys, dishes, and grooming equipment may or may not be appropriate to donate. Call the shelter and review what you have with them.

Another way to memorialize your pet is to make a renewed effort to take care of yourself. After all, your pet would want you to be healthy and happy! Quit smoking. Start exercising. Restore contact with an estranged relative or former friend. Your desire to honor your pet's memory might give you the extra oomph you need to really accomplish the task.

Living, Loving, and Enjoying

When you memorialize your pet in some way, you are "emotionally relocating" it. It's not the removal of the departed one from our consciousness but the relocation. We are taking it from our everyday consciousness and placing it into memory. Even as we focus on the pet for a service, an event, or a creative endeavor, we are saying goodbye. We are putting it in the past so we can move into the future.

It's also important to realize that the past fuels the future. The loves and losses of our history help to shape us, to make us ready for whatever we encounter in the days ahead. And this might turn out to be the most important legacy your pet leaves: you.

You can talk about loyalty, companionship, and the time your pet almost ate a whole ball of string, but what you're saying is that your pet helped you enjoy life. So, as you consider the most effective ways to honor your friend, here's the ultimate memorial:

Be the person your pet helped you to be. Live. Love. Enjoy.

What Grieving Looks Like

Grief can affect your life in any of the following ways.

❋　❋　❋　❋

PHYSICAL: YOU MIGHT lose your appetite or feel nauseous. Some people find it hard to sleep. Or perhaps you feel aches and pains in your body.

Emotional: You might find yourself crying at the drop of a hat. Your self-esteem may sag. You also might be sensitive to feelings of guilt, anger, or impatience—even if the situation has nothing to do with your pet.

Psychological: You might forget that your pet is gone and mistakenly set out food or call for it. Perhaps you imagine you hear your pet's sounds or catch a glimpse of your pet out of the corner of your eye. You might want to keep your pet's things around the house for quite a while—or feel a sudden impulse to trash it all.

Mental: You might find it hard to concentrate. Perhaps you feel that each day just drags along. You might reevaluate decisions you made in regards to your pet and wonder, What if I had done things differently?

Spiritual: You might question long-held beliefs. Perhaps you express anger toward God. You might withdraw from your religious group in some way. Or, conversely, you find yourself becoming more spiritual.

Social: You might withdraw from close relationships, or perhaps you'll rely more heavily on certain people. Some feel a need to busy themselves with social activities as a way to distract themselves from their grief.

The Stages of Grief

In 1969, psychiatrist Dr. Elisabeth Kübler-Ross gave the counseling world a great gift with her seminal book On Death and Dying. *As she studied terminally ill patients, she recognized a process that occurred as they struggled to deal with their illnesses and mortality.*

✳ ✳ ✳ ✳

A T FIRST, THE patients couldn't believe their prognoses, and they tried to act as if it weren't true. As they began to accept reality, they would often become angry—with themselves, at the doctors, at loved ones, at God, or even at the disease. This would lead to an energetic period in which they would try to beat the disease by means of aggressive treatment, radical lifestyle changes, and prayer. When these efforts failed, the patients would typically lose energy and become very sad. There was nothing to be done. Finally, at the depths of this malaise, some patients would find a strange kind of calm, as they finally accepted what was happening to them and tried to make the best of it.

In essence, Kübler-Ross identified what she called the five stages of grief: denial, anger, bargaining, depression, and acceptance. In the years since, counselors have applied these stages to bereavement, addiction, divorce, and virtually any upheaval in life. In general, the model fits a wide range of human experiences. Some have tried to place timelines on the different stages—if you were divorced a year ago, you still have six months of depression left —but this sort of math is fraught with difficulty. While the stages of grief identify a general pattern, each person is different, and each crisis is different. The stages don't run like clockwork.

Observers have also found that the stages don't always proceed in a certain order. In fact, some people will show signs of all five stages on the same day. Other times, stages may lie dormant within the psyche until you experience something that triggers that stage and its related emotions. For example, someone cuts you off on the highway, and suddenly you're feeling every bit of anger you've stored up for the past six months—not just at that driver, but at your parents, at the IRS, at your losing sports team, at the companies that make the lids of pickle jars too tight, and at your vet for not finding the problem with your pet sooner.

When you're in that mind frame, it certainly doesn't matter whether the anger is totally misplaced or not.

Kübler-Ross said that the stages she identified were "never meant to help tuck messy emotions into neat packages," so be wary of anyone who tells you how you should feel at any point in the grieving process. Emotions are messy; sometimes we revisit a stage we thought we were done with. This is normal too. With that said, the stages of grief can help us to understand the general process, the sort of journey our emotions take as they come to terms with loss.

In the decades since Kübler-Ross's groundbreaking observations, others have tried to tweak the model or present entirely new ways of looking at grief. Some experts have suggested that one who grieves is really doing two different things: letting go of what's lost and building a new life without it. Some experts talk about "integration" of one's memories into the fabric of a new life; we want to move forward but we also search for a way to carry what we've lost. As we grieve, we're constantly dealing with both the past and the future.

In recent years, some experts have tucked two additional stages into the classic model. In the first of these new stages, denial is broken down into feelings of pain and guilt. The other stage, wedged in between depression and acceptance, is one in which people try to rebuild their lives. Let's go through these "seven stages of grief" and see how they apply specifically to the loss of a pet. Keep in mind, however, that this is not an agenda or a schedule. It's a general observation of how many people process grief. You may see yourself in these descriptions, but don't be alarmed if you don't. Your grieving experience is unique.

Stage 1: Shock and Denial

This can begin the first moment you recognize a problem.

❋ ❋ ❋ ❋

MAYBE YOU FEEL a lump under your cat's skin or you notice a limp. You don't want to deal with a problem, so you tell yourself it doesn't exist. Denial can also occur at several points thereafter. Although the vet explains that there's a minimal chance of survival, you don't really take it in—you're confident that your pet will defy the odds.

Or perhaps the death was sudden and unexpected, and you simply can't accept that it happened. Expected or not, even after a pet's death, some owners continue to live as if he or she were still with them, keeping the pet's belongings around, perhaps even keeping the water bowl fresh. It's difficult for them to give in to the reality of the loss.

The addition of shock to the denial stage is very helpful, because these feelings aren't just mind games. With the loss of a pet, especially if it's a sudden death, you might find it difficult to function, walking around in a daze. People in this stage often seem disengaged from life.

Why does this happen? When the human body sustains an injury, it responds with numbness in the area of the injury and sometimes a general state of shock. This is because when the body can't deal with pain, it temporarily shuts down its pain receptors. It's a survival mechanism. The same sort of thing happens with our emotions when we face loss. We disengage temporarily from the world that has brought us this pain.

This is perfectly normal. But in some cases, a person's denial goes on too long or the shock strikes too deep, and it keeps that person from normal functioning. However, if denial and shock are temporary symptoms, it's typically nothing to worry about.

Stage 2: Pain and Guilt

It is not uncommon for someone to cry steadily for two or three days after losing a beloved pet.

✳ ✳ ✳ ✳

THIS TOO IS a healthy expression of the pain of loss. Thoughts and regrets rapidly crash through one's mind as you "wake up" from your denial. Numbness is wearing off; your emotions are extraordinarily raw. Any little reminder can set you off on another crying jag.

One thing that intensifies the sorrow is that, in previous times of grief, you've had your pet there for comfort, and now you don't. "You're never really alone when you have a pet. Whether you come in super excited and dancing around over an awesome first date or when you're chest-deep in tissues over the loss of a family member, your pet is there in times when there is absolutely no way you'd want another person to see you," says animal rescuer Jennifer Wesh. "They know us in a way no one else does, and that is why that relationship and bond is so hard to lose."

In many cases, added to the sorrow is a sense of guilt. It can be easy to find reasons to blame yourself (whether it's rational or not). You think of all the things you could have done differently. Perhaps you wonder what your pet thought of you in its final moments, or you worry that your actions made things worse for your family. You even blame yourself for crying too much— which makes you cry more. This blame game can become a vicious cycle.

Stage 3: Anger

Anger often arises over a sense of injustice, toward yourself or someone else.

✳ ✳ ✳ ✳

IN ANGER YOU feel that you don't deserve this, and your pet certainly didn't deserve this. Anger can turn this way and that, seeking someone to blame. As with the guilt in the previous stage, anger is not always rational. You feel like you want to lash out. Perhaps you get mad at the veterinarian for not trying harder. Or maybe it's another family member for falling short in their responsibility toward the pet.

It's even possible that you will become angry at your cat for leaving you. This is especially true in a situation where the pet is missing, ran off into traffic, or when the animal has just become ill. You blame the pet, and then you blame yourself for blaming the innocent pet.

Often this anger revolves around yourself, and you get a second helping of guilt. Why didn't you use your X-ray vision to see that tumor before it grew? Why don't you earn enough money to pay for the expensive operation that had a slight chance of saving your pet's life? It might not make sense, but you are heated up, and you need to fire away at someone.

The danger is the anger state is that you will do something foolish and drive people away from you. There have been marriages that have broken up in the aftermath of a pet's death. There have been lawsuits filed against innocent veterinarians. And there have been millions of harsh words uttered against people who don't deserve them.

Stage 4: Bargaining

This stage is often the hardest to understand.

✳ ✳ ✳ ✳

YOUR MAIN MOTIVE in the bargaining stage is to fix the problem as fast as possible. You want to stop feeling such sadness, and so you reach for a quick cure. If you get to this stage while your pet is still alive, this is where you push for the experimental operation that will hopefully make everything all better. For those whose pets have died, their instinct might be to run out and get a new pet just like the old one, expecting that this would set things right again.

Of course that's not the answer. Grief is something you work through over time; there's no way to magically beam yourself out of it. Another pet might be a great idea eventually, but you know that no creature can fully replace the one you've lost. You still have to go through the experience of loss.

In the bargaining stage, people are especially susceptible to escapist addictions. If they have issues with drugs or alcohol, they may be tempted to "medicate" their grief in these ways. Others distract themselves from their grief with behavioral addictions, including gambling, shopping, or sex. These attempts to shut down the sadness may work in the short term, but the normal feelings of loss will inevitably creep up again.

On a positive note, bargaining is an attempt to deal with the reality of the loss and to get back to "normal" in some sense. The problem is often in the griever's lack of patience—the "quick fix" mentality won't really fix anything, and it could get you into even more trouble.

Stage 5: Depression

Well, if a quick fix won't work, what will?

❋ ❋ ❋ ❋

WHEN YOU REACH the stage of depression, you finally realize that life can't go back to the way it was. What's lost is lost. You feel powerless to change anything about your situation, and you're stuck in your sadness.

This stage can often resemble the shock of the first stage of denial as you wander around with little energy to do anything useful. It may also feel a lot like the sorrow of the second stage of guilt as you cry yourself to sleep each night. But this sorrow runs deeper. It exposes a deep sense of emptiness. You're not enjoying the things you used to; you barely can taste the foods you love. You may feel like you have no more emotional resources to cope with the loss. Obviously, this stage is not enjoyable, but this is where you "hit bottom"—and you must bottom out in order to move upward again. You will heal from this ordeal.

Stage 6: Testing and Reconstruction

In Kübler-Ross's original model, depression gave way to acceptance.

❋ ❋ ❋ ❋

FOR MANY PEOPLE, this transformation was so sudden that it felt almost magical: They woke up one morning and literally smelled the coffee. It's as if their quota of grieving had been met and they could begin to enjoy life again.

But newer paradigms reflect a different reality as many people continue to function as the "walking wounded." For them, there isn't a sudden moment where the gray skies turn blue. Instead, they gradually begin to put their lives back together. They start doing things with people again, rather than rushing home to hibernate. They allow themselves to have a little fun. This is a testing process, and there is some trial-and-error. Painful memories may resurface at any time, driving them back to their private grieving. Still, they're slowly rebuilding.

Stage 7: Acceptance

First, let's discuss what acceptance does not mean.

✳ ✳ ✳ ✳

ACCEPTANCE DOESN'T MEAN that the mourner is glad that the pet is gone. It doesn't mean the person won't still burst into tears now and then. The key here is that in this stage, the person integrates the loss into his or her life. The memory of the pet is carried along as the person moves into new adventures.

There might always be a sense of sadness over the loss, but this is matched and exceeded by a sense of gratitude for the time they were able to have with the pet. They might wonder if they'll ever see their pet again in some future heaven, but they're not consumed by this thought. They step forward into robust earthly lives, confident it's what their dear, departed pet would want them to do.

Complicated Grieving

There are, however, some complicating factors that can extend the grieving process.

✳ ✳ ✳ ✳

WHEN THE PERSON feels strong guilt over the pet's death. People can generally deal with the "phantom guilt" that accompanies a loss ("I should have done more sooner"), but if they feel their actions or negligence directly caused the pet's death, the early stages of grief may take longer.

When the attachment to the animal is especially strong. In this case, we're talking about not just love for the pet but a practical or emotional dependency. This would be true in the case of service animals, and in other situations where the person's life has revolved around the pet. It will take longer to reconstruct one's life without such a pet in it.

When the pet was associated with another person. If the pet serves as a reminder of, say, a departed spouse or a distant child who used to care for it, then the task of grieving doubles, for you're not only mourning the pet but also the person.

When the loss was especially traumatic. A sudden shock, a gruesome accident—these can keep a person at the denial stage for longer than usual.

When the person has few other friends or family for support. It's very hard to reconstruct a life without the pet, when the pet was all that mattered. Supportive friends keep grieving people moving through the stages, and they're a crucial component of the reconstruction process that frequently pulls a griever out of depression. A person can get through the grief without any outside support; it simply may take a bit longer.

Whether or not these extenuating circumstances apply to your situation, it's essential to realize that healing takes time. Just as a broken bone or a scraped knee requires a certain period of recuperation, so does a heart broken by the loss of a dear companion.

The Tasks of Grief

In the last decade or two, some counselors have grown
dissatisfied with the classic "stages of grief" model. In a sense,
there was something too geographical about it. "You are here
(at this stage) now. You'll be here for a while, and there's nothing
you can do about it. When the time is right, you'll be over there."
Wasn't there something more proactive that people could do to
work through their grief? Was it really just a matter of waiting out
their feelings, like a hockey player's trip to the penalty box or a
young child's "time out?"

✳   ✳   ✳   ✳

WHILE THE CLASSIC stages are still used, and other counselors prefer to speak of the "phases" of grief, there's
increased talk about the "tasks" of the grieving process. In his
book *Grief Counseling and Grief Therapy*, psychologist William
Worden writes about a theory he calls "The Four Tasks of
Mourning." This has widely caught on among counselors who
recognize that it brings a more energetic sense to grief therapy.

"The tasks approach gives the mourner some sense of leverage
and hope that there is something that he or she can actively do,"
writes Worden, " . . . although this may seem overwhelming to the person in the throes of acute grief, it can, with the
facilitation of a counselor, offer hope that something can be
done and that there is a way through it. This can be a powerful antidote to the feelings of helplessness that most mourners
experience."

In this theory, you have several jobs to do as you recover. It's
still a process, and it still takes time, but you are actively working through it. You are adapting and adjusting to a new kind
of life without your departed companion. There is a general
order, but the tasks often overlap. "Tasks can be revisited and
reworked over time," says Worden. "Various tasks can also

be worked on at the same time. Grieving is a fluid process." According to Worden, there are four tasks of grief.

Task 1: Accept the Reality of the Loss

This is the flip side of denial. Since denial is a normal first reaction in the grieving process, there's no shame in being there—just as long as you don't stay there. Your task over the coming weeks and months is to accept the reality of your pet's death.

This is not just an intellectual acceptance, but an emotional one as well. You may know that your pet is gone, but still half-expect it to come bounding around the corner. There are many stories of pet owners who "forget" their pets are gone, and call out to them. If this has happened to you, don't feel bad. It doesn't mean you're crazy. It just means you still have a little work to do on this task.

Worden notes that acceptance needs to encompass the basic fact of the loss suffered, its meaning, and its irreversibility. When people deny the meaning of a loss, they may downplay the importance of the departed one. A pet owner says, "Well, it was only an animal. I didn't care that much anyway." While this may temporarily shield a person from the sorrow of losing a beloved pet, it's still a form of denial. The acceptance required in this first task means owning up to the importance of the pet in your life. It means fully facing your loss.

What can you do to accomplish this task?

Have a memorial service. In general, rituals move us through the transitions of life. It might help you deal with this transition if you set up a little gathering for family and friends who knew the departed pet. You don't need to make it a big production; just take the opportunity to express your appreciation for your pet and ask your friends for support as you grieve. This is especially helpful if you were not present at your pet's actual death, if you haven't seen the body, or if the pet has run away and is presumed dead. A service can provide closure.

Set a date to let go of your pet's things. You may want to keep your pet's things—leash, bowls, cage, or what have you—around for a few days or even weeks, but don't keep them much longer than that. Put a date on your calendar to get rid of the items and stick with it. It will be an emotional time for you, so you might ask a friend to help.

Don't overreact to slip-ups. So you forget and put out a bowl of food for your pet. Don't make a big deal of it. It's just your heart's way of saying a long goodbye to a cherished friend. This isn't a race; don't put too much pressure on yourself to hustle through your grief. Healing takes time.

Task 2: Experience the Pain of Grief

This might be harder than you think. Society tends to frown on outward displays of emotion. Break down in tears and people might look oddly in your direction, as if you're not "normal"—which is ironic, because it's really the holding back of emotion that's abnormal. We were made to express our feelings, and we are healthier when we do so.

You may feel a certain pressure to be further along in your recovery than you are, so you'll stifle your tears or angry outbursts. You want people to think you're doing just fine. This too is ironic, because your effort to appear healthy is actually hurting your health.

Perhaps you're afraid to give in to your emotions because they might pull you down into a pit of depression. As a result, you hold back your true feelings, you just don't "go there." If this is the case, you might have a backlog of unspent emotion, perhaps from previous losses that were never adequately mourned. If so, you may want to talk with a professional counselor. He or she can help you unpack those emotions and dismantle those emotional blocks. (And don't worry that a counselor will laugh at you for grieving over a "mere" pet. If they have any training at all, they'll know how difficult this can be.)

Perhaps you find it uncomfortable to experience your grief because you don't know how. You would classify yourself as an "unemotional" person. Tears don't come easily to you. And maybe that's true. Or maybe you've become such an expert at holding back your feelings that it's now second nature to you. Don't force it. After all, no one benefits from a phony display of emotion. But you might want to start talking more about what you feel, whatever you feel. Let the walls fall down as you discuss how you really feel.

The only way through this grief is *through* it. Stop avoiding it, hiding it, or barricading it. Feel it. Yes, it will hurt. A lot. But that's the only way to accomplish this task.

What can you do to accomplish this task?

Talk about your feelings. Look for friends who will let you sob in their presence. Right now, you need listeners who won't try to cheer you up or calm you down, but will let you feel the way you really feel. If you don't have someone like that in your life, then look to a counselor or minister.

Join a pet bereavement group. If not in person, you can find chat rooms online in which you can share and read others' experiences. Run a search for "pet loss" and try some of the sites that pop up.

Express yourself in the arts. If talking isn't your thing, try writing about your feelings. Or painting. Or sculpting. Or making music. You don't need to create a masterpiece for public consumption; just let your emotions spill out. Work with the assumption that no one else will ever see this—and then take a chance with what you create. Dig up those feelings you have a hard time discussing.

Get physical. Exercise is good for you, of course, and it's easy to overlook it in a time of grief. But if you have a swarm of feelings buzzing within you, a good workout will get that energy out.

Walk, run, swim, lift , spin, or hit a punching bag, and let your motion be powered by emotion.

"Steer into the skid." If you've ever driven in an icy climate, you might have heard the advice "steer into a skid." It sounds counterintuitive. If your car starts to slide one way, you want to steer yourself out of it, don't you? Nope. That would make you lose control; the car would spin. Steering into a skid allows you to regain control of the vehicle and drive safely out of danger. Emotionally, you might find yourself "skidding." You're getting into frightening territory, feeling shades of grief you're not sure you can handle. Your instinct is to protect yourself from pain or embarrassment by shutting down the feelings. But think of that sliding car. Allow yourself to steer into that emotion.

Task 3: Adjust to an Environment in Which the Deceased Is Missing

Worden discusses three types of adjustments that are necessary in dealing with grief: external, internal, and spiritual.

External adjustments have to do with the functions of everyday life. If in the past your dog always fetched your slippers, you'll need to get them yourself. One of the immediate challenges for many pet mourners is the change in schedule. For example, if your pet had a certain feeding time, walking time, or perhaps playing time, it might take some time to get used to life without those activities or timetables.

Internal adjustments have to do with your sense of self. This may or may not come into play for a pet owner. Without her cat, a woman who describes herself as the "crazy cat lady" might have to rethink that description. A man who shows up in the park as "Rover's owner" will need to find another way to introduce himself. If there were any guilt issues involved in the pet's death, this too might require some internal adjustments. For instance, a person who chose not to go forward with a pet's surgery or who put their pet to sleep might wrestle with guilt. But that person could also put a positive spin on the situation:

"I am a person capable of making life-or-death decisions." We learn about ourselves in trying times.

Spiritual adjustments have to do with religion, fate, and the world. The death of someone close to us—whether human or animal—challenges the basic assumption many people have: that the world is fair and friendly. We may go through life expecting that good things will happen to us because we're good people, and then we suffer the sudden illness and death of a pet we love. *Why did this happen? Didn't we deserve better? Didn't our innocent pet deserve better?* Now the world doesn't make as much sense; it seems cruel and dangerous. It's a crisis of belief in ourselves, God, or the world around us that may require a major adjustment.

For many children, adjustments like these are a memorable part of the growing-up process. Years later, you'll hear people saying, "I learned as a child that the world is a nasty place," or, "I figured I must have done something very bad to have my pet taken away like that."

This task requires a certain ability to "roll with the punches." We must accept that the world looks different after this tragedy, and that we must change with it. We struggle to make sense of things, but the breakthrough might come in finally accepting that life doesn't always make sense. Questions go unanswered. The world is not a neat equation. After your loss, you may be faced with this realization.

What can you do to accomplish this task?

Change your routine. This is a simple adjustment you can make. Go out for a walk, but at a different time than when you used to walk the dog, and take another route. Routines you had established with your pet should be changed a bit, so that you can move on. (Of course, this isn't such a good idea if you still have other pets that depend on that routine.)

Be careful with medication of all types. Adjusting is hard work, and you might be tempted to escape into alcohol, illegal drugs, or even misuse of prescription drugs. But try to abstain—you'll need to stay sober to take these important emotional steps.

Call for reinforcements. Talk with the people who know you best. Ask them what they like best about you. That might seem odd to fish for compliments, but think about it this way: For some time now, you've enjoyed the unconditional love of a pet who thought you were divine. Now you need to get that support from people.

Find a new adventure. Learn more about yourself. What makes you you? What skills do you have? What interests? What's on your "bucket list" of things to do someday? Now's the time to start cultivating those things! Learn a language. Start a new hobby. Travel. Maybe it was difficult to travel when you had a pet to care for, but now you're building a new life independent of the one you've lost.

Task 4: "Emotionally" Relocate the Deceased and Move on with Your Life

What does it mean to "relocate" your departed cat? We're talking about your heart and mind here; where do you hold their memories?

Psychologist and writer William Worden called this task to "withdraw emotional energy and reinvest it." That may sound sort of clinical or confusing, but the idea is that it's time to stop investing your emotional resources in the one who's gone and time to start investing in your future. Worden got this idea from Sigmund Freud, who wrote, "Mourning has a quite precise physical task to perform: its function is to detach the survivors' hopes and memories from the dead."

But it's not really a matter of "detaching." You don't remove the departed one from your heart—you can't. But you can "relocate" the deceased. You can put them in a place where you can always think of them fondly, but without being distracted by those memories. You're able to focus on building a new life. It's like taking a video screen off the dashboard of your car and putting it in the back seat. You still know it's there, and maybe you'll pull over sometime and watch what's on the screen. But if you want to get anywhere, it can't be right in front of you. Relocation is crucial.

This sounds easier than it is. Many people are afraid that if they take their memories of the deceased off the "dashboard" of their lives, so to speak, they'll forget them entirely. They feel it would somehow dishonor the departed to stop thinking about them. But nothing could be further from the truth, especially in the case of a departed pet.

Think about it. Your pet loved you. Your pet was fully invested in helping you live your life. Okay, it liked food and exercise and maybe a scratch behind the ears, too, but apart from that, it wanted what was best for you. Your pet was there for you in the midst of some difficult times. Well, this is a difficult time, and you're at a point where you need to move forward, not backward. You need to put memories of your pet in their place and focus on what's ahead. That's what's best for you now. And really, your pet would be more than willing to jump in the back seat and let you drive.

What can you do to accomplish this task?

Create a memorial. Find a fitting way to honor your departed cat—create a photo collage, name a small part of your home after your pet ("Champ's Corner"), or use a favorite pet toy to decorate the garden. Don't make this memorial an all-consuming passion; the idea is to show your love for your pet.

Write a brief history of your life with your pet. This is another kind of memorial. Don't worry about grammar or spelling. This probably won't be for public consumption, but it could be your personal tribute. It will be especially effective if you conclude with a section like "What my pet taught me," or "How my pet prepared me for the future." This is part of "relocating"—honoring the pet in the past, while you focus on moving forward.

Work on your human relationships. It's possible that in your time of grief you've let your human relationships slide a little. This is the time to take stock with the handful of people closest to you. Do you need to reconnect with them, patch things up, or start anew?

Rediscover your creative, adventurous, fun side. You've been through the wringer emotionally. You've had your time to mourn, but now it's time to dance—or it will be soon. Plan some fun experiences for the near future. Start enjoyable projects. Hang out with people who delight you. You've been distancing yourself from the joy of life; soon you'll be ready to move into really living again.

Give of yourself.

Here's a secret: Pain and loss equip you to help others. You have now "been there," and that enables you to commiserate with anyone else who is going through a rough patch. One of the surest ways to climb out of your pain is to care about someone else's. Try volunteering as a tutor, mentor, or helper for some nonprofit organization. Or connect with a community group or place of worship. Stay on the lookout for people experiencing grief, because you now have the qualifications to help.

Recovering, Reformatting, and Replacing

"By the time we realized how sick Frankie was, it was too late," *says Lynette about the cat she got when she was 12. It was just a* *year later that he started having health problems.* *"We took him* *to the vet's office and left him there. He died there the next day."*

✳   ✳   ✳   ✳

L YNETTE WAS VERY upset, and took her anger out on those closest to her. "You're probably glad he died," she told her mother. "You never liked him anyway."

A crisis brings out utterances and feelings we normally keep quiet. At the time, Lynette felt she had good reason to suspect this. She had received Frankie as a gift from a friend, and her mother had never been very excited about it. Grudgingly she had allowed the cat to stay, but its care was entirely Lynette's responsibility, and it was never allowed to enter Mom's room.

Now the pain of losing her pet worsened the already difficult relationship Lynette had at the time with her mother. In her darker moments, she suspected her mother of poisoning the cat, a charge which she now, years later, admits was groundless.

"At the time, my life was pretty bad. I was in eighth grade and that whole experience was nasty. My parents were close to divorcing, and I think my mom and sister were also having issues, so even before Frankie died, there weren't many positives going on. Losing the cat was a big blow," says Lynette. "I cried myself to sleep a lot—over the cat's death, but also because of how miserable my mother was in general as a result of everything else going on in her life."

Owning a pet doesn't occur in a vacuum. There is a life you are living, with friends and neighbors, with jobs and responsibilities, with bills to pay and appointments to keep. A pet becomes a part of that broader life. Perhaps the whole family enjoys the pet together, or friends come over and greet your pet even before they greet you. But there are other times when your pet provides a refuge from the harsh realities of life. This was certainly the case with Lynette, and when Frankie died, she felt she didn't have much of a life to go back to.

"Pets to us are purity," says Dr. Donna Alberici, a professor of psychology. "They never tell us we look bad. They're always happy to see us. When my pet 'waves' to me, it's all for me."

Alberici notes that there's a kind of "perfection" in this relationship. "We grant attributes to them that we don't give to humans." We see our pets as perfectly loyal, perfectly supportive—and when there's a lack of loyalty or support in the world around us, this is especially important.

Psychologist Thomas Whiteman talks about the "bonding" between a pet and its owner. "It's possible for someone to own a pet and not bond with it, but when there is a connection made, it's positive. They communicate with you, but not with words."

In this way, pets "say" exactly what we need to hear, especially when we're feeling emotionally needy. We're grateful for their support, idealizing them as the perfect friends. "With other people, we have good and bad memories," Whiteman says, "but there are only pleasant memories with pets."

He notes that this is especially important for single people or senior citizens who may not have much human companionship. A pet provides much-needed support in these social situations, and when that pet passes on, the grief can be overwhelming

Under these circumstances, grieving becomes even more difficult. It's not just about "getting over" an emotional loss; it means reconstructing your life, a post-pet existence in which support must come from somewhere else. It also requires a certain kind of reformatting: We must process the world—and our place in it—differently.

Should You Get Another Cat?

Early in the recovery process you might be tempted to "replace" your departed pet with a new one, perhaps even one of the same breed and color. However, this is a classic example of bargaining, where you hope a quick fix will cure your grief.

✳   ✳   ✳   ✳

I**T MAY TAKE** a while before you're emotionally ready to open your heart to a new pet. In addition, it's not fair to expect a new pet to take the departed one's place, as if it were simply a replica. Wait until you're ready to love a new pet for his or her own personality.

It's possible that a well-meaning friend or relative will buy you a new pet to replace the old one. This also is not a good idea—only you know when you're ready to take on a new pet. Let them know you appreciate the gesture, but you're not quite there yet.

Sometimes children will beg and plead for a new pet, to replace the old one. It's advisable to hold out for now, at least during the early stages of grief. Instead, teach your children the importance of honoring their departed pet. Help them deal with the loss in a healthy way first, before getting a new pet.

Eventually, getting a new pet could be a good step forward. It will require you to open up your heart again. When you think you might be ready, visit an animal shelter—but at first you should only look around, not adopt. If you're feeling positive after the shelter visit, and you're still feeling good after you've thought about it for a few days, then maybe you're ready to make another commitment to a new animal friend.

Family Matters

It was Christmas Day, and Brad and Rachel watched as their two sons ripped through the carefully wrapped packages. Jason, 11, and Sam, 9, were having a blast with their new toys and gadgets. Finally, someone said, "Where's Pookie?"

❋   ❋   ❋   ❋

No one had seen the family cat all morning, which was unusual. Well, they figured, maybe it was spooked by all the early-morning merriment. They looked all through the house. They checked outside. They searched the neighborhood, calling out for Pookie.

What began as a festive day became increasingly frantic as Brad drove through the streets, hoping to catch a glimpse of the family's lost cat. Rachel went out to the backyard and prayed.

The boys went to bed that night terribly worried, and it was hard for them to get to sleep. "Maybe Pookie's just out exploring, and he'll come back tomorrow," said their parents. "That sort of thing happens all the time. We'll look again in the morning."

The next day, the family woke to a foot of snow on the ground, which hindered their search efforts. Their hearts ached as they imagined Pookie somewhere outside, cold and confused.

"Why would he run off like that?" the younger son, Sam, wondered.

"That's what cats do sometimes," said Rachel. "They're curious."

"Yeah," added his older brother. "Haven't you heard, 'Curiosity killed the cat'?"

They all knew it—death—was a distinct possibility, but they didn't want to think about it.

The next week brought a strange mixture of emotions for the whole family—sadness, but also a certain energy in trying to solve the mystery. Rachel figured that the cat must have scampered away when she took out the trash late on Christmas Eve. She knew it wasn't really her fault, but she still felt guilty. Meanwhile, the boys acted out a little. After a week, the family figured that Pookie was gone for good. Jason thought that the cat probably had been run over by a car. Sam disagreed; he was sure Pookie had joined the other cats behind the nearby supermarket and was probably having the time of his life.

Brad put the cat's favorite cardboard box in the backyard, along with a dish of water and some dry cat food. If Pookie did wander back, he'd be welcome, but the family was ready to assume the worst and move forward.

When Children Lose the Pets They Love

Jason and Sam each had his own relationship with Pookie, and they dealt with the cat's disappearance differently. Each boy will have his own way of finding closure in the matter—coming to the realization that Pookie is gone for good—and each will have his own way of grieving.

Although the whole family has been shaken by this loss, Brad and Rachel have a responsibility as parents to shore up their family life, to manage the collective grief process, and to make sure their children have the resources they need for healthy mourning. It's a daunting task for any parent.

Children will grieve differently according to their ages, personalities, previous experiences, closeness to the pet, and circumstances of the pet's departure. There's no standard seven-step course that every family must go through. Your situation requires careful observation of your children, communication, patience, and wisdom. Along the way, you will find the "right answers" for your family, or at least discover some helpful ideas to get you through this difficult period.

For many children, the loss of a pet is their first experience with death. Younger children really don't know what death is; they have no category in which to place this event and so have no understanding of it. The pet is there, and then it's not, and everybody's sad. What's up? Somewhat older children may see death on TV and in video games but still be untouched by it personally. Others may not realize death's permanence.

All of this means that parents (or grandparents) may have to take on the role of teacher, instructing their children in this basic aspect of life—that is, death. It must be done carefully and sensitively, but also clearly.

For many children, this is also their first experience with grief. They are feeling emotions they've never felt before. Again, they lack descriptive language and the ability to identify and categorize their feelings. As adults, we are able to say, "Oh, I'm going through a bad time. I'm stressed. I'm grieving." But children don't know how to do that yet. They may find themselves angry or listless or restless, and they don't know why. They feel an ache in the pit of their stomach, or perhaps they begin thinking of their parents', or their own, mortality. Such complicated feelings are often new, and for the very young (toddlers), it may even be beyond their developmental abilities to effectively comprehend or cope with.

Parents should act as counselors and guides through this difficult time. They might need to demonstrate "good grief"—for example, by having a healthy cry or maybe forgiving some stressed out behavior. By their own example, parents can teach children how to identify their feelings and express them in words, as language and comprehension go hand in hand. And children need regular reassurance that things will be better in the future, and that grief eventually gives way to normalcy.

These are teaching opportunities for some of the most important lessons of life. What children learn from this experience will help them to know themselves and to engage with the world in a healthy way. "Children look for personal meaning in everything," write Michael Stern and Susan Cropper in *Loving and Losing a Pet*, "and when they struggle to deal with sad and previously unfamiliar events, they are in danger of reaching erroneous conclusions that open the door for self-blame, guilt, and misunderstanding, which in turn can have far-reaching implications for behavior and adjustment."

You may find that challenge a little bit intimidating. But why not turn that around to the positive? Yes, if you leave children to engage in this emotional struggle alone, without any guidance, negative emotional and psychological effects may occur later. But if you pay attention to your children, talk with them, and take the time to answer their questions and discuss their fears, you will be building a mature, well-adjusted person. And isn't that what parenting is all about?

Age Considerations

It's not like clockwork, but children do go through certain developmental stages. Use this as a general guide to help your children deal with grief at their level.

✳   ✳   ✳   ✳

0–2 YEARS OLD

There's little to no understanding of death at this early age, but very young children will pick up on the emotions of people around them. If there's a lot of crying or tension in the air, these youngsters may feel anxious or worried. Reassure them with lots of hugs and calming words.

2–5 years old

At this age, children may not understand that death is permanent. Be direct about this. They may also worry that the pet is gone as a result of something they did. You may be tempted to shield children this young from the harsh reality of the situation, but they'll know something is going on, and their fears might be harsher than the reality. Be honest, but simple, in your explanations. Don't be surprised if those children exhibit regressive behavior—crying, thumb-sucking, or bed-wetting (that is, if they've already grown out of it). They are merely seeking pathways for their grief with a behavior that seemed to work for them or comfort them in the past.

5–9 years old

Children's minds are blossoming in this stage, and they're often very curious. They'll ask about (or imagine) the details of the pet's illness and death, and they may wonder about their own death or yours. This may border on "morbid fascination," but do your best to deal openly with the questions. Children sometimes bear some feelings of guilt and worry that they caused the pet's death in some way. They may also feel angry if they blame you or someone else for the death. If you euthanized the pet, you may need to review that decision with them step by step. This is also a time of "magical thinking" for children, in which they imagine a pet coming back or think that someone caused the death by wishing it. In this stage, grief often gets acted out socially in the form of rebellious behavior at school or violent actions with playmates. Give them healthier ways to channel these feelings—for example, by talking, writing, drawing, or playing sports.

10–12 years old

From this age on, children are mentally able to comprehend death, but they're probably inexperienced at dealing with it emotionally. They look to parents as models for processing their grief. They might feel denial, sadness, anger, bargaining, and depression but not necessarily understand those feelings. Give this child as much permission to experience these feelings as you give yourself—perhaps more. Be open and expressive about your own grieving process, and explain it as you go. "I know it's been a while, but I'm still sad about losing Butters. Maybe you are, too." Remember that your child's grieving process might be on a different timetable than your own. Don't rush kids through their feelings—just nudge them along.

13 and up

Everything from the previous age group applies here, with one big addition: the need for peer acceptance. Teenagers often live and die by their place in social groups, and so they're likely to let those concerns affect the grieving process. With a handful of close friends, perhaps pet owners themselves, who understand and support your teen, he or she should do just fine. But if the larger group mocks or scorns your child for mourning a "mere animal," your teen may squelch his or her natural feelings of grief. Feelings should never be buried when they can be healthfully expressed and released—to do so can have damaging consequences later in life.

An additional complication is the adolescent's need to find and express his or her own identity. You probably know already that the least effective way to get something done is to flat-out tell your teenager to do it. You'll find the same thing is true if you order them to let out their feelings.

The point is this: Your teen needs to find his or her own way to grieve. Keep checking in and continue communicating with your child. You can reveal your own grieving process, but let your teen find his or her unique pathway.

General Guidelines

Be honest and direct. Avoid the euphemisms for death we commonly use as adults, as children might not understand them. "Putting an animal to sleep" might seem like a fine way to gently break the news, but it might make a child worry at bedtime—What if I don't wake up? Don't say the animal ran away if it didn't. Don't blame it on the vet if he or she did nothing wrong. Tell the truth.

There are multiple problems with these well-meant "white lies." Young children will extrapolate from what you tell them, and they'll misunderstand what's going on. If you need an operation and anesthesia "puts you to sleep," they might get frantic. Or perhaps they'll wonder what they did to scare the pet away forever. They might learn to distrust doctors, or even God. But they might also learn not to trust you, once they learn the truth. It's much better to establish open communication with children early on.

"At all ages, honesty is the best policy," says bereavement counselor Marty Tously. "That means using the words 'death' and 'dying,' and explaining the permanence of death. You do it gently but without confusing them as to what dying really means."

With that said, you should be sensitive to what children can take in at any particular stage of their lives. Be honest and direct, but don't give more information than they can handle. It's a good idea to ask them if they have any questions. And, since they might not know which questions to ask, it's even better to ask your children periodically to explain to you what happened. This will give you a glimpse of what they're thinking and an opportunity to fill in details or clear up any misconceptions.

Be authentic. You have your own grieving process to go through. If you stifle it for the sake of your kids, you hurt yourself emotionally, and you give your kids a bad model of mourning. Let the grieving happen, and talk about it openly with your children.

Talking is especially important. If you try to contain it, your grief can release in bouts of crying or displays of anger. Your kids will wonder if they're the ones making you sad or angry (and maybe they are, a little), so it's important to talk about it. "I was a little upset with you for not cleaning your room, but I yelled at you too much, and I'm sorry for that. I think it's because I still miss Mittens." That kind of talk will help them deal with their own grief-based anger at some point.

There is one slight caveat to this guideline: As a parent, you're still in charge, and you're still responsible for the family. Especially in their time of grief, your children need to know that they're secure and that the family is operational. You need to let them know that you're not going to have a complete melt-down or leave them—both of which can be very scary to kids. So even if you're sad, angry, or depressed, you still need to cook dinner, drive them to school, and help them with homework, or at least see that those tasks get done. Don't burden the children with your woes or make them worry about the future of the household, but do be open about the process of grieving.

Be there. Even if you have nothing to say, your presence is cru-cial in this time of need. Your child has suffered an important loss and may feel abandoned, rejected, or forsaken. You need to do all you can to counter those feelings. You don't need to have all the answers. You don't need to know all the right things to do. Be there and good things will happen as a result. Doing so puts you in a position to monitor your child's grief, and you can answer your child's questions as they arise.

As children get older and grow into the middle school and teen years, "being there" becomes more of a challenge. Your pres-ence doesn't need to be as frequent, but it should be a priority. Children in this age group need time away from their parents for their own individuation, but awareness and communication within the family are still necessary. In a time of grief, some older children will want to spend less time at home, where they see constant reminders of the lost pet. Even so, being avail-able is still extremely important, for them and for you. Studies have shown the strength of families that routinely have dinner together. Perhaps that's an option that will help your family to work in some "together time."

Be patient and permissive. Wait—permissive? Well, not in the sense that you let your children do whatever they want, but that you give them permission to grieve as they need to. You may encounter a frustrating time of denial when they talk about the pet coming back. As long as you've clearly explained the facts, you don't need to rush them out of denial. Don't try to keep kids from crying or asking questions. Even if you've had enough, realize that apparently they haven't. Be wise in the way that you deal with their anger. Understand that this is a way of coping with their loss, but you may also want to teach them about controlling their actions when they feel angry. This process may not develop the way you thought it would, and it may last longer than you want, but allow it to run its course. If you try to inhibit their emotions, the process may last even longer.

Be perceptive. Most likely you are already an expert on your children—after all, you've been reading their emotional and physical responses since birth. But in a time of grief, you need to be especially attuned to their reactions. They are navigating uncharted waters here. "It is not uncommon for children to present a blank facade that can be interpreted as indifference or as no emotional reaction at all when anger or bitterness is clearly part of the experience," say authors Michael Stern and Susan Cropper. "Similarly, children may appear to return to a normal routine rather quickly, yet the loss continues to have its impact in subtle ways."

It's sometimes assumed that children aren't very serious about their grief when they move quickly from tears to laughter, but that's not necessarily the case. It can be their way of managing strange new emotions. In order to keep from

being overwhelmed with sadness, they might "rescue" themselves with laughter.

All of this requires careful study and insightful perception on the part of parents. Stop, look, and listen to your children. Understand when they've received enough information for one day. Recognize when they have questions they don't know how to ask. Sense when they need a hug rather than an explanation. No one knows your children like you do, so trust your intuition, but keep studying and perceiving. What was true of them yesterday may not be true today.

Be a wise leader. As a parent, you steer this vessel we call a family. You make decisions that affect the whole family. So when the household is dealing with the loss of a pet, you have a certain responsibility to manage the recovery. You can't dictate how each family member will grieve, but you can take certain steps that might facilitate the process.

One important task is to set a tone of mutual support within the family. When there are multiple children in the household, some may appear to go through grief very quickly, while others carry the sadness for quite some time. You will need to foster an understanding among the family that grieving is an important task, and that each person has the right to do it in his or her own way.

You may have already made decisions regarding the death and burial or cremation of your pet. Perhaps you have also made decisions about whether to involve your family in those events. Doubts or concerns may be raised, even by you, but one role of a leader is to keep moving forward.

You might want to consider some sort of funeral or memorial for the lost cat in which the family can participate. Whether an event or an artwork or a monument, it might help your family to both honor the pet and gain a sense of closure so they can "let the pet go" and retain good memories. Lead the way forward—what do you think the family needs?

Also, be wise about whether and when to get a new cat. Your kids may want one right away, but this may not be a good idea. You need to gauge when they're sufficiently moved on so that a new pet is not just a quick stand-in for the old one but a unique being that can be loved in its own right.

Family Conflict

When a cat dies, it may stir up tension within the family. The emotional turmoil during the aftermath may give rise to resentment and bitterness, guilt and blame, whether spoken or not. If these feelings are brought into the open, they can be discussed and dealt with, confessed, forgiven, and released. If not, the negative feelings can continue to fester, poisoning family relationships for years to come. Let's take a look at some of these adverse reactions.

✳   ✳   ✳   ✳

GUILT CAN BE a problem because it's not always rational. As we've seen, children can feel responsible for a pet's death (or disappearance) even if they had nothing to do with it. In the same way, adults can second-guess themselves for their decisions (such as putting a pet to sleep), even if those choices were legitimate. There's always another way to look at things—you may feel bad for putting a pet down too soon or too late, for involving the kids in the process or not, and even for the decision whether to cremate or bury. There is plenty of "phantom guilt" to be found in these matters.

It gets a bit more complicated when the guilt might actually be deserved. Maybe Pookie wouldn't have gotten out at night if Rachel had been more careful with the back door. Maybe. Perhaps you had a choice between paying for a pet's surgery and getting the new car you needed, and you chose the car.

Maybe you left the dog in the car or the cat in the basement with unforeseen disastrous results. What can you do about those feelings of guilt?

Nancy fights back tears as she talks about an event that occurred several years earlier. She had two cats—an older, worldly outdoor cat and a younger one she had always kept inside. This double standard became hard to enforce, and so she began to let the younger cat outside during the day, trusting the older cat to teach it how to survive in the "wilderness" of her suburban community. One evening, Nancy called for the cats to come indoors. The older one came quickly, but the younger one didn't. As it turned out, it had been hit by a car and killed.

Nancy still feels guilt about the incident. The younger cat wasn't ready to be outside at night, she says. She should have called it in before dark. Her sense of regret runs deep. A friend tried to console her. "You wanted to give that cat a certain kind of life where it could run and play freely outside. There's nothing wrong with that. Your cat would forgive you," he said.

That's really what guilt requires, isn't it? Forgiveness. The problem with guilt in a family situation is that it puts up walls. The guilty person withdraws from the others, whether or not they're being blamed. How do you break down those walls? By talking about the issue. Allow the guilty person to confess; let the others consider, and say, "We understand what you've done and we see your pain, and we will continue to love you. Let's put the matter aside."

Resentment is the flip side of that coin. This occurs when people blame others and hold grudges. "You never liked that cat anyway. You intentionally left the door open." This reasoning is often irrational and unspoken. "I can't prove it, but I know."

Children sometimes feel resentment toward their parents if they're kept out of the euthanasia decision. All they know is that mom or dad took the pet to the vet and it didn't come back. Often children make the deduction that their parents must have killed it. Without knowing the whole story, it's easy for children to attribute negative motives. This can also happen with older children living away from home at college or elsewhere. If they hear that the pet was put to sleep, they might suspect that the parents were just tired of caring for *their* pet.

As we've seen, there are often financial decisions regarding the health of a cat, and they can also create resentment within the family. How important is the health of the pet compared to other pressing financial matters? Children often don't understand why healing a pet is less important than, say, paying the mortgage. Similarly, this can also be a source of tension between couples.

It's a mistake to think that issues like this will just go away over time. It's best to open up and talk about them. When all of the elements—blame and explanations, pain and confessions—are out in the open, it's easier for people to reconcile with one another and with the loss. Forgiveness becomes one of those elements.

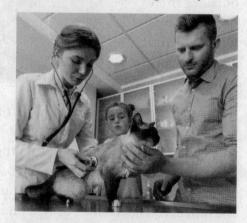

Favoritism can spawn a certain kind of resentment that surfaces when a family loses a pet. Sometimes pets become associated with certain family members. It's "Maria's kitty" or "Johnny's dog," even if other family members love and care for the pet as well. When that pet passes, attention and sympathy may be showered on the one person associated with it, but not on others who also hurt. This can even be true of parents—often it's Mom or Dad who feeds the pet and provides most of the care. They can feel left out of the sympathy. It's important to see how everyone is struggling with the loss of the pet. Spread the sympathy around, and you'll avoid this type of resentment.

Wounds of the grieving process deserve mention as well. We've already seen how grief can lead to anger and depression. When one family member is experiencing these feelings, the rest of the family is affected as well. One sibling, hurt by the angry words of another, may respond in kind. A parent may resent the way a depressed teen "shut down" after a pet's death and now refuses to do anything around the house. Grief can sometimes blind people to the needs of others, and in a family in which everyone is suffering from the same loss, some people can feel neglected.

Once again, communication is key. If the family keeps sharing their feelings, they can help each other through the process.

Singles and Seniors

When we talk about "family matters," we sometimes overlook certain households; often these are the ones most deeply affected by the loss of a cat.

✳ ✳ ✳ ✳

SINGLE PEOPLE, ESPECIALLY those who live alone, can find the grief devastating. A cat can do a great deal to keep loneliness at bay. It's something to talk to, something to care for, and something to cuddle with. A pet can bring a measure of wholeness to the lives of some singles. When that pet is gone, everything is shaken. The routines of life are thrown off.

The owner has to deal not only with grief, but also loneliness and possibly a feeling of purposelessness. "For singles, the loss of a pet is like the loss of a child," says Thomas Whiteman, a psychologist who has written on the needs of divorced and single people. "That's their companion."

Further, the single person sometimes lacks a support network to provide comfort in this difficult time. The pet is the companion who was there for the owner in previous crises, and now the pet is gone. If you're a single person touched by the death of a beloved pet, what can you do? Here are some thoughts.

* **Don't take it lightly.** Your emotions are slamming you right now, and you may be uncomfortable with those feelings. *I shouldn't feel this bad. Does this mean I'm abnormal?* There is nothing abnormal about feeling thrown by the loss of a primary companion. You have nothing to apologize for.

* **Change your routine.** Presumably you did a number of things on a regular basis that involved your pet, whether it was walking the dog or watching your favorite TV show with your cat on your lap. These activities can remind you of your pet and drag you deeper into sadness. Find a different way to get exercise. Go to a friend's house to watch your show. Whenever possible, get out and engage with the world around you, rather than sit at home with your memories.

* **Write down your feelings.** You could also record your feelings or sing them or paint them—the point is to let them out. Many pet owners talk to their pets (and those pets are

probably pretty good listeners!). Without that sounding board, it's easy to allow thoughts and feelings to stagnate within you. Let them out by journaling, composing, blogging, or by other means.

* **Find a support network.** Start with one friend who understands your pain—maybe it's a relative, a neighbor, or a coworker. If you're already connected to some sort of singles group, whether in a community or a church, look there for sympathetic friends. If not, consider joining one. (Just make sure the group is focused on friendship and not solely on matchmaking.) Groups are also available, online and in person, for those who have lost pets.

* **Watch out for a "rebound."** The grieving process makes you emotionally vulnerable. It's rather easy to get into an unhealthy romantic relationship when you are feeling needy. As with any new relationship, it's wise to go slowly.

* **Control your addictions.** This is another danger. When you're hurting, it's easy to seek relief or escape in alcohol, drugs, gambling, pornography, or games. As a single person you have less accountability to others, especially if you live alone, so addictions are especially tempting.

* **Seek your purpose.** As you find yourself pulling out of the downward spiral of grief, it might be a good time to do some heavy thinking about your purpose in life. Is it rooted in your job, your hobby, your faith, or your friendships? Is there something you could be doing to pursue your purpose more directly?

* **Get another pet.** You'll know when you're ready. You already know that no other animal can replace the one you lost, but when the time is right, visit a shelter and make a home in your heart for another companion.

Senior citizens have many of the same issues as singles, even if they're married. Cats become part of the rhythm of their lives, and that comfortable routine is sorely missed when the pet is gone. In some cases, the pet has aged along with them, and they have a long history together. That makes the pain all the greater. It also brings an unwelcome reminder of their mortality. For widows and widowers, the pet might serve as a connection to the departed spouse, and so the grief doubles when the pet dies.

The social networks of seniors often shrink as they age, and now they find themselves without a good support system. It's difficult to get the comfort they need. For seniors that are married, the loss of the pet can leave both people emotionally needy. It helps to have a third party offer understanding and consolation.

If you're a senior citizen affected by the loss of a cat you loved, what can you do? First, read over the advice to singles, because many of the same ideas apply to you. In addition, consider the following ideas.

* **Memorialize the cat.** Make a scrapbook of pictures or craft some sort of shrine—not to worship the pet, but to honor its memory. Especially if the pet was with you for many years, you'll have a lot of memories, and you don't want to forget them.

* **Enjoy your freedom.** Were there activities, such as travel, that you couldn't do before, or were more difficult, because you had the pet? Exploring new adventures might be a good way to take your mind off your loss.

* **Consider the practical effects.** What did your cat do for you that is now missing in your life? Did it remind you of certain things in your schedule? It wouldn't hurt to list these things and then think about how they will still be accomplished.

* **Talk about any guilt you feel.** If you're on a fixed income, perhaps you lacked the resources to pay for the pet's surgery.

Or maybe it was too difficult to get the pet in for check-ups as often as you should have. Whatever the case, you might be feeling some guilt over your pet's death. The best way to deal with this is to talk it out, if not with your spouse, then with a friend or counselor.

* **Don't feel bad about crying.** This might not apply to you, but there are a number of older folks, especially men, who have learned not to show emotion. Some people may see tears as a sign of weakness. If that's your assumption as well, it may keep you from getting over your pet's death. So if you feel like crying, go ahead and cry. Tears are healthy when you are facing a loss. Holding them back is what hurts you.

* **Think through the issues of getting a new pet.** It may be a little more complicated for a senior citizen—considering income, living quarters, and the energy needed to care for an animal—but having a new pet can be very rewarding. For instance, you may want to share custody of a new pet with a younger person or family—a solution that would ease the burden on you and still provide some much-needed love and joy. If getting a baby animal such as a puppy or kitten seems daunting or just not right for you, consider adopting an adult pet. It's harder for shelters to find homes for grown pets, and getting an animal that's already housetrained can be a benefit to a senior.

* **Renew relationships.** Consider a renewed connection with children and grandchildren. You invested a lot of love in your pet, and now you don't know where to put that energy. Think about whether there are others in your life— humans or animals— who might benefit from your attention.

Chapter 10

Cats in Popular Culture

Puddy Tat

Appearing in more than 100 Warner Bros. animated shorts between 1945 and 1966, Sylvester the Cat was the fourth most frequently featured character in the cartoons, after Bugs Bunny, Porky Pig, and Daffy Duck. The poor cat also holds the unfortunate record for "dying" more often than any other Looney Tunes *character.*

✳ ✳ ✳ ✳

From No Name to Famous Name

The scientific name for a domestic cat is *Felis silvestris catus*. So when animator Chuck Jones needed a name for a new Looney Tunes cat character in the 1948 short *Scaredy Cat*, he decided to use a play on "silvestris" and called the cat Sylvester (Sylvester James Pussycat Sr., to be more specific). But Scaredy Cat wasn't Sylvester's first appearance in cartoons; the character underwent several evolutions before he became the black and white, red-nosed, lisping feline we've come to know so well.

Sylvester's first appearance was in director Friz Freleng's 1945 short *Life with Feathers*, in which a pessimistic bird attempts suicide by trying to get the cat to eat him. But the cat, suspicious of this easy meal, believes the bird must be poisoned and refuses to take a nibble. Although the cat would soon be known as Sylvester, at this point he had no name.

In 1946, Sylvester popped up in director Bob Clampett's *Kitty Kornered*, which also featured Porky Pig. Again unnamed, the cat had a black nose and yellow eyes, giving him a slightly different appearance than the one he is now known for. The next year, the still-unnamed cat was featured in two cartoons by director Arthur Davis, titled *Doggone Cats* and *Catch as Cats Can*. Also in 1947, Sylvester made his debut in several Robert McKimson cartoons, where he was often paired with a baby kangaroo named Hippety Hopper. In these cartoons, the cat mistakes the kangaroo for a giant mouse, and the kangaroo mistakes the cat's attempts to catch him as a game of roughhousing. Cartoonish shenanigans ensue, of course.

Feathered Sidekick

While 1948's *Scaredy Cat* was the first cartoon where Sylvester had an official name, 1947's *Tweetie Pie* introduced another character that would soon become Sylvester's cute little nemesis: Tweety the yellow canary. Created by Clampett and Freleng, the little bird appeared in 46 cartoons, most of them with Sylvester, and became famous for his catchphrase, "I tawt I taw a puddy tat!" *Tweetie Pie* earned Warner Bros. its first Academy Award for Best Animated Short Film.

Tweety wasn't the only character with a catchphrase—or a speech impediment, for that matter. The first words Sylvester ever uttered in his cartoons were "Sufferin' succotash," said with his famous, heavy lisp, and the exclamation became his trademark. The cat's voice was originally provided by Mel Blanc, who also voiced Bugs Bunny, Daffy Duck, and Porky Pig. Interestingly, Blanc's son, Noel, once stated that of all the characters his father brought to life, Sylvester was the one that sounded most like his natural voice (but without the lisp!).

While Sylvester "died" in at least 16 of his cartoons, the most of any Looney Tunes character, he is also the Looney Tunes character who starred in the most Oscar-winning shorts. *Tweetie Pie*, 1955's *Speedy Gonzales*, and 1957's *Birds Anonymous* all won Academy Awards for Best Animated Short Film. Not bad for a cat competing with Bugs Bunny and Daffy Duck.

Since the original cartoons aired, Sylvester has appeared in the WB network's *The Sylvester* and *Tweety Mysteries*, and Cartoon Network's *The Looney Tunes Show*, and been in films like *Who Framed Roger Rabbit* and *Space Jam*. The cat with the red nose and the lisping catchphrase, as well as his feathered sidekick, will continue to entertain new generations of cartoon fans.

Fancy Felines on Film

Notable for being the last film project personally approved by Walt Disney before his death in 1966, The Artistocats *was first released on Christmas Eve 1970. Although not as popular as Disney hits* The Jungle Book *and* 101 Dalmatians, *the film is considered no less iconic today.*

✳ ✳ ✳ ✳

Ideas Wanted

WALT DISNEY'S ANIMATED television series *Wonderful World of Color* debuted in 1961 on NBC, taking advantage of the network's new ability to broadcast in color. The series aired cartoons featuring Disney characters like Mickey Mouse, Goofy, and Chip 'n' Dale, as well as a new character named Ludwig Von Drake, said to be Donald Duck's uncle. The character was the first Disney character created solely for television, but Disney didn't want to stop with just one. He believed the new color television show could use a few more original ideas.

So Disney asked writers Tom McGowan and Tom Rowe, as well as producer Harry Tytle, to come up with some animal story ideas for the *Wonderful World of Color* show. McGowan found a story he thought would be a good fit, about a mother cat and her kittens that was set in New York City. Tytle liked the idea, but suggested the story take place in Paris. And Rowe, an American who was living in Paris at the time, took on the task of writing a story using McGowan's and Tytle's ideas.

Bumps in the Road

The result was a rough draft of a story featuring a butler and a maid who work for a wealthy old heiress. In her will, the heiress leaves her fortune to the butler and maid, but only after her beloved cats die. This vexes the greedy butler and maid, who plot ways to kill the cats, but of course their clumsy, bumbling efforts are futile

By the summer of 1962, the script was completed; but strangely, when it was forwarded to an executive at Disney studios, it was rejected. This prompted Tytle to take it straight to Walt Disney himself, who approved it, but with a few revisions. By the time the script had been rewritten and reworked, Tytle and Disney had made the decision to use the story for a feature film, instead of the original intention of using it for television. But, since *The Jungle Book* was already in production, the story about the feline heirs to a fortune would have to wait.

A Film Worth the Wait

In 1966, work on the film, titled *The Aristocats*, finally began. The story remained much the same as Rowe's original idea, with a few changes: in Paris, a cat named Duchess lives with her three kittens, Marie, Berlioz, and Toulouse, in the mansion of retired opera singer Madame Adelaide Bonfamille. In her will, Madame leaves her fortune to Duchess and her kittens, and asks her butler, Edgar, to care for the cats for the rest of their lives. Only then will he have access to Madame's wealth. Edgar, unwilling to wait for the money, drugs the cats and leaves them out in the French countryside, but Duchess meets an alley cat named Thomas O'Malley who helps the aristocratic cats return to their home in Paris. In the end, Madame not only changes her will to exclude Edgar and include Thomas O'Malley, but she starts a charity to provide a home for Paris's stray cats.

When it was released at the end of 1970, *The Aristocats* was praised for the voice work of its actors, especially Eva Gabor, who provided the voice of the elegant, caring Duchess, and Phil Harris, who voiced the streetwise Thomas O'Malley. With charming feline characters and a happy ending, *The Aristocats* is worth a modern viewing by cat lovers young and old.

A Lion in Your Lap

Hollywood embraced 3-D technology in the 1950s to counter a decline at the box office.

✳ ✳ ✳ ✳

STEREOSCOPIC CINEMATOGRAPHY, OR 3-D, is a process that emphasizes the illusion of depth by making the foreground, middle ground, and background of an image seem separate or spatially distinct.

Imagery in 3-D existed as far back as the late 19th century, when stereoscopic photographs were available as popular parlor items. Hollywood dabbled with 3-D movies as early as the 1920s. However, 3-D is most frequently associated with the 1950s, when Hollywood embraced this process to counter a loss of revenue due to competition from television and a change in the makeup of the moviegoing audience. Studios were determined to give audiences spectacle and novelty—to offer something they couldn't get from television. The history of 3-D in Hollywood is tied to its value as a novelty.

Studios exploited the 3-D technique by producing films that featured spears, rocks, animals, and human fists flying toward the audience. In 1953, during the publicity for *Bwana Devil*—the film that jump-started the 3-D craze—Gulu Productions promised viewers "A lion in your lap!" Unfortunately, audiences didn't necessarily want lions in their laps, and they grew weary of having projectiles tossed toward them. Exploitative rather than imaginative, the 3-D effects often got in the way of story-telling and character development.

The stereoscopic process of the 1950s used polarized lenses to create the 3-D effect, and audiences wore polarized eyepieces to experience the binocular vision. The glasses caused headaches and eye strain. Between these negative physical effects and the lackluster moviemaking, 3-D waned in popularity after a mere 18 months.

Periodically, the film industry introduces an improved 3-D process, generally at a time when box office revenues are in decline. Yet 3-D is a filmmaking technology rather than a filmmaking technique; its obviousness interferes with standard filmmaking practices such as editing and *mise-en-scene*, dooming it to the margins of the industry.

Dick Whittington

The pantomime story of Dick Whittington and his cat is a British classic and has been told since the fifteenth century. Penniless Dick walked to London in search of fortune. He found work with a rich merchant and used his first earnings to buy a cat. When one of the merchant's trading vessels set sail, he asked all his servants to contribute something to sell. Poor Dick had only his cat, and he offered his companion reluctantly. He continued to work but became miserable and decided to run away. When he reached Highgate Hill, he heard the bells of the city calling "Turn again, Whittington, Lord Mayor of London." He returned and discovered the ship had traded on an island overrun with rats, which his cat had vanquished. Dick was rewarded with a princely sum in exchange for letting the king of the island keep his cat. (And in fact, a man named Dick Whittington did hold the office of Lord Mayor of London—four times.)

Who Is Catwoman?

Catwoman is a DC Comics character hailing from the Batman series.

❋　❋　❋　❋

ORIGINALLY KNOWN AS "The Cat" she was intended to be an antagonist for Batman. However, just like a real cat, her loyalties and motives were sometimes ambiguous, and she was known to abhor killing. Catwoman's "real" name is Selina Kyle, named after the ancient lunar deity Selene.

Julie Newmar played Catwoman for the first two seasons on TV, but Lee Meriwether replaced her for the movie, due to a scheduling conflict on Newmar's part. Eartha Kitt eventually replaced Newmar in the third season of the TV series.

Catwoman's costume has undergone numerous changes over the years. In the first season, she wore a theaterlike cat mask that covered her entire face. Later, she wore a dress, and soon after that she exchanged the dress for a bodysuit. The bodysuit was changed to green in the 1960s and a body-molding purple in the 1990s. The most popular catwoman suit of all time may be that worn by sultry actress Michelle Pfeiffer in the 1992 *Batman Returns* movie. *Catwoman* the movie, starring Halle Berry, was released in 2004, but the bikini-topped costume was generally agreed to look like something the cat dragged in.

Caterwauling

❋ One of the most famous pieces of "cat music" is Edward Lear's verse "The Owl and the Pussycat," set to music by Stravinsky.

* Rossini composed "Duetto Buffo Dei Due Gatti," a duet for two female singers who vocalize solely on the word meow.

* Domenico Scarlatti's "Cat Fugue" was inspired by his feline running over the piano keyboard. The cat's paw-tread became the underlying theme in the piece.

* Tchaikovsky's *Sleeping Beauty* ballet includes a beautiful pas de deux for two fairy-tale cat figures.

Do You Mind?

Cats often appeared as companions in the portraits of painters, including the works of Pierre-Auguste Renoir, Henri Rousseau, and Pierre Bonnard. But before them, Gottfried Mind (1767–1814) was the first painter to specialize in portraits of cats themselves rather than their owners. Mind always worked with his favorite cat nearby and her kittens draped over his shoulder. In 1809, an outbreak of rabies resulted in the destruction of all cats in the city. Mind managed to hide and save his beloved cat Minette.

It Was a Dark, Stormy Night . . .

Perhaps due to their feline mystique or their wily ways, cats have always been popular in "who-done-it" mystery novels, usually solving the crime despite the "help" of a bumbling human partner. Some "hair-raising" mystery books with cat protagonists:

* The Cat Who . . . series by Lilian Jackson Braun features detective James Owilleran and his twin Siamese cats Koko and Yum Yum.

* The Felidae novels by Akif Pirinçi feature Francis as the feline detective.

* Carole Nelson Douglas has brought fame to Midnight Louie and his daughter, Midnight Louise, in a series of novels that follow amateur human sleuth and cat lover Temple Barr.

* Author Rita Mae Brown coauthors her books with her cat Sneaky Pie Brown as they write about feline sleuth Mrs. Murphy.

* Shirley Rousseau Murphy's feline investigator, Joe Grey, gets help from his fellow talking cats, who call in tips to the local police.

* Marian Babson uses various feline finders in her novels.

Kellogg's Cats

Kellogg's first feline advertising success came along in 1914, when they used a picture of a child holding a gray cat alongside the slogan "For Kiddies not Kitties" to market Toasted Corn Flakes.

But their big hit came in 1952 when Tony the Tiger came bounding onto the scene as the spokesperson er, spokescat) for Kellogg's Sugar Frosted Flakes (later, just "Frosted Flakes"). Tony was originally one of four animated creatures in a campaign that included Katy the Kangaroo, Newt the Gnu, and Elmo the Elephant. But the blue-nosed, orange-and-black striped Tony—along with his trademark roar, "They're Grrrreat!"—quickly vaulted to solo status as the king feline of the cereal world.

The Enduring Love of *Cats*

At one time the longest running show on Broadway, Cats has been described as everything from ridiculous and nonsensical to exhilarating and brilliant. But one thing is certain: there is nothing else like it.

* * * *

Poetic Inspiration

IN 1977, FAMED composer Andrew Lloyd Webber, known for musicals including *Evita*, *Sunset Boulevard*, and *The Phantom of the Opera*, decided to write some songs based on T.S. Eliot's *Old Possum's Book of Practical Cats*. The book, published in 1939, features a collection of whimsical poems about the nature of cats, and features felines with fanciful names like Jennyanydots, Rum Tum Tugger, and Skimbleshanks.

Lloyd Webber considered the book a childhood favorite, and simply wanted to try setting some of the poems to music. At first, it was nothing more than an experiment, and he only shared his compositions with friends and family. But a few years later, he began considering expanding on what he'd written, and approached theater producer Cameron Mackintosh with the idea. After some brainstorming, Lloyd Webber came up with a whimsical plot to go along with the whimsical mood of Eliot's poems, and by spring 1981, the show was ready to open in London's West End. Investors refused to contribute to the show's budget, unconvinced that the public would embrace the strange story; but Lloyd Webber was so confident that his unusual musical would be a hit that he took out a second mortgage on his house and used his own money to finance it.

A Strange Plot

It's hard to blame those skeptical investors, though, who no doubt thought the plot of Cats was a bit quirky. The show, which is entirely sung-through, centers around what Eliot dubbed "Jellicle" cats. While neither Eliot nor Lloyd Webber makes it entirely clear what a "Jellicle" cat is, the term supposedly stemmed from Eliot's very young niece trying to pronounce "dear little cat." In Cats, these Jellicle cats gather in a junkyard one night and sing songs about their lives, with each cat hoping to be chosen to enter the Heaviside Layer—the cat version of heaven—where the chosen feline is reborn as a younger cat.

Overseeing these proceedings is a wise, elderly cat named Old Deuteronomy, and each cat gets a chance to state their case for why they should be chosen to ascend to the Heaviside Layer. The showstopper comes in the second act, when the old, disheveled Grizabella takes the stage and sings a melancholy plea to be chosen by the other cats. The song she sings, "Memory," is not only the best-known song in the show, but by some estimates is the most successful song ever written for a musical. Grizabella's impassioned song wins over the other cats, and she is chosen to ascend to the Heaviside Layer.

Nine Lives . . . and Beyond

With such an unusual, perhaps even silly, plotline, it may have surprised no one if *Cats* had been a bomb at the box office. But the show had the opposite effect, becoming an immediate hit. It ran for 21 years and 8,949 performances in London's West End, as well as 18 years and 7,485 performances on Broadway. In 1997, *Cats* became the longest-running show on Broadway, a record it held until 2006, when another Lloyd Webber musical, *The Phantom of the Opera*, surpassed it. The musical has been staged all over the world, translated into multiple languages, and was adapted into a film in 2019. While the film adaptation, which stared Judi Dench as Old Deuteronomy and Jennifer Hudson as Grizabella, was widely panned, there's little doubt that the magic of this musical will endure. After all, cats have nine lives.

The Animated Odd Couple

What do you get when you combine two different personalities into one? Well, in the case of the 1998 Nickelodeon animated show, you get the quirky CatDog.

✳   ✳   ✳   ✳

Two Heads, One Body

ACCORDING TO ONE story, Peter Hannan, the creator of the animated series *CatDog*, had an unusual dog when he was growing up. The dog, named Tipper, had lost a leg in a car accident, but managed life with three legs quite well. So well, in fact, that when Tipper accidentally got a leg caught in his collar one day, he was able to toddle home on two legs. Needless to say, Hannan, who is also known for creating the educational PBS series *Let's Go Luna!*, was no stranger to odd animals. And CatDog, the star of the series by the same name, is certainly an odd animal.

Years before Hannan came up with his concept for *CatDog*, he had been toying around with some ideas for a book about superheroes. He wanted the superheroes to be a bit inept and clumsy, not the usual confident crusaders we're used to seeing in the comics. One of these clumsy heroes was dubbed "The Amazing Catdog Man," and Hannan envisioned him as a character with a man's body and a cat and dog head. The two heads would argue with each other about how they should go about rescuing citizens in distress, but their arguing would distract them from their superhero duties. Hannan never finished the book, but the idea of two personalities sharing a body stuck with him. He eventually pitched the idea for *CatDog*, a show about conjoined twins—one a cat, one a dog—to Nickelodeon, and the show debuted in 1998.

Opposites Attract

The cat and dog in *CatDog*, who share the same body with no tails or hind legs, have wildly different personalities, giving the show a theme similar to Neil Simon's *The Odd Couple*. But in the case of *CatDog*, the two personalities are literally stuck together. Dog, voiced by Tom Kenny, is the more fun-loving, enthusiastic, and naïve character of the pair. Cat, voiced by Jim Cummings, is cunning and cantankerous, and, according to Hannan, was created to be the more "human" of the duo. A typical dog, Dog enjoys chasing cars, chewing on bones, and eating food, and frequently ignores Cat's warnings of looming trouble. Cat, on the other hand, prefers a calmer lifestyle, and enjoys reading, listening to music, and gardening. Easygoing Dog is well-liked by the other characters on the show, while uptight Cat is often ridiculed. Of course, the challenge for Cat and Dog is navigating life permanently stuck together, regardless of these differing personalities.

Enjoy the Show

The show aired its first episode on April 4, 1998, following the Kids' Choice Awards, and ran for 68 episodes over seven years. Set in the town of Nearburg, the show also featured characters like a Brooklyn-accented mouse named Winslow, a group of street dogs named Cliff, Shriek, and Lube, Eddie the squirrel, and Rancid the rabbit. But Cat and Dog were the main feature, drawing viewers in with their spats and exploits, while providing kids (and even adults!) with humor and heart. *CatDog* was nominated for an Annie Award in 1998, and for two Kids' Choice Awards in 1999 and 2000.

Amusingly, Hannan has said that the question he is most asked about *CatDog* is "how does CatDog go to the bathroom?" A fair question, since Cat and Dog are conjoined with no hind-quarters. The answer? Nobody knows, not even Hannan. He suggests that viewers set aside their disbelief and simply enjoy the show. Perhaps in the case of *CatDog*, it's best if some things remain a mystery.

Salem and the Silly Superstitions

The only character aside from the teen witch herself to appear in every episode of Sabrina the Teenage Witch, *Salem the cat was not only a loyal sidekick to Sabrina, but also a favorite character with fans of the show. His popularity continues on Netflix, where he appears on* Chilling Adventures of Sabrina.

✳ ✳ ✳ ✳

Unfairly Maligned

BLACK CATS HAVE long been associated with witches and have even been accused of being witches themselves. One of the earliest depictions of such a claim comes from a Middle Ages folklore tale that described an injured black cat who wandered into the house of a woman believed to be a witch. The next day, villagers saw the woman limping and bruised, and said that she and the cat were one and the same. Thus, the idea that a witch could turn into a black cat planted itself into the Middle Ages psyche, spreading across Europe like wildfire.

Other stories from the time suggested that while black cats weren't necessarily witches themselves, the fluffy felines were in cahoots with practitioners of dark magic, operating as assistants and companions to witches. Over time, black cats became symbols of evil and portents of bad luck, even when the innocent animals were just chasing mice or sleeping in piles of hay.

Regardless of how harmless they seemed, the superstitious belief that black cats are unlucky—and might even be witches—stuck around, and even today some people refuse to keep black cats as pets. But the irrational fears about the felines have also given us numerous stories, novels, films, and television shows that reflect these fears and beliefs.

Comic Relief Cat

Fortunately, the black cat trope isn't always taken so seriously these days. And there may have been no better depiction of a witch's helper than Salem Saberhagen, the American Shorthair cat who was featured in the 1990s show *Sabrina the Teenage Witch* starring Melissa Joan Hart. Salem's original appearance was actually decades earlier, in the 1962 comic *Archie's Mad House*. Surprisingly, he was first depicted as an orange tabby in the comic; but the creators of Sabrina decided to stick with the folklore and make Salem a black cat. They also created a history and backstory for the cat, and, although he was a silent sidekick in the comic, gave him the power of speech, complete with sassy one-liners and a sharp wit.

During the course of the show, viewers learn that Salem is a very old witch, perhaps as old as 500. (This may not be considered terribly old to a witch, however. After all, Sabrina's aunts are said to be 600 years old!) Twenty-five years before the beginning of the series, the human Salem attempted to take over the world using his supernatural powers. As a punishment, he was sentenced to 100 years as a cat and stripped of his magic. He becomes Sabrina's "familiar," an animal believed to assist witches in their practice of magic, and he provides much of the comic relief in the show.

Fan Favorite

Salem quickly became a fan favorite on *Sabrina*, winning the "Favorite Animal Star" award at the Kids' Choice Awards three years in a row. While four real black cats played the role throughout the show, animatronic cats were also used, especially when Salem spoke. But in the newer Netflix series *Chilling Adventures of Sabrina*, Salem is no longer a human trapped in a cat's body, but rather a familiar who, so far, does not speak. And sadly, Kiernan Shipka, the actress who plays Sabrina in *Chilling Adventures of Sabrina*, is allergic to cats, so her version of Sabrina isn't as cuddly with Salem as Hart's Sabrina.

Salem transformed the superstitious belief of the evil, cursed black cat into a cheeky, lovable character. *Sabrina the Teenage Witch* would not be the same without him!

The Coolest Cat on the Internet

Only in the age of the internet could a video of a cat playing a keyboard become an overnight sensation. But surprisingly, Keyboard Cat's road to stardom began long before Google, YouTube, and "meme" were household words.

✳ ✳ ✳ ✳

A Cat and a Camcorder

CHARLIE SCHMIDT WAS bored. The struggling graphic designer, who had studied art at Washington State University, was hanging out with friends and trying to come up a way to pass the time. But with little money to spend on recreation, the options were limited. So the group decided to pick up a video camera and take turns making silly videos just for fun, something the creative, artistic Schmidt enjoyed.

He had no idea, however, that the video he was about to make would one day change his life.

The year was 1984. At the time, videos had to be played on VCRs, and that was only if you were lucky enough to own one. The idea that one day videos would be shared around the globe instantaneously would've seemed like a crazy notion in the 80s. But that didn't stop camcorders from becoming hugely popular during the decade, and it certainly didn't stop amateur videographers from creating home movies.

After Schmidt's friends had played around with the camera, it was his turn to create a video; but first he needed inspiration. Glancing around his living room, he spotted his beloved orange tabby cat, Fatso, curled up next to his electronic keyboard, and he had an idea. First, he recorded a simple upbeat tune on the keyboard. Then he dressed Fatso in a little blue shirt, propped her up in front of the keys, and replayed the recorded song while he manipulated her legs under the shirt to make it look like she was playing the keyboard. The finished product made for a cute video and Schmidt and his friends had a laugh about it, but it was soon forgotten and stored in a plastic bin with other videos Schmidt had made.

A YouTube Star Is Born

Then, in 1998, 11 years after Fatso had passed away, Schmidt, who was now married with a two-year-old daughter named Sydney, made the smart decision to transfer all of his old videos to digital format. He also began sharing them with Sydney, who loved the video of Fatso at the keyboard. Seven years later, YouTube debuted, and soon people around the world were sharing videos of everything from mundane life moments to exciting vacation videos. Schmidt remembered how much Sydney had loved Fatso's video and thought maybe others would enjoy it, too, so on June 7, 2007, he uploaded his digital copy to YouTube with the title "Cool Cat."

Schmidt's video was being viewed dozens of times a day, but it wasn't until 2009, when it caught the attention of video website syndication manager Brad O'Farrell, that it reached viral status. O'Farrell got Schmidt's permission to add Fatso's video to the end of a blooper video, with the title *Play Him Off, Keyboard Cat.* The idea was that the video was like a version of a vaudevillian "hook" that removed unwanted performers from a stage.

Gone Viral

O'Farrell's version of the video made Schmidt, and Fatso, an overnight hit. Not only did the video start attracting millions of hits, but celebrities, brands, and news shows all wanted to know more about Keyboard Cat. The video was such a success that Schmidt went to an animal shelter and found another orange tabby, who he named Bento, to follow in Fatso's footsteps. Bento appeared in ads for Wonderful Pistachios, Delta, Starburst, and more, and even played in the halftime show of Animal Planet's 2014 Puppy Bowl.

Bento died in 2018, but Schmidt is continuing the Keyboard Cat tradition with a new tabby named Skinny, whose videos are posted to Schmidt's Keyboard Cat 2020 YouTube channel. The original Keyboard Cat video has amassed more than 60 million views and is still going strong.

A Feline Pastime

Almost a third of Americans own at least one cat, and there are more than 94 million furry felines living in households around the country. Is it any wonder that cats have become one of our favorite subjects on the internet?

✳ ✳ ✳ ✳

For the Love of Cats

O N MAY 22, 2005, YouTube co-founder Steve Chen uploaded the very first cat video to the site. Titled "Pajamas and Nick Drake," the video shows Pajamas the cat playing with a string while a Nick Drake song plays in the background. It may have been unremarkable, but the humble little video paved the way for what would soon be a rather strange obsession around the world: cats on the internet.

Surprisingly, the practice of using cats in memes is nothing new, going all the way back to the early days of photography. In the 1870s, photographers like Harry Pointer and Harry Whittier Frees created photos featuring cats in funny costumes, complete with amusing captions. Fast forward to the 2000s, and the same concept was launched on the internet in the form of "lolcats." A combination of "LOL" (laugh out loud) and "cat," lolcats became wildly popular when the website "I Can Has Cheezburger?" was launched in 2007. The site featured a collection of cat memes, most with funny, intentionally misspelled and grammatically incorrect captions.

Unintentionally Famous

Around the same time that lolcats began to entertain internet visitors, Keyboard Cat made her first appearance. The video of the orange tabby "playing" a keyboard became an overnight sensation, and suddenly, the internet wasn't just obsessed with random cats; they were obsessed with a specific cat. But Keyboard Cat wasn't the only musical cat to make waves online; she had some competition from Nora the Piano Cat, a gray tabby from Camden, New Jersey. In Nora's first YouTube video, she climbed up on her owner's piano bench and softly pawed the keys, creating a surprisingly melodious tune.

The next cat to take over the internet did so by, quite simply, being a cat. Maru, a Scottish Fold cat from Japan, made his first appearance on YouTube in 2008. Posted under the account "mugumogu," Maru's videos often feature the cat squeezing himself into small boxes or paper bags, and generally acting the way cats act. But the adorable feline has attracted a huge following, even earning a Guinness World Record for the most YouTube views of a single animal. Maru's videos have racked up more than 405 million views.

Cranky but Cute

But perhaps there is no more famous internet cat than the humorously nicknamed "Grumpy Cat." Officially named Tardar Sauce by her owner, Tabatha Bundesen, the cat was born in 2012 in Arizona. Tardar Sauce had a form of feline dwarfism, which made her undersized and gave her face an unusual appearance. When Bundesen posted a picture of her to the social news website Reddit, Tardar Sauce was immediately dubbed "Grumpy Cat" due to the permanent look of annoyance on her face. But it was a face that won the hearts of internet users around the world, and soon, Grumpy Cat was appearing on news shows, in advertisements, and at the famous South by Southwest (SXSW) festival in Austin, Texas. She even starred in her own made-for-television movie, titled *Grumpy Cat's Worst Christmas Ever*, which aired on the Lifetime network.

Sadly, Grumpy Cat died in 2019 at the age of seven. In her heyday, she was earning a six-figure salary for Bundesen, who took a leave of absence from her job to manage the popular cat's busy schedule. Today, Grumpy Cat's famous face can still be found on t-shirts, mugs, calendars, and other merchandise, proving that for some, internet fame is just one picture away.

Vote for a Cause

Politics can often be a contentious issue, with candidates trading insults and barbs, and voters feeling trapped into choosing between the "lesser of two evils." But a mayoral candidate in Halifax, Nova Scotia, in 2012 found a way to bring citizens together, while also raising money and awareness for a cause.

✳ ✳ ✳ ✳

A Problem with a Black and White Solution

RETIRED HALIFAX VETERINARIAN Hugh Chisholm and his wife, Kathy, were distressed about a problem in their city. All over Halifax, stray cats were living on the streets, encountering other stray cats, and having kittens, creating a never-ending cycle of feral felines. These cats wandered the city, enduring cold weather, predators, and the ever-present threat of cars and trucks, all while continuing to make the situation worse.

But the Chisholms realized there was something they could do about the sad state of feral cats in their city, and the key to their solution was living in their home. His name was Tuxedo Stan, a black and white cat who had come from the same lowly roots as the cats on the streets. Stan's mom was abandoned and pregnant with four kittens, but she was rescued and taken to a veterinary hospital. After Stan and his siblings were born, the Chisholms adopted him and the lucky kitten moved into a house with four other cats, two dogs, two guinea pigs, and several fish.

The Chisholms, knowing that most people love furry friends, started a political party they dubbed the "Tuxedo Party," and entered a candidate into the mayoral race in Halifax. The candidate? Tuxedo Stan! Stan, of course, already had plenty of experience with listening to different opinions, having grown up with his many animal siblings. And his platform was very straightforward: improving the lives of abandoned and neglected cats in the city. The Chisholms soon created stickers, posters, and t-shirts, proclaiming "Tuxedo Stan for Mayor; Because neglect isn't working," and the campaign was underway.

Clawing Their Way Into Office

It may be surprising to learn that Tuxedo Stan was not the first cat to run for office. It may be even more surprising to learn that some of these furry felines have won their political races. A cat named Stubbs was named mayor of the small Alaskan town of Talkeetna in 1997. Stubbs faithfully served his community for 20 years, drawing in tourists who were often eager to meet the "mayor." After his death in 2017, another cat, Denali, took his place. In 2018, a cat named Sweet Tart was elected to serve as mayor of Omena, Michigan. The small, unincorporated village holds regular elections, which are also fundraisers for the historical society, to select one of the citizens' pets to be mayor. And the quirky town of Guffey, Colorado, has two political parties: the DemoCATS and the RePUPlicans. Citizens of Guffey have elected dogs and cats to serve as mayors for decades, with the post currently held by Monster the cat.

Winning the Popular Vote

Obviously, Tuxedo Stan was in good company when his run for office began. He immediately drew the attention of local media, and soon everyone in Halifax knew about the cat running for mayor. At a party where he announced his candidacy, attendees were so enthusiastic it was standing room only. And soon, media worldwide picked up on the story, as well. Anderson Cooper and Ellen DeGeneres even publicly endorsed Tuxedo Stan, and his story was the talk of the internet.

Of course, as it turned out, municipal laws in Halifax require that candidates be human, so Tuxedo Stan's run was mostly symbolic. But the Tuxedo Party succeeded in its mission of calling attention to the plight of abandoned cats in Halifax, and Stan raised tens of thousands of dollars for local animal shelters and to provide spaying and neutering services. Stan died of kidney cancer in 2013, but his legacy lives on in the nonprofit

Tuxedo Party of Canada Cat Welfare Society, which continues to care for the cats of Halifax.

Cat in a Box

Quantum mechanics seems like a rather dry and heavy subject to those of us outside the scientific realm. But Austrian-Irish physicist Erwin Schrodinger's famous paradoxical "cat" thought experiment so thoroughly captured imaginations that even decades after its original description, Schrodinger's Cat is still found in our pop culture.

✳   ✳   ✳   ✳

Our Strange Universe

IN 1935, SCIENTISTS Albert Einstein, Boris Podolsky, and Nathan Rosen published an article, nicknamed the EPR Article, in which they discussed the odd behaviors of quantum superpositions. This principle of quantum mechanics states that a physical system can be in one of many configurations, and until the system is observed and measured, its properties are not well defined. So, it is said to exist in a "superposition" of states, with any of its possible states being just as likely as any others. In fact, a theory called the Copenhagen interpretation suggests that particles on a microscopic level do not have any properties until they are observed or measured.

Einstein was troubled by the uncertainty of such an idea. How would the universe know if it was being observed or measured? He and Schrodinger, who had won the Nobel Prize in physics in 1933 for his work in quantum mechanics, exchanged letters about the topic. Like Einstein, Schrodinger felt that the idea of particles being in a state of superposition until they are observed seemed absurd. And to illustrate this absurdity, he came up with a thought experiment.

Illustrating Absurdity

In a paper titled "The Current Situation in Quantum Mechanics," Schrodinger wrote about what he called a "ridiculous" scenario in which a cat is closed in a steel box. Inside the box there is a sealed vial of cyanide, a small amount of radioactive material, a Geiger counter, and a suspended hammer. During the course of the experiment – Schrodinger suggested it be left alone for one hour – the radioactive substance may or may not decay. If it does, the Geiger counter triggers the hammer to break the vial of poison, and the cat dies. But there is just as much of a chance that the radioactive substance will not decay, and the cat will live. Since the only way to know if the cat has lived or died is to open the box and observe the cat, quantum mechanics would suggest that the cat is in a state of superposition, and can be thought of as both alive and dead.

Of course, Schrodinger's experiment has never literally been carried out, and certainly no scientist would be cruel enough to try it. But the idea of the living and dead cat in the box immediately sparked discussions in the scientific community. Einstein even brought it up again in a 1950 letter to Schrodinger, proving that the paradoxical nature of superposition continued to vex the scientific community.

Living (or Dying) in Pop Culture

But perhaps even more interesting than Schrodinger's Cat itself is the effect the thought experiment had on pop culture. The cat has been mentioned numerous times in literature and has been especially popular with science fiction writers. Douglas Adams, best known for *The Hitchhiker's Guide to the Galaxy*, wrote about the cat in *Dirk Gently's Holistic Detective Agency*. Likewise, bestselling authors Terry Pratchett and Neil Gaiman have made references to the famous experiment in their novels.

Schrodinger's Cat has also popped up in poetry and artwork, and has been referenced in films like *Mean Girls 2*, *The Prestige*, and *Repo Men*, and in television shows including *Rick and*

Morty, *Stargate SG-1*, *Futurama*, and *Bones*. But perhaps the most famous references have come from the popular television show *The Big Bang Theory*, where the cat is mentioned in several episodes. Schrodinger's cat may not exist, but it's certainly one of the most famous felines in the world.

Fat Cat

First published in 1978, Garfield has become one of the world's most widely syndicated comic strips. The popularity of the lasagna-loving cat has spawned television shows, films, video games, and even a food delivery service, and Garfield's creator, Jim Davis, has won multiple awards for the comic.

✳   ✳   ✳   ✳

The Early Comics

CARTOONIST JIM DAVIS was born in Marion, Indiana, in 1945, and grew up on a farm in nearby Fairmount. While attending Fairmount High School in the 1960s, he drew his first comic strip, which appeared in the school's 1963 yearbook. This was the first hint of his future career in art and comics.

By 1969, Davis was assisting with artist Tom Ryan's comic strip *Tumbleweeds*, and in 1973, he created his own strip, titled *Gnorm Gnat*. The comic, which featured a group of insects, was published for three years in *The Pendleton Times* in Pendleton, Indiana, but Davis was unable to sell the strip for syndication. After an editor told him that bugs weren't "relatable," he put *Gnorm Gnat* aside and began drawing a new strip. The new strip, titled *Jon*, focused on a man of the same name who owned a wisecracking, orange tabby-striped cat. The cat delivered the punchline in each strip, and Davis soon realized that his comic strip wasn't actually about Jon, it was about Jon's cat: Garfield.

A Huge Success

On September 1, 1977, United Feature Syndicate accepted *Garfield* for national distribution, and the first strip made its nationwide debut on June 19, 1978, in 41 newspapers. The strip was an immediate hit, drawing fans in with Garfield's snarky attitude, rotund belly, and unusual love of lasagna. It was so popular that the *Chicago Sun–Times* was inundated with complaints after they decided to drop the comic strip, and they were forced to reinstate it to keep readers happy.

Other publications soon caught on to *Garfield's* popularity, and within three years, the strip appeared in 850 newspapers. Davis also founded a comic studio called Paws, Inc., to help him keep up with the burgeoning success of his creation, which had brought in $15 million in merchandise. But *Garfield* was far from finished: after decades of steady growth, *Garfield* earned the Guinness World Record in 2002 for being the world's most widely syndicated comic strip, appearing in more than 2,500 newspapers and journals.

A Cat with Character

Davis modeled Garfield – and named him – after his own grandfather, James A. Garfield Davis, a man Davis called "large and cantankerous." His grandfather was named after President James A. Garfield, giving everyone's favorite wisecracking cat a presidential connection. Another inspiration for the comic strip came from Davis's upbringing on his family's farm, which was home to 25 cats. He reportedly incorporated characteristics from several of his furry childhood friends into the Garfield character.

Garfield has appeared in films, television shows, and commercials, and has been featured on a huge amount of merchandise, making the *Peanuts* characters his only rivals in comic character profitability. All of the *Garfield* comic strip books have reached number one on the *New York Times* Bestseller list, with 1980's *Garfield at Large* spending an astounding 100 weeks at number one. But perhaps most interesting are the Garfield-themed "ghost restaurants" that opened in Dubai and Toronto in 2018 and 2019. These "restaurants" are actually food delivery services in which customers order online through apps. Available for delivery are Garfield-shaped pizzas, Garfield-shaped chocolate bars, "Garfuccinos," and, of course, lasagna. The app even allows users to play games or watch Garfield television shows while they wait for their food.

Today, Davis is mostly retired, but he has a team of cartoonists who help bring Garfield to life. For those who grew up with *Garfield*, it's reassuring to know that the fat cat will stick around for a while, and that new generations can be introduced to the wisecracking, lasagna-loving character.

Friends Forever

Many kids have a favorite stuffed toy that fuels their imagination, becoming a sleepover buddy, car ride companion, and a comforting presence during scary thunderstorms. And there may be no comic strip that better captured the silliness, the humor, and the importance of "furever" friends than Calvin and Hobbes.

✳ ✳ ✳ ✳

A Shaky Start

DRAWING CALVIN AND *Hobbes* was not cartoonist Bill Waterson's first choice for a career. Although he loved art and drew his first cartoon at the age of eight, Waterson, who was born in Washington, D.C., planned to use his talents to draw political cartoons. He attended Kenyon College in Gambier, Ohio, and graduated with a degree in political science in 1980, intending to use his degree as a way to get his foot in the door of editorial cartooning.

One of Waterson's influences was the work of editorial cartoonist Jim Borgman, who worked for *The Cincinnati Enquirer* and encouraged Waterson in his ambitions. Shortly after graduating from Kenyon, Waterson was hired by the *Enquirer's* competitor, *The Cincinnati Post*. But the job turned out to be much more challenging than he'd realized, especially since the Washington, D.C. native knew relatively little about the Cincinnati political scene. He was fired nearly before the ink on his cartoons was dry.

A Boy and His Tiger

Disillusioned by the political cartoon scene, Waterson moved on to advertising, but he wasn't much happier there. In his spare time, he began drawing comic strips in the hopes that someone would want to syndicate his work. After he drew a strip that included a brief appearance by a little boy with a stuffed tiger, an editor encouraged him to feature the two as main characters. Waterson obliged, and on November 18, 1985, the first *Calvin and Hobbes* comic strip was published in 35 newspapers across the country. It took less than a year for the instantly popular comic to reach 250 papers, including some outside the United States.

And it's not hard to understand the appeal of *Calvin and Hobbes*. The strip features the adventures of Calvin, a mischievous, precocious six-year-old boy, and his stuffed tiger, Hobbes, who comes to life – but only for Calvin – and shares in the antics of his best friend. While Calvin, who Waterson has described as "a little too intelligent for his age," is the main character in the comic, it is the anthropomorphic Hobbes who adds elements of heart and friendship to each strip. Seen as a regular stuffed tiger to the other characters in the comic, which include Calvin's parents and his classmate Susie Derkins, Hobbes morphs into a living tiger when he is alone with Calvin. He is the more reasonable of the pair, often warning Calvin that one of his schemes might not be the best idea, but in the end, he usually goes along with the mischief anyway.

Is He Real?

Waterson modeled Hobbes after his own cat, Sprite, who had a playful personality and a habit of jumping out of nowhere to scare his owner. He incorporated this feline attitude into Hobbes, who occasionally attacks Calvin by pouncing on him and tackling him to the ground. Hobbes revels in his feline prowess, often saying how lucky he is to be a tiger and not human, giving the impression that he, like Calvin, also believes he is alive. Waterson never confirms whether or not Hobbes is real, preferring to leave that up to the reader to decide.

The last *Calvin and Hobbes* comic strip was published on December 31, 1995, to the disappointment of its many fans. But Waterson believes he ended the strip at just the right time, preferring to end on a high note. And with 18 *Calvin and Hobbes* books on the market, including a complete collection of the strips encompassing 1,440 pages, fans can continue to laugh at the antics of Calvin and his imaginary (or possibly real) tiger Hobbes for years to come.

Made in Japan

With an instantly recognizable face that adorns more than 50,000 products in 130 countries, Hello Kitty is one of the most ubiquitous cartoon characters in the world. What makes this cat (who, surprisingly, may not actually be a cat) so popular?

✴ ✴ ✴ ✴

Cuteness Sells

IN 1962, SHINTARO Tsuji, the founder of the Yamanashi Silk Company in Japan, was looking to expand his new company's products. Tsuji decided to add rubber sandals to the company's offerings, painting them with colorful flowers. The cute design was a huge hit, and Tsuji wondered how else he might be able to capitalize on the success of the sandals, especially considering the *kawaii* culture in Japan.

Kawaii is the Japanese love of all things "cute," and its modern practice can be traced back to the 1950s, when illustrator Rune Naito found fame for his drawings of "baby-faced" girls and cartoon animals. Tsuji hired several designers to create "cute" characters for his merchandise, and over the next decade, the Yamanashi Silk Company grew, until silk was no longer its focus. Tsuji changed the name of the company to Sanrio in 1973, and the company became well-known for its cute merchandise that centered around gift-giving occasions.

Well, Hello There!

In 1974, designer Yuko Shimizu created a new character: a simple, white, cat-like character with a bow in her hair, and, interestingly, no mouth. Shimizu named the character after a passage in Lewis Carroll's *Through the Looking Glass*, when Alice plays with a cat she calls Kitty. But Tsuji also wanted the new character to reflect Sanrio's motto, "social communication," and added "Hello" to the name, dubbing it Hello Kitty.

Hello Kitty made her first appearance on a vinyl coin purse in 1974, which immediately sold well in Japan. Two years later, the character was introduced to America, and soon, Hello Kitty's rise in popularity reached stratospheric heights. Although she was originally marketed toward young girls, the character gained newfound popularity among teens and even adults by the 1990s, as those who remembered her from childhood purchased Hello Kitty merchandise with a sense of nostalgia. Recognizing the character's appeal to older consumers, Sanrio began licensing Hello Kitty for a more mature audience. Instead of only finding the cute face on dolls, stickers, and school supplies, Hello Kitty could also be found on laptops, televisions, and expensive jewelry.

By 2014, more than 50,000 Hello Kitty product lines were available, covering everything from clothing and greeting cards to watches and wine. The cute character has been painted onto several commercial planes, and Hello Kitty cafes are found in many locations around the world, including in Seoul, South Korea, Adelaide, Australia, and Irvine, California.

A Big Surprise

According to Sanrio, Hello Kitty was created to be a symbol of friendship to everyone, regardless of nationality or gender. Her missing mouth means she can't speak in any language (her creators say this is so she can "speak from the heart"), making her appeal universal. But it may be surprising to learn that Hello Kitty, with her pointy ears, whiskers, and seemingly paw-like appendages, is not meant to be a cat at all, but rather a girl. The character's creators say that her full name is Kitty White, she was born in London, England, and she has a twin sister named Mimmy. Kitty dreams of being a pianist or a poet, and she loves her mother's apple pie (although how she eats it without a mouth is unexplained). She even has a pet cat of her own, named Charmmy Kitty.

But while the revelation that this beloved cute cat is not, in fact, a cat may have shocked some fans, it certainly has not lessened Hello Kitty's popularity.

A Finicky Icon

Quite possibly the most famous cat in advertising, Morris the cat has been the face of 9Lives cat food for decades. With his handsome looks, snarky attitude, and rags-to-riches story, Morris is quite the character!

✳ ✳ ✳ ✳

The Search for Morris

IT WAS 1968, and the creative team at Chicago-based advertising agency Leo Burnett was thinking about cat food. The agency, known for creating memorable commercial characters including the Keebler Elves, the Pillsbury Doughboy, and Kellogg's Tony the Tiger, had just landed the 9Lives cat food account, with an ad campaign about "the world's most finicky cat." Now they just needed to find a "spokescat" to be the face of the brand.

Professional animal trainer Bob Martwick was tasked with the assignment of finding the perfect cat for the "finicky" role, so he headed out to the Hinsdale Humane Society, an animal shelter near Chicago. There, Martwick told staff members about the 9Lives campaign and explained the kind of cat he was looking for, and the Hinsdale staff immediately thought of Lucky, an orange tabby living at the shelter. When Martwick met Lucky, he was struck by the cat's charming demeanor, and set up an audition for the furry feline. At his casting call, the affable Lucky jumped up on a table, sauntered over to the art director, and gave him a head bump. After the audition, the delighted art director exclaimed, "He's the Clark Gable of cats!" And Lucky—who certainly lived up to his name—was about to go from a shelter cat without a home to a famous star.

Top Star

The first commercial featuring Lucky, who was renamed Morris, debuted in 1969. Voiced by John Erwin, who was also known for performing the voice of He-Man, Morris exuded the pickiness that many cats are known for, refusing all food except 9Lives. The public loved the cat's finicky, sarcastic persona, and over the next nine years, Morris appeared in 58 television commercials. The cat was so popular that a secretary was hired to read through and answer his mountains of fan mail. He even had the opportunity to star in Hollywood films, making his debut in the comedy *The Long Goodbye*, then appearing alongside Burt Reynolds in *Shamus*, both released in 1973. The talented feline was also awarded two PATSY awards—which stands for Picture Animal Top Star of the Year or Performing Animal Television Star of the Year—for his work in television and film.

Cat with a Cause

Inevitably, Lucky, the original Morris the cat, passed away in 1978 at the age of 17. But that wasn't the end of Morris. Martwick found a second cat to play the part in 1979, adopting him from another shelter. Three cats have played the part of Morris so far, all of them rescues. In fact, pet adoption has become one of Morris's favorite causes, and in 2006, he became the "spokescat" for a campaign called Morris' Million Cat Rescue, a 9Lives-sponsored effort to find loving homes for shelter cats. Morris also "authored" three books about cat care.

Morris even gained fame overseas, when his 9Lives commercials began airing on British television in the late 1970s. Amusingly, his voice in Britain was provided by television presenter Johnny Morris, leading some viewers to assume the cat had been named after him. But Morris is a unique personality in his own right, a fact that was honored in 2015 at the Museum of Broadcast Communications in Chicago. Morris was one of 10 mascots named in "A Salute to Advertising's Greatest Icons." Today, Morris can be found on Twitter and Facebook, where he continues to advocate for pet adoptions.

The Furry Face of Evil

It's a common movie trope for the evil mastermind in a film to have a cat sidekick, like Vito Corleone and his cat Cannoli in The Godfather, *or Dolores Umbridge and her office full of cats in the* Harry Potter *series. And the* Austin Powers *films, written and produced by their star, Mike Myers, were no exception, introducing filmgoers to Mr. Bigglesworth.*

✳ ✳ ✳ ✳

Bond and Blofeld

Any JAMES BOND fan is familiar with the superspy's arch nemesis, Ernst Stavro Blofeld. Appearing in three James Bond novels and seven films, Blofeld is the head of the evil corporation SPECTRE, an acronym

for Special Executive for Counter-intelligence, Terrorism, Revenge, and Extortion. As if running an international organized crime syndicate wasn't enough, Blofeld was also responsible for murdering the only woman Bond ever married, Tracy, in *On Her Majesty's Secret Service*. Needless to say, the two share a mutual dislike and distrust of each other.

Blofeld, who has been played by various actors throughout the James Bond franchise including Donald Pleasance, Telly Savalas, Max Von Sydow, and, most recently, Christoph Waltz, is not only known for his ongoing conflict with Bond. He is also known for his ever-present sidekick, a white Persian cat who made its first appearance in 1963's *From Russia With Love*. In fact, in this first introduction to the character of Blofeld, the audience is not shown the evil mastermind's face; we only see the cat. Interestingly, the cat is not a part of Blofeld's character in the James Bond books. But legend has it that director Terence Young added the cat so that viewers would have something to look at during Blofeld's scenes. It was a smart decision: The image of Blofeld calming stroking his Persian cat while simultaneously planning Bond's destruction became an iconic part of the film series.

Iconic Parody

It was such an iconic image that when actor, producer, and screenwriter Mike Myers created the *Austin Powers* franchise, he made sure his villain had a cat. In the *Austin Powers* films, which Myers has said were created in part as an homage to James Bond, the British spy title character faces off with his adversary, the aptly named Dr. Evil. And of course, being the villain, Dr. Evil has a cat, with the not-so-evil name Mr. Bigglesworth.

When he is first introduced in *Austin Powers: International Man of Mystery*, Mr. Bigglesworth, like Blofeld's cat, is a long-haired white Persian who sits on Dr. Evil's lap. But at the end of the movie, Dr. Evil and Mr. Bigglesworth are forced to escape in a cryogenic chamber, where they remain frozen for 30 years. After they are thawed out for the sequel, *Austin Powers: The Spy Who Shagged Me*, Mr. Bigglesworth, like Dr. Evil, is bald, thanks to "an error in the thawing process."

Are the Puns Too Much?

This bald cat is, of course, a Sphynx, a breed that is naturally hairless, and the cat used for the part was humorously named Ted Nudegent. But Ted wasn't the only Sphynx to appear in the film: After Dr. Evil creates a miniature clone of himself called Mini-Me, played by actor Verne Troyer, the clone also gets a (much smaller) cat sidekick. Mini-Me's cat was dubbed—what else?—Mini Mr. Bigglesworth, and he was played by a trio of kittens named Mel Gibskin, Skindiana Jones, and Paul Nudeman.

It may seem like Ted Nudegent had an easy acting job, since his character's part called for simply lying in a lap. But his trainer, Tammy Maples, pointed out that cats are notoriously difficult to train. Still, Ted delivered a star performance as the other actors hammed it up for the camera, sometimes staying still for 45 minutes at a time, and even occasionally dozing off in Myers' lap. Perhaps life as an evil mastermind's sidekick isn't so bad.

Goodbye, Dick and Jane

With more than 10 million copies printed, Dr. Seuss's classic The Cat in the Hat *is arguably one of the best-known, and best-loved, books ever written. So how did this simple bit of prose skyrocket to such great success?*

✳ ✳ ✳ ✳

The Doctor Is In

THEODORE SEUSS GEISEL was forced to come up with a pen name after a rather scandalous event. In the early 1920s, the young Geisel was attending Dartmouth College, where he was the editor-in-chief of the school's humor magazine, the *Dartmouth Jack-O-Lantern*. One night, Geisel was caught drinking gin in his dorm room with several friends. Since this was during Prohibition, the penalty was extra harsh: Geisel was forbidden from working on the school magazine. So, to work around this banishment, Geisel began writing for the magazine under a pen name: Seuss. Several years later, after accepting a job as a writer and illustrator for the magazine *Judge*, he added "Dr." to the name, and an icon was born.

Dr. Seuss began his career by drawing political cartoons, and later he drew illustrations for advertising agencies. But in 1936, he published his first children's book, *To Think That I Saw It on Mulberry Street*. This was followed by *If I Ran the Zoo*, *Horton Hears a Who!*, and *If I Ran the Circus*. Dr. Seuss was becoming a household name.

Limited Vocabulary

But as Dr. Seuss's books were gaining popularity, another set of children's books were being criticized. In 1954, an article in *Life* magazine lamented the use of "Dick and Jane" primers in elementary school classrooms, questioning why children only had these "boring" books to read, and not the "strange and wonderful" characters found in stories by illustrators like Walt Disney and Dr. Seuss.

When the director of Houghton Mifflin's education division, William Spaulding, read the article, he had an idea. He contacted Dr. Seuss and challenged him to create an exciting children's book using only a limited vocabulary of around 200 words. Dr. Seuss accepted, but the task turned out to be more demanding than he'd imagined. After struggling to come up with a story, he finally simply chose the first two rhyming words on the list—cat and hat—and began crafting a story around them. The finished story, titled *The Cat in the Hat*, used just 236 different words.

"Strange and Wonderful"

In the story, two children are stuck at home alone on a rainy day, when suddenly, an anthropomorphic cat in a red and white striped top hat appears. The Cat offers to show the children some tricks he knows, to the objection of their pet fish, but the Cat begins entertaining the children anyway. He then brings in a box that contains two blue-haired characters, Thing One and Thing Two, who wreak havoc around the house. When the children see their mother returning home, the Cat in the Hat quickly cleans up the mess, to the amazement of the children and their fish, and leaves just before their mother arrives.

Not only was *The Cat in the Hat* an immediate hit when it was released in 1957, it led to the creation of publishing house Beginner Books, which produced similar books to help kids learn to read. Dr. Seuss later said that this was the book he was most proud of, because it helped to end the reign of the Dick and Jane primers. Ten million copies of the book have been printed in more than 12 languages, and it has spawned television shows, a live-action film, a stage play, and even a Russian cartoon. All of this would be impressive for any book; but for a book that only uses 236 different words, it's remarkable.

Fables, Felines, and Footwear

Most of us have heard of, if not seen, the 2011 DreamWorks Animation film Puss in Boots, *featuring the voice of Antonio Banderas as the titular cat. But it might be surprising to discover that the origins of the cat with the fancy footwear go back hundreds of years.*

✳   ✳   ✳   ✳

A Goose and a Cat

IN A COLLECTION of Hindu tales from the second century titled *Panchatantra*, or "Five Principles," stories about various animals, including cats, are used as a way to convey morality and a concept called *niti*, which is translated as "the wise conduct of life." In short, *Panchatantra* is one of the earliest examples of animal fables. Today, we often think of "Mother Goose" when we think of animal fables, and our concept of an old woman telling stories to captivated children owes its existence to one tale in particular: *Puss in Boots*.

The earliest version of this feline fable traces back to the mid-1500s, when Italian writer Giovanni Francesco Straparola included the tale in a collection of stories called *The Facetious Nights of Straparola*. The work is often cited as being the first European book to contain fairytales, and Straparola is said to have influenced writers like the Brothers Grimm. His work also influenced French writer Charles Perrault, who included the "puss in boots" story in his 1697 publication, *Histoires ou contes du temps passé, avec des moralités* or *Contes de ma mère l'Oye*.

This wordy title translates to *Stories or Tales from Past Times, with Morals* or *Mother Goose Tales*, and the earliest English editions include a drawing of an old woman telling stories to a group of children. Mother Goose soon became synonymous with fairytales and fables. And the most famous fable in Perrault's collection was "The Master Cat" or "The Booted Cat," which later became known simply as "Puss in Boots."

A Crafty Cat with an Enduring Story

In Perrault's story, a miller dies and leaves each of his three sons an inheritance. The oldest son is given a mill, the middle son a donkey, and the youngest son a cat. At first, the youngest son is unhappy with his inheritance and considers killing the cat; but the cat promises to make his young master rich if he will spare his life. When his master agrees, the cat asks for a pair of boots, which he then dons before setting off on cunning adventures.

First, the cat traps rabbits and other game animals and gifts them to the king, saying they are from his fictional master, the Marquis de Carabas. The mysterious, generous benefactor intrigues the king. The cat then arranges an "accidental" meeting between his master and the king's daughter, who immediately falls in love with the "Marquis de Carabas." Together, the king, his daughter, and the master take a carriage ride on a country road, where the cat runs ahead and orders the farmers and peasants in the area to say that the land belongs to the Marquis de Carabas.

Finally, the cat stumbles upon a castle occupied only by a magical ogre, who can transform himself into any animal. The cat tricks him into transforming into a mouse, and quickly dispatches him, leaving the castle empty. When the king's carriage arrives, the king believes he is at the home of the Marquis de Carabas and allows his daughter to wed the cat's master. Just like the cat promised, he has made his master rich.

Puss in Boots is one of the most popular fairytales featuring an animal "donor," which is a type of character that helps, or provides magical assistance, to the hero of a story. Its popularity has stood the test of time, inspiring artwork, songs, picture books, animated shorts, a television series, and of course, feature films.

For the Love of Cats

T.S. Eliot wrote some of the best-known dramatic poems and plays in the English language, including The Love Song of J. Alfred Prufrock *and* The Waste Land, *earning him a Nobel Prize in Literature in 1948. But when it came to writing for fun, one of his favorite subjects was much less serious and much more frivolous: cats.*

✳ ✳ ✳ ✳

A Feline Obsession

IN 1982, JUST before the Andrew Lloyd Webber musical *Cats* opened on Broadway with the largest advanced ticket sales the industry had ever seen, T.S. Eliot's widow, Valerie, told the press that her late husband was an animal lover. He loved dogs, as many people do, and he also had an affinity for pigs.

He even wrote a few poems about pigs, which is an honor rarely afforded the mud-caked creatures. But Eliot's true love was neither canine nor porcine; it was feline. In fact, some Eliot scholars have insisted that the writer was "obsessed" with the furry animals.

This "obsession" prompted Eliot to begin writing whimsical poems about cats in the 1930s. At first, he only shared the verses with his young godchildren and the children of several of his associates at Faber and Faber, the London publishing house where he worked. He signed the poems "Old Possum," a nickname given to him by fellow poet Ezra Pound. The fanciful poems were later collected and published in a book, *Old Possum's Book of Practical Cats*, in 1939.

What's in a Name?

The collection of poems—originally 14, with a fifteenth poem added in the 1952 edition—use nonsense verse to profile the eccentricities and quirks of felines. With titles like "The Old Gumbie Cat," "Growltiger's Last Stand," and "Mungojerrie and Rumpleteazer," even a cursory glance at the verses provides a reader with a taste of the imaginative world Eliot created.

The first poem in the collection, titled "The Naming of Cats," kicks things off with the emphatic declaration that "a cat must have THREE DIFFERENT NAMES." One is an "everyday" name, one is "particular," and the last name is "secretive." According to the poem, "everyday" names can include "Peter, Augustus, Alonzo, or James," or "fancier" names, like, "Plato, Admetus, Electra" or "Demeter." Eliot's "particular" names are a bit more imaginative, including invented monikers like "Quaxo," "Bombalurina," and "Jellylorum." But the "secretive" names are just that: a secret. These "deep and inscrutable" names are known only to cats themselves.

Book to Musical

Despite the obvious fun and whimsy found in Eliot's poems, *Old Possum's Book of Practical Cats* attracted little attention when it was first published. Some readers, familiar with the writer's more serious work, even wondered if Eliot was a bit out of his mind, considering he published such a strange and silly work just as the world was grappling with the outbreak of war. But the truth was that Eliot, as his widow would state years later, simply loved cats.

And surprisingly, Eliot's love of felines spilled over into his other works, as well. For instance, a description of fog in *The Love Song of J. Alfred Prufrock* uses decidedly cat-like language. In the poem, the fog "made a sudden leap," before it "curled once about the house and fell asleep." Similarly, Eliot mentions cats in the poems *Rhapsody on a Windy Night and Five-Finger Exercises*, and in the play *The Rock*.

Eliot's quirky cat poetry may have faded into obscurity had it not been for one particular fan of his work: Andrew Lloyd Webber. Lloyd Webber's musical *Cats* opened in London in 1981 and on Broadway in 1982, and featured lyrics that came straight from *Old Possum's Book of Practical Cats*. Thanks to the musical, generations of theater-goers have been introduced to a fanciful feline world, first envisioned by a poet who really, *really* loved cats.

Cats in the Belfry

It's a common trope: an old woman, living alone, possibly crazy, and surrounded by cats. But how did the idea of the "crazy cat lady" start? And more importantly, can this negative stereotype be transformed into a positive one?

✳ ✳ ✳ ✳

Single with Cats

IF YOU'VE EVER watched the animated show *The Simpsons*, you are no doubt familiar with the character of Eleanor Abernathy. The character is a gray-haired, unkempt old woman, who is dressed in a frumpy outfit and often speaks nothing but gibberish. But Eleanor's most striking characteristic is, of course, the fact that she is always covered in cats.

And Eleanor Abernathy is far from the only "crazy cat lady" in pop culture. In the television comedy *The Office*, the character Angela Martin, often depicted as stodgy, stern, and dull, loves her cats so much that she keeps an eye on them with a nanny cam. Robert De Niro once donned a gray wig and an oversized sweatshirt to play the role of "Margie," a *Saturday Night Live* character who sat on an afghan-covered couch with her cadre of cats. And in an episode of *30 Rock*, Tina Fey's hilarious protagonist Liz Lemon decides to embrace "spinsterhood" by wearing a fanny pack, putting her hair up with a chip clip, and adopting a cat she names Emily Dickinson.

Dark Roots

While these examples are certainly amusing, the stereotype of the "crazy cat lady" has some dark roots. All the way back to the dark ages, in fact. In medieval times, cats were often believed to be associated with witches, and sometimes were even thought to be witches themselves. Folkloric tales told of witches who transformed into cats, and vice versa, giving women who owned cats a bad reputation. Especially women who lived alone, since no one could vouch for their comings and goings. Who was to say whether the lonely woman in the village turned into a cat at night, roaming the streets, mumbling curses?

Over time, that fearsome idea of a "crazy cat lady," morphed into the stereotype of the lonely, frumpy woman we know today. Although no longer associated with witchcraft, being called a "crazy cat lady" isn't always a compliment. And unfortunately, there is a certain element of truth found in the idea. For instance, while men and women are equally affected by generalized hoarding disorder, women are three times more likely than men to succumb to animal hoarding. These sorts of facts have made the "crazy cat lady" stereotype stick around, giving it a ring of plausibility while projecting a negative image.

Flip the Script

But recently, a new trend is emerging: call them crazy, but cool, cat ladies. A younger generation of cat lovers have embraced both their cats and modern media, in an effort to take the "crazy cat lady" moniker and turn it on its head. Books like *Girls & Their Cats*, by BriAnne Wills, and *Cat Lady Chic* by Diane Lovejoy feature photographs of successful, independent, and career-driven women and their cats. Magazines like *Cat People* interview fashion designers, artists, and writers about their love of cats. And CatCon Worldwide, a conference celebrating all things feline, states that one of its goals is "changing the negative perception of the 'crazy cat lady' and proving that it is possible to be hip, stylish, and have a cat, simultaneously."

While the image of the "crazy cat lady" will no doubt continue to be used for laughs, those of us who love our cats know there's no shame in the label. And now that popular culture is starting to agree, it may not be long before the world understands that "crazy" cat ladies are perfectly sane.

A Twist on *Twist*

The twenty-seventh film developed by Walt Disney Feature Animation, Oliver & Company *was released in 1988 and featured the voices of Joey Lawrence and Billy Joel. The film reimagined the classic story of* Oliver Twist, *featuring an adorable kitten in the role of the street savvy orphan.*

❋   ❋   ❋   ❋

A Timeless Classic

IN CHARLES DICKENS' classic novel *Oliver Twist*, the title character is a young orphaned boy who is raised in a workhouse, where he and the other orphans in the house are treated horribly. Eventually, Oliver runs away and makes his way to London, where he meets a pickpocket by the name of Jack Dawkins, who is better known by his nickname, "the Artful Dodger." The Dodger tells Oliver that he knows of an "old gentleman" who will provide him with food and lodging. The "gentleman" turns out to be a criminal named Fagin, and before he knows it, Oliver is ensnared in Fagin's world of pickpockets and robbers. But happily, after some struggle and hardship, Oliver is adopted by a kindly man named Mr. Brownlow, and at last has a family of his own.

The classic story has sparked dozens of adaptations, including six silent film versions, a musical, several full-length movies, and at least three miniseries. So it's no surprise that in 1985, when CEO of the Walt Disney Company Michael Eisner and studio chairman Jeffrey Katzenberg were looking for new ideas for animated films, a story artist named Pete Young suggested creating "Oliver Twist with dogs." Katzenberg loved the idea and approved the project, handing over directing duties to George Scribner. Scribner decided to make one change, however: instead of a dog, Oliver would be an abandoned kitten.

An Old Story with a New Hero

Oliver & Company begins with orphaned Oliver alone on Fifth Avenue in New York City. He wanders the streets, hoping someone will adopt him, and meets a dog named Dodger who teaches him how to steal food. Dodger, of course, is the dog version of Dickens' Artful Dodger; and just like in the book, Dodger takes Oliver to meet Fagin. Fagin remains human in the animated film, but Dodger also introduces Oliver to a gang of stray dogs.

Here, the movie takes a turn from the book, when Oliver happens to meet a rich young girl named Jenny. Jenny immediately adopts Oliver, taking him home and outfitting him with a fancy new collar. But his new dog friends are convinced he's been kidnapped and needs to be rescued, so they steal him away from Jenny's home and return him to Fagin. When Fagin sees Oliver's fancy collar, he sees an opportunity, and sends Jenny a ransom note demanding money for the return of the kitten. In the end, of course, Oliver and Jenny are reunited, Dodger and the gang of dogs turn out to be great friends to Oliver, and even Fagin ends up having a kind heart.

Joey Lawrence, best known for playing Joey Russo in the early-90s comedy *Blossom* and Joe Longo in the ABC Family series *Melissa and Joey*, provided the voice for Oliver, while singer-songwriter Billy Joel lent his voice for Dodger. The film, which was released in 1988, also featured songs by Joel, Barry Manilow, and Huey Lewis, and was nominated for a Golden Globe for Best Original Song for the song "Why Should I Worry." Today, this sweet retelling of Dickens' classic, with its feline hero, is available for streaming on Disney+, so a whole new generation of cat lovers can cheer for Oliver.

Cat and Mouse

The names Jasper and Jinx may not sound familiar, but chances are, we've all seen these two characters many times, chasing each other onscreen in more than 160 short films. But this antagonistic pair are now known by more familiar names: Tom and Jerry.

✳ ✳ ✳ ✳

Been There, Done That

IN 1937, ANIMATORS Joseph Barbera and William Hanna were working in the animation department of MGM, the largest studio in Hollywood at the time. MGM co-owner Louis B. Mayer was looking for suggestions for some new cartoon characters, and Barbera and Hanna were tossing around ideas. One idea was to create a cartoon pair who were constantly at odds with each other, like a fox and a dog. In the end, however, the creative team settled on the classic pairing of cat and mouse.

Animators got to work, and a short film, titled *Puss Gets the Boot*, was released in early 1940. In the animated film, a mangy street cat named Jasper and a skinny mouse named Jinx chase each other and cause general mayhem, banging into walls, smashing flowerpots, and crashing dishes along the way.

While the cartoon was fun and well-liked by audiences, there were no plans to create more of the same, as the "cat and mouse" pairing was considered a bit stale.

Back to Work

Even after *Puss Gets the Boot* was nominated for an Academy Award, Barbera and Hanna concentrated on other cartoons, assuming Jasper and Jinx had run their brief course. But then MGM received a letter from a woman named Bessa Short, who was the head of a major Texas movie chain. Short requested "more of the delightful cat and mouse cartoons," and suddenly, the idea didn't seem so "stale" anymore. MGM commissioned a series of the cat and mouse cartoons, and the animators were back in business.

But they still weren't sold on the names "Jasper" and "Jinx" for their cat and mouse rivals, so they decided to hold a contest to choose new names. The winner was animator John Carr, who won $50 (worth more than $900 today!) for his suggestions: Tom and Jerry. Legend has it that Carr chose the names as a nod to a Christmastime cocktail popular in the 19th and early 20th centuries that combined eggnog, brandy, and rum, and was known as a "Tom and Jerry." But "Tom and Jerry" was also an early 19th century British term for rowdy youngsters, and another version of Carr's story suggests that this was his influence for picking the names.

The Rivalry Continues

Of course, there's another explanation for Tom's name: "Tom Cat" is, obviously, a tomcat, a term used to describe male cats. He appears to be a domestic gray and white shorthair, who, over the years, has morphed from walking on all fours to being almost exclusively bipedal, like a human. Although Tom rarely talks in the cartoons, with the exception of screeches and screams when he is fighting with Jerry, the character has been voiced by dozens of actors, including Hanna, famed Bugs Bunny voice actor Mel Blanc, Warner Bros. cartoonist Chuck

Jones, and *SpongeBob SquarePants* voice actor Tom Kenny. The poor cat rarely wins in his skirmishes against Jerry, but occasionally he manages to outwit the crafty mouse.

The original run of *Tom and Jerry* cartoons, which spanned from 1940 to 1958, earned seven Academy Awards for Animated Short Film. The cartoons were revived in the 1960s, where they became so popular they surpassed *Looney Tunes* to become the highest-grossing animated short film series of the time. Since then, *Tom and Jerry* has sparked several television shows and a feature length movie, with more in the works, proving that this game of cat and mouse is far from over.

Say Cheese

While it would be easy to assume that "grinning like a Cheshire cat" originated with Lewis Carroll's Alice's Adventures in Wonderland, *the phrase was popular before the book was published. But Carroll's classic guaranteed that the "Cheshire cat," and its iconic grin, would find a place in popular culture.*

✳ ✳ ✳ ✳

Unknown Origin

LEWIS CARROLL WAS born Charles Lutwidge Dodgson on January 27, 1832, in Daresbury, a village in Cheshire, England. Even before he was born, the phrase "grin like a Cheshire cat" was well-known, with the residents of Cheshire believing it originated thanks to their abundance of dairy farms, which keep the local cats well-fed and happy with plenty of milk and cream. Another theory claims that a sign painter once attempted to paint grinning lions on the signboards of inns in the area, but the finished product much more resembled smiling housecats. Still another idea claims that a cheesemaker in Cheshire used to sell blocks of cheese which were molded to the form of a grinning cat.

However it began, the phrase was first published in 1788, in Francis Grose's unorthodox lexicon of slang words and phrases, *A Classical Dictionary of the Vulgar Tongue*. In his book, Grose says that the phrase "he grins like a Cheshire cat" is "said of anyone who shows his teeth and gums in laughing." The phrase was seen in print several more times before Carroll published *Alice's Adventures in Wonderland* in 1865, but there's no doubt that Alice's encounter with the Cheshire Cat is much more beloved than Grose's dictionary definition.

A Girl, a Grin, and a Galaxy

In Carroll's novel, a young girl named Alice falls down a rabbit hole and encounters a world of magical food and drink, talking animals, riddles, and a bad-tempered queen. The strange and varied animals she meets include a white rabbit, a caterpillar, a frog, a gryphon, and, of course, the Cheshire Cat. Alice's first encounter with the cat occurs at the house of a character called The Duchess. After leaving the Duchess's house, Alice again sees the cat in a tree, where it directs her to the house of another animal, the March Hare. As it sits in the branches of the tree, the Cheshire Cat demonstrates its ability to disappear and reappear at will. When it disappears, it leaves behind its distinctive grin, resulting in one of the most oft-quoted lines in the book: *"Well! I've often seen a cat without a grin,"* thought Alice; *"but a grin without a cat! It's the most curious thing I ever saw in all my life!"*

The Cheshire Cat poses questions to Alice that are philosophical and sometimes confusing, causing her a bit of consternation. But he ultimately directs her to the famous Mad Hatter's tea party at the March Hare's house, and later appears next to her on the Queen of Heart's croquet field, where the furious queen orders his beheading. But the clever cat performs his disappearing act, until only his head is visible; the confounded executioner muses that he can't behead the cat, since his head is all that can be seen.

Since its original appearance in Carroll's novel, the Cheshire Cat has been depicted dozens of times, including in Disney's 1951 animated film *Alice in Wonderland*, where it was voiced by Sterling Holloway, a 1999 television adaptation voiced by Whoopi Goldberg, and Tim Burton's 2010 film adaptation voiced by Stephen Fry. The cat is also found in video games, comic books, and artwork, and has even lent its name to a cluster of galaxies in the constellation Ursa Major, dubbed the "Cheshire Cat galaxy group" by astronomers.

The Original Animated Star

These days, the animated stars of our favorite movies enjoy a popularity that can eclipse that of their human counterparts. But before Buzz Lightyear, Elsa, Moana, or even Mickey Mouse made their mark on the big screen, their path to fame was paved by the original animated movie star, Felix the Cat.

✳ ✳ ✳ ✳

A New Pastime

THE FIRST MOVIE theater in the United States opened on June 19, 1905 in Pittsburgh, Pennsylvania. Called a "nickelodeon," after the five-cent coin (the price of admission) and the Greek word *oideion*, an ancient theater, the space was the first indoor movie theater similar to the modern theaters we have today. Nickelodeons began popping up all over the country, numbering in the thousands just a few years later. By 1915, the smaller nickelodeons were usurped by larger, more ornate "movie palaces," like the Mark Strand Theater in New York City and the Million Dollar Theater in Los Angeles.

Movies at this time were silent, of course—*The Jazz Singer*, the first film with synchronized dialogue, wasn't released until 1927—but audiences still filled theaters to watch performers like Charlie Chaplin, Mary Pickford, Roscoe "Fatty" Arbuckle, and Lillian Gish on the big screen. But in 1919, a new entertainer debuted, to surprisingly enthusiastic crowds. Because this commanding screen presence wasn't a human, but rather an animated cat.

Happy, but Controversial

The first film to feature the cat was a Paramount Pictures short titled *Feline Follies*, which debuted to rave reviews. The animated cat, who was originally named "Master Tom," then appeared in a second film, *Musical Mews*, which was just as popular as the first. Australian cartoonist Pat Sullivan, who owned the animation studio responsible for the short films, realized he had a hit on his hands, but the animated cat needed a better name. Sullivan, and cartoonist and director Otto Messmer, eventually settled on the moniker "Felix," and the third film, *The Adventures of Felix*, officially introduced the new character on December 14, 1919.

Felix's creation came with a couple points of controversy, which are still debated today. First is the origin of his name, which Messmer claimed was suggested by John King of Paramount Magazine as an homage to the Latin words *felis* and *felix*, which mean "cat" and "happy." But Sullivan insisted he came up with the name as a nod to "Australia Felix," or "happy Australia," a term coined by explorer Thomas Livingstone Mitchell when he first came upon Victoria in the southeastern part of the country.

The second controversy concerns who deserves the credit for originally creating Felix: Sullivan or Messmer. While he was alive, Sullivan claimed that he created Felix and had been inspired by both his wife's love of cats, and Rudyard Kipling's *The Cat that Walked by Itself*. But after his death, employees who worked at Sullivan's animation studio began coming forward to credit Messmer with the creation of Felix, saying that the cat was based on an animated version of Charlie Chaplin that Messmer had drawn.

Famous Face

While these disputes have never been resolved, there is one thing everyone agreed on: Felix the cat, a short black cat with big white eyes and a huge grin, was loved by audiences. By 1923, the cat branched out from films to comic strips, and his likeness was found on everything from toys to Christmas ornaments, earning around $100,000 per year—or $1.5 million in modern day money.

Felix became so popular in the 1920s that he was named as mascot for many different organizations, including the U.S. Navy, the 1922 New York Yankees, and the Felix Chevrolet car dealer in Los Angeles, where the cartoon cat still stands over the door to welcome car shoppers today. Despite his controversial beginnings, Felix the cat remains one of the most recognizable characters ever created.

"Kat" the Mouse

A strange, surreal comic filled with slapstick humor and idiosyncratic language, Krazy Kat's final strip appeared more than 75 years ago. But with fans including Calvin and Hobbes' Bill Watterson and Bloom County's Berkeley Breathed, the comic continues to influence modern cartoonists.

✳ ✳ ✳ ✳

A Comic Career

GEORGE HERRIMAN WAS born in New Orleans on August 22, 1880, but moved with his family to Los Angeles when he was ten. In 1897, shortly after graduating from a Catholic boys' high school, he sold his first piece of artwork—a sketch of Hotel Petrolia in Santa Paula, California—to the *Los Angeles Herald*. This led to a job with the newspaper, where he was able to use his talents in the engraving department. But he believed, as many artists do, that his chances at success would be greater in New York City, so he moved to the metropolis in 1900.

Herriman's hunch was correct, and within two years, he had established a career for himself, with his first recurring comic strip, *Musical Mose*, debuting in February 1902. This was soon followed by the creation of other comics, including *Professor Otto and His Auto*, *Acrobatic Archie*, *Two Jolly Jackies*, and *Major Ozone's Fresh Air Crusade*.

Filling Space

Herriman enjoyed steady work as a cartoonist over the next eight years, including a stint back in California at the *Los Angeles Examiner*, where his artwork was solely responsible for an increase in the newspaper's sales. In 1910, his former colleagues in New York convinced him to return, and within six days of arriving back in New York City, Herriman began drawing a strip titled *The Dingbat Family*. While the strip was not a huge hit with critics, it would lead to something much bigger.

The Dingbat Family featured a character named E. Pluribus Dingbat and his family, who often quarreled with their upstairs neighbors. In the July 26, 1910, comic strip, Herriman also drew a cat into the scene, which was, in his words, "to fill up the waste space." As the comic unfolded, the main characters interacted at the top of each panel, while the cat, and a sneaky mouse, sat at the bottom, drawn so small they could almost be overlooked. In the strip, the mouse creeps up to the cat and throws a projectile at its head. It seems like something that would barely be worth mentioning, if not for the fact that it launched Herriman's most famous comic, *Krazy Kat.*

Love/Hate Relationship

The adventures of *Krazy Kat* and the projectile-tossing mouse, named Ignatz, continued in their unassuming form in the lower panels of *The Dingbat Family* until 1913, when Krazy Kat debuted as a strip of its own. But Krazy Kat's very first appearance in *The Dingbat Family* set the tone for the new strip and the story it told: Krazy Kat, whose gender is purposely left ambiguous, loves Ignatz the mouse, but Ignatz hates Krazy Kat and often throws bricks at the cat's head. Krazy Kat, however, misconstrues each brick-tossing as a profession of affection. To muddy the waters further, Herriman introduced a third character, Officer Pupp, who falls in love with Krazy and frequently hauls Ignatz off to jail.

Herriman set Krazy Kat in Coconino County, Arizona, where the innocent, hopelessly lovelorn Krazy pined for Ignatz in a surreal landscape that the cartoonist changed from frame to frame. He also used unique, whimsical language for his characters, and experimented with unconventional page layouts, a technique that *Krazy Kat* fan Watterson is particularly fond of.

Although *Krazy Kat* never achieved much mainstream success—when Herriman died in 1944, the strip only appeared in 35 newspapers—it enjoyed a level of critical acclaim rarely seen by other comics. And with fans through the decades that include Pablo Picasso, F. Scott Fitzgerald, Cyndi Lauper, and Quentin Tarantino, this "Kat" continues to inspire artists today.

The Anti-Garfield

Most cartoonists would probably have a difficult time creating a mangy, scraggly, and brain damaged cat that comes across as more hilarious than heartbreaking; but Berkeley Breathed, creator of Bloom County, *took on that challenge and succeeded, gifting the comic world with Bill the Cat.*

✳ ✳ ✳ ✳

Lofty Inspiration

HARPER LEE, THE Pulitzer Prize-winning author of *To Kill a Mockingbird*, has inspired plenty of writers and artists over the years. But it's a bit surprising to learn that she also inspired a comic strip that features a talking penguin, a 10-year-old newspaper reporter, a chain-smoking lawyer, and a nearly unresponsive orange tabby cat. These are all characters, of course, in *Bloom County*, a comic strip created by cartoonist Berkeley Breathed in 1980.

Breathed, who was born in California and raised in Texas, published his first comic strip, *The Academia Waltz*, in 1978 while he was a student at the University of Texas. In fact, the comic was so popular that he was able to use profits from selling collections of the strip to pay his tuition, and it also caught the attention of editors at the *Washington Post*, who asked the young cartoonist to create a nationally syndicated comic strip.

So, on December 8, 1980, the first *Bloom County* strip debuted. At its inception, the comic featured several of the characters from *The Academia Waltz*, including Steve Dallas, a womanizing lawyer who, despite his penchant for sexism and cigarettes, would soon become a fan favorite. The comic was set in a small town, and Breathed would later state that he was inspired by the Maycomb, Alabama, setting in *To Kill a Mockingbird*.

The book's young protagonist, Scout, also inspired Breathed to create another popular character: Opus the Penguin.

Unmarketable?

But it wasn't Harper Lee who provided the catalyst for *Bloom County's* flea-bitten Bill the Cat, who debuted in the comic in the summer of 1982. Rather, it was Breathed's distaste for another orange comic cat, Garfield, that inspired the *Bloom County* character. Breathed felt that Garfield had become much too commercialized and was used mostly as a marketing ploy to sell toys and calendars. So he devised Bill as a bit of a Garfield parody—a cat so far removed from the lovable lasagna-loving feline that no one would ever want to use him for marketing purposes.

Breathed certainly succeeded in making Bill the Cat an unusual character in the world of comic strips. Although at first the cat was able to speak, over the course of the comic Bill has become mostly mute and unresponsive, with explanations for his near catatonic state ranging from drug use to a car accident. Bill's escapades have included joining a cult, singing for a rock band called "Billy and the Boingers," and becoming a televangelist. He has also run for President of the United States several times, and in a series of strips in the late 80s, had his brain replaced with Donald Trump's. Bill was even said to have had affairs with Princess Diana, former diplomat Jeane Kirkpatrick, and President Bill Clinton's cat, Socks.

Prize-Worthy

While Breathed's ragged, unappealing, and possibly brain damaged cat was unlike the cuddly cartoon characters usually chosen to be commercialized, surprisingly, his assumption that no one would ever want to market Bill the Cat was wrong. The mangy feline is found on t-shirts, mugs, and calendars, and for a time, was even available as a plush doll.

Bloom County, with its collection of quirky characters and witty study of politics and social issues, earned Breathed a Pulitzer

Prize in 1987. Although he ended the original strip in 1989, he revived it in 2015, ensuring that Bill the Cat will find a whole new generation of fans who appreciate eccentric characters.

A Dandy Cat

One of the most recognizable comic characters in Great Britain, Korky the Cat helped popularize The Dandy, *a children's comic magazine. Running from 1937 to 2012, the magazine, and its famous cat, have entertained generations of British fans.*

* * * *

A Desperado and a Cat

THE FIRST ISSUE of *The Dandy*, originally titled *The Dandy Comic*, was published on December 4, 1937 by D.C. Thompson and Co. The publication set itself apart from other comics in a very simple way—by using speech balloons in the frames instead of captions underneath. The debut issue featured two comic strips, the first of which was called *Desperate Dan*. The title character was a desperado from the Wild West, who was so strong he could lift a cow with one hand. Desperate Dan became a hugely popular character in his own right, and a statue of the desperado can be found in the D.C. Thompson headquarters city of Dundee, Scotland.

The other comic strip featured in *The Dandy's* debut issue was *Korky the Cat*, which was given the honor of appearing on the front page of the magazine. At the time, audiences had been enjoying the antics of silent film star Felix the Cat for almost two decades. Felix creators Pat Sullivan and Otto Messmer had given their feline cartoon character plenty of personality even without sound, and artist James Crighton, who drew the first version of Korky, took his cues from the success of *Felix the Cat*. The comic strip depicted the cat in pantomime, with plenty of slapstick antics to amuse readers.

A Gradual Evolution

At first, Korky was decidedly cat-like, but it didn't take long for Crighton to start anthropomorphizing the cat to give him a more human-like quality. The artist also added more supporting characters, including police officers, neighborhood kids, and soldiers (this was during World War II, after all), rounding out Korky's comic universe. Then, in the October 5, 1940, issue, Crighton decided to make Korky even more human-like by giving him dialogue, using *The Dandy's* unique speech balloons. Korky's first words were, "Let's ask the butcher for some sausages!" in a comic where the cat, standing on two legs like a human, is helping hungry street dogs procure a meal.

Korky continued to evolve as the years passed, eventually standing upright at all times and sporting nearly human proportions. He even moved into a modern, furnished house with a manicured yard, and of course interacted with the humans in the comic strip, who never seemed alarmed that Korky was a giant, talking cat.

Crighton drew Korky all throughout the wartime years, when the comic would often depict Korky helping out with the war effort, and continued drawing the comic in the 1950s, which would prove to be the most popular era for *The Dandy*. During this decade, *Korky the Cat* introduced Nip, Lip, and Rip, Korky's kitten nephews, also known as the Kits. The trio of kittens became so popular that for a time the comic was renamed *Korky the Cat and the Kits*.

Decades of Popularity

Korky the Cat's early success was certainly bolstered by Crighton's artwork, but in 1962 he passed the baton to artist Charles Grigg, who brought his own style to Korky. The cat was drawn with a friendlier look, and comics with Grigg's cover artwork are considered by many to be the definitive *Korky the Cat* collector's items. Grigg drew the comic for twenty years, after which the longstanding strip was drawn by David Gudgeon, Robert Nixon, and, finally, Phil Corbett.

Korky the Cat was so popular that he appeared on the cover of *The Dandy* for 47 straight years, until he was replaced in 1984 by Desperate Dan. Although the last issue of *The Dandy* was published in 2012, Korky the Cat remains instantly recognizable in the U.K., even to those who have never picked up a comic book.

A Comic First

It would be easy to assume that the widely syndicated Garfield, *one of the most recognizable comics in the world, has been around longer than any other orange cartoon cat. But Garfield wasn't the first orange tabby to appear in comics; that honor belongs to Heathcliff.*

✳ ✳ ✳ ✳

A Born Cartoonist

GEORGE GATELY, BORN in Queens, New York, in 1928, was surrounded by a family of comic lovers. His father enjoyed doodling for fun, while his older brother, John, worked as a professional cartoonist. This artistic upbringing led him to pursue an art degree at the Pratt Institute in Brooklyn, New York, after which he worked in advertising for more than a decade. Gately envied the accomplishments of his cartooning older brother, and in 1957, decided to try his hand at comics.

In the late 1960s, Gately found modest success with the comic strips *Hapless Harry* and *Hippy*, which both ran in newspapers for several years. But then, in 1973, he created what would become his biggest success: *Heathcliff*, a comic strip about a rotund orange cat. The comic became such a hit that Gately was unable to keep up with demand for the daily strips on his own, so he asked artist Bob Laughlin to help with drawing the comic. Later, he also recruited his brother, having surpassed even the successes of his one-time idol. Eventually, *Heathcliff* was distributed to more than 1,000 newspapers worldwide.

Neighborhood Cat

The comic takes place in a town called Westfinster, where Heathcliff, a slightly overweight orange cat with black tiger stripes, lives with an older couple named Mr. and Mrs. Nutmeg. The Nutmegs also have a grandson named Iggy, who makes many appearances in the comic. Unlike Garfield, who often simply hangs out at home eating and sleeping, Heathcliff enjoys getting out into his community. He is especially fond of pestering the owner of the local fish market, provoking neighborhood dogs and giving them up to the dog catcher, turning over garbage cans, and tricking the milkman into giving him bottles of milk.

Other characters who pop up in the comic include Iggy's friends Willy and Marcy, friendly, face-licking dog Chauncey, and neighborhood bully Muggsy Faber. Muggsy's bulldog, Spike, is usually in tow, but Heathcliff often outwits him. Pops Heathcliff, the orange tabby's father, also shows up occasionally. Pops wears a black-and-white striped prison uniform, although it's never clear why, if he's out of prison, he doesn't change clothes!

Heathcliff also has a girlfriend—a female cat named Sonja. While Heathcliff loves Sonja and showers her with gifts and affection, Sonja's owner, Herb Jablonski, is not at all taken with the cat. Herb sees Heathcliff as a nuisance, even when his wife points out the chivalrous actions of the gallant, lovestruck cat.

Books, Television, and Film

Since its inception, *Heathcliff* has been presented as a single-panel comic during the week, with an expanded, multiple-panel format on Sundays under the title *Sunday with Heathcliff*. Gately drew the comic until he retired in 1998, when his nephew Peter Gallagher took over. Today, the strip is found not only in daily newspapers, but also in digital form on websites such as GoComics. But Heathcliff hasn't been limited to its newspaper comic form: Marvel Comics began producing a *Heathcliff* comic book in 1985 that ran for 56 issues, and two animated series, one in 1980 and one in 1984, featured the voice of Mel Blanc as the orange cat. Seven episodes from the 1984 series were collected for an anthology film, *Heathcliff: The Movie*, which was released in 1986.

While Garfield may get much of the spotlight, Heathcliff is the cat who paved his way. With millions of copies of *Heathcliff* comic books in print and generations of delighted fans, this orange cat deserves his own moment in the limelight.

A Comic Legend

Before he was known for writing graphic novels and comic books including The League of Extraordinary Gentlemen, V for Vendetta, *and* Watchmen, *Alan Moore tried his hand at drawing cartoons for a younger audience in the comic strip* Maxwell the Magic Cat. *However, the comic may not have been as innocent as it appeared.*

✳ ✳ ✳ ✳

A Bit of a Rebel

ALAN MOORE, BORN in Northampton, England, in 1953, has described himself as an occultist, a ceremonial magician, and an anarchist; hardly the descriptors one would imagine using to depict the creator of a comic strip. But Moore has not always been a typical cartoonist. Growing up in a poverty-stricken area of Northampton, Moore loved reading and writing as a child, and devoured comic books like *The Flash* and *Fantastic Four*. Although he was a good student in primary school, he grew less interested in education as he got older, considering it a form of "indoctrination."

By the time he was a teenager, Moore was publishing his own poetry and essays in fanzines, and established his own fanzine called *Embryo*. He also began dabbling in LSD, a practice that got him expelled from school. For Moore, who was apathetic toward formal education, this merely meant that it was time to find a job. He cleaned toilets, he worked in a tannery, and he worked an office job, but none of these brought him any fulfillment.

Settling Down

In the late 1970s, now married with a newborn daughter, Moore made the decision to quit his office job and to start writing and illustrating comics fulltime. But even after selling a few drawings, Moore and his family struggled financially. He finally scored a weekly gig creating the series *Roscoe Moscow* for the magazine *Sounds*, which he wrote under the pseudonym Curt Vile—a pun on the name of German composer Kurt Weill—but also collected unemployment benefits to scrape by.

Then, in 1979, Moore went to the local newspaper, the *Northants Post*, and pitched an idea to them. It was a comic called *Nutter's Ruin*, which Moore envisioned as an adult-oriented strip. But the *Post* had another idea: they requested he create a comic for children, instead. So, Moore developed a comic strip featuring a talking cat named Maxwell and his human companion, Norman Nesbit, and the first *Maxwell the Magic Cat* comic was published in the *Post* on August 25, 1979.

Comic Anarchy

But Moore didn't exactly take the request for a children's comic entirely to heart. For starters, he published the comic under the pseudonym "Jill de Ray," a play on the name of an infamous 15th century child serial killer named Gilles de Rais, which Moore called a "sardonic joke." But in addition to this obvious expression of disdain for his employer's insistence that he produce children's comics, Moore also introduced more sophisticated themes and language into his comic, addressing issues like politics, social issues, and organized religion.

According to writer Andrew Edwards, Moore's overall theme in *Maxwell the Magic Cat* was that "mankind's own sense of superiority is grossly misguided." Which would seem to be a rather heavy theme for a children's comic. Still, Moore drew inspiration from a beloved children's comic strip, *Peanuts*, as well as British comics like *Korky the Cat*, when drawing his characters.

Maxwell the Magic Cat provided Moore with the opportunity to polish his skills and develop his comedic abilities before diving into more serious subject matter. It also provided him with enough financial security that he was able to end his unemployment benefits and take care of his family. Though not his most well-known comic, Moore's *Maxwell the Magic Cat* opened the door to a lucrative career for this writer and artist. Not bad for a self-proclaimed anarchist.

The Pastry and Tom Puss

The star of a Dutch comic series featuring an anthropomorphic white cat and his pipe-smoking bear sidekick, Tom Puss owes his existence to Felix the Cat, Argentina, and a delicious pastry.

✳ ✳ ✳ ✳

A Lifechanging Voyage

CONSIDERED THE MOST successful comic artist in the Netherlands, Marten Toonder is honored today with a monument that stands in his hometown of Rotterdam. Toonder was born in the city in 1912, and at an early age loved reading classic novels and poetry. His father was a sea captain who sailed the world and frequently returned home with foreign comic books, which the young Toonder would also devour. After high school, Toonder wanted to head off to university, but his father had hopes that his son would follow in his footsteps and pursue a nautical career. In an effort to introduce 19-year-old Toonder to the adventure of seafaring, his father took him on a voyage from the Netherlands to Argentina. The trip would change Toonder's life; but not in the way his father hoped.

One day, when Toonder was in Buenos Aires, he met a man named Jim Davis (no relation to the future *Garfield* cartoonist). Davis was an American animator who had worked for Pat Sullivan and Otto Messmer, the creators of *Felix the Cat*. Toonder and Davis struck up a conversation about comics and animation, and the American gave Toonder a few lessons in drawing. He also introduced Toonder to the work of a local comic legend named Dante Quinterno and provided him with a written animation course that Quinterno had authored.

Growing Career

The Argentina trip proved to be the catalyst that launched Toonder's career. Back in Rotterdam, he began studying the work of artists from around the world, including *Felix the Cat* and the work of Walt Disney. By 1933, Toonder was creating drawings and cartoons for publications and newspapers throughout the Netherlands, and soon became a full-time illustrator for a printing and publishing house in the town of Leiden. In the late 1930s, he decided to go off on his own, becoming an independent artist and working with clients throughout Europe.

Then, in 1940, the Nazis invaded the Netherlands and banned the import of American and British comics. Toonder, seeing an opportunity in the midst of a terrible situation, realized that with other competitors gone, this was the perfect time to debut a new character he'd been developing: Tom Puss, or, in Dutch, Tom Poes.

Around the World

Toonder's wife, fellow cartoonist Phiny Dick, chose the name for the character as a play on a popular Dutch pastry called a *tompouce*. The pastry's namesake, Tom Poes, a small, intelligent, white cat, was introduced on March 16, 1941, in the Dutch newspaper *De Telegraaf*. The first comic was titled *Het Geheim der Blauwe Aarde*, or "The Secret of the Blue Earth," and replaced a Mickey Mouse comic that had previously run in its place. In the third installment of the comic, published on July 12, 1941, Tom meets his sidekick, a rich, nobleman bear by the name of Bommel.

Tom's world is an ambiguous fairy tale world, where sometimes clothing and architecture looks medieval, but other times modern objects such as cars and televisions appear. He and Bommel go on adventures where they meet wizards, fairies, and other animals. But perhaps the oddest part of Toonder's comic was his creation of new words and expressions that were adopted into the Dutch language, with some added to the dictionary.

After the war, Tom Poes was given his own magazine, and the comic was published around the world in many languages, including French, German, Spanish, Indonesian, and English, where he was called Tom Puss. In 1954, Toonder was honored with a membership in the *Maatschappij der Nederlandse Letterkunde*, or the Society of Dutch Literature, and Tom Poes is still considered to be the only Dutch comic worthy of being called literature.

Jazz Paws

What do you get when you combine jazz, the Prohibition Era, and cats? Well, in the case of the comic world, you get Lackadaisy, *a webcomic that mixes the drama of the 1930s with the whimsy of anthropomorphic felines.*

✳   ✳   ✳   ✳

Breaking the Comic Ceiling

THE COMIC WORLD is often dominated by men. From Marvel Comic legend Stan Lee to Charles Schulz of *Peanuts* fame, male artists and writers have mostly controlled the comic market from the moment the very first Felix the Cat and Mickey Mouse films debuted. And while there's no doubt that these gentlemen have made invaluable contributions to pop culture, sometimes it's refreshing to see a woman's artistic talent shine.

Case in point: Tracy J. Butler, creator of the webcomic *Lackadaisy*. Butler was born in Springfield, Massachusetts, on August 3, 1980, and as a child, she loved to draw. In school, she was constantly doodling and drawing characters on her notebooks, which often took the form of cats. After graduating from high school, Butler spent a year studying biology at Elms College, but realized that her true love was art. She dropped out of school to focus on illustration, graphic design, and 3D animation, eventually landing a job at a St. Louis, Missouri, game development company.

Inspiration Strikes

But even after tackling the "real world" as an adult, Butler never stopped carrying around a sketchbook. Calling it a "security blanket," the artist would jot down sketches and drawings when inspiration struck. She settled in to her new city of St. Louis, where she bought a 100-year-old house and began researching its history, and she developed a love of jazz music—which was perhaps not surprising, living in the city where greats like Miles Davis and Duke Ellington used to play. But what may have been surprising, even to Butler herself, was how the combination of learning about St. Louis history and listening to jazz music called up memories of those childhood cat drawings. Ideas began to form, a story was created, and soon, Butler published her first *Lackadaisy* comic strip.

Butler set her comic in St. Louis in the mid-1920s, when the prohibition of alcohol led to the creation of speakeasies, where bootlegged alcohol was secretly sold. The Lackadaisy is one such speakeasy, located in a subterranean limestone cavern underneath a legitimate eatery, the Little Daisy Café. As the comic opens, the proprietor of the Little Daisy, Atlas May, has been mysteriously killed and management of both the café and the speakeasy are taken over by his widow, Mitzi. While the Lackadaisy was a popular establishment when Atlas May was alive, it struggles after his death, leaving the remaining employees, including bootleggers and rumrunners, grappling with how to keep the illegal operation going.

Distinctive Style

The strip is already a unique addition to the comic world, but what sets *Lackadaisy* apart from other stories even more is the fact that every character in the comic is an anthropomorphized cat. In addition to Atlas and Mitzi, these include reckless rumrunner Rocky Rickaby, Rocky's impressionable cousin Calvin McMurray, brother and sister pair Nicodeme and Serafine Savoy, jazz singer Ivy Pepper, and a quartet of inept pig farmers named Avery, Avril, Emery, and Benjy.

Butler sketches each comic with pencil first, then scans, adjusts, and assembles them with Photoshop, finishing each panel with a sepia tone to give the comic a true 1920s feel. The result is a beautifully detailed comic that immerses the reader in the mystery, intrigue, and history of the Prohibition Era, with the twist of feline charm. After it debuted in 2006, *Lackadaisy* won multiple Web Cartoonists' Choice Awards, and in 2020, production began on a short film based on the comic. The cats of *Lackadaisy* have proven that Butler has more than earned her place in the male-dominated world of comic strips.

Call PETA

The "Great Cat Massacre," surely one of the strangest incidents in French history, was exactly what it sounds like. But perhaps even more disturbing than the event itself was an observer's insistence that the massacre was "funny."

✳   ✳   ✳   ✳

It's a Hard-Knock Life

THERE'S NO QUESTION that the lives of the printing apprentices working in 1730s Paris were extremely difficult. Particularly tormented were those working in the Latin Quarter on the Rue Saint-Severin at the shop of Jacques Vincent.

The apprentices were berated and beaten by the master of the house, given only kitchen scraps to eat, and forced to sleep in freezing, dirty rooms. Every morning, after a night of little sleep, they rose before the sun to begin running errands, while the printer and his wife slept in late, cozy in a warm bed.

To add insult to injury were the many well-fed cats that roamed the neighborhood. In fact, the "bourgeois," as the apprentices called the wealthy printers and their families, adored the cats and welcomed them into their homes. One member of the bourgeois on the Rue Saint-Severin was said to have taken 25 cats into his home, where he had their portraits painted and fed them roasted meat at his dining table. Jacques Vincent and his wife weren't nearly as obsessed, but the printer's wife did have a particular fondness for one cat, *la grise*, or the gray. In short, the cats ate better and slept better than the apprentices, specifically because the bourgeois devoted more care and attention to the felines.

All of that was difficult enough, but the cats threw one more monkey wrench into the lives of the apprentices. Every night, as the exhausted apprentices struggled to sleep in their cold room, alley cats would howl and screech just outside the window. A good night's sleep was never to be found. No doubt the frustration and stress grew more unbearable with each passing day.

A Plan for Terrible Revenge

So, one day, after once again being tormented by caterwauling overnight, the apprentices on Rue Saint-Severin finally decided they'd had enough. One of them, a man by the name of Leveille, was not only an exceptional climber, but also a master of mimicry. He waited until the printer and his wife retired for the evening, then climbed over the roof until he was perched over their bedroom window. He then did his best imitation of a howling alley cat, and ensured that the printer and his wife were awake all night.

Leveille repeated his prank for days, until the master of the house was certain that the cats in the neighborhood were possessed. After all, there was still a pervasive belief at the time that cats were associated with witches, and some were thought to have magical powers. The distressed printer ordered the apprentices and other workers in the printshop to round up all the cats they could find—except for his wife's favorite, *la grise*— and dispose of them.

In a modern sense, it was disturbing how quickly and enthusiastically the apprentices set off on their task. They ignored the printer's order to overlook *la grise*; the poor gray cat was one of the first to be killed. They then set out along the Rue Saint-Severin, beating cats with sticks and bars and throwing them in sacks. After rounding up as many cats as they could find, they brought them back to the printshop, held a mock trial, found the cats "guilty," and hung them.

For months afterwards, the workers would reenact the cat massacre as they howled with laughter, knowing they'd hit the bourgeois hard, without ever throwing a punch. And while it's easy to understand the frustration and pain the neglected apprentices faced on a daily basis, it's still hard to understand their "revenge." Let's hope the events that occurred in the print shop on Rue Saint-Severin will never be repeated.

What's in a Name?

Every hero needs a villain, and every villain needs a sidekick. James Bond's foe Goldfinger had Oddjob; Jafar, Aladdin's nemesis, had Iago; and even Dr. Evil of Austin Powers *fame had his clone, Mini Me. But none of them have a name quite as terrifying as Gargamel's cat in the popular comic and cartoon,* The Smurfs.

✳ ✳ ✳ ✳

Belgian Import

THE WORD "SMURFS" has a bit of a silly ring to it, giving readers of *The Smurfs* comic or viewers of the cartoon show a hint of the cute absurdity contained in the stories. Originally a comic series created by Belgian artist Pierre Culliford (better known by his penname, Peyo), *The Smurfs* began as a spinoff of another Peyo series titled *Johan et Pirlouit*. The artist created the tiny, blue-skinned humanoid creatures for a *Johan et Pirlouit* story published in 1958 and called them "Schtroumpfs." The characters were an instant hit, and stories exclusively featuring the "Schtroumpfs," which was translated to "Smurfs" for the Dutch version of the comic, debuted in 1959.

Throughout the 60s and 70s, the Smurfs gained popularity, not only in Belgium, but also in France, Germany, Turkey, and the Netherlands. Peyo published 31 volumes of Smurf comics, and two films were released featuring the characters. Then, in 1981, the Smurfs crossed the Atlantic and found a new audience in the United States when Hanna-Barbera Productions began airing the Saturday morning cartoon, *The Smurfs*. A whole new generation of fans was introduced to the tiny blue creatures and their weekly adventures.

Smurfy Smurfs

These adventures often take place in the forest where the Smurfs live in mushroom-shaped houses in a forest, where they eat sarsaparilla leaves and "smurfberries." They are described as being "three apples high," and mostly dress in white outfits with white hats. Each Smurf has a name that matches their characteristics, such as Jokey Smurf, the practical joker, Brainy Smurf, the village intellectual, and Handy Smurf, who takes care of building and maintaining things in Smurf village. There's also Smurfette, one of the few female characters in the comic, and Papa Smurf, the leader of the group, who stands out from the others with his red hat and pants and white beard.

Of course, Peyo couldn't simply create an idyllic village of Smurfs without also creating a villain to torment them. Enter Gargamel, an evil wizard who lives in a run-down stone castle and spends his days plotting ways to capture the Smurfs. Sometimes he wants to eat the Smurfs, and sometimes he wants to use them in magic potions; but he always hates them. But Gargamel isn't the only one who dreams of eating a Smurf: his feline sidekick, Azrael, would like nothing more.

Angel, or Devil?

Azrael may look like a scruffy, mangy orange cat, but his name belies a much more sinister personality lurking underneath. The name "Azrael" is associated with both Islamic and Jewish traditions, where it is the name given to the angel of death. Azrael records the names of mortals at birth and erases them at death, before transporting the souls of the dead. There is a catch, however: Azrael may only take the souls of those God has commanded him to take.

So how does this relate to Azrael the cat? Well, in the cartoon, if Azrael catches a Smurf, as much as he'd like to chomp down on the little guys, he must first take them to Gargamel. Of course, the Smurfs always manage to escape before either of the bad guys can consume them, but in a sense, Azrael the cat is Gargamel's own "angel of death," procuring Smurf souls, but, thanks to his master's inept plans, he is never able to transport them to the afterlife.

Azrael may be "just a cat," but the meaning of his name makes him one of the most terrifying, albeit fluffy, villain sidekicks in the pop culture world.

A Roaring Success

The names Slats, Jackie, Tanner, Telly, Coffee, George, and Leo may not ring any bells, but you've no doubt seen the work of these Hollywood legends. They're better known as the MGM lions.

✳ ✳ ✳ ✳

The Silent One

THE IMAGE OF a majestic lion and the sound of its intimidating roar has become synonymous with Hollywood studio Metro-Goldwyn-Mayer. But the very first lion, chosen before Metro Pictures and Louis B. Mayer added their names to Samuel Goldwyn's Goldwyn Pictures, didn't utter a sound. The reason, of course, is that the first lion, Slats, debuted in 1916, during the silent film era.

The original logo for Goldwyn Pictures was designed by Howard Dietz, a publicist who had studied journalism at Columbia University. In honor of his alma mater, whose mascot is a lion, Dietz created a logo that featured the giant cat. Slats, a lion born at the Dublin Zoo in Ireland, was chosen to be featured in the first logo, and Hollywood animal trainer Volney Phifer worked with the lion to get the right look for the finished logo. Slats appeared in the Goldwyn Pictures logo until 1924, when the company became Metro-Goldwyn-Mayer, or MGM. He then became the first of the famous MGM lions, appearing before the film *He Who Gets Slapped*.

Sound and Color

Slats retied in 1928, the only MGM lion to never roar in the logo. His successor, Jackie, made his first appearance before the film *White Shadows in the South Seas*. Although the film was silent, it was released with a prerecorded soundtrack, making it the first MGM production with sound. It was also the first time audiences heard the roaring lion in the MGM logo, a sound that would soon become legendary. Jackie then reached another milestone when he appeared in Technicolor before 1939's *The Wizard of Oz*. But Jackie's claim to fame doesn't stop at Hollywood. The tough cat became renowned for surviving several accidents, including an explosion in the studio, two train wrecks, an earthquake, a sinking ship, and a plane crash, earning him the nickname, "Leo the Lucky."

Jackie appeared in all of MGM's black and white films until 1956, but in 1934 MGM began producing color films, as well. A new lion, Tanner, was brought in to become the face (and roar) of color films. Tanner first appeared before the 1934 short film *Holland in Tulip Time*, and his first feature length film was four years later before *Sweethearts*. Tanner's logo became the most commonly used MGM logo throughout the Golden Age of Hollywood, and his roar was often used as a sound effect for animated films produced by the studio.

The Furry Face of MGM

Slats, Jackie, and Tanner were three of the longest-appearing lions used for the MGM logo, but three others—Telly, Coffee, and George—also had their moments in the spotlight. Telly and Coffee appeared sporadically in the late 1920s and early 1930s as MGM began dabbing in color film, and George was briefly introduced in 1956. Although he only appeared before films for two years, George held the record for "biggest mane" of the MGM lions.

But the longest-used lion, and the one most of us are familiar with, is Leo, who has been featured before MGM films since 1957. Like the original MGM lion, Slats, Leo was born at the Dublin Zoo in Ireland, and later purchased from animal importer Henry Trefflich. Besides his work as the face of MGM, Leo had a long career in films, as well, appearing in *King of Kings*, *The Lion*, *Zebra in the Kitchen*, several *Tarzan* movies, and more.

Chapter 11

People and Their Cats

Angel with an Attitude

She hated him when he first arrived. Old, grouchy, fat, and loud, Angela's new cat was not the sweet little kitten she had always wanted. Terminally ill, Angela had longed for a "buddy" to keep her company. Cancer is a lonely disease, no matter how many people love and care for you, and her sister, Annie, understood Angela's need for a feline companion. Annie's baby sister was only 28 years old, and Angela didn't have much time left. Their family wanted to accommodate her and make her feel comfortable in any way they could. If getting her a kitten would make Angela feel even a little bit better, then they were happy to provide one.

✳   ✳   ✳   ✳

UNFORTUNATELY, THE CAT their mother brought home for Angela was not what she had been hoping for. Oreo had an air of independence, and he "argued" with everyone in an ornery tone. Right away Annie figured out that Angela and Oreo were kindred spirits; it just took them a little while to realize it.

Angela's new buddy wanted nothing to do with her; she wanted nothing to do with him. "Take him back, Mom!" she ordered after a couple of days. "He hates me, and he never shuts up!"

But Oreo stayed, complaining loudly all the while. He and Angela had no choice but to get used to one another.

Annie thought that when you meet someone a lot like you, you either love them or you hate them.

When Annie arrived at Angela's house each morning, Oreo was waiting at the door, and he would bolt past her the instant the door opened wide enough for him to escape. She gathered that he reciprocated Angela's feelings for him. Until the day she fell.

Her morning caregiver didn't show up that day, and Angela was so happy to have some "alone time" that she didn't call Annie or anyone else to let them know. Because her brain tumor had paralyzed her entire right side, she often fell, so they never left her by herself.

When Annie pulled up to the house, she noticed all the blinds were still shut. She immediately knew something was wrong. Running into the house, her heart racing, she rushed to Angela's room and found her unconscious, the right side of her face swollen and cut. Oreo was standing on top of her, meowing loudly at Annie as if to say, "Where have you been?" His back was arched; he was rigid and protective. If a cat can have a "worried" expression, this one had it.

Angela was never the same after that fall, and her time on earth drew to an end only a couple months later. But her guardian feline never left her side.

Whenever Annie was able to get Angela into the living room for some sunshine and a new view, Oreo followed them. As soon as Annie got her sister seated or lying down, Oreo would climb gracefully to his place of guardianship on her lap or chest. With disdain, he would glare at anyone who tried to move him, including Angela. Annie hadn't envisioned a "buddy" as committed as this one, but she had to admit, the cat had tenacity.

As time went by and Angela became too weak to leave her bed, Oreo stayed near her at all times, leaving only for eating and brief trips outside. During Angela's last 24 hours on earth, Oreo didn't leave her once. He never ate, never went outside, never moved from his spot on Angela's chest. Somehow he knew her time was near, and he was determined to be her protector. Angela died surrounded by family and friends who loved her. And Oreo, the guardian angel with an attitude, was with her to the last breath.

Presidential Pets

More than two dozen children, both children and grandchildren of presidents, have called the White House home. And along with clothes, toys, and schoolbooks, the First Families have brought their pets to the White House.

✳   ✳   ✳   ✳

DURING SOME ADMINISTRATIONS the White House has resembled the National Zoo. President Theodore Roosevelt and his six children assembled the largest menagerie: dogs, cats, birds, guinea pigs, rats, a badger, a pig, a flying squirrel, a rabbit, horses, and snakes. Algonquin, their Icelandic pony, was famous for his elevator ride (at the urging of young Quentin) to visit Archie, confined with the measles in an upper-floor bedroom.

Soviet Union Premier Nikita Khrushchev gave Caroline Kennedy a puppy called Pushinka. Her mother Strelka was one of the first dogs in space. Since it was the height of the Cold War, the poor pup was checked for bugs— and not the kind with  six legs. Pushinka and another Kennedy dog, Charlie the Welsh terrier, had multiple puppies, or pupniks, as JFK called them.

Although dogs are the most common White House animal, many exotic animals have wandered the halls as well. In 1929, Herbert Hoover's son, Allan Henry, brought a pair of alligators with him. They weren't even the first alligators to call the White House home. When the Marquis de Lafayette visited the White House in 1826, he brought along a gator who lived in the East Room for two months.

In 1863, a friend sent the Lincolns a live turkey for Christmas dinner. Before the ax could fall, son Tad named the newcomer Jack. And if you've got a name, you're a dinner guest, not a dinner entrée. Jack wasn't the only dinner-turned-pet. Upon receiving a raccoon for his Thanksgiving dinner, Calvin Coolidge promptly named her Rebecca. Rebecca had an annoying habit—unscrewing lightbulbs as she wandered through the White House.

One day, strollers on Pennsylvania Avenue witnessed President Benjamin Harrison barreling down the street brandishing a cane. He was in pursuit of the family goat. Whiskers had made a break for freedom—while harnessed to a cart containing several of the president's grandchildren!

Hemingway's Cats

The great American author and proverbial "man's man" Ernest Hemingway was a big fan of bullfighting, boxing, and hunting— and also of cats. Ever since he was given Snowball, a six-toed feline (known as a polydactyl) by a ship's captain in the 1930s, Hemingway allowed cats to multiply with abandon in his Key West, Florida, home.

✳   ✳   ✳   ✳

IN 2003, THE Hemingway Home and Museum, where the writer lived and worked for ten years on novels including *To Have and Have Not* and short stories such as "The Snows of Kilimanjaro," became embroiled in a dispute over its nearly 60 resident felines. All of these cats are descendants of Snowball, and they all carry the gene for polydactylism; only half, however, have extra toes.

Just Trying to Help

The legal battle began after the local Society for the Prevention of Cruelty to Animals (SPCA) cited animal welfare legislation requiring any business employing animals in acts or advertisements to have a special license. The Hemingway cats,  many named after literary and entertainment celebrities (such as Audrey Hepburn, Emily Dickinson, Simone de Beauvoir, and Charlie Chaplin), are featured on the museum's website and are a huge tourist attraction, but they do not exactly perform, per se. The museum faced huge fines and confiscation of the cats by the Department of Agriculture if it didn't cage the furry creatures. A local animal shelter official thought she was doing a good deed by taking the cats in to be neutered; the museum fought to stop her, saying she had left almost no cats able to continue Snowball's bloodline.

The hard-fought battle of the little-six-toed-guy against the big-bad-government made its way through the courts, ending with a 2007 victory for the beleaguered and bewhiskered: The cats still freely roam the grounds, and the tourists keep coming to enjoy the cats.

Mabel Stark: The Ultimate Cat Lady

Barely five feet tall in her signature white leather suit and knee-high boots, Mabel Stark didn't look fierce enough to train tigers. But some girls won't back down from a catfight.

✳ ✳ ✳ ✳

TALK ABOUT A caveat: The young woman who'd previously held Mabel Stark's position as an assistant to the tiger trainer for the Barnes Circus met a grisly fate: attacked and eaten by a tiger in the ring. But Stark couldn't sign up for the gig fast enough. Training tigers is what she'd wanted to do her whole life.

Born Mary Haynie sometime between 1889 and 1904—she was cagey about her real age, and dubious about many facts of her life—to Kentucky tobacco farmers who died when she was 13, the orphaned girl was shipped off to Louisville to live with an aunt and uncle who never wanted her around. Stark took to spending her afternoons at the zoo, dreaming about becoming a wild animal trainer. But societal conventions held sway, and the petite blonde headed to nursing school when she was (supposedly) 18 years old.

What happens next is subject to some debate, but both stories end with Mabel in the ring with tigers.

The Lady or the Tiger?

By her own account, Stark headed to Los Angeles in 1911 on a post-graduation trip, where, on her first night, she ran into Barnes Circus owner A. G. Barnes. Stark was hired on the spot and the next day reported to work as an animal trainer—but she was upset to find that she'd been assigned to train a horse. When her contract came up for another year, Stark demanded she work with tiger trainer Louis Roth to learn his trade.

In another version, historians say Mabel left nursing school in 1911 to become a stripper in the Great Parker Carnival, working under the name Mabel Aganosticus. (This was possibly the last name of her first ex-husband; she would go on to collect four or five more.) A year later, she left to marry a "rich Texan," but the relationship quickly went kaput.

In keeping with the second story, now using the surname "Stark," Mabel returned to the carnival where she hung around the animals and befriended their trainer, Al Barnes. A year later, Barnes left to start his own circus and took Mabel with him as an animal trainer—but she was upset to find that she'd been assigned to train goats. To convince tiger trainer Roth to hire her as a replacement for his assistant who'd been devoured, she married him.

In the early 1900s, Ivan Pavlov hadn't yet done his experiment with dogs and bells, so no one knew for sure how to train an animal to do something. But Roth had a hunch. While most animal trainers at the time beat their subjects into submission, Roth used a method called "gentling," rewarding tigers for good behavior with fresh horse meat.

Roth devolved into alcoholism, and the two divorced. Stark took the gentling method into the ring, though she also packed a whip and a pistol that fired blanks, noisy enough to frighten the tigers.

Maim Attraction

Over the decades, Stark made a name for herself, performing her "cat act" with Barnes, Ringling Brother's Barnum and Bailey, and several small circuses before landing with the JungleLand theme park in Thousand Oaks, California.

Stark firmly believed that tigers could never be tamed, only subdued, and only when they felt like it. Eighteen times Stark was mauled, yet she never blamed the cats for acting out—only herself for not paying attention. And though nearly every inch of her body was eventually covered with scars, she continued working well into old age.

Stark Says Goodbye

Stark once said she couldn't live without her tigers, and that would prove true. Stark's demise was shrouded in rumor, much like her beginnings. In 1968, JungleLand closed its doors. Also, some say Stark's favorite tiger, Rajah, whom Barnes had given to her as a cub and whom she'd brought home and walked like a dog around her neighborhood, had died. Three months after the park closed, Stark was found dead in her home of an apparent barbiturate overdose—an unfortunate end to an exciting life.

Florida Man and Cat

A Florida man and his cat, Misty, were surprised by a pet-friendly Christmas miracle in 2016. Cat-owner Jonathan was devastated when Misty disappeared in October, but after weeks of searching for her with no luck, he decided to head to the Jacksonville Humane Society and adopt a new feline friend.

The humane society thought they had the perfect cat for the distraught cat lover. "Bon Bon"—a pretty tortoiseshell-colored cat—

had been at the shelter for months. Although she was very sweet, no one seemed to want to adopt her.

The staff couldn't understand why until Jonathan saw her: Bon Bon was his own tortoiseshell cat, Misty! As far as everyone at the humane society was concerned, it was simply holiday magic that brought the two back together. And human and cat were able to enjoy Christmas together again!

An Amazing Journey

Sugar was a cream Persian who became famous when her family moved from California to Oklahoma—and she followed.

✳ ✳ ✳ ✳

THE FAMILY STARTED the journey with Sugar in the car, but the Persian was so obviously ill and terrified that the family reluctantly turned around and left Sugar in the care of trusted neighbors. Fighting back tears, the family waved goodbye to Sugar as they set out once again for Oklahoma.

Fifteen days later the neighbors wrote to say Sugar had disappeared, and despite their frantic attempts to locate her, she was nowhere to be found.

Fast-forward 14 months. Sugar's original owner was doing the family wash when a bedraggled Persian jumped through an open window and landed on her shoulder. Upon examination, the owner joyously recognized the cat as Sugar. Sugar had been injured years earlier in a road accident and had an unmistakable scar on her hind leg.

In order to be reunited with her family, Sugar had walked more than 1,500 miles, crossing not only the Great American Desert but the Rocky Mountains as well. Prior to this incredible journey, Sugar had never strayed farther than the next-door neighbor's backyard.

Surviving "Cat"astrophes

In New Brunswick, teenage girls saved the lives of two kittens by performing an emergency C-section on a cat that had been hit and killed by a car. The teens recognized the animal and knew it was pregnant. When they checked and found that the cat's body was still warm, they decided to try and save the kittens, even though neither girl had any knowledge of cat anatomy. The girls were able to rescue two of the four kittens, bundling them in a sweater and taking them home. Later that same evening, a neighborhood cat that had recently delivered kits heard the meows of the newborns and adopted them.

Samuel Clemens's Felines

Samuel Clemens, commonly known as Mark Twain, had a deep and abiding love and respect for cats and often referred to them in his writing. He gave his cats tongue-twisting monikers to help children practice pronunciation. At one time, he shared his house with cats named Buffalo Bill, Beelzebub, Blather-skite, and Apollinaris. Twain's property adjoined that of Harriet Beecher Stowe (author of Uncle Tom's Cabin), who also loved and cherished her cats. Since the two sets of felines often visited each other, the authors had the cats "write" letters to one another.

Betty White's Cats

Betty White has been a pet lover her whole life. She found a stunning black cat hanging out in her backyard shortly after her husband, Allen Ludden, passed away. In typical cat fashion, the feline vanished if White so much as looked at it. However, the cat seemed fascinated by Timmy, White's little black poodle. Eventually, the homeless cat started accepting food from Betty. Then one day the stray kitty followed Timmy inside. It took a long time to win the cat's trust, but Timmy eventually made friends with the black cat. Betty promptly adopted the feline and named him T.K. for Timmy's Kitty.

Helpful Humans

President Calvin Coolidge had three cats: Timmie, Tiger, and Blacky. Tiger was a wanderer. One day when Tiger didn't come home, Coolidge asked a local radio station for help in locating his cat. The station broadcast Tiger's description and passed on the President's request to help find the cat. Tiger was soon discovered at the Navy building (perhaps trying to enlist?) and was returned to the grateful President.

Angel

Emma and her husband, Jim, have always felt blessed with a house full of cats. They've shared their home with 11 feline friends, all of whom were strays or from an animal shelter. And they always run an "outdoor café" on their porch to feed countless other strays.

❋　❋　❋　❋

WEENIE, THEIR OLDEST and dearest cat, died in the fall of 2016, an especially painful time for them because Emma had recently suffered the loss of her entire family. Over a period of 11 months, her mother, father, and brother had all died of cancer. She was becoming increasingly depressed and could not bear the thought of the normally joyous holiday season without her family and Weenie.

Her downward slide became apparent at work, especially to a dear young man named Patrick. He and Emma had formed a friendship immediately after she started her job. His great sense of humor and love for laughter and practical jokes had instantly drawn her to him—he reminded her a great deal of her younger brother. Emma was also one of the few people who could see through the comedian on the outside to find the hurting teenager on the inside, crying out for attention and understanding. They were both from broken homes and had an overwhelming need to be loved. Perhaps that is what had really drawn her to him—in many ways, she understood his pain. It disturbed him to see Emma so depressed, especially at Christmastime. Knowing of her great affection for cats and how much the recent loss of Weenie had added to her depression, Patrick decided to take action.

He had heard about a poor little kitten that had been left to die, but miraculously someone had heard her faint cries and rescued her. She was taken to a local veterinary clinic, where she was first fed through an eyedropper and then eventually raised on a baby bottle. She spent the first three months of her life in the clinic, receiving constant love and attention from the staff. Patrick chose the perfect "mama" for this special kitten.

On December 23, he called Emma into the kitchen at work and gave her a handsomely wrapped package. Immediately being suspicious of a prank, she shook it. The familiar sound of a box of cat food rattled through the kitchen. Everyone who had gathered started laughing, so she went along with Patrick's joke. She ripped off the paper and was holding a box of Kitten Chow. By this time, she was laughing, too, and thanked him. "Well, at least it's something I can always use!"

At that moment, he took Emma by the hand and led her around the corner. There stood another coworker holding the most adorable little kitten she had ever seen. She was so shocked and surprised, and she couldn't believe how kind and thoughtful her young friend had been. There aren't many people who would go to such lengths to give such a meaningful gift, she thought.

Patrick looked at her and said, "I figured this was the one thing you needed to cheer you up and help you make it through this Christmas. Having a new kitten to care for will occupy your mind and bring you the happiness you deserve." Emma was laughing and crying and hugging him at the same time. For once in her life, she was speechless.

As she walked closer to the kitten, their eyes met. There was an instant connection, and Emma knew in her heart that this kitten was meant for her. The kitty scrambled into Emma's arms and crawled up the front of her Christmas cat sweatshirt until her little head was resting on Emma's right shoulder. It was there that she stayed for the rest of the afternoon, purring. Others tried to take her from Emma, but the feline held on to her for dear life. The kitten had adopted Emma, and she named her Angel. Everyone agreed that it was the perfect name for this tiny gift—and, of course, Patrick.

Emma took Angel home and introduced her to her new brothers and sisters and her stunned but pleased husband. There was no period of adjustment as there had been with the other cats. Angel walked around as though she owned the place. It seemed so familiar to her, as if she had been here before.

During Angel's first night at home, she wasn't satisfied to sleep in the cozy little bed they had carefully prepared for her downstairs. Instead, she followed Emma up the steps and took her place on her pillow. And she did the same thing every night afterward. She placed her paws around Emma's head as if holding her safely and protecting her from the world. Emma began to sleep more soundly and peacefully than she had in a very long time.

As Angel grew, they needed to change the sleeping arrangements because Emma no longer had a place on her pillow for herself. Now Angel sleeps right next to her, lengthwise with her head on the pillow, nestled close to Emma. This gives Angel close access to her owner's face when she feels the need for hugs and kisses during the night. If Emma makes the "mistake" of trying to roll over and face away from Angel, Angel is forced to get up and properly throw herself down again on the other side, letting Emma know of her displeasure at being disturbed.

Angel always seems to sense when Emma is having an especially bad day because she makes it a point to stay as close as possible to her and smother her with extra kisses. It's as if Angel gives her the strength and courage she needs to go on for another day.

Patrick is always anxious to hear of Angel's latest escapades and devilish behavior. She makes them both laugh, even more than they did before, and that is quite an accomplishment. Because of her angel, Angel, Emma is certain that she has been able to recover from her tremendous losses and once again is able to enjoy life. She was sent the best gift of all that Christmas, and Patrick was the delivery person.

First Cat Socks

After 12 "catless" years at the White House, First Cat Socks took the country by storm. Socks was given to President Bill Clinton's daughter Chelsea by one of her elementary school friends when he was just a kitten. A distinguished black-and-white cat, Socks had his own newsletter and fan club.

Feline Foes

❋ Johannes Brahms refused to go near cats.

❋ President Dwight Eisenhower banished cats from the White House and gave standing orders that cats trespassing on White House grounds should be shot on sight.

❋ Alexander the Great despised cats (perhaps making him not so great).

❋ Shakespeare had nothing good to say (or write) about cats.

❋ Napoleon Bonaparte suffered from a clinical cat phobia and was said to become hysterical when faced with a feline.

Cat Fanciers

* Anne Frank shared cramped quarters with a white-socked cat named Boche.

* Winston Churchill kept a succession of cats, including Nelson, Margate, and a marmalade cat named Jock.

* At one time, Florence Nightingale had more than 60 Persians who she named after public figures, such as Bismarck, Gladstone, and Disraeili.

* The prophet Mohammed was very fond of a little cat he called Muezza. Mohammed is reported to have cut off his sleeve rather than disturb the cat, which was sleeping on it.

Cassie's Kittens

Taylor sighed as she looked around their four-room apartment. It hadn't been updated in 50 years. Gray paint cracked on top of layers of spongy wallpaper, the varnish was worn off the cabinets, and the linoleum on the kitchen floor was so badly cracked it was hard to scrub it clean.

✳ ✳ ✳ ✳

WORST OF ALL, Taylor and her husband's three youngest children and their beagle shared one bedroom. They had squeezed two sets of bunk beds into the bedroom, and they were occupied by their 15-year-old daughter, Karen, their 12-year-old son, Kendal, and their 6-year-old daughter, Cassie. Luckily, Dan, their oldest, had already moved away from home or they'd have been even more crowded. The children got some privacy by changing clothes in the bathroom, and their daughter Karen did her nightly studying at the city library. Still, none of them were coping very well with their new living situation.

Their family business had failed, leaving Taylor and her husband deeply in debt with few options. They had to sell the lovely home that they had spent the past nine years remodeling. She and her husband each had new jobs, and they knew they'd slowly climb out of their financial hole, but for now they were living in an old apartment building that they were attempting to renovate.

Taylor's deepest concern was for her daughter, Cassie. They had adopted her when she was four. Her early years had been difficult and left her traumatized. Now, just when she was beginning to feel comfortable and secure, they had moved into this ugly, crowded living space. Each member of the family was grieving their individual losses, and tempers were running short. Taylor knew Cassie didn't need this added stress.

Cassie came up with her own cure for the sadness she felt. She decided she needed a kitten to snuggle and love. She stubbornly refused to listen when Taylor tried to explain that they didn't have room for another pet.

Winter approached, and the family continued to make the best of their less-than-desirable living situation. Cassie and Taylor decided to pray—Cassie for a kitten and Taylor for an answer. One evening Taylor went out to the garage to pull some boxes of winter clothing out of storage. The box with Cassie's clothes was near the floor, and the lid had come off. Taylor could hardly believe her eyes when she saw what was in that box: A mother cat had made her bed there, and she was nursing two tiny gray kittens.

It seemed that their prayers were answered with not one kitten, but two. Cassie said it was a double blessing. Once the mama cat left her kittens and Taylor brought them inside, she was amazed at how much joy they brought to their household. The children took turns feeding and brushing them, and everyone enjoyed watching their playful antics. Even their beagle seemed happy to have them around.

Cassie had been right. Having the kittens gave them something fun to focus on, so they didn't feel as unhappy about their dreary home.

Trim: First Cat Around the World

A glossy 12-pound black cat with four white feet and a white star on his chest, Trim was the first cat to tour the globe and circumnavigate Australia.

✳ ✳ ✳ ✳

TRIM WAS BORN at sea on a ship called *Roundabout* in 1799 and became the beloved cat of explorer Matthew Flinders (1774–1814), famous in his own right for being the first person to circumnavigate Australia—as well as name it.

Raised at sea, Trim demonstrated no fear of the water. He was an adept swimmer, and if he ever fell overboard while perusing the slippery deck, crew members would simply throw him a rope so he could scurry up to the safety of the ship.

After four happy years of adventures, 1803 marked the last year Trim set sail with Matthew Flinders. Sailing for England aboard the ship Cumberland, the pair were shipwrecked on a coral reef in the Indian Ocean. Matthew Flinders and Trim were rescued but imprisoned on the French island of Mauritius, where Flinders was held as a spy. After two weeks of captivity, Trim went missing and was presumed dead. Flinders was nearly inconsolable. Later in life, Flinders wrote, "I can never speak of cats without a sentiment of regret for my poor Trim, the favourite of all our ship's company."

A statue of Trim looking up at the statue of his master, Matthew Flinders, was erected in Sydney in 1995.

From Abandoned to Adored

With patches of orange and brown fur and constantly squinting eyes, Nanny the kitten was barely old enough to eat on her own. Still, she was found abandoned on the street. As is the case with abandoned animals, the local shelter picked up little Nanny, which could have been the end of this kitten's life. However, one of the shelter workers knew of a kind person named Catherine who took on special cases like this little one.

✳   ✳   ✳   ✳

IT TURNED OUT that Nanny had been born with disfigured eyelids, and she was constantly squinting because of how irritated her eyes had become. This was likely the reason that the original owner abandoned her. Some people want "perfect" pets.

Thanks to Catherine, who took Nanny into her home and welcomed her into the family, the kitty received drops in her eyes daily and corrective surgery on her eyelids when she was old enough. Although they still do not look completely healed and "normal," her eyes no longer bother her to the point of constant whimpering and squinting.

Through all her discomfort and pain and the necessary treatment to relieve it, Nanny has never been anything but a truly happy kitten. It is as if she has no idea that there is anything wrong or different about her. She runs, jumps, and plays just like any other happy, healthy feline. Nanny loves being petted, snuggling, and curling up to Catherine for her daily snoozes. She climbs up Catherine's pant leg to oversee what's cooking on the stove, and the close supervision of her owner is exactly how she got her name. To say Nanny has personality is an understatement.

Because of all the things she has overcome, Nanny is now taken around to various local events by the family that adopted her. By her very presence, Nanny proves a point: Although a little different, she still has a big spirit and a loving personality to share. The colorful kitten has sat in the laps of small children as they learn to read, offering an encouraging purr or blink. She has been stroked and lovingly called "imperfectly perfect." Nanny has inspired people to see past her differences and realize that she and other special-needs animals like her are just as loving and deserving of a good home as any so-called "normal" pet.

People miss out when they demand perfection—in animals or in other people. Often there's far more joy to be found in someone who's a little different or has walked a more difficult road. That's what Nanny teaches us. This abandoned kitten turned into an adorable cat—and she is adored by not just her family, but by all who meet her and have a chance to pet those soft patches of orange and brown fur.

An Unlikely Truce

"Retirement does not have to be this boring," Carol told her nine-year-old Boston terrier, Bailey, a few weeks after she retired.

❋   ❋   ❋   ❋

THE TWO HAD spent those weeks in a state of confusion. Every morning at 7:45, Bailey would stand by the back door to be let out for the day. When Carol would call her to come inside ten minutes later, Bailey would give her that "Who, me?" look. For the rest of the day, Bailey would pace around the house until 5:30 in the evening, the time Carol used to come home from work. Then Bailey would revert to her normal self, bringing toys for Carol to toss, snuggling with her on the sofa, and begging for treats.

"We need more action around here," Carol told Bailey. And according to Carol, what spelled action more than a kitten? She always wanted to adopt another furry friend, and she thought there was no better time than now.

Later that week, Carol set a half-grown feline fur ball she adopted from the shelter next to Bailey and said, "This is Dasher. Treat him gently."

Carol expected more out of Bailey than the dog's aggrieved-princess routine. Bailey would disdainfully sniff Dasher then yelp at the claw scratch the kitten gave her on the nose. When Dasher drank from Bailey's water bowl, Bailey would bark from a safe distance until he had lapped up his fill. The pooch refused to snuggle with Carol on the sofa when Dasher was on her lap.

Although the kitty was undaunted by living with a jealous dog, Carol bought Dasher a plush red cat bed so he could have a place of his own. As soon as it was unwrapped and set on the floor, Bailey occupied it. Her head hung off one end, her tail off the other. Dasher snatched one of Bailey's toys and played with it enthusiastically while Bailey glowered from the cat bed.

Carol finally had the "action" she was craving, but she felt badly that it was at her beloved dog's expense. One afternoon Carol pulled out the dog leash, which she thought would be the only thing that would get Bailey out of the cat bed, and the two headed out the door for the second love of Bailey's life: a walk. (Food had always been her first, but at this point Carol figured it might have been replaced by that cat bed.) Dasher slipped out the door and followed them. Carol couldn't catch Dasher to bring him back inside the house, and he refused to desert the group. Bailey plodded along the riverbank, tail drooping, too dispirited to bark at the geese Dasher was chasing.

Even though Carol's pets had not become the fast friends she had hoped they would be, eventually the two reached an uneasy truce. Each animal staked out and defended his or her own territory, and they seemed to be learning the basic rules of pet cohabitation. Carol's friends told her that it would be a kindness to her elderly dog to get rid of the cat, but by then

Carol knew that Dasher had become a permanent part of their dysfunctional little family.

While Carol's atypical brood had certainly grown closer, it took a cooking disaster to make them a real family. One evening Carol was cooking chili for dinner when she forgot that it was heating on the stove, and the smell of smoke quickly alerted her that her meal was boiling over. The cornbread in the oven was also charred and smoke billowed from the oven when she opened it. The smoke detector shrieked.

While Carol was opening the windows and fanning the air with the cat bed, firemen alerted by a neighbor charged through the door. They hustled Carol out of the house so quickly that she did not have time to grab her purse. Bailey was trailing behind her, and the dog paced between Carol and the men in boots. Carol did not see flames licking curtains and walls, but the fire chief ordered her to stay outside. At that point Carol must have been too flustered to think about Dasher even when Bailey ran back inside. Bailey quickly returned with a snarling, clawing Dasher in her mouth. She dropped the cat at Carol's feet, sat beside her, and nudged her knee for a pat. Carol hugged and praised her heroic dog while Dasher stalked off to bother some birds that were congregating in the yard.

The cat bed still belongs to Bailey, but now the two furry pals play together and share the water bowl like collaborative colleagues, if not best friends. At night they snuggle with Carol on the sofa, one on each side. Carol's Christmas card photo surprised friends with whom she had shared stories about their domestic strife. In the photo, Carol is kneeling beside the Christmas tree with a dog on one side and a cat on the other, both wearing Christmas ribbon and rather pleasant expressions. The caption wrote itself: "All is calm."

The Ministerial Mouser

Political offices, such as the Oval Office in the White House or the Prime Minister's office at 10 Downing Street in London, are often considered serious, no-nonsense places of business. But sometimes, a cat is just the ticket to providing a bit of levity in an otherwise formal setting.

✳ ✳ ✳ ✳

Cats and Kings

WE SOMETIMES ASSUME that the British are a bit serious and stodgy. Their reputation for maintaining a cool, calm demeanor did, after all, inspire the idiom, "keep a stiff upper lip," and our impression of British heads of state is colored by the stoicism of hundreds of years of enduring tradition. So perhaps the last place we would expect to see cat hair on the furniture is in the offices of 10 Downing Street, the headquarters of the Government of the United Kingdom. Yet this office is home to Larry, a brown and white tabby cat believed to have been born around 2007. Even more impressive, Larry has his own official title: Chief Mouser to the Cabinet Office.

Surprisingly, keeping a cat in English government offices is not a new practice. On the contrary, there have been cats living amongst the rulers of England at least since the 1500s, when King Henry VIII allowed Lord Chancellor Cardinal Thomas Wolsey to keep his cat at his side, even during judicial proceedings. Throughout history, these cats have not only been companions for kings, queens, and heads of state, but they've served a practical purpose, as well, chasing mice and rats and keeping the vermin population under control.

A New Appointee

And it was a vermin problem that brought Larry to 10 Downing Street in 2011. After rats were seen scurrying around outside the building during a televised news report, officials realized they needed to deal with the unwanted visitors.

Downing Street staff members adopted Larry from the Battersea Dogs and Cats Home, one of the U.K.'s oldest animal shelters, and Prime Minister David Cameron and his family approved of the new addition. Larry's adoption was big news in the country, and the animal shelter saw a 15 percent increase in cat adoptions over the next year.

Larry, who is the first Downing Street cat to be given a title, wasn't immediately confident in his job duties, preferring instead to explore the corridors and rooms of his new home. But after staff members gave him a stuffed mouse to play with, he started to get into the groove of his occupation, catching his first mouse two months after joining Downing Street. After that, it was every mouse for himself, as the Chief Mouser began seeking out intruders, quickly dispatching them and occasionally dropping them on the front lawn.

Cat Fights and Cat Naps

Like most political appointees, Larry's tenure has not been without controversy. On his very first day at Downing Street, the overwhelmed cat scratched a reporter who got a little too

close for comfort. Larry then ran under a table and hid the rest of the day. Fortunately, he has improved his relationship with people over the years, but the same can't be said for his colleague Palmerston, the Chief Mouser of the Foreign and Commonwealth Office. The two cats have been in numerous fights over the years, with one particularly nasty brawl

requiring police intervention. Although both cats were able to keep their jobs, they no doubt received a reprimand from human—or rather feline—resources.

Larry's official job description on the 10 Downing Street website includes "greeting guests to the house, inspecting security defenses and testing antique furniture for napping quality." It sounds like a tough job, but this fluffy Brit is definitely up for the challenge.

Who Says Cats Don't Care?

Zipper was one of two dogs that lived on the Jensen farm along with his canine sister, Molly. The two were born in the same litter and were indisputably the best of friends. When Molly got sick, it was a cat that took matters into her own paws to make Zipper's life worth living again.

✳   ✳   ✳   ✳

FROM THE EARLIEST weeks, when they would tumble over each other to get to their mother's milk, Zipper and Molly were inseparable. The family who owned the farm sold four of the puppies from their litter, but they knew better than to try to separate these two.

For 12 years Zipper and Molly were a dynamic duo. They ate together, they snuggled together, and they played together. Where one went, the other followed. They got along with the cats living on the farm, but neither paid them much attention. Why should they? They had each other.

One day Molly became sick. She lived another three weeks, and at the ripe old age of 84 in dog years, she passed away. Of course the Jensens were sad to lose their beloved pooch, but Zipper was devastated. Without his best friend, he moped around the farm as if life were barely worth living. He rarely ate, and he certainly didn't want to play. The only thing he did was sleep all day long.

The Jensens were worried about Zipper. He was, after all, the same age as Molly, and he seemed to have lost his cheerful and buoyant personality. He was losing weight, and his once-mischievous eyes were now clouded over. The Jensens weren't sure what to do.

Around that time, Cassie, a black-and-white Persian cat, started to pay attention to Zipper. She would bring him valuable gifts—like mice that she carried in her mouth—and gently lay them at his feet. She would take her nap by him and follow him whenever he ventured outside. She would even carry bits of cat food to his bowl, and Cassie would eat during those rare times that Zipper ate.

At first Zipper ignored the cat, but little by little he began to take an interest in her—and in his life again. The first step was eating some of his food, which gave him strength. In time, he slowly started to play again, either with his new feline friend or the other animals in the Jensen menagerie.

Zipper, the dog that had shared so much with his littermate, suddenly had a new best friend. Whether he realized that his new friend was feline rather than canine is unknown. Whatever the reason, the now 13-year-old Zipper is living the life of a much younger dog. All because of a cat that cared.

Mess-Kit, the VIP Cat

Elaine was a U.S. Army nurse during World War II, serving with the 131st General Hospital at Blandford Camp close to Bournemouth, England. She was honored to serve her country and especially proud of the soldiers, who gave their all for the cause.

* * * *

DURING ELAINE'S TOUR of duty, a mother cat chose to have her litter near the camp's kitchen. Elaine asked for permission to keep one of the kittens and chose a long-haired, striped one, which she named Mess-Kitt. She was a lively kitty who often got Elaine in trouble by scattering the contents of her wastebasket throughout the barracks. But she was worth the trouble. Mess-Kitt learned to meet her when she got off duty, which always brightened Elaine's day. She would get down on one knee, and Mess-Kitt would jump from that knee to her shoulder and curl around her neck like a fur piece. It was an immense blessing to have something to write home about other than the war.

Mess-Kitt enjoyed the care packages Elaine received, especially the canned Vienna sausages. Elaine used the cartons as litter boxes, filling them with sandy ground from a nearby field.

Sometimes Mess-Kitt would visit Elaine's ward. There she'd spend the day with "her boys," the wounded soldiers. They were alone, injured, and in a foreign country. They desperately needed someone to love, and Mess-Kitt filled that void, giving them something to think about besides the war.

One day Mess-Kitt started to have a seizure, and Elaine asked the colonel for permission to call a vet, even though she knew this would be a luxury that probably wouldn't be allowed. Imagine Elaine's surprise when he sent his own driver to take the ailing Mess-Kitt for treatment. It was clear that this morale-boosting kitty had worked her way into even the colonel's heart.

When the war eventually ended, it was time for Elaine to go home. She sadly gave Mess-Kitt to a friend she had met while in England, who wrote to Elaine for years after that, keeping her up-to-date on Mess-Kitt's mischievous antics.

So if anyone should hear some elderly veteran telling stories about a cat that comforted him in an Army hospital in England during the war, they should believe him—he's telling the truth.

Better Together

Candice had two beloved pets. Ironically, one of them was deaf and the other was blind. But together, they were perfect.

❋   ❋   ❋   ❋

A TRUE ANIMAL LOVER, Candice has always had one or two pets ever since she was a little girl. Unlike some pet owners, she didn't consider herself a "dog person" or a "cat person." She loved them all the same.

Truman came to her first. A basset hound with long, floppy ears and soulful eyes, he was a devoted dog. In his puppy years, he was lively and playful. He adored Candice, and the feeling was mutual.

One day while watching the local news, Candice caught a segment about a stray cat that needed a home. A bit shy, the calico kitty avoided human contact until a determined cook finally captured her in the alley with the offer of leftover tuna casserole. She was turned over to the local Humane Society, where they soon discovered she was deaf.

When the little cat arrived at the shelter, she was in bad shape. Skinny with ratty fur, a host of worms, and two small cuts on her ear, they called her Tatters. They bathed her, dewormed her, and brushed her until her coat was soft and fluffy. She was ready for a forever home. The trouble was that no one seemed willing to take in a stray cat that couldn't hear.

But Candice was touched by the story. Knowing that it might be hard to find a home for Tatters, she called the Humane Society and offered to adopt the kitten.

When she first arrived at her new home, Tatters was afraid of everything. She hid under the bed for two days, eating only what was placed close enough to her that she didn't need to come out into the open.

Truman, on the other hand, was a natural with the kitten, and he welcomed the new arrival with open paws. He would inch close to the cat and calmly rest his head between his paws—the canine version of "This place is safe and calm. You'll like it here." And sure enough, Tatters did.

The two quickly became friends. With no hearing, Tatters seemed to have sharpened her other senses. Candice could tell that the kitten felt even the slightest breeze or when the floorboards vibrated and that she saw everything through eagle eyes. And Truman was always at her side and alerted her to danger.

As Truman grew older, his eyesight began to get bad, until one day he could see only shadows. Tatters seemed to realize that it was her turn to be the protector, and the deaf kitty became Truman's seeing-eye cat. She slept by his side, led him slowly to his food, and helped him navigate around the house. Together, they could do anything.

6 Top Cats

Some people are cat people. They take pictures of their cats, tell stories about their cats, and feed their cats designer food. For a cat lover, even the most unremarkable cat is special, but the following cats have been singled out for extra-noteworthy achievements or distinctions.

✳   ✳   ✳   ✳

1. **Cat Most in Need of a Babysitter: Bluebell:** Bluebell, a Persian cat from South Africa, gave birth to 14 kittens in one litter. She holds the record for having the most kittens at once, with all of her offspring surviving—rare for a litter so large.

2. **Most Aloof Cat: Big Boy:** When Hurricane George hit Gulfport, Mississippi, in 1998, Big Boy was blown up into a big oak tree. In 2001, Big Boy's owner claimed the cat

never left the tree. The feline eats, sleeps, and eliminates in the tree and climbs from branch to branch for exercise.

3. **Big Mama: Dusty:** In 1952, a seemingly ordinary tabby cat gave new meaning to the term "maternal instinct." Texas-born Dusty set the record for birthing more kittens than any other cat in history. Dusty had more than 420 kittens before her last litter at age 18.

4. **Best-dressed Cat: The Birman:** The Birman cat breed originally came from Burma (now Myanmar) where these longhairs were bred as companions for priests. A Birman cat can be identified by its white "gloves." All Birmans have four white paws, which give them that oh-so-aristocratic look.

5. **Cat Most in Need of a Diet: Himmy:** According to the Guinness Book of World Records, the heaviest cat in recorded history was an Australian kitty named Himmy that reportedly weighed more than 46 pounds in 1986. If the data is accurate, Himmy's waistline measured about 33 inches. Guinness has removed this category from their record roster, so as not to encourage people to overfeed their animals.

6. **First Cat: The Eocene Kitty:** Fossils from the Eocene period show that cats roamed the earth more than 50 million years ago. Sure, they looked a little different, but these remains show that today's domestic cats have a family tree that goes way, way back.

Chapter 12

Cat Poems and Stories

Kittenhood

Nineteenth century British children's author Alfred Elwes wrote a charming book titled The Adventures of a Cat, and a Fine Cat Too! *The following is an excerpt from the book.*

✳   ✳   ✳   ✳

THERE IS NOTHING like beginning at the very commencement of a story, if we wish it to be thoroughly understood; at least, I think so; and, as I wish my story to be clear and intelligible, in order that it may furnish a hint or a warning to others, I shall at least act up to my opinion, and begin at the beginning,—I may say, at the very tip of my tale.

Being now a Cat of some years' standing (I do not much like remembering how many), I was of course a Kitten on making my entry into life,—my first appearance being in company with a brother and three sisters.

We were all declared to be "the prettiest little darlings that ever were seen;" but as the old Puss who made the remark had said precisely the same thing at sight of every fresh Kitten she beheld, and she was accustomed to see ten or twelve new ones every week, the observation is no proof of our being very charming or very beautiful.

I cannot remember what passed during the first few days of my existence, for my eyes were close-shut till the ninth morning.

I have an indistinct recollection however of overhearing a few words which passed between my mother and a friend of the family who had dropped in for a little chat, on the evening of the eighth day.

The latter had been remarking on my efforts to unclose my lids, to obtain a little peep at what was going on, when my good parent exclaimed, "Ah! yes, she tries hard enough to stare at life now, because she knows nothing of it; but when she is as old as you or I, neighbour, she will wish more than once that she had always kept her eyes closed, or she is no true Cat."

I could not of course, at the time, have any notion what my mother meant, but I think, indeed I am sure, that I have discovered her meaning long ago; and all those who have lived to have sorrow,—and who has not?—will understand it too.

I had found my tongue and my legs, and so had my brother and sisters, before we got the use of our eyes. With the first we kept up a perfect concert of sounds; the legs we employed in dragging our bodies about our capacious cradle, crawling over each other, and getting in everybody's way, for we somehow managed, in the dark as we were, to climb to the edge of our bed and roll quickly over it, much to our astonishment and the amusement or annoyance of the family, just as they happened to be in the humour.

Our sight was at last granted us. On that eventful morning our mother stepped gently into our bed, which she had left an hour before; and, taking us one by one in her maternal embrace, she held us down with her legs and paws, and licked us with more affection and assiduity than she had ever bestowed on our toilet before. Her tongue, which she rendered as soft for the occasion as a Cat's tongue can be made, I felt pass and repass over my eyes until the lids burst asunder, and I could see!

And what a confusion of objects I first beheld! It seemed as if everything above was about to fall upon my head and crush me, and that everything around was like a wall to prevent my moving; and when, after a day or two, I began to understand better the distance that these objects were from me, I fell into the opposite error, and hurt my nose not a little through running it against a chair, which I fancied to be very much further off. These difficulties however soon wore away. Experience, bought at the price of some hard knocks, taught me better; and, a month after my first peep at the world, it seemed almost impossible I could ever have been so ignorant.

No doubt my brother and sisters procured their knowledge in a similar way: it is certain that it cost them something. One incident, which happened to my brother, I particularly remember; and it will serve to prove that he did not get his experience for nothing.

We were all playing about the room by ourselves, our mother being out visiting or marketing, I do not know which, and the nurse, who was charged to take care of us, preferring to chat to the handsome footman in the tortoise-shell coat over the way, to looking after us Kittens.

A large pan full of something sticky, but I do not remember what, was in a corner; and as the edge of it was very broad, we climbed on to it and peeped in.

Our brother, who was very venturesome, said he could jump over it to the opposite brim. We said it was not possible, for the pan was broad and rather slippery; and what a thing it would be if he fell into it! But the more we exclaimed about its difficulty, the more resolved he was to try.

Getting his legs together, he gave a spring; but, slipping just as he got to the other side, his claws could not catch hold of anything to support himself, and he went splash backwards into the sticky mess. His screams, and indeed ours, ought to have been enough to call nurse to our assistance; but she was making such a noise herself with the tortoise-shell footman, that my brother might have been drowned or suffocated before she would have come to his assistance. As it was, he managed to drag himself to the edge without any help at all; and as we feared that all of us would get punished if the adventure were known, my sisters and myself set to work and licked him all over; and then getting into bed, we cuddled up together to make him dry, and were soon fast asleep.

Although the accident was not known at the time, we all suffered for it; for my brother caught a dreadful cold, and myself and sisters were ill for several days, through the quantity of the stuff we had licked off my brother's coat, and one of us nearly died through it.

As we grew stronger and older, we were permitted, under the care of our nurse, to go into the country for a few hours to play. It may be perhaps thought, from what I have said, that nurse's care was not worth much, and that we might just as well have looked after ourselves, as the poorer Kittens of our city were accustomed to do. But this was not precisely the case; for when nurse had nobody to chat with she was very strict with us, I assure you, and on such occasions made up for her inattention at other times. That unlucky fondness of hers however for gossiping, was the cause of a great deal of mischief; and about this time it partly occasioned a sad misfortune in our family. I said partly, because the accident was also due to an act of disobedience; and as the adventure may serve as a double warning, I will briefly relate it.

It was a lovely morning in early summer; the sun shone gaily upon the city, looked at his brilliant face in the river, danced about among the leaves of the trees, and polished the coats of every Cat and Dog which came out to enjoy the beautiful day he was making.

To our great delight we were allowed to take a long walk in the country. Two of our cousins, and a young Pussy who was visiting at our house, were to accompany us; and nurse had strict charge to prevent our getting into mischief. Before we started our mother called us and said, that, although she had desired nurse to look after us, and take care that no harm should happen while we were out, she desired also that we should take care of ourselves, and behave like Kittens of station and good-breeding, not like the young Cats about the streets, poor things! who had no home except the first hole they could creep into, no food but what they could pick up or steal, and no father or mother that they knew of to teach them what was good. Such creatures were to be pitied and relieved, but not imitated; and she hoped we would, by our behaviour, show that we bore her advice in mind. "Above all," she added, "do not let me hear of your climbing and racing about in a rude and extravagant way, for a great deal of mischief is often done by such rough modes of amusement." We hastily promised all and everything. If we had kept our words, we should have been perfect angels of Cats, for we declared in a chorus that we would do only what was good, and would carefully avoid everything that was evil; and with these fine promises in our mouths, we started off in pairs under the guidance of nurse.

We soon came to the wood, situated at some distance from the city; and, walking into it, shortly arrived at an open space, where some large trees stood round and threw broad patches of shade over the grass.

We at once commenced our gambols. We rolled over one another, we sprang over each other's backs, and hid behind the great beech trunks for the pleasure of springing out upon our companions when they stealthily came to look for us.

In the midst of our fun we observed that nurse had gone. We had been so busied with our own diversions that not one of us had observed her departure; but now that we found it out, we set off to discover where she had strolled to. We observed her, after a few minutes, cosily seated on a bank of violets, near the very same tortoise-shell footman, who lived opposite our house, although how he came there we could not imagine. Nor indeed did we much trouble ourselves to guess. Seeing she was so engaged we returned at once to our sport, and played none the less heartily because nurse was not there to curb us.

I remember, as if it were only yesterday, the scene which followed. I was amusing myself with one of my pretty cousins, who was dressed in white, and was about my own age. I had thrown her down on the grass, and was patting her with my paws, when I heard a scream; I turned quickly round, just in time to see one of my sisters falling from a tall tree, to which she had climbed with our young visitor, when, all of us running up, we discovered that, on reaching the ground, she had struck her head against a sharp stone, and was now bleeding and without motion.

Our cries brought nurse to the spot, who, as soon as she discovered all the mischief that had been done, without saying a word started off with all swiftness, with her tail in the air. We thought she had gone to fetch assistance or to inform our mother of what had occurred; but as she did not come back, and evening was fast setting in, we thought it best to proceed towards home, although we did not much like meeting our parents after what had happened.

There was no help for it however; so, giving a last frightened look at our poor little sister, who was now quite dead and cold, we walked sadly homewards, and reached the house just as night was falling.

I pass over what ensued,—my mother's grief, and her anger against nurse, who, by the bye, never came back to express her sorrow; I pass over also my mother's remarks upon the occasion; but I may observe, that they, added to the sad accident itself, made so deep an impression upon me, that whenever I felt inclined to disobey my good mother's admonitions, the image of my dead sister would rise up before me, and, although it did not, alas! always prevent my being wicked, it often did so, and on every occasion made me feel repentance for my error.

(Alfred Elwes)

"Kitten's Night Thought" (A Poem)

English writer and cat lover Oliver Herford has been dubbed "The American Oscar Wilde".

✳   ✳   ✳   ✳

When Human Folk put out the light,
And think they've made it dark as night,
A Pussy Cat sees every bit
As well as when the lights are lit.
When Human Folk have gone upstairs,
And shed their skins and said their prayers,
And there is no one to annoy,
Then Pussy may her life enjoy.
No Human hands to pinch or slap,
Or rub her fur against the nap,
Or throw cold water from a pail,
Or make a handle of her tail.
And so you will not think it wrong
When she can play the whole night long,
With no one to disturb her play,
That Pussy goes to bed by day.

(Oliver Herford)

Ban-Ban, The Bold

American author Marion Ames Taggart was a children's author who published the majority of her work in the early twentieth century. The following excerpt comes from her book Pussy-Cat Town.

✳ ✳ ✳ ✳

H E WAS REALLY very beautiful. High-born, too,—a pure Maltese! He had a short, saucy face; a square little nose, with which he was apt to pry into other people's business; and he saw everything with his bright eyes, and understood most things with his quick wit. But he had almost no patience at all, and he was as full of pranks as a monkey—indeed, that's what gave him his name.

A boy? Mercy, no! Whoever heard of a pure Maltese boy? A cat, of course, but such a beauty! He was as quick as he could be, and ran very fast, and jumped like a flash—flashes do jump, so that's all right. Did you never see a flash of lightning jump from one cloud to another? Well, this Maltese kitten was so quick that his little master called him Bandersnatch—out of "Through the Looking-Glass", you know, where the White King says: "You might as well try to catch a Bandersnatch," or, in another place: "You might as well try to stop a Bandersnatch." So that is where quick little Ban-Ban got his first name. And the second Ban was short for Bandarlog, the name of the monkey people in the Jungle Book, because he was so much more like a monkey than a quiet, purry, furry, mild-mannered kitten.

Ban-Ban had the very best home a cat could have; indeed, he was a good deal spoiled. In this home he grew up to be three years old, but it was only his body that grew bigger. Inside that Maltese body he wore a kitten's heart, getting younger every minute, loving play better, and cutting up more didoes all the time, instead of settling down into a staid cat, as any one would have expected him to do who saw the purple shades in his dark gray suit!

Now Ban-Ban loved his little master very much—not that he ever thought of him as his "master;" no cat ever would admit having a master. Ban-Ban considered the little boy as a friend whom he, a prince of the Maltese Royal Family, allowed to play with him. He was more useful than kitten friends because he could open doors, drag strings around, hide sticks under the edges of rugs, get milk from the refrigerator, cut up meat, play hide-and-go-seek better than cats, and shake up soft knitted things into fine beds on cold days, besides scratching a person under the chin and on the side of the cheek in a way that made a person stick out his little red tongue and purr, no matter how much he felt like playing. But that is not having a master; that is really keeping a very useful and devoted servant. Ban-Ban hated of all things to show that he loved little Rob; he liked to pretend that he was only polite to him, and often, when he meant to get up in Rob's lap for a little talk, if Rob saw him coming, Ban-Ban would sit down and wash his face, trying to look as if he had never once thought of being loving. You see he was independent.

Because he was independent, and so very impatient, it all came about.

One day Ban-Ban had an idea dart into his brain. Ban-Ban's ideas always darted, they never came slowly; they were just like everything else about him, "as fast as a Bandersnatch." "If two-legged people can build towns and live in them without asking the help of us cats, why can't we cats have a town of our own, and not ask the help of the two-legged people? They are more clumsy and stupid than we are—except Rob; he isn't clumsy or stupid."

It was such a wonderful thought that it half-stunned even Ban-Ban. For as much as five minutes he sat perfectly still, with only the tippest tip of his tail moving. Then he started up with a leap, as if he were jumping after those lost five minutes just as he jumped for butterflies, and away he ran down the garden to find some of his friends.

Bidelia was one of these friends. She was a little creature, very young, a tortoise-shell cat, not pretty, but so clever that no one who didn't know her could believe how clever she was. Her cat acquaintances suspected that she wrote stories on the sly, for her sides were always spattered with big black spots on a yellow ground, and her friends believed she got ink on her yellow clothes writing stories for the magazines, because she was so very clever, and people who are very clever and write books are apt to be untidy with their ink.

Though she was younger than Ban-Ban by nearly two years she had three children, and they were already two months old: Nugget, all yellow, Puttel, black with a white thumb-mark under her chin, and Dolly Varden, with a tortoise-shell dress like her mother's. Bidelia had good reason to be as proud of her children as she was!

Another of Ban-Ban's friends was Mr. Thomas Traddles, a tiger cat, who was so wise and had such remarkable judgment that every one came to him for advice. He was older than Ban-Ban, and he was one of that queer sort of friends which we all have: people whom we do not really like, but whom we respect heaps and heaps, and without whom we cannot get along. Not that there was any reason why Ban-Ban should not like Tommy Traddles; his disposition was perfect, and his manners of the best. Perhaps it was because Tom was so sensible and grave, and Ban-Ban was such a little firebrand, for we none of us really like people who make us feel that we are in the wrong, not unless we are far more humble-minded folk than was proud little Ban-Ban.

There, too, was Wutz-Butz, whose name didn't mean much, but that the little girl who owned him liked to mix up letters and call him by queer sounds. He was a gray and white cat who would let the little girl whom he thought he owned, but who thought that she owned him, do anything under the sun to him, and he would stand it with a perfect mush of patience, but out among the cats he was a warrior. He fought every one that he happened to dislike, and Ban-Ban was always thankful Wutz-Butz liked him—and Ban-Ban was not a coward, either. Wutz-Butz had a big, round head, and a short, thick-set body, and his complexion was apt to get rumpled up—can complexions get rumpled? Well, at any rate this cat's complexion looked rumpled—because of the many strong arguments he had with Ruth's grandmother's big white cat with the gray ears. Ruth was the little girl who owned Wutz-Butz, or whom he owned, according to whether you believe from her or his side of the question.

Ban-Ban had another friend to whom he was bound by ties of the highest respect and gratitude. This was Madam Laura, a sweet, kindly middle-aged lady,—perhaps a trifle past middle age,—to whom all the cats went for comfort and teaching. She was a widow lady, so she wore a great deal of black over her white sides and back, laid on in big spots. She had had a great many sons and daughters, but they had all gone to make their own way in the world, and Madam Laura was said to be quite wealthy, with no one dependent upon her for mice. She was a cat with a mother's heart for all the mewing world, and no cat could be so scratchy as not to love this gentle lady.

The last and dearest of Ban-Ban's friends was Kiku, the snow-white cat, whose name was a Japanese word that means chrysanthemum, and whose nature was as flower-like as his name. He lived next door to Ban-Ban, and played with him most of the time. His little mistress was Rob's dearest friend, his cousin, and her name was Lois. She was a year younger than Rob, which made her only seven years old, but she was not the least bit careless or rough with her pets, as some children are, and Kiku was a very lucky "kitteny-wink, little white lambkin," as Lois called him.

Kiku was always called "Kiku-san," because "san" is a mark of honour among the Japanese, and white Kiku was so gentle and lovely-mannered that no one could deny him the respectful title that his Japanese name suggested. Kiku-san wore white garments with pink trimmings, and he kept them snowy white, for he only went out to play in the grass in fine weather, and slept at night cuddled close in Lois's arms. He puckered his mouth when he was spoken to, and brought his lids down over his amber eyes as if he knew he was most sweet and lovable, fully deserving all the praise which he received—and so he did, for nothing would tempt him to scratch; he never lost his temper, unless he had lost it for good and all when he was born, and had never found it again, which seemed to be the case, for no one had ever seen him cross.

These were Ban-Ban's friends, and it was to find them, or all of them that he could find, that he ran so fast down the garden after his wonderful idea struck him.

He came upon Bidelia, who was sitting in the sunshine letting the children play with her tail.

"Oh, Bidelia!" cried Ban-Ban, "have you seen any of the others?"

"How out of breath you are!" said Bidelia, reproachfully. She was so little that she could jump about all day and never lose her breath. "Tommy Traddles is sunning himself on the fence. Madam Laura is singing a few Felines on the garden bench." A Feline is a kind of cat hymn.

"Do you think you could trust one of the kittens to hunt up Wutz-Butz, and Kiku-san, and ask them to join us here? I have something catelovelant to tell them," said Ban-Ban. "Catelovelant" means "lovely for cats."

"I think Nugget could go; he is getting very plump and reliable," returned Bidelia. "Puttel, go and ask Madam Laura if she would kindly come over here when she has finished her Felines. And, Dolly Varden, go waken Mr. Traddles and ask him to come.

If he is very sound asleep you may stand up on your hind legs and pull his tail—very gently," she added, as Dolly spun around three times rapidly, "and with the greatest respect."

The three kittens scampered off, and Ban-Ban with much effort kept himself from pouring out to Bidelia the Great Idea. Fortunately the kittens so quickly got together the cats for whom they were sent that Ban-Ban was saved from choosing between telling or having a fit.

You had something to say to us, my dear?" hinted Madam Laura after they were all seated. Her voice sounded like rolls of butter rolling, it was so soft and smooth.

"Yes," said Ban-Ban, his fur beginning to stick up all over and his tail to swell, as it always did when he was excited. "I have had a Great Idea."

"You were clever from your kittenhood, Bannie," said Madam Laura, who had known his grandmother.

"Human beings," Ban-Ban continued, trying to keep back the little puffing spits which he often gave when he was stirred, "Human beings build towns and live in them. They never ask our help; they feel that they own the towns. Very likely they do; but as their cats always own the human beings, it doesn't matter. What I have to suggest is that there is no reason why cats should not build and own a city just as the human beings do. I think that we should be the ones to do this. Let us, all of us here, go away to some lovely spot and build a city. Let us ask all the poor, homeless cats, who don't own any human beings, and so have very little food and no warm places to live, to join us. Let us have a city of cats, and let us hand our names down in all future categories and catalogues and histories as the Fathers—and Mothers"—he added, bowing to Madam Laura and Bidelia—"of Our Country, Glory of Our Race."

"Hear, hear!" cried Wutz-Butz. He pronounced it: "He-ar, He-ar!" It sounded like a mew.

"Bandersnatch-Bandarlog, you are indeed A Great Mind," said Tommy Traddles, gravely.

"It will be lovely!" cried Bidelia, joyously. "I want a more extended field."

"And more field-mice," added Laura, who was not clever, only good, which is better than mere cleverness, as all properly taught cats know.

"Then you agree?" asked Ban-Ban, not able, this time, to keep from ending in a "P-pst!" of pure excitement.

"Yes, yes," cried all the cats together.

"Yes," added Kiku-san alone, "but I am afraid that Lois will need me."

"Our human beings will soon get other cats," said Ban-Ban, wisely. "I have always noticed they soon get another cat to wait upon, when they lose the one they have had. Not that I shall leave Rob long without me," he added. "Rob and I are friends. But the founding of this city is a duty; it will be a haven for oppressed cats. When shall we go?"

"On the third day from this one," said Tommy Traddles, promptly. "In the meantime we will eat all that we can, and get together as many provisions as we can carry."

"Before we part," said Bidelia, "let us sing a song. Wait; I will make one for this occasion."

It was the custom of these cats to sing each night before separating, so the others all willingly sat down to wait while Bidelia wrote the words which were to commemorate their newly taken and important resolution.

Soon that clever little cat announced the song ready, and they sang the following words to the air of the "Battle Hymn of the Republic:"

"We'll put our fur in order and brave Pilgrim-cats we'll be;
With whiskers out and tails erect we'll march courageously.
We'll found a town for other cats, less fortunate than we:
　　　Each cat shall have his day!

"We love the friends that love us, and our hearts to them are true;
We'll ne'er forget the kindly folk beside whose hearths we grew,
But though our friends are good to us, mankind is cruel, too:
　　　Each cat must have his day!

"Then, onward, Pilgrim-cats, nor pause to cast a look behind,
For duty calls our velvet paws our kindred's wounds to bind;
In Pussy-Town all homeless cats a home and peace may find:
　　　Each cat shall have his day."

(*Marion Ames Taggart*)

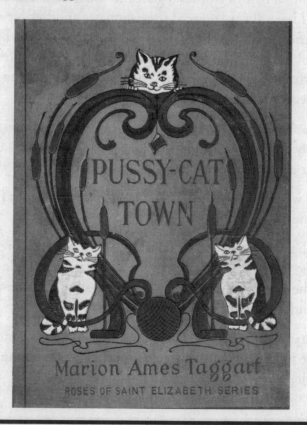

"The Kitten and the Falling Leaves" (A Poem)

William Wordsworth was a famous English Romantic writer and author of hundreds of poems. In this poem, he describes a kitten's playful side.

✳   ✳   ✳   ✳

That way look, my Infant, lo!
What a pretty baby-show!
See the kitten on the wall,
Sporting with the leaves that fall,
Withered leaves, one, two, and three
From the lofty elder-tree!
Through the calm and frosty air
Of this morning bright and fair,
Eddying round and round they sink
Softly, slowly: one might think,
From the motions that are made,
Every little leaf conveyed
Sylph or Faery hither tending,
To this lower world descending,
Each invisible and mute,
In his wavering parachute.
But the Kitten, how she starts,
Crouches, stretches, paws, and darts!
First at one, and then its fellow
Just as light and just as yellow;
There are many now, now one
Now they stop and there are none
What intenseness of desire
In her upward eye of fire!
With a tiger-leap half way
Now she meets the coming prey,

Lets it go as fast, and then
Has it in her power again:
Now she works with three or four,
Like an Indian conjurer;
Quick as he in feats of art,
Far beyond in joy of heart.
Were her antics played in the eye
Of a thousand standers-by,
Clapping hands with shout and stare,
What would little Tabby care
For the plaudits of the crowd?
Over happy to be proud,
Over wealthy in the treasure
Of her own exceeding pleasure!
'Tis a pretty baby-treat;
Nor, I deem, for me unmeet;
Here, for neither Babe nor me,
Other play-mate can I see.
Of the countless living things,
That with stir of feet and wings
(In the sun or under shade,
Upon bough or grassy blade)
And with busy revellings,
Chirp and song, and murmurings,
Made this orchard's narrow space,
And this vale so blithe a place;
Multitudes are swept away
Never more to breathe the day:
Some are sleeping; some in bands
Travelled into distant lands;
Others slunk to moor and wood,
Far from human neighborhood;
And, among the Kinds that keep
With us closer fellowship,

With us openly abide,
All have laid their mirth aside.
Where is he that giddy Sprite,
Blue-cap, with his colors bright,
Who was blest as bird could be,
Feeding in the apple-tree;
Made such wanton spoil and rout,
Turning blossoms inside out;
Hung, head pointing towards the ground
Fluttered, perched, into a round
Bound himself, and then unbound;
Lithest, gaudiest Harlequin!
Prettiest Tumbler ever seen!
Light of heart and light of limb;
What is now become of Him?
Lambs, that through the mountains went
Frisking, bleating merriment,
When the year was in its prime,
They are sobered by this time.
If you look to vale or hill,
If you listen, all is still,
Save a little neighboring rill,
That from out the rocky ground
Strikes a solitary sound.
Vainly glitter hill and plain,
And the air is calm in vain;
Vainly Morning spreads the lure
Of a sky serene and pure;
Creature none can she decoy
Into open sign of joy:
Is it that they have a fear
Of the dreary season near?
Or that other pleasures be
Sweeter even than gaiety?

Yet, whate'er enjoyments dwell
In the impenetrable cell
Of the silent heart which Nature
Furnishes to every creature;
Whatsoe'er we feel and know
Too sedate for outward show,
Such a light of gladness breaks,
Pretty Kitten! from thy freaks,
Spreads with such a living grace
O'er my little Dora's face;
Yes, the sight so stirs and charms
Thee, Baby, laughing in my arms,
That almost I could repine
That your transports are not mine,
That I do not wholly fare
Even as ye do, thoughtless pair!
And I will have my careless season
Spite of melancholy reason,
Will walk through life in such a way
That, when time brings on decay,
Now and then I may possess
Hours of perfect gladsomeness.
Pleased by any random toy;
By a kitten's busy joy,
Or an infant's laughing eye
Sharing in the ecstasy;
I would fare like that or this,
Find my wisdom in my bliss;
Keep the sprightly soul awake,
And have faculties to take,
Even from things by sorrow wrought,
Matter for a jocund thought,
Spite of care, and spite of grief,
To gambol with Life's falling Leaf.
(William Wordsworth)

"Good and Bad Kittens" (A Poem)

Is your kitten good or bad?

* * * *

Kittens, you are very little,
And your kitten bones are brittle,
If you'd grow to Cats respected,
See your play be not neglected.

Smite the Sudden Spool, and spring
Upon the Swift Elusive String,
Thus you learn to catch the wary
Mister Mouse or Miss Canary.

That is how in Foreign Places
Fluffy Cubs with Kitten faces,
Where the mango waves sedately,
Grow to Lions large and stately.

But the Kittencats who snatch
Rudely for their food, or scratch,
Grow to Tomcats gaunt and gory,—
Theirs is quite another story.

Cats like these are put away
By the dread S. P. C. A.,
Or to trusting Aunts and Sisters
Sold as Sable Muffs and Wristers.
(Oliver Herford)

Good Cat

Bad Cat

"The Three Little Kittens"
(A Poem)

Try this nursery rhyme on your young kitten!

✳   ✳   ✳   ✳

There were three little kittens
Put on their mittens
To eat some Christmas pie.
Mew, mew,
Mew, mew,
Mew, mew, mew.

These three little kittens
They lost their mittens,
And all began to cry.
Mew, mew, mew.

"Go, go, naughty kittens,
And find your mittens,
Or you shan't have any pie."
Mew, mew, mew.

These three little kittens
They found their mittens,
And joyfully they did cry.
Mew, mew, mew.

"O Granny, dear!
Our mittens are here,
Make haste and cut up the pie!"
Purr-rr, purr-rr, purr-rr-rr.
(*Walter Crane*)

"Pangur Bán" (A Poem)

A narrator compares himself to a cat in this ancient Irish poem.

* * * *

I and Pangur Bán, each of us two at his special art:
his mind at hunting (mice), my own mind is in my special craft.

I love to rest—better than any fame—at my booklet with
diligent science:
not envious of me is Pangur Bán: he himself loves his
childish art.

When we are—tale without tedium—in our house, we two
alone,
we have—unlimited (is) feat-sport—something to which to
apply our acuteness.

It is customary at times by feat of valour, that a mouse sticks
in his net,
and for me there falls into my net a difficult dictum with
hard meaning.

His eye, this glancing full one, he points against the
wall-fence:
I myself against the keenness of science point my clear eye,
though it is very feeble.

He is joyous with speedy going where a mouse sticks in his
sharp-claw:
I too am joyous, where I understand a difficult dear question.

Though we are thus always, neither hinders the other:
each of us two likes his art, amuses himself alone.

He himself is the master of the work which he does every day:
while I am at my own work, (which is) to bring difficulty to
clearness.
(Anonymous)

"She sights a Bird— she chuckles—" (A Poem)

Dickinson's short poem describes a cat's cunning hunting skills.

✳ ✳ ✳ ✳

She sights a Bird — she chuckles —
She flattens — then she crawls —
She runs without the look of feet —
Her eyes increase to Balls —

Her Jaws stir — twitching — hungry —
Her Teeth can hardly stand —
She leaps, but Robin leaped the first —
Ah, Pussy, of the Sand,

The Hopes so juicy ripening —
You almost bathed your Tongue —
When Bliss disclosed a hundred Toes —
And fled with every one —
(Emily Dickinson)

"Ode on the Death of a Favourite Cat Drowned in a Tub of Goldfishes" (A Poem)

Gray's poem parodies the popular heroic-style poetry of the eighteenth century.

✳ ✳ ✳ ✳

'Twas on a lofty vase's side,
Where China's gayest art had dyed
The azure flowers that blow;
Demurest of the tabby kind,
The pensive Selima, reclined,
Gazed on the lake below.

Her conscious tail her joy declared;
The fair round face, the snowy beard,
The velvet of her paws,
Her coat, that with the tortoise vies,
Her ears of jet, and emerald eyes,
She saw; and purred applause.

Still had she gazed; but 'midst the tide
Two angel forms were seen to glide,
The genii of the stream;
Their scaly armour's Tyrian hue
Through richest purple to the view
Betrayed a golden gleam.

The hapless nymph with wonder saw;
A whisker first and then a claw,
With many an ardent wish,
She stretched in vain to reach the prize.

What female heart can gold despise?
What cat's averse to fish?

Presumptuous maid! with looks intent
Again she stretch'd, again she bent,
Nor knew the gulf between.
(Malignant Fate sat by, and smiled)
The slippery verge her feet beguiled,
She tumbled headlong in.
Eight times emerging from the flood
She mewed to every watery god,
Some speedy aid to send.
No dolphin came, no Nereid stirred;
Nor cruel Tom, nor Susan heard;
A Favourite has no friend!

From hence, ye beauties, undeceived,
Know, one false step is ne'er retrieved,
And be with caution bold.
Not all that tempts your wandering eyes
And heedless hearts, is lawful prize;
Nor all that glisters, gold.
(*Thomas Gray*)

"The Tyger" (A Poem)

Blake's famous poem uses a big cat to ponder religious ideas.

✳ ✳ ✳ ✳

Tyger Tyger, burning bright,
In the forests of the night;
What immortal hand or eye,
Could frame thy fearful symmetry?

In what distant deeps or skies,
Burnt the fire of thine eyes?
On what wings dare he aspire?
What the hand dare seize the fire?

And what shoulder, and what art,
Could twist the sinews of thy heart?
And, when thy heart began to beat,
What dread hand and what dread feet?

What the hammer? what the chain?
In what furnace was thy brain?
What the anvil? what dread grasp,
Dare its deadly terrors clasp?

When the stars threw down their spears,
And watered heaven with their tears,
Did He smile His work to see?
Did He who made the Lamb make thee?

Tyger Tyger, burning bright,
In the forests of the night,
What immortal hand or eye,
Dare frame thy fearful symmetry?
(*William Blake*)

The Owl and the Pussy-Cat

Edward Lear was an illustrator and poet whose works are some of the best-known from the nineteenth century English writers. His nonsense poetry was very popular, and he made the limerick a well-known style of verse.

＊　＊　＊　＊

EDWARD LEAR WAS born in London on May 13, 1812, to a middle-class family. He had twenty brothers and sisters. His parents could not afford to raise all of the children. When he

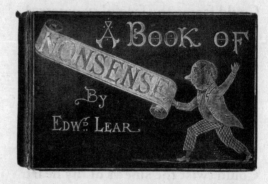

was four years old, his oldest sister Ann, who was twenty-five, took him to live with her and became his mother figure. Lear was frequently ill as a child and had poor health his entire life. He suffered from epilepsy and had seizures that left him with feelings of guilt and shame well into adulthood. His various illnesses caused him frequent periods of deep depression that he called "The Morbids."

Lear is remembered for his brilliant and witty nonsense poetry, the most famous of which is "The Owl and the Pussycat." The poem was published in an 1871 collection called *Nonsense Songs, Stories, Botany and Alphabets* and begins:

"The Owl and the Pussy-cat went to sea
In a beautiful pea green boat,
They took some honey, and plenty of money,
Wrapped up in a five pound note."

Lear's poetry was a celebration of words, both real and imaginary. His best-known invention is the word "runcible," which he incorporated into several of his poems. The word has no fixed meaning, and Lear himself never was clear on what the definition might be. Lear was one of the first major writers to use limericks widely, and is responsible for their popularity. He was also a gifted artist who illustrated his and other books of poetry, and published several travelogues with beautiful illustrations of Greece and Italy. Lear died on January 29, 1888, in Italy.

The Brazilian Cat
British writer Arthur Conan Doyle talks up big cats with this chilling short story.

✳ ✳ ✳ ✳

IT IS HARD luck on a young fellow to have expensive tastes, great expectations, aristocratic connections, but no actual money in his pocket, and no profession by which he may earn any. The fact was that my father, a good, sanguine, easy-going man, had such confidence in the wealth and benevolence of his bachelor elder brother, Lord Southerton, that he took it for granted that I, his only son, would never be called upon to earn a living for myself. He imagined that if there were not a vacancy for me on the great Southerton Estates, at least there would be found some post in that diplomatic service which still remains the special preserve of our privileged classes. He died too early to realize how false his calculations had been. Neither my uncle nor the State took the slightest notice of me, or showed any interest in my career. An occasional brace of pheasants, or basket of hares, was all that ever reached me to remind me that I was heir to Otwell House and one of the richest estates in the country. In the meantime, I found myself a bachelor and man about town, living in a suite of apartments in Grosvenor Mansions, with no occupation save that of pigeon-shooting and polo-playing at Hurlingham. Month by month I realized that it was more and more difficult to get the brokers to renew my bills, or to cash any further post-obits upon an unentailed property. Ruin lay right across my path, and every day I saw it clearer, nearer, and more absolutely unavoidable.

What made me feel my own poverty the more was that, apart from the great wealth of Lord Southerton, all my other relations were fairly well-to-do. The nearest of these was Everard King, my father's nephew and my own first cousin, who had spent an adventurous life in Brazil, and had now returned to this country to settle down on his fortune. We never knew how he made his money, but he appeared to have plenty of it, for he bought the estate of Greylands, near Clipton-on-the-Marsh, in Suffolk. For the first year of his residence in England he took no more notice of me than my miserly uncle; but at last one summer morning, to my very great relief and joy, I received a letter asking me to come down that very day and spend a short visit at Greylands Court. I was expecting a rather long visit to Bankruptcy Court at the time, and this interruption seemed almost providential. If I could only get on terms with this unknown relative of mine, I might pull through yet. For the family credit he could not let me go entirely to the wall. I ordered my valet to pack my valise, and I set off the same evening for Clipton-on-the-Marsh.

After changing at Ipswich, a little local train deposited me at a small, deserted station lying amidst a rolling grassy country, with a sluggish and winding river curving in and out amidst the valleys, between high, silted banks, which showed that we were within reach of the tide. No carriage was awaiting me (I found afterwards that my telegram had been delayed), so I hired a dogcart at the local inn. The driver, an excellent fellow, was full of my relative's praises, and I learned from him that Mr. Everard King was already a name to conjure with in that part of the county. He had entertained the school-children, he had thrown his grounds open to visitors, he had subscribed to charities—in short, his benevolence had been so universal that my driver could only account for it on the supposition that he had parliamentary ambitions.

My attention was drawn away from my driver's panegyric by the appearance of a very beautiful bird which settled on a telegraph-post beside the road. At first I thought that it was a jay, but it was larger, with a brighter plumage. The driver accounted for its presence at once by saying that it belonged to the very man whom we were about to visit. It seems that the acclimatization of foreign creatures was one of his hobbies, and that he had brought with him from Brazil a number of birds and beasts which he was endeavouring to rear in England. When once we had passed the gates of Greylands Park we had ample evidence of this taste of his. Some small spotted deer, a curious wild pig known, I believe, as a peccary, a gorgeously feathered oriole, some sort of armadillo, and a singular lumbering in-toed beast like a very fat badger, were among the creatures which I observed as we drove along the winding avenue.

Mr. Everard King, my unknown cousin, was standing in person upon the steps of his house, for he had seen us in the distance, and guessed that it was I. His appearance was very homely and benevolent, short and stout, forty-five years old, perhaps, with a round, good-humoured face, burned brown with the tropical sun, and shot with a thousand wrinkles. He wore white linen clothes, in true planter style, with a cigar between his lips, and a large Panama hat upon the back of his head. It was such a figure as one associates with a verandahed bungalow, and it looked curiously out of place in front of this broad, stone English mansion, with its solid wings and its Palladio pillars before the doorway.

"My dear!" he cried, glancing over his shoulder; "my dear, here is our guest! Welcome, welcome to Greylands! I am delighted to make your acquaintance, Cousin Marshall, and I take it as a great compliment that you should honour this sleepy little country place with your presence."

Nothing could be more hearty than his manner, and he set me at my ease in an instant. But it needed all his cordiality to atone for the frigidity and even rudeness of his wife, a tall, haggard woman, who came forward at his summons. She was, I believe, of Brazilian extraction, though she spoke excellent English, and I excused her manners on the score of her ignorance of our customs. She did not attempt to conceal, however, either then or afterwards, that I was no very welcome visitor at Greylands Court. Her actual words were, as a rule, courteous, but she was the possessor of a pair of particularly expressive dark eyes, and I read in them very clearly from the first that she heartily wished me back in London once more.

However, my debts were too pressing and my designs upon my wealthy relative were too vital for me to allow them to be upset by the ill-temper of his wife, so I disregarded her coldness and reciprocated the extreme cordiality of his welcome. No pains had been spared by him to make me comfortable. My room was a charming one. He implored me to tell him anything which could add to my happiness. It was on the tip of my tongue to inform him that a blank cheque would materially help towards that end, but I felt that it might be premature in the present state of our acquaintance. The dinner was excellent, and as we sat together afterwards over his Havanas and coffee, which later he told me was specially prepared upon his own plantation, it seemed to me that all my driver's eulogies were justified, and that I had never met a more large-hearted and hospitable man.

But, in spite of his cheery good nature, he was a man with a strong will and a fiery temper of his own. Of this I had an example upon the following morning. The curious aversion which Mrs. Everard King had conceived towards me was so strong, that her manner at breakfast was almost offensive. But her meaning became unmistakable when her husband had quitted the room.

"The best train in the day is at twelve-fifteen," said she.

"But I was not thinking of going today," I answered, frankly—perhaps even defiantly, for I was determined not to be driven out by this woman.

"Oh, if it rests with you—" said she, and stopped with a most insolent expression in her eyes.

"I am sure," I answered, "that Mr. Everard King would tell me if I were outstaying my welcome."

"What's this? What's this?" said a voice, and there he was in the room. He had overheard my last words, and a glance at our faces had told him the rest. In an instant his chubby, cheery face set into an expression of absolute ferocity.

"Might I trouble you to walk outside, Marshall?" said he. (I may mention that my own name is Marshall King.)

He closed the door behind me, and then, for an instant, I heard him talking in a low voice of concentrated passion to his wife. This gross breach of hospitality had evidently hit upon his tenderest point. I am no eavesdropper, so I walked out on to the lawn. Presently I heard a hurried step behind me, and there was the lady, her face pale with excitement, and her eyes red with tears.

"My husband has asked me to apologize to you, Mr. Marshall King," said she, standing with downcast eyes before me.

"Please do not say another word, Mrs. King."

Her dark eyes suddenly blazed out at me.

"You fool!" she hissed, with frantic vehemence, and turning on her heel swept back to the house.

The insult was so outrageous, so insufferable, that I could only stand staring after her in bewilderment. I was still there when my host joined me. He was his cheery, chubby self once more.

"I hope that my wife has apologized for her foolish remarks," said he.

"Oh, yes—yes, certainly!"

He put his hand through my arm and walked with me up and down the lawn.

"You must not take it seriously," said he. "It would grieve me inexpressibly if you curtailed your visit by one hour. The fact is—there is no reason why there should be any concealment between relatives—that my poor dear wife is incredibly jealous. She hates that anyone—male or female—should for an instant come between us. Her ideal is a desert island and an eternal tete-a-tete. That gives you the clue to her actions, which are, I confess, upon this particular point, not very far removed from mania. Tell me that you will think no more of it."

"No, no; certainly not."

"Then light this cigar and come round with me and see my little menagerie."

The whole afternoon was occupied by this inspection, which included all the birds, beasts, and even reptiles which he had imported. Some were free, some in cages, a few actually in the house. He spoke with enthusiasm of his successes and his failures, his births and his deaths, and he would cry out in his delight, like a schoolboy, when, as we walked, some gaudy bird would flutter up from the grass, or some curious beast slink into the cover. Finally he led me down a corridor which extended from one wing of the house. At the end of this there was a heavy door with a sliding shutter in it, and beside it there projected from the wall an iron handle attached to a wheel and a drum. A line of stout bars extended across the passage.

"I am about to show you the jewel of my collection," said he. "There is only one other specimen in Europe, now that the Rotterdam cub is dead. It is a Brazilian cat."

"But how does that differ from any other cat?"

"You will soon see that," said he, laughing. "Will you kindly draw that shutter and look through?"

I did so, and found that I was gazing into a large, empty room, with stone flags, and small, barred windows upon the farther wall. In the centre of this room, lying in the middle of a golden patch of sunlight, there was stretched a huge creature, as large as a tiger, but as black and sleek as ebony. It was simply a very enormous and very well-kept black cat, and it cuddled up and basked in that yellow pool of light exactly as a cat would do. It was so graceful, so sinewy, and so gently and smoothly diabolical, that I could not take my eyes from the opening.

"Isn't he splendid?" said my host, enthusiastically.

"Glorious! I never saw such a noble creature."

"Some people call it a black puma, but really it is not a puma at all. That fellow is nearly eleven feet from tail to tip. Four years ago he was a little ball of back fluff, with two yellow eyes staring out of it. He was sold me as a new-born cub up in the wild country at the head-waters of the Rio Negro. They speared his mother to death after she had killed a dozen of them."

"They are ferocious, then?"

"The most absolutely treacherous and bloodthirsty creatures upon earth. You talk about a Brazilian cat to an up-country Indian, and see him get the jumps. They prefer humans to game. This fellow has never tasted living blood yet, but when he does he will be a terror. At present he won't stand anyone but me in his den. Even Baldwin, the groom, dare not go near him. As to me, I am his mother and father in one."

As he spoke he suddenly, to my astonishment, opened the door and slipped in, closing it instantly behind him. At the sound of his voice the huge, lithe creature rose, yawned and rubbed its round, black head affectionately against his side, while he patted and fondled it.

"Now, Tommy, into your cage!" said he.

The monstrous cat walked over to one side of the room and coiled itself up under a grating. Everard King came out, and taking the iron handle which I have mentioned, he began to turn it. As he did so the line of bars in the corridor began to pass through a slot in the wall and closed up the front of this grating, so as to make an effective cage. When it was in position he opened the door once more and invited me into the room, which was heavy with the pungent, musty smell peculiar to the great carnivora.

"That's how we work it," said he. "We give him the run of the room for exercise, and then at night we put him in his cage. You can let him out by turning the handle from the passage, or you can, as you have seen, coop him up in the same way. No, no, you should not do that!"

I had put my hand between the bars to pat the glossy, heaving flank. He pulled it back, with a serious face.

"I assure you that he is not safe. Don't imagine that because I can take liberties with him anyone else can. He is very exclusive in his friends—aren't you, Tommy? Ah, he hears his lunch coming to him! Don't you, boy?"

A step sounded in the stone-flagged passage, and the creature had sprung to his feet, and was pacing up and down the narrow cage, his yellow eyes gleaming, and his scarlet tongue rippling and quivering over the white line of his jagged teeth. A groom entered with a coarse joint upon a tray, and thrust it through the bars to him. He pounced lightly upon it, carried it off to the corner, and there, holding it between his paws, tore and wrenched at it, raising his bloody muzzle every now and then to look at us. It was a malignant and yet fascinating sight.

"You can't wonder that I am fond of him, can you?" said my host, as we left the room, "especially when you consider that I have had the rearing of him. It was no joke bringing him over from the centre of South America; but here he is safe and sound—and, as I have said, far the most perfect specimen in Europe. The people at the Zoo are dying to have him, but I really can't part with him. Now, I think that I have inflicted my hobby upon you long enough, so we cannot do better than follow Tommy's example, and go to our lunch."

My South American relative was so engrossed by his grounds and their curious occupants, that I hardly gave him credit at first for having any interests outside them. That he had some, and pressing ones, was soon borne in upon me by the number of telegrams which he received. They arrived at all hours, and were always opened by him with the utmost eagerness and anxiety upon his face. Sometimes I imagined that it must be the Turf, and sometimes the Stock Exchange, but certainly he had some very urgent business going forwards which was not transacted upon the Downs of Suffolk. During the six days of my visit he had never fewer than three or four telegrams a day, and sometimes as many as seven or eight.

I had occupied these six days so well, that by the end of them I had succeeded in getting upon the most cordial terms with my cousin. Every night we had sat up late in the billiard-room, he telling me the most extraordinary stories of his adventures in America—stories so desperate and reckless, that I could hardly associate them with the brown little, chubby man before me. In return, I ventured upon some of my own reminiscences of London life, which interested him so much, that he vowed he would come up to Grosvenor Mansions and stay with me. He was anxious to see the faster side of city life, and certainly, though I say it, he could not have chosen a more competent guide. It was not until the last day of my visit that I ventured to approach that which was on my mind. I told him frankly about my pecuniary difficulties and my impending ruin, and I asked his advice—though I hoped for something more solid. He listened attentively, puffing hard at his cigar.

"But surely," said he, "you are the heir of our relative, Lord Southerton?"

"I have every reason to believe so, but he would never make me any allowance."

"No, no, I have heard of his miserly ways. My poor Marshall, your position has been a very hard one. By the way, have you heard any news of Lord Southerton's health lately?"

"He has always been in a critical condition ever since my childhood."

"Exactly—a creaking hinge, if ever there was one. Your inheritance may be a long way off. Dear me, how awkwardly situated you are!"

"I had some hopes, sir, that you, knowing all the facts, might be inclined to advance——"

"Don't say another word, my dear boy," he cried, with the utmost cordiality; "we shall talk it over tonight, and I give you my word that whatever is in my power shall be done."

I was not sorry that my visit was drawing to a close, for it is unpleasant to feel that there is one person in the house who eagerly desires your departure. Mrs. King's sallow face and forbidding eyes had become more and more hateful to me. She was no longer actively rude—her fear of her husband prevented her—but she pushed her insane jealousy to the extent of ignoring me, never addressing me, and in every way making my stay at Greylands as uncomfortable as she could. So offensive was her manner during that last day, that I should certainly have left had it not been for that interview with my host in the evening which would, I hoped, retrieve my broken fortunes.

It was very late when it occurred, for my relative, who had been receiving even more telegrams than usual during the day, went off to his study after dinner, and only emerged when the household had retired to bed. I heard him go round locking the doors, as custom was of a night, and finally he joined me in the billiard- room. His stout figure was wrapped in a dressing-gown, and he wore a pair of red Turkish slippers without any heels. Settling down into an arm-chair, he brewed himself a glass of grog, in which I could not help noticing that the whisky considerably predominated over the water.

"My word!" said he, "what a night!"

It was, indeed. The wind was howling and screaming round the house, and the latticed windows rattled and shook as if they were coming in. The glow of the yellow lamps and the flavour of our cigars seemed the brighter and more fragrant for the contrast.

"Now, my boy," said my host, "we have the house and the night to ourselves. Let me have an idea of how your affairs stand, and I will see what can be done to set them in order. I wish to hear every detail."

Thus encouraged, I entered into a long exposition, in which all my tradesmen and creditors from my landlord to my valet, fig-ured in turn. I had notes in my pocket-book, and I marshalled my facts, and gave, I flatter myself, a very businesslike statement of my own unbusinesslike ways and lamentable position. I was depressed, however, to notice that my companion's eyes were vacant and his attention elsewhere. When he did occasionally throw out a remark it was so entirely perfunctory and pointless, that I was sure he had not in the least followed my remarks. Every now and then he roused himself and put on some show of interest, asking me to repeat or to explain more fully, but it was always to sink once more into the same brown study. At last he rose and threw the end of his cigar into the grate.

"I'll tell you what, my boy," said he. "I never had a head for figures, so you will excuse me. You must jot it all down upon paper, and let me have a note of the amount. I'll understand it when I see it in black and white."

The proposal was encouraging. I promised to do so.

"And now it's time we were in bed. By Jove, there's one o'clock striking in the hall."

The tingling of the chiming clock broke through the deep roar of the gale. The wind was sweeping past with the rush of a great river.

"I must see my cat before I go to bed," said my host. "A high wind excites him. Will you come?"

"Certainly," said I.

"Then tread softly and don't speak, for everyone is asleep."

We passed quietly down the lamp-lit Persian-rugged hall, and through the door at the farther end. All was dark in the stone corridor, but a stable lantern hung on a hook, and my host took it down and lit it. There was no grating visible in the passage, so I knew that the beast was in its cage.

"Come in!" said my relative, and opened the door.

A deep growling as we entered showed that the storm had really excited the creature. In the flickering light of the lantern, we saw it, a huge black mass coiled in the corner of its den and throwing a squat, uncouth shadow upon the whitewashed wall. Its tail switched angrily among the straw.

"Poor Tommy is not in the best of tempers," said Everard King, holding up the lantern and looking in at him. "What a black devil he looks, doesn't he? I must give him a little supper to put him in a better humour. Would you mind holding the lantern for a moment?"

I took it from his hand and he stepped to the door.

"His larder is just outside here," said he. "You will excuse me for an instant won't you?" He passed out, and the door shut with a sharp metallic click behind him.

That hard crisp sound made my heart stand still. A sudden wave of terror passed over me. A vague perception of some monstrous treachery turned me cold. I sprang to the door, but there was no handle upon the inner side.

"Here!" I cried. "Let me out!"

"All right! Don't make a row!" said my host from the passage. "You've got the light all right."

"Yes, but I don't care about being locked in alone like this."

"Don't you?" I heard his hearty, chuckling laugh. "You won't be alone long."

"Let me out, sir!" I repeated angrily. "I tell you I don't allow practical jokes of this sort."

"Practical is the word," said he, with another hateful chuckle. And then suddenly I heard, amidst the roar of the storm, the creak and whine of the winch-handle turning and the rattle of the grating as it passed through the slot. Great God, he was letting loose the Brazilian cat!

In the light of the lantern I saw the bars sliding slowly before me. Already there was an opening a foot wide at the farther end. With a scream I seized the last bar with my hands and pulled with the strength of a madman. I WAS a madman with rage and horror. For a minute or more I held the thing motionless. I knew that he was straining with all his force upon the handle, and that the leverage was sure to overcome me. I gave inch by inch, my feet sliding along the stones, and all the time I begged and prayed this inhuman monster to save me from this horrible death. I conjured him by his kinship. I reminded him that I was his guest; I begged to know what harm I had ever done him. His only answers were the tugs and jerks upon the handle, each of which, in spite of all my struggles, pulled another bar through the opening. Clinging and clutching, I was dragged across the whole front of the cage, until at last, with aching wrists and lacerated fingers, I gave up the hopeless struggle. The grating clanged back as I released it, and an instant later I heard the shuffle of the Turkish slippers in the passage, and the slam of the distant door. Then everything was silent.

The creature had never moved during this time. He lay still in the corner, and his tail had ceased switching. This apparition of a man adhering to his bars and dragged screaming across him had apparently filled him with amazement. I saw his great eyes staring steadily at me. I had dropped the lantern when I seized the bars, but it still burned upon the floor, and I made a movement to grasp it, with some idea that its light might protect me. But the instant I moved, the beast gave a deep and menacing growl. I stopped and stood still, quivering with fear in every limb. The cat (if one may call so fearful a creature by so homely a name) was not more than ten feet from me. The eyes glimmered like two disks of phosphorus in the darkness. They appalled and yet fascinated me. I could not take my own eyes from them. Nature plays strange tricks with us at such moments of intensity, and those glimmering lights waxed and waned with a steady rise and fall. Sometimes they seemed to be tiny points of extreme brilliancy—little electric sparks in the black obscurity—then they would widen and widen until all that corner of the room was filled with their shifting and sinister light. And then suddenly they went out altogether.

The beast had closed its eyes. I do not know whether there may be any truth in the old idea of the dominance of the human gaze, or whether the huge cat was simply drowsy, but the fact remains that, far from showing any symptom of attacking me, it simply rested its sleek, black head upon its huge forepaws and seemed to sleep. I stood, fearing to move lest I should rouse it into malignant life once more. But at least I was able to think clearly now that the baleful eyes were off me. Here I was shut up for the night with the ferocious beast. My own instincts, to say nothing of the words of the plausible villain who laid this trap for me, warned me that the animal was as savage as its master. How could I stave it off until morning? The door was hopeless, and so were the narrow, barred windows. There was no shelter anywhere in the bare, stone- flagged room. To cry for assistance was absurd. I knew that this den was an outhouse, and that the corridor which connected it with the house was at least a hundred feet long. Besides, with the gale thundering outside, my cries were not likely to be heard. I had only my own courage and my own wits to trust to.

And then, with a fresh wave of horror, my eyes fell upon the lantern. The candle had burned low, and was already beginning to gutter. In ten minutes it would be out. I had only ten minutes then in which to do something, for I felt that if I were once left in the dark with that fearful beast I should be incapable of action. The very thought of it paralysed me. I cast my despairing eyes round this chamber of death, and they rested upon one spot which seemed to promise I will not say safety, but less immediate and imminent danger than the open floor.

I have said that the cage had a top as well as a front, and this top was left standing when the front was wound through the slot in the wall. It consisted of bars at a few inches' interval, with stout wire netting between, and it rested upon a strong stanchion at each end. It stood now as a great barred canopy over the crouching figure in the corner. The space between this iron shelf and the roof may have been from two or three feet. If I could only get up there, squeezed in between bars and ceiling, I should have only one vulnerable side. I should be safe from below, from behind, and from each side. Only on the open face of it could I be attacked. There, it is true, I had no protection whatever; but at least, I should be out of the brute's path when he began to pace about his den. He would have to come out of his way to reach me. It was now or never, for if once the light were out it would be impossible. With a gulp in my throat I sprang up, seized the iron edge of the top, and swung myself panting on to it. I writhed in face downwards, and found myself looking straight into the terrible eyes and yawning jaws of the cat. Its fetid breath came up into my face like the steam from some foul pot.

It appeared, however, to be rather curious than angry. With a sleek ripple of its long, black back it rose, stretched itself, and then rearing itself on its hind legs, with one forepaw against the wall, it raised the other, and drew its claws across the wire meshes beneath me. One sharp, white hook tore through my trousers—for I may mention that I was still in evening dress— and dug a furrow in my knee. It was not meant as an attack, but rather as an experiment, for upon my giving a sharp cry of pain he dropped down again, and springing lightly into the room, he began walking swiftly round it, looking up every now and again in my direction. For my part I shuffled backwards until I lay with my back against the wall, screwing myself into the small- est space possible. The farther I got the more difficult it was for him to attack me.

He seemed more excited now that he had begun to move about, and he ran swiftly and noiselessly round and round the den, passing continually underneath the iron couch upon which I lay. It was wonderful to see so great a bulk passing like a shadow, with hardly the softest thudding of velvety pads. The candle was burning low—so low that I could hardly see the creature. And then, with a last flare and splutter it went out altogether. I was alone with the cat in the dark!

It helps one to face a danger when one knows that one has done all that possibly can be done. There is nothing for it then but to quietly await the result. In this case, there was no chance of safety anywhere except the precise spot where I was. I stretched myself out, therefore, and lay silently, almost breathlessly, hoping that the beast might forget my presence if I did nothing to remind him. I reckoned that it must already be two o'clock. At four it would be full dawn. I had not more than two hours to wait for daylight.

Outside, the storm was still raging, and the rain lashed continually against the little windows. Inside, the poisonous and fetid air was overpowering. I could neither hear nor see the cat. I tried to think about other things—but only one had power enough to draw my mind from my terrible position. That was the contemplation of my cousin's villainy, his unparalleled hypocrisy, his malignant hatred of me. Beneath that cheerful face there lurked the spirit of a mediaeval assassin. And as I thought of it I saw more clearly how cunningly the thing had been arranged. He had apparently gone to bed with the others. No doubt he had his witness to prove it. Then, unknown to them, he had slipped down, had lured me into his den and abandoned me. His story would be so simple. He had left me to finish my cigar in the billiard-room. I had gone down on my own account to have a last look at the cat. I had entered the room without observing that the cage was opened, and I had been caught. How could such a crime be brought home to him? Suspicion, perhaps—but proof, never!

How slowly those dreadful two hours went by! Once I heard a low, rasping sound, which I took to be the creature licking its own fur. Several times those greenish eyes gleamed at me through the darkness, but never in a fixed stare, and my hopes grew stronger that my presence had been forgotten or ignored. At last the least faint glimmer of light came through the windows—I first dimly saw them as two grey squares upon the black wall, then grey turned to white, and I could see my terrible companion once more. And he, alas, could see me!

It was evident to me at once that he was in a much more dangerous and aggressive mood than when I had seen him last.

The cold of the morning had irritated him, and he was hungry as well. With a continual growl he paced swiftly up and down the side of the room which was farthest from my refuge, his whiskers bristling angrily, and his tail switching and lashing. As he turned at the corners his savage eyes always looked upwards at me with a dreadful menace. I knew then that he meant to kill me. Yet I found myself even at that moment admiring the sinuous grace of the devilish thing, its long, undulating, rippling movements, the gloss of its beautiful flanks, the vivid, palpitating scarlet of the glistening tongue which hung from the jet-black muzzle. And all the time that deep, threatening growl was rising and rising in an unbroken crescendo. I knew that the crisis was at hand.

It was a miserable hour to meet such a death—so cold, so comfortless, shivering in my light dress clothes upon this gridiron of torment upon which I was stretched. I tried to brace myself to it, to raise my soul above it, and at the same time, with the lucidity which comes to a perfectly desperate man, I cast round for some possible means of escape. One thing was clear to me. If that front of the cage was only back in its position once more, I could find a sure refuge behind it. Could I possibly pull it back? I hardly dared to move for fear of bringing the creature upon me. Slowly, very slowly, I put my hand forward until it grasped the edge of the front, the final bar which protruded through the wall. To my surprise it came quite easily to my jerk. Of course the difficulty of drawing it out arose from the fact that I was clinging to it. I pulled again, and three inches of it came through. It ran apparently on wheels. I pulled again . . . and then the cat sprang!

It was so quick, so sudden, that I never saw it happen. I simply heard the savage snarl, and in an instant afterwards the blazing yellow eyes, the flattened black head with its red tongue and flashing teeth, were within reach of me. The impact of the creature shook the bars upon which I lay, until I thought (as far as I could think of anything at such a moment) that they were coming down. The cat swayed there for an instant, the head and front paws quite close to me, the hind paws clawing to find a grip upon the edge of the grating. I heard the claws rasping as they clung to the wire-netting, and the breath of the beast made me sick. But its bound had been miscalculated. It could not retain its position. Slowly, grinning with rage, and scratching madly at the bars, it swung backwards and dropped heavily upon the floor. With a growl it instantly faced round to me and crouched for another spring.

I knew that the next few moments would decide my fate. The creature had learned by experience. It would not miscalculate again. I must act promptly, fearlessly, if I were to have a chance for life. In an instant I had formed my plan. Pulling off my dress-coat, I threw it down over the head of the beast. At the same moment I dropped over the edge, seized the end of the front grating, and pulled it frantically out of the wall.

It came more easily than I could have expected. I rushed across the room, bearing it with me; but, as I rushed, the accident of my position put me upon the outer side. Had it been the other way, I might have come off scathless. As it was, there was a moment's pause as I stopped it and tried to pass in through the opening which I had left. That moment was enough to give time to the creature to toss off the coat with which I had blinded him and to spring upon me. I hurled myself through the gap and pulled the rails to behind me, but he seized my leg before I could entirely withdraw it. One stroke of that huge paw tore off my calf as a shaving of wood curls off before a plane. The next moment, bleeding and fainting, I was lying among the foul straw with a line of friendly bars between me and the creature which ramped so frantically against them.

Too wounded to move, and too faint to be conscious of fear, I could only lie, more dead than alive, and watch it. It pressed its broad, black chest against the bars and angled for me with its crooked paws as I have seen a kitten do before a mouse-trap.

It ripped my clothes, but, stretch as it would, it could not quite reach me. I have heard of the curious numbing effect produced by wounds from the great carnivora, and now I was destined to experience it, for I had lost all sense of personality, and was as interested in the cat's failure or success as if it were some game which I was watching. And then gradually my mind drifted away into strange vague dreams, always with that black face and red tongue coming back into them, and so I lost myself in the nirvana of delirium, the blessed relief of those who are too sorely tried.

Tracing the course of events afterwards, I conclude that I must have been insensible for about two hours. What roused me to consciousness once more was that sharp metallic click which had been the precursor of my terrible experience. It was the shooting back of the spring lock. Then, before my senses were clear enough to entirely apprehend what they saw, I was aware of the round, benevolent face of my cousin peering in through the open door. What he saw evidently amazed him. There was the cat crouching on the floor. I was stretched upon my back in my shirt-sleeves within the cage, my trousers torn to ribbons and a great pool of blood all round me. I can see his amazed face now, with the morning sunlight upon it. He peered at me, and peered again. Then he closed the door behind him, and advanced to the cage to see if I were really dead.

I cannot undertake to say what happened. I was not in a fit state to witness or to chronicle such events. I can only say that I was suddenly conscious that his face was away from me—that he was looking towards the animal.

"Good old Tommy!" he cried. "Good old Tommy!"

Then he came near the bars, with his back still towards me.

"Down, you stupid beast!" he roared. "Down, sir! Don't you know your master?"

Suddenly even in my bemuddled brain a remembrance came of those words of his when he had said that the taste of blood would turn the cat into a fiend. My blood had done it, but he was to pay the price.

"Get away!" he screamed. "Get away, you devil! Baldwin! Baldwin! Oh, my God!"

And then I heard him fall, and rise, and fall again, with a sound like the ripping of sacking. His screams grew fainter until they were lost in the worrying snarl. And then, after I thought that he was dead, I saw, as in a nightmare, a blinded, tattered, blood-soaked figure running wildly round the room—and that was the last glimpse which I had of him before I fainted once again.

******

I was many months in my recovery—in fact, I cannot say that I have ever recovered, for to the end of my days I shall carry a stick as a sign of my night with the Brazilian cat. Baldwin, the groom, and the other servants could not tell what had occurred, when, drawn by the death-cries of their master, they found me behind the bars, and his remains—or what they afterwards discovered to be his remains—in the clutch of the creature which he had reared. They stalled him off with hot irons, and afterwards shot him through the loophole of the door before they could finally extricate me. I was carried to my bedroom, and there, under the roof of my would-be murderer, I remained between life and death for several weeks. They had sent for a surgeon from Clipton and a nurse from London, and in a month I was able to be carried to the station, and so conveyed back once more to Grosvenor Mansions.

I have one remembrance of that illness, which might have been part of the ever-changing panorama conjured up by a delirious brain were it not so definitely fixed in my memory. One night, when the nurse was absent, the door of my chamber opened, and a tall woman in blackest mourning slipped into the room.

She came across to me, and as she bent her sallow face I saw by the faint gleam of the night-light that it was the Brazilian woman whom my cousin had married. She stared intently into my face, and her expression was more kindly than I had ever seen it.

"Are you conscious?" she asked.

I feebly nodded—for I was still very weak.

"Well; then, I only wished to say to you that you have yourself to blame. Did I not do all I could for you? From the beginning I tried to drive you from the house. By every means, short of betraying my husband, I tried to save you from him. I knew that he had a reason for bringing you here. I knew that he would never let you get away again. No one knew him as I knew him, who had suffered from him so often. I did not dare to tell you all this. He would have killed me. But I did my best for you. As things have turned out, you have been the best friend that I have ever had. You have set me free, and I fancied that nothing but death would do that. I am sorry if you are hurt, but I cannot reproach myself. I told you that you were a fool—and a fool you have been." She crept out of the room, the bitter, singular woman, and I was never destined to see her again. With what remained from her husband's property she went back to her native land, and I have heard that she afterwards took the veil at Pernambuco.

It was not until I had been back in London for some time that the doctors pronounced me to be well enough to do business. It was not a very welcome permission to me, for I feared that it would be the signal for an inrush of creditors; but it was Summers, my lawyer, who first took advantage of it.

"I am very glad to see that your lordship is so much better," said he. "I have been waiting a long time to offer my congratulations."

"What do you mean, Summers? This is no time for joking."

"I mean what I say," he answered. "You have been Lord Southerton for the last six weeks, but we feared that it would retard your recovery if you were to learn it."

Lord Southerton! One of the richest peers in England! I could not believe my ears. And then suddenly I thought of the time which had elapsed, and how it coincided with my injuries.

"Then Lord Southerton must have died about the same time that I was hurt?"

"His death occurred upon that very day." Summers looked hard at me as I spoke, and I am convinced—for he was a very shrewd fellow—that he had guessed the true state of the case. He paused for a moment as if awaiting a confidence from me, but I could not see what was to be gained by exposing such a family scandal.

"Yes, a very curious coincidence," he continued, with the same knowing look. "Of course, you are aware that your cousin Everard King was the next heir to the estates. Now, if it had been you instead of him who had been torn to pieces by this tiger, or whatever it was, then of course he would have been Lord Southerton at the present moment."

"No doubt," said I.

"And he took such an interest in it," said Summers. "I happen to know that the late Lord Southerton's valet was in his pay, and that he used to have telegrams from him every few hours to tell him how he was getting on. That would be about the time when you were down there. Was it not strange that he should wish to be so well informed, since he knew that he was not the direct heir?"

"Very strange," said I. "And now, Summers, if you will bring me my bills and a new cheque-book, we will begin to get things into order."

(Arthur Conan Doyle)

"For I will consider my Cat Jeoffry" (A Poem)

Eighteenth century English poet Christopher Smart celebrates his cat in this lively poem.

✳   ✳   ✳   ✳

For I will consider my Cat Jeoffry.

For he is the servant of the Living God duly and daily serving him.

For at the first glance of the glory of God in the East he worships in his way.

For this is done by wreathing his body seven times round with elegant quickness.

For then he leaps up to catch the musk, which is the blessing of God upon his prayer.

For he rolls upon prank to work it in.

For having done duty and received blessing he begins to consider himself.

For this he performs in ten degrees.

For first he looks upon his forepaws to see if they are clean.

For secondly he kicks up behind to clear away there.

For thirdly he works it upon stretch with the forepaws extended.

For fourthly he sharpens his paws by wood.

For fifthly he washes himself.

For sixthly he rolls upon wash.

For seventhly he fleas himself, that he may not be interrupted upon the beat.

For eighthly he rubs himself against a post.

For ninthly he looks up for his instructions.

For tenthly he goes in quest of food.

For having consider'd God and himself he will consider his neighbour.

For if he meets another cat he will kiss her in kindness.
For when he takes his prey he plays with it to give it a chance.
For one mouse in seven escapes by his dallying.
For when his day's work is done his business more properly begins.
For he keeps the Lord's watch in the night against the adversary.
For he counteracts the powers of darkness by his electrical skin and glaring eyes.
For he counteracts the Devil, who is death, by brisking about the life.
For in his morning orisons he loves the sun and the sun loves him.
For he is of the tribe of Tiger.
For the Cherub Cat is a term of the Angel Tiger.
For he has the subtlety and hissing of a serpent, which in goodness he suppresses.
For he will not do destruction, if he is well-fed, neither will he spit without provocation.
For he purrs in thankfulness, when God tells him he's a good Cat.
For he is an instrument for the children to learn benevolence upon.
For every house is incomplete without him and a blessing is lacking in the spirit.
For the Lord commanded Moses concerning the cats at the departure of the Children of Israel from Egypt.
For every family had one cat at least in the bag.
For the English Cats are the best in Europe.
For he is the cleanest in the use of his forepaws of any quadruped.
For the dexterity of his defence is an instance of the love of God to him exceedingly.

For he is the quickest to his mark of any creature.

For he is tenacious of his point.

For he is a mixture of gravity and waggery.

For he knows that God is his Saviour.

For there is nothing sweeter than his peace when at rest.

For there is nothing brisker than his life when in motion.

For he is of the Lord's poor and so indeed is he called by benevolence perpetually—Poor Jeoffry! poor Jeoffry! the rat has bit thy throat.

For I bless the name of the Lord Jesus that Jeoffry is better.

For the divine spirit comes about his body to sustain it in complete cat.

For his tongue is exceeding pure so that it has in purity what it wants in music.

For he is docile and can learn certain things.

For he can set up with gravity which is patience upon approbation.

For he can fetch and carry, which is patience in employment.

For he can jump over a stick which is patience upon proof positive.

For he can spraggle upon waggle at the word of command.

For he can jump from an eminence into his master's bosom.

For he can catch the cork and toss it again.

For he is hated by the hypocrite and miser.

For the former is afraid of detection.

For the latter refuses the charge.

For he camels his back to bear the first notion of business.

For he is good to think on, if a man would express himself neatly.

For he made a great figure in Egypt for his signal services.

For he killed the Ichneumon-rat very pernicious by land.

For his ears are so acute that they sting again.

For from this proceeds the passing quickness of his attention.

For by stroking of him I have found out electricity.

For I perceived God's light about him both wax and fire.

For the Electrical fire is the spiritual substance, which God sends from heaven to sustain the bodies both of man and beast.

For God has blessed him in the variety of his movements.

For, tho he cannot fly, he is an excellent clamberer.

For his motions upon the face of the earth are more than any other quadruped.

For he can tread to all the measures upon the music.

For he can swim for life.

For he can creep.

(Christopher Smart)

The Patient Cat

A nest tests a cat's patience is this short story.

✳ ✳ ✳ ✳

WHEN THE SPOTTED cat first found the nest, there was nothing in it, for it was only just finished. So she said, "I will wait!" for she was a patient cat, and the summer was before her. She waited a week, and then she climbed up again to the top of the tree, and peeped into the nest. There lay two lovely blue eggs, smooth and shining.

The spotted cat said, "Eggs may be good, but young birds are better. I will wait." So she waited; and while she was waiting, she caught mice and rats, and washed herself and slept, and did all that a spotted cat should do to pass the time away.

When another week had passed, she climbed the tree again and peeped into the nest. This time there were five eggs. But the spotted cat said again, "Eggs may be good, but young birds are better. I will wait a little longer!"

So she waited a little longer and then went up again to look. Ah! there were five tiny birds, with big eyes and long necks, and yellow beaks wide open. Then the spotted cat sat down on the branch, and licked her nose and purred, for she was very happy. "It is worth while to be patient!" she said.

But when she looked again at the young birds, to see which one she should take first, she saw that they were very thin,—oh, very, very thin they were! The spotted cat had never seen anything so thin in her life.

"Now," she said to herself, "if I were to wait only a few days longer, they would grow fat. Thin birds may be good, but fat birds are much better. I will wait!"

So she waited; and she watched the father-bird bringing worms all day long to the nest, and said, "Aha! they must be fattening fast! they will soon be as fat as I wish them to be. Aha! what a good thing it is to be patient."

At last, one day she thought, "Surely, now they must be fat enough! I will not wait another day. Aha! how good they will be!"

So she climbed up the tree, licking her chops all the way and thinking of the fat young birds. And when she reached the top and looked into the nest, it was empty!

Then the spotted cat sat down on the branch and spoke thus, "Well, of all the horrid, mean, ungrateful creatures I ever saw, those birds are the horridest, and the meanest, and the most ungrateful! Mi-a-u-ow!!!!"

(*Laura E. Richards*)

"The Cat" (A Poem)

Every cat owner can relate to the mischievous cat in this poem.

✳ ✳ ✳ ✳

Stop, naughty pussy! that's not fair!
Jump down this minute from the chair!
You've eaten my nice slice of bread.
And here are only crumbs instead.

I for a minute left the room
To listen to the "Buy a broom,"
And now I think it's quite too bad
That you my luncheon should have had.

Her mother said, "My dear, if you
Had done what you were told to do,
And put the plate upon the shelf,
You might have had the bread yourself.

"But if you have no thought nor care,
And leave your luncheon on a chair,
You must not blame poor pussy-cat;
She knows no better, dear, than that.

"The one who left her bread about
Upon the chair, while she went out,—
The one who hangs her head for shame,—
My little girl's the one to blame!"
(*H.P. Nichols*)

"Verses On a Cat" (A Poem)

This famous Romantic poet ponders the life of a cat.

✳   ✳   ✳   ✳

1. A cat in distress,
   Nothing more, nor less;
   Good folks, I must faithfully tell ye,
   As I am a sinner,
   It waits for some dinner
   To stuff out its own little belly.

2. You would not easily guess
   All the modes of distress
   Which torture the tenants of earth;
   And the various evils,
   Which like so many devils,
   Attend the poor souls from their birth.

3. Some a living require,
   And others desire
   An old fellow out of the way;
   And which is the best
   I leave to be guessed,
   For I cannot pretend to say.

4. One wants society,
   Another variety,
   Others a tranquil life;
   Some want food,
   Others, as good,
   Only want a wife.

5. But this poor little cat
   Only wanted a rat,
   To stuff out its own little maw;
   And it were as good
   SOME people had such food,
   To make them HOLD THEIR JAW!
   (Percy Bysshe Shelley)

"The Cats Have Come to Tea" (A Poem)

What's something that both cats and humans share? A love of a tasty afternoon snack, of course.

* * * *

What did she see oh, what did she see,
As she stood leaning against the tree?
Why all the Cats had come to tea.

What a fine turn out from round about,
All the houses had let them out,
And here they were with scamper and shout.

"Mew mew mew!" was all they could say,
And, "We hope we find you well to-day."

Oh, what should she do oh, what should she do?
What a lot of milk they would get through;
For here they were with "Mew mew mew!"

She didn't know oh, she didn't know,
If bread and butter they'd like or no;
They might want little mice, oh! oh! oh!

Dear me oh, dear me,
All the cats had come to tea.
(Kate Greenaway)

The Black Cat

*Edgar Allan Poe scares up another creepy yarn in this unsettling
short story.*

✳ ✳ ✳ ✳

FOR THE MOST wild, yet most homely narrative which I
am about to pen, I neither expect nor solicit belief. Mad
indeed would I be to expect it, in a case where my very senses
reject their own evidence. Yet, mad am I not—and very surely
do I not dream. But to-morrow I die, and to-day I would
unburthen my soul. My immediate purpose is to place before
the world, plainly, succinctly, and without comment, a series
of mere household events. In their consequences, these events
have terrified—have tortured—have destroyed me. Yet I will
not attempt to expound them. To me, they have presented
little but Horror—to many they will seem less terrible than
barroques. Hereafter, perhaps, some intellect may be found
which will reduce my phantasm to the common-place—some
intellect more calm, more logical, and far less excitable than
my own, which will perceive, in the circumstances I detail with
awe, nothing more than an ordinary succession of very natural
causes and effects.

From my infancy I was noted for the docility and humanity of
my disposition. My tenderness of heart was even so conspicu-
ous as to make me the jest of my companions. I was especially
fond of animals, and was indulged by my parents with a great
variety of pets. With these I spent most of my time, and never
was so happy as when feeding and caressing them. This pecu-
liarity of character grew with my growth, and in my manhood,
I derived from it one of my principal sources of pleasure. To
those who have cherished an affection for a faithful and sagacious dog, I need hardly be at the trouble of explaining the
nature or the intensity of the gratification thus derivable. There
is something in the unselfish and self-sacrificing love of a brute,

which goes directly to the heart of him who has had frequent occasion to test the paltry friendship and gossamer fidelity of mere Man.

I married early, and was happy to find in my wife a disposition not uncongenial with my own. Observing my partiality for domestic pets, she lost no opportunity of procuring those of the most agreeable kind. We had birds, gold-fish, a fine dog, rabbits, a small monkey, and a cat.

This latter was a remarkably large and beautiful animal, entirely black, and sagacious to an astonishing degree. In speaking of his intelligence, my wife, who at heart was not a little tinctured with superstition, made frequent allusion to the ancient popular notion, which regarded all black cats as witches in disguise. Not that she was ever serious upon this point—and I mention the matter at all for no better reason than that it happens, just now, to be remembered.

Pluto—this was the cat's name—was my favorite pet and playmate. I alone fed him, and he attended me wherever I went about the house. It was even with difficulty that I could prevent him from following me through the streets.

Our friendship lasted, in this manner, for several years, during which my general temperament and character—through the instrumentality of the Fiend Intemperance—had (I blush to confess it) experienced a radical alteration for the worse. I grew, day by day, more moody, more irritable, more regardless of the feelings of others. I suffered myself to use intemperate language to my wife. At length, I even offered her personal violence. My pets, of course, were made to feel the change in my disposition. I not only neglected, but ill-used them. For Pluto, however, I still retained sufficient regard to restrain me from maltreating him, as I made no scruple of maltreating the rabbits, the monkey, or even the dog, when by accident, or through affection, they came in my way. But my disease grew upon me—for what disease is like Alcohol!—and at length even Pluto, who was now becoming old, and consequently somewhat peevish—even Pluto began to experience the effects of my ill temper.

One night, returning home, much intoxicated, from one of my haunts about town, I fancied that the cat avoided my presence. I seized him; when, in his fright at my violence, he inflicted a slight wound upon my hand with his teeth. The fury of a demon instantly possessed me. I knew myself no longer. My original soul seemed, at once, to take its flight from my body and a more than fiendish malevolence, gin-nurtured, thrilled every fibre of my frame. I took from my waistcoat-pocket a pen-knife, opened it, grasped the poor beast by the throat, and deliberately cut one of its eyes from the socket! I blush, I burn, I shudder, while I pen the damnable atrocity.

When reason returned with the morning—when I had slept off the fumes of the night's debauch—I experienced a sentiment half of horror, half of remorse, for the crime of which I had been guilty; but it was, at best, a feeble and equivocal feeling, and the soul remained untouched. I again plunged into excess, and soon drowned in wine all memory of the deed.

In the meantime the cat slowly recovered. The socket of the lost eye presented, it is true, a frightful appearance, but he no longer appeared to suffer any pain. He went about the house as usual, but, as might be expected, fled in extreme terror at my approach. I had so much of my old heart left, as to be at first grieved by this evident dislike on the part of a creature which had once so loved me. But this feeling soon gave place to irritation. And then came, as if to my final and irrevocable overthrow, the spirit of PERVERSENESS. Of this spirit philosophy takes no account. Yet I am not more sure that my soul lives, than I am that perverseness is one of the primitive impulses of the human heart—one of the indivisible primary faculties, or sentiments, which give direction to the character of Man. Who has not, a hundred times, found himself committing a vile or a silly action, for no other reason than because he knows he should not? Have we not a perpetual inclination, in the teeth of our best judgment, to violate that which is Law, merely because we understand it to be such? This spirit of perverseness, I say, came to my final overthrow. It was this unfathomable longing of the soul to vex itself—to offer violence to its own nature—to do wrong for the wrong's sake only—that urged me to continue and finally to consummate the injury I had inflicted upon the unoffending brute. One morning, in cool blood, I slipped a noose about its neck and hung it to the limb of a tree;—hung it with the tears streaming from my eyes, and with the bitterest remorse at my heart;—hung it because I knew that it had loved me, and because I felt it had given me no reason of offence;—hung it because I knew that in so doing I was committing a sin—a deadly sin that would so jeopardize my immortal soul as to place it—if such a thing wore possible—even beyond the reach of the infinite mercy of the Most Merciful and Most Terrible God.

On the night of the day on which this cruel deed was done, I was aroused from sleep by the cry of fire. The curtains of my bed were in flames. The whole house was blazing. It was with great difficulty that my wife, a servant, and myself, made our escape from the conflagration. The destruction was complete. My entire worldly wealth was swallowed up, and I resigned myself thenceforward to despair.

I am above the weakness of seeking to establish a sequence of cause and effect, between the disaster and the atrocity. But I am detailing a chain of facts—and wish not to leave even a possible link imperfect. On the day succeeding the fire, I visited the ruins. The walls, with one exception, had fallen in. This exception was found in a compartment wall, not very thick, which stood about the middle of the house, and against which had rested the head of my bed. The plastering had here, in great measure, resisted the action of the fire—a fact which I attributed to its having been recently spread. About this wall a dense crowd were collected, and many persons seemed to be examining a particular portion of it with very minute and eager attention. The words "strange!" "singular!" and other similar expressions, excited my curiosity. I approached and saw, as if graven in bas relief upon the white surface, the figure of a gigantic cat. The impression was given with an accuracy truly marvellous. There was a rope about the animal's neck.

When I first beheld this apparition—for I could scarcely regard it as less—my wonder and my terror were extreme. But at length reflection came to my aid. The cat, I remembered, had been hung in a garden adjacent to the house. Upon the alarm of fire, this garden had been immediately filled by the crowd—by some one of whom the animal must have been cut from the tree and thrown, through an open window, into my chamber. This had probably been done with the view of arousing me from sleep. The falling of other walls had compressed the victim of my cruelty into the substance of the freshly-spread plaster; the lime of which, with the flames, and the ammonia from the carcass, had then accomplished the portraiture as I saw it.

Although I thus readily accounted to my reason, if not altogether to my conscience, for the startling fact just detailed, it did not the less fail to make a deep impression upon my fancy. For months I could not rid myself of the phantasm of the cat; and, during this period, there came back into my spirit a half-sentiment that seemed, but was not, remorse. I went so far as to regret the loss of the animal, and to look about me, among the vile haunts which I now habitually frequented, for another pet of the same species, and of somewhat similar appearance, with which to supply its place.

One night as I sat, half stupified, in a den of more than infamy, my attention was suddenly drawn to some black object, reposing upon the head of one of the immense hogsheads of Gin, or of Rum, which constituted the chief furniture of the apartment. I had been looking steadily at the top of this hogshead for some minutes, and what now caused me surprise was the fact that I had not sooner perceived the object thereupon. I approached it, and touched it with my hand. It was a black cat—a very large one—fully as large as Pluto, and closely resembling him in every respect but one. Pluto had not a white hair upon any portion of his body; but this cat had a large, although indefinite splotch of white, covering nearly the whole region of the breast. Upon my touching him, he immediately arose, purred loudly, rubbed against my hand, and appeared delighted with my notice. This, then, was the very creature of which I was in search. I at once offered to purchase it of the landlord; but this person made no claim to it—knew nothing of it—had never seen it before.

I continued my caresses, and, when I prepared to go home, the animal evinced a disposition to accompany me. I permitted it to do so; occasionally stooping and patting it as I proceeded. When it reached the house it domesticated itself at once, and became immediately a great favorite with my wife.

For my own part, I soon found a dislike to it arising within me. This was just the reverse of what I had anticipated; but—I know not how or why it was—its evident fondness for myself rather disgusted and annoyed. By slow degrees, these feelings of disgust and annoyance rose into the bitterness of hatred. I avoided the creature; a certain sense of shame, and the remembrance of my former deed of cruelty, preventing me from physically abusing it. I did not, for some weeks, strike, or otherwise violently ill use it; but gradually—very gradually—I came to look upon it with unutterable loathing, and to flee silently from its odious presence, as from the breath of a pestilence.

What added, no doubt, to my hatred of the beast, was the discovery, on the morning after I brought it home, that, like Pluto, it also had been deprived of one of its eyes. This circumstance, however, only endeared it to my wife, who, as I have already said, possessed, in a high degree, that humanity of feeling which had once been my distinguishing trait, and the source of many of my simplest and purest pleasures.

With my aversion to this cat, however, its partiality for myself seemed to increase. It followed my footsteps with a pertinacity which it would be difficult to make the reader comprehend. Whenever I sat, it would crouch beneath my chair, or spring upon my knees, covering me with its loathsome caresses. If I arose to walk it would get between my feet and thus nearly throw me down, or, fastening its long and sharp claws in my dress, clamber, in this manner, to my breast. At such times, although I longed to destroy it with a blow, I was yet withheld from so doing, partly by a memory of my former crime, but chiefly—let me confess it at once—by absolute dread of the beast.

This dread was not exactly a dread of physical evil—and yet I should be at a loss how otherwise to define it. I am almost ashamed to own—yes, even in this felon's cell, I am almost ashamed to own—that the terror and horror with which the animal inspired me, had been heightened by one of the merest chimaeras it would be possible to conceive. My wife had called my attention, more than once, to the character of the mark of white hair, of which I have spoken, and which constituted the sole visible difference between the strange beast and the one I had destroyed. The reader will remember that this mark, although large, had been originally very indefinite; but, by slow degrees—degrees nearly imperceptible, and which for a long time my Reason struggled to reject as fanciful—it had, at length, assumed a rigorous distinctness of outline. It was now the representation of an object that I shudder to name—and for this, above all, I loathed, and dreaded, and would have rid myself of the monster had I dared—it was now, I say, the image of a hideous—of a ghastly thing—of the GALLOWS!—oh, mournful and terrible engine of Horror and of Crime—of Agony and of Death!

And now was I indeed wretched beyond the wretchedness of mere Humanity. And a brute beast —whose fellow I had contemptuously destroyed—a brute beast to work out for me—for me a man, fashioned in the image of the High God—so much of insufferable wo! Alas! neither by day nor by night knew I the blessing of Rest any more! During the former the creature left me no moment alone; and, in the latter, I started, hourly, from dreams of unutterable fear, to find the hot breath of the thing upon my face, and its vast weight—an incarnate Night-Mare that I had no power to shake off—incumbent eternally upon my heart!

Beneath the pressure of torments such as these, the feeble remnant of the good within me succumbed. Evil thoughts became my sole intimates—the darkest and most evil of thoughts. The moodiness of my usual temper increased to hatred of all things and of all mankind; while, from the sudden, frequent, and ungovernable outbursts of a fury to which I now blindly abandoned myself, my uncomplaining wife, alas! was the most usual and the most patient of sufferers.

One day she accompanied me, upon some household errand, into the cellar of the old building which our poverty compelled us to inhabit. The cat followed me down the steep stairs, and, nearly throwing me headlong, exasperated me to madness. Uplifting an axe, and forgetting, in my wrath, the childish dread which had hitherto stayed my hand, I aimed a blow at the animal which, of course, would have proved instantly fatal had it descended as I wished. But this blow was arrested by the hand of my wife. Goaded, by the interference, into a rage more than demoniacal, I withdrew my arm from her grasp and buried the axe in her brain. She fell dead upon the spot, without a groan.

This hideous murder accomplished, I set myself forthwith, and with entire deliberation, to the task of concealing the body. I knew that I could not remove it from the house, either by day or by night, without the risk of being observed by the neighbors.

Many projects entered my mind. At one period I thought of cutting the corpse into minute fragments, and destroying them by fire. At another, I resolved to dig a grave for it in the floor of the cellar. Again, I deliberated about casting it in the well in the yard—about packing it in a box, as if merchandize, with the usual arrangements, and so getting a porter to take it from the house. Finally I hit upon what I considered a far better expedient than either of these. I determined to wall it up in the cellar—as the monks of the middle ages are recorded to have walled up their victims.

For a purpose such as this the cellar was well adapted. Its walls were loosely constructed, and had lately been plastered throughout with a rough plaster, which the dampness of the atmosphere had prevented from hardening. Moreover, in one of the walls was a projection, caused by a false chimney, or fireplace, that had been filled up, and made to resemble the red of the cellar. I made no doubt that I could readily displace the bricks at this point, insert the corpse, and wall the whole up as before, so that no eye could detect any thing suspicious. And in this calculation I was not deceived. By means of a crow-bar I easily dislodged the bricks, and, having carefully deposited the body against the inner wall, I propped it in that position, while, with little trouble, I re-laid the whole structure as it originally stood. Having procured mortar, sand, and hair, with every possible precaution, I prepared a plaster which could not be distinguished from the old, and with this I very carefully went over the new brickwork. When I had finished, I felt satisfied that all was right. The wall did not present the slightest appearance of having been disturbed. The rubbish on the floor was picked up with the minutest care. I looked around triumphantly, and said to myself—"Here at least, then, my labor has not been in vain."

My next step was to look for the beast which had been the cause of so much wretchedness; for I had, at length, firmly resolved to put it to death. Had I been able to meet with it, at the moment, there could have been no doubt of its fate; but it appeared that the crafty animal had been alarmed at the violence of my previous anger, and forebore to present itself in my present mood. It is impossible to describe, or to imagine, the deep, the blissful sense of relief which the absence of the detested creature occasioned in my bosom. It did not make its appearance during the night—and thus for one night at least, since its introduction into the house, I soundly and tranquilly slept; aye, slept even with the burden of murder upon my soul!

The second and the third day passed, and still my tormentor came not. Once again I breathed as a freeman. The monster, in terror, had fled the premises forever! I should behold it no more! My happiness was supreme! The guilt of my dark deed disturbed me but little. Some few inquiries had been made, but these had been readily answered. Even a search had been instituted—but of course nothing was to be discovered. I looked upon my future felicity as secured.

Upon the fourth day of the assassination, a party of the police came, very unexpectedly, into the house, and proceeded again to make rigorous investigation of the premises. Secure, however, in the inscrutability of my place of concealment, I felt no embarrassment whatever. The officers bade me accompany them in their search. They left no nook or corner unexplored. At length, for the third or fourth time, they descended into the cellar. I quivered not in a muscle. My heart beat calmly as that of one who slumbers in innocence. I walked the cellar from end to end. I folded my arms upon my bosom, and roamed easily to and fro. The police were thoroughly satisfied and prepared to depart. The glee at my heart was too strong to be restrained. I burned to say if but one word, by way of triumph, and to render doubly sure their assurance of my guiltlessness.

"Gentlemen," I said at last, as the party ascended the steps, "I delight to have allayed your suspicions. I wish you all health, and a little more courtesy. By the bye, gentlemen, this—this is a very well constructed house." [In the rabid desire to say something easily, I scarcely knew what I uttered at all.]—"I may say an excellently well constructed house. These walls—are you going, gentlemen?—these walls are solidly put together;" and here, through the mere phrenzy of bravado, I rapped heavily, with a cane which I held in my hand, upon that very portion of the brick-work behind which stood the corpse of the wife of my bosom.

But may God shield and deliver me from the fangs of the Arch-Fiend! No sooner had the reverberation of my blows sunk into silence, than I was answered by a voice from within the tomb!—by a cry, at first muffled and broken, like the sobbing of a child, and then quickly swelling into one long, loud, and continuous scream, utterly anomalous and inhuman—a howl—a wailing shriek, half of horror and half of triumph, such as might have arisen only out of hell, conjointly from the throats of the dammed in their agony and of the demons that exult in the damnation.

Of my own thoughts it is folly to speak. Swooning, I staggered to the opposite wall. For one instant the party upon the stairs remained motionless, through extremity of terror and of awe. In the next, a dozen stout arms were toiling at the wall. It fell bodily. The corpse, already greatly decayed and clotted with gore, stood erect before the eyes of the spectators. Upon its head, with red extended mouth and solitary eye of fire, sat the hideous beast whose craft had seduced me into murder, and whose informing voice had consigned me to the hangman. I had walled the monster up within the tomb!
(Edgar Allan Poe)

"Sonnet To Mrs. Reynolds's Cat" (A Poem)

From youth to old age, cats are admirable creatures.

✻ ✻ ✻ ✻

Cat! who hast pass'd thy grand climacteric,
How many mice and rats hast in thy days
Destroy'd? How many tit bits stolen? Gaze
With those bright languid segments green, and prick
Those velvet ears, but pr'ythee do not stick
Thy latent talons in me, and upraise
Thy gentle mew, and tell me all thy frays,
Of fish and mice, and rats and tender chick.
Nay, look not down, nor lick thy dainty wrists
For all thy wheezy asthma, and for all
Thy tail's tip is nick'd off, and though the fists
Of many a maid have given thee many a maul,
Still is that fur as soft, as when the lists
In youth thou enter'dest on glass bottled wall.

(John Keats)

The Cat That Walked By Himself

In praise of the independent cat.

* * * *

HEAR AND ATTEND and listen; for this befell and behappened and became and was, O my Best Beloved, when the Tame animals were wild. The Dog was wild, and the Horse was wild, and the Cow was wild, and the Sheep was wild, and the Pig was wild—as wild as wild could be—and they walked in the Wet Wild Woods by their wild lones. But the wildest of all the wild animals was the Cat. He walked by himself, and all places were alike to him.

Of course the Man was wild too. He was dreadfully wild. He didn't even begin to be tame till he met the Woman, and she told him that she did not like living in his wild ways. She picked out a nice dry Cave, instead of a heap of wet leaves, to lie down in; and she strewed clean sand on the floor; and she lit a nice fire of wood at the back of the Cave; and she hung a dried wild-horse skin, tail-down, across the opening of the Cave; and she said, "Wipe you feet, dear, when you come in, and now we'll keep house."

That night, Best Beloved, they ate wild sheep roasted on the hot stones, and flavoured with wild garlic and wild pepper; and wild duck stuffed with wild rice and wild fenugreek and wild coriander; and marrow-bones of wild oxen; and wild cherries, and wild grenadillas. Then the Man went to sleep in front of the fire ever so happy; but the Woman sat up, combing her hair. She took the bone of the shoulder of mutton—the big fat blade-bone—and she looked at the wonderful marks on it, and she threw more wood on the fire, and she made a Magic. She made the First Singing Magic in the world.

Out in the Wet Wild Woods all the wild animals gathered together where they could see the light of the fire a long way off, and they wondered what it meant.

Then Wild Horse stamped with his wild foot and said, "O my Friends and O my Enemies, why have the Man and the Woman made that great light in that great Cave, and what harm will it do us?"

Wild Dog lifted up his wild nose and smelled the smell of roast mutton, and said, "I will go up and see and look, and say; for I think it is good. Cat, come with me."

"Nenni!" said the Cat. "I am the Cat who walks by himself, and all places are alike to me. I will not come."

"Then we can never be friends again," said Wild Dog, and he trotted off to the Cave. But when he had gone a little way the Cat said to himself, "All places are alike to me. Why should I not go too and see and look and come away at my own liking?" So he slipped after Wild Dog softly, very softly, and hid himself where he could hear everything.

When Wild Dog reached the mouth of the Cave he lifted up the dried horse-skin with his nose and sniffed the beautiful smell of the roast mutton, and the Woman, looking at the blade-bone, heard him, and laughed, and said, "Here comes the first. Wild Thing out of the Wild Woods, what do you want?"

Wild Dog said, "O my Enemy and Wife of my Enemy, what is this that smells so good in the Wild Woods?"

Then the Woman picked up a roasted mutton-bone and threw it to Wild Dog, and said, "Wild Thing out of the Wild Woods, taste and try." Wild Dog gnawed the bone, and it was more delicious than anything he had ever tasted, and he said, "O my Enemy and Wife of my Enemy, give me another."

The Woman said, "Wild Thing out of the Wild Woods, help my Man to hunt through the day and guard this Cave at night, and I will give you as many roast bones as you need."

"Ah!" said the Cat, listening. "This is a very wise Woman, but she is not so wise as I am."

Wild Dog crawled into the Cave and laid his head on the Woman's lap, and said, "O my Friend and Wife of my Friend, I will help Your Man to hunt through the day, and at night I will guard your Cave."

"Ah!" said the Cat, listening. "That is a very foolish Dog." And he went back through the Wet Wild Woods waving his wild tail, and walking by his wild lone. But he never told anybody.

When the Man waked up he said, "What is Wild Dog doing here?" And the Woman said, "His name is not Wild Dog any more, but the First Friend, because he will be our friend for always and always and always. Take him with you when you go hunting."

Next night the Woman cut great green armfuls of fresh grass from the water-meadows, and dried it before the fire, so that it smelt like new-mown hay, and she sat at the mouth of the Cave and plaited a halter out of horse-hide, and she looked at the shoulder of mutton-bone—at the big broad blade-bone—and she made a Magic. She made the Second Singing Magic in the world.

Out in the Wild Woods all the wild animals wondered what had happened to Wild Dog, and at last Wild Horse stamped with his foot and said, "I will go and see and say why Wild Dog has not returned. Cat, come with me."

"Nenni!" said the Cat. "I am the Cat who walks by himself, and all places are alike to me. I will not come." But all the same he followed Wild Horse softly, very softly, and hid himself where he could hear everything.

When the Woman heard Wild Horse tripping and stumbling on his long mane, she laughed and said, "Here comes the second. Wild Thing out of the Wild Woods what do you want?"

Wild Horse said, "O my Enemy and Wife of my Enemy, where is Wild Dog?"

The Woman laughed, and picked up the blade-bone and looked at it, and said, "Wild Thing out of the Wild Woods, you did not come here for Wild Dog, but for the sake of this good grass."

And Wild Horse, tripping and stumbling on his long mane, said, "That is true; give it me to eat."

The Woman said, "Wild Thing out of the Wild Woods, bend your wild head and wear what I give you, and you shall eat the wonderful grass three times a day."

"Ah," said the Cat, listening, "this is a clever Woman, but she is not so clever as I am." Wild Horse bent his wild head, and the Woman slipped the plaited hide halter over it, and Wild Horse breathed on the Woman's feet and said, "O my Mistress, and Wife of my Master, I will be your servant for the sake of the wonderful grass."

"Ah," said the Cat, listening, "that is a very foolish Horse." And he went back through the Wet Wild Woods, waving his wild tail and walking by his wild lone. But he never told anybody.

When the Man and the Dog came back from hunting, the Man said, "What is Wild Horse doing here?" And the Woman said, "His name is not Wild Horse any more, but the First Servant, because he will carry us from place to place for always and always and always. Ride on his back when you go hunting."

Next day, holding her wild head high that her wild horns should not catch in the wild trees, Wild Cow came up to the Cave, and the Cat followed, and hid himself just the same as before; and everything happened just the same as before; and the Cat said the same things as before, and when Wild Cow had promised to give her milk to the Woman every day in exchange for the wonderful grass, the Cat went back through the Wet Wild Woods waving his wild tail and walking by his wild lone, just the same as before. But he never told anybody. And when the Man and the Horse and the Dog came home from hunting and asked the same questions same as before, the Woman said, "Her name is not Wild Cow any more, but the Giver of Good Food. She will give us the warm white milk for always and always and always, and I will take care of her while you and the First Friend and the First Servant go hunting."

Next day the Cat waited to see if any other Wild thing would go up to the Cave, but no one moved in the Wet Wild Woods, so the Cat walked there by himself; and he saw the Woman milking the Cow, and he saw the light of the fire in the Cave, and he smelt the smell of the warm white milk.

Cat said, "O my Enemy and Wife of my Enemy, where did Wild Cow go?"

The Woman laughed and said, "Wild Thing out of the Wild Woods, go back to the Woods again, for I have braided up my hair, and I have put away the magic blade-bone, and we have no more need of either friends or servants in our Cave."

Cat said, "I am not a friend, and I am not a servant. I am the Cat who walks by himself, and I wish to come into your cave."

Woman said, "Then why did you not come with First Friend on the first night?"

Cat grew very angry and said, "Has Wild Dog told tales of me?"

Then the Woman laughed and said, "You are the Cat who walks by himself, and all places are alike to you. Your are neither a friend nor a servant. You have said it yourself. Go away and walk by yourself in all places alike."

Then Cat pretended to be sorry and said, "Must I never come into the Cave? Must I never sit by the warm fire? Must I never drink the warm white milk? You are very wise and very beautiful. You should not be cruel even to a Cat."

Woman said, "I knew I was wise, but I did not know I was beautiful. So I will make a bargain with you. If ever I say one word in your praise you may come into the Cave."

"And if you say two words in my praise?" said the Cat.

"I never shall," said the Woman, "but if I say two words in your praise, you may sit by the fire in the Cave."

"And if you say three words?" said the Cat.

"I never shall," said the Woman, "but if I say three words in your praise, you may drink the warm white milk three times a day for always and always and always."

Then the Cat arched his back and said, "Now let the Curtain at the mouth of the Cave, and the Fire at the back of the Cave, and the Milk-pots that stand beside the Fire, remember what my Enemy and the Wife of my Enemy has said." And he went away through the Wet Wild Woods waving his wild tail and walking by his wild lone.

That night when the Man and the Horse and the Dog came home from hunting, the Woman did not tell them of the bargain that she had made with the Cat, because she was afraid that they might not like it.

Cat went far and far away and hid himself in the Wet Wild Woods by his wild lone for a long time till the Woman forgot all about him. Only the Bat—the little upside-down Bat—that hung inside the Cave, knew where Cat hid; and every evening Bat would fly to Cat with news of what was happening.

One evening Bat said, "There is a Baby in the Cave. He is new and pink and fat and small, and the Woman is very fond of him."

"Ah," said the Cat, listening, "but what is the Baby fond of?"

"He is fond of things that are soft and tickle," said the Bat. " He is fond of warm things to hold in his arms when he goes to sleep. He is fond of being played with. He is fond of all those things."

"Ah," said the Cat, listening, "then my time has come."

Next night Cat walked through the Wet Wild Woods and hid very near the Cave till morning-time, and Man and Dog and Horse went hunting. The Woman was busy cooking that morning, and the Baby cried and interrupted. So she carried him outside the Cave and gave him a handful of pebbles to play with. But still the Baby cried.

Then the Cat put out his paddy paw and patted the Baby on the cheek, and it cooed; and the Cat rubbed against its fat knees and tickled it under its fat chin with his tail. And the Baby laughed; and the Woman heard him and smiled.

Then the Bat—the little upside-down bat—that hung in the mouth of the Cave said, "O my Hostess and Wife of my Host and Mother of my Host's Son, a Wild Thing from the Wild Woods is most beautifully playing with your Baby."

"A blessing on that Wild Thing whoever he may be," said the Woman, straightening her back, "for I was a busy woman this morning and he has done me a service."

That very minute and second, Best Beloved, the dried horse-skin Curtain that was stretched tail-down at the mouth of the Cave fell down—whoosh!—because it remembered the bargain she had made with the Cat, and when the Woman went to pick it up—lo and behold!—the Cat was sitting quite comfy inside the Cave.

"O my Enemy and Wife of my Enemy and Mother of my Enemy," said the Cat, "it is I: for you have spoken a word in my praise, and now I can sit within the Cave for always and always and always. But still I am the Cat who walks by himself, and all places are alike to me."

The Woman was very angry, and shut her lips tight and took up her spinning-wheel and began to spin. But the Baby cried because the Cat had gone away, and the Woman could not hush it, for it struggled and kicked and grew black in the face.

"O my Enemy and Wife of my Enemy and Mother of my Enemy," said the Cat, "take a strand of the wire that you are spinning and tie it to your spinning-whorl and drag it along the floor, and I will show you a magic that shall make your Baby laugh as loudly as he is now crying."

"I will do so," said the Woman, "because I am at my wits' end; but I will not thank you for it."

She tied the thread to the little clay spindle whorl and drew it across the floor, and the Cat ran after it and patted it with his paws and rolled head over heels, and tossed it backward over his shoulder and chased it between his hind-legs and pretended to lose it, and pounced down upon it again, till the Baby laughed as loudly as it had been crying, and scrambled after the Cat and frolicked all over the Cave till it grew tired and settled down to sleep with the Cat in its arms.

"Now," said the Cat, "I will sing the Baby a song that shall keep him asleep for an hour." And he began to purr, loud and low, low and loud, till the Baby fell fast asleep. The Woman smiled as she looked down upon the two of them and said, "That was wonderfully done. No question but you are very clever, O Cat."

That very minute and second, Best Beloved, the smoke of the fire at the back of the Cave came down in clouds from the roof—puff!—because it remembered the bargain she had made with the Cat, and when it had cleared away—lo and behold!—the Cat was sitting quite comfy close to the fire.

"O my Enemy and Wife of my Enemy and Mother of My Enemy," said the Cat, "it is I, for you have spoken a second word in my praise, and now I can sit by the warm fire at the back of the Cave for always and always and always. But still I am the Cat who walks by himself, and all places are alike to me."

Then the Woman was very very angry, and let down her hair and put more wood on the fire and brought out the broad blade-bone of the shoulder of mutton and began to make a

Magic that should prevent her from saying a third word in praise of the Cat. It was not a Singing Magic, Best Beloved, it was a Still Magic; and by and by the Cave grew so still that a little wee-wee mouse crept out of a corner and ran across the floor.

"O my Enemy and Wife of my Enemy and Mother of my Enemy," said the Cat, "is that little mouse part of your magic?"

"Ouh! Chee! No indeed!" said the Woman, and she dropped the blade-bone and jumped upon the footstool in front of the fire and braided up her hair very quick for fear that the mouse should run up it.

"Ah," said the Cat, watching, "then the mouse will do me no harm if I eat it?"

"No," said the Woman, braiding up her hair, "eat it quickly and I will ever be grateful to you."

Cat made one jump and caught the little mouse, and the Woman said, "A hundred thanks. Even the First Friend is not quick enough to catch little mice as you have done. You must be very wise."

That very moment and second, O Best Beloved, the Milk-pot that stood by the fire cracked in two pieces—ffft—because it remembered the bargain she had made with the Cat, and when the Woman jumped down from the footstool—lo and behold!—the Cat was lapping up the warm white milk that lay in one of the broken pieces.

"O my Enemy and Wife of my Enemy and Mother of my Enemy," said the Cat, "it is I; for you have spoken three words in my praise, and now I can drink the warm white milk three times a day for always and always and always. But still I am the Cat who walks by himself, and all places are alike to me."

The Woman laughed and set the Cat a bowl of the warm white milk and said, "O Cat, you are as clever as a man, but remember that your bargain was not made with the Man or the Dog, and I do not know what they will do when they come home."

"What is that to me?" said the Cat. "If I have my place in the Cave by the fire and my warm white milk three times a day I do not care what the Man or the Dog can do."

That evening when the Man and the Dog came into the Cave, the Woman told them all the story of the bargain while the Cat sat by the fire and smiled. Then the Man said, "Yes, but he has not made a bargain with me or with all proper Men after me." Then he took off his two leather boots and he took up his little stone axe (that makes three) and he fetched a piece of wood and a hatchet (that is five altogether), and he set them out in a row and he said, "Now we will make our bargain. If you do not catch mice when you are in the Cave for always and always and always, I will throw these five things at you whenever I see you, and so shall all proper Men do after me."

"Ah," said the Woman, listening, "this is a very clever Cat, but he is not so clever as my Man."

The Cat counted the five things (and they looked very knobby) and he said, "I will catch mice when I am in the Cave for always and always and always; but still I am the Cat who walks by himself, and all places are alike to me."

"Not when I am near," said the Man. "If you had not said that last I would have put all these things away for always and always and always; but I am now going to throw my two boots and my little stone axe (that makes three) at you whenever I meet you. And so shall all proper Men do after me!"

Then the Dog said, "Wait a minute. He has not made a bargain with me or with all proper Dogs after me." And he showed his teeth and said, "If you are not kind to the Baby while I am in the Cave for always and always and always, I will hunt you till I catch you, and when I catch you I will bite you. And so shall all proper Dogs do after me."

"Ah," said the Woman, listening, "this is a very clever Cat, but he is not so clever as the Dog."

Cat counted the Dog's teeth (and they looked very pointed) and he said, "I will be kind to the Baby while I am in the Cave, as long as he does not pull my tail too hard, for always and always and always. But still I am the Cat that walks by himself, and all places are alike to me."

"Not when I am near," said the Dog. "If you had not said that last I would have shut my mouth for always and always and always; but now I am going to hunt you up a tree whenever I meet you. And so shall all proper Dogs do after me."

Then the Man threw his two boots and his little stone axe (that makes three) at the Cat, and the Cat ran out of the Cave and the Dog chased him up a tree; and from that day to this, Best Beloved, three proper Men out of five will always throw things at a Cat whenever they meet him, and all proper Dogs will chase him up a tree. But the Cat keeps his side of the bargain too. He will kill mice and he will be kind to Babies when he is in the house, just as long as they do not pull his tail too hard. But when he has done that, and between times, and when the moon gets up and night comes, he is the Cat that walks by himself, and all places are alike to him. Then he goes out to the Wet Wild Woods or up the Wet Wild Trees or on the Wet Wild Roofs, waving his wild tail and walking by his wild lone.

(Rudyard Kipling)

The Tiger and the Monkeys

This Indian folk tale features a lovesick tiger who learns an important lesson.

❋ ❋ ❋ ❋

AT THE BEGINNING of time the animals were free and living wild and unruly lives, but there were so many disputes and quarrels that they convened a council to choose a king to reign over them. With one accord they nominated the tiger to be king, not for any special wisdom or merit which he possessed, but because of his great strength, by which he would be able to subdue the turbulent beasts.

Although he possessed greater strength than any of his kindred, the tiger was more ignorant of the ways and habits of his subjects than any of the animals. He was so self-absorbed that he never troubled himself to study the ways of others, and this caused him to act very foolishly at times and to make himself ridiculous, for the animals were tempted to take advantage of his great ignorance and to play tricks upon him whenever they thought they could do so undetected. This tale relates how the monkeys played a cunning trick on their king which caused mortal enmity to spring up between him and them forever.

One hot day the tiger walked abroad to take an airing, but, the sun being so hot, he turned aside to shelter under some leafy trees and there he fell asleep. Presently he awoke, and on awaking he heard coming from overhead very melodious singing to which he listened enraptured. It was the little insect, Shalymmen, chirping on a leaf, but she was so small the tiger could not see her, and, being so ignorant, he had no idea whose voice it was. He peered to the branches right and left trying to discover the singer, but he only saw a company of monkeys at play in the trees, so he began to question them who it was that was singing above him.

Now the monkeys and all the jungle animals were perfectly voice from afar. They thought it very contemptible in the king to be more ignorant than themselves, and one audacious young monkey, in a spirit of mischief, answered that the singer was their youngest sister.

The other monkeys were perturbed when they heard their brother giving such an impudent answer, thinking that the tiger would be offended and would punish them with his great strength. They were preparing to run away when, to their amazement, they heard the tiger replying to their rash young brother in a gentle voice and with most affable manners and saying to him, "You are my brother-in-law. Your sister has the most beautiful voice in the jungle; I will make her my wife."

If the predicament of the monkeys was bad at the beginning, it was doubly so now, for they felt that, things having taken such an unexpected turn, it would be impossible to conceal from the knowledge of the tiger their brother's offence. They determined, however, not to desert the young culprit, and if possible to try and rescue him, so they approached the tiger, and with much seeming courtesy and honor they put forward the excuse that their sister was very young and not yet of marriageable age. This excuse made no impression on the king, for he said:

"So much the better. As she is young, I can mold her to my own ways, and bring her up according to my own views, which would not be so easy if she were fully matured."

To which the monkeys replied, "Our sister is not amenable to instruction. She is indolent and fond of her own will."

The tiger, however, was so lovesick that no argument had weight with him. He thought the brothers were severe in their judgement, and expressed his conviction that she could not be as slothful as they said, for she was forgoing her midday repose for the sake of making music to cheer the animals. He ordered them to come down from the trees and to lead their sister to him.

After this the monkeys feared to argue further, so they pretended to agree to his commands; but they craved a boon from him, and asked for a little time to make preparations, as it would not be becoming for one of such a high degree to join himself with a poor family like theirs without their showing him adequate honor such as was due to his rank. This request the tiger granted, and it was arranged between them that he was to come and claim his bride at the time of the full moon, a week from that day, and so the tiger departed with goodwill.

As soon as they found themselves alone the monkeys began to think out some plans by which they could meet the situation and escape exposure. They decided to call together a council of the whole tribe of monkeys, for they well foresaw that the whole tribe would be in peril if the tiger found out what they had done. So the monkeys came to hold a council, and in that council it was decided that they must continue to keep up the duplicity begun, and in order to hoodwink the tiger still further they planned to make a clay image after the fashion of a woman and to present her to the tiger as his bride. So they made preparations for a great feast, but they did not invite anybody except their own tribe to attend.

During the succeeding days the monkeys busied themselves collecting clay and molding it into an image, which they propped against a tree. They were unable to make the head of one piece with the body, so they molded the head separately, and when it was finished they placed it loosely on the body of the image. They then proceeded to dress the image in all the finery they could procure, and they carefully covered the head and face with a veil so as to hide it from the eyes of the bridegroom.

The night of the full moon arrived, and all the monkey family were assembled at the appointed place, where with much clatter and seeming joy they awaited the arrival of the tiger, though they were really very anxious about the consequences.

Everything was in readiness, and the place laid out with many kinds of food, so as to lead the tiger to think that they were sincere in their welcome.

He came early, very gorgeously arrayed, and carrying over his shoulder a net full of betel nut and pan leaves, and was received with loud acclamation by his prospective relatives. But the tiger hardly deigned to give them a greeting, so impatient was he to meet his bride, and he demanded to be taken to her immediately. The monkeys led him with great ceremony to the clay image, but their hearts were beating fast with fear lest he should discover their fraud.

When they reached the image they said, "This is our sister. Take her and may she be worthy of the great honor you have conferred upon her." Thereupon they retired to a safe distance.

When the tiger saw how finely dressed she was and how modestly she had veiled herself, he felt a little timid, for she was so much finer than the little grey monkey he had been picturing to himself. He came up to her and said deferentially, as he slung the net of betel nut round her neck:

"You are the chief person at this feast, take the pan and the betel nut and divide them among the company according to custom."

The bride, however, remained motionless and mute, seeing which, the tiger asked the monkeys in a displeased voice, "Why doth not your sister answer me nor obey my commands?"

"She is very young," they replied, "perhaps she has fallen asleep while waiting for you; pull the string of the net and she will awaken."

Upon this the tiger gave the string a sharp tug, and the loose head of the image rolled on to the floor, whereupon the monkeys, uttering the most piercing shrieks, pounced upon the tiger in a mob, declaring that he had killed their sister, and that he had only made a pretense of marrying her in order to get hold of her to kill her. A fierce and bloody fight ensued in which the tiger was nearly killed, and ever since then the tiger has feared the monkeys, and they are the only animals in the jungle that dare challenge him to fight. He never discovered their duplicity, but he learned one very effective lesson, for he has never committed the indiscretion of proposing marriage with an unknown bride since that unfortunate affair with the monkeys; while the monkeys are rejoicing in the cunning by which they saved their brother and their tribe from punishment.

(*Indian Folk Tale*)

Cat and Mouse in Partnership
Can you always trust your cat?

* * * *

A CERTAIN CAT HAD made the acquaintance of a mouse, and had said so much to her about the great love and friendship she felt for her, that at length the mouse agreed that they should live and keep house together.

"But we must make a provision for winter, or else we shall suffer from hunger," said the cat; "and you, little mouse, cannot venture everywhere, or you will be caught in a trap some day." The good advice was followed, and a pot of fat was bought, but they did not know where to put it. At length, after much consideration, the cat said: "I know no place where it will be better stored up than in the church, for no one dares take anything away from there. We will set it beneath the altar, and not touch it until we are really in need of it."

So the pot was placed in safety, but it was not long before the cat had a great yearning for it, and said to the mouse: "I wantto tell you something, little mouse; my cousin has brought a little son into the world, and has asked me to be godmother; he is white with brown spots, and I am to hold him over the font at the christening. Let me go out today, and you look after the house by yourself."

"Yes, yes," answered the mouse, "by all means go, and if you get anything very good to eat, think of me. I should like a drop of sweet red christening wine myself."

All this, however, was untrue; the cat had no cousin, and had not been asked to be godmother. She went straight to the church, stole to the pot of fat, began to lick at it, and licked the top of the fat off. Then she took a walk upon the roofs of the town, looked out for opportunities, and then stretched herself in the sun, and licked her lips whenever she thought of the pot of fat, and not until it was evening did she return home.

"Well, here you are again," said the mouse, "no doubt you have had a merry day."

"All went off well," answered the cat.

"What name did they give the child?"

"Top off!" said the cat quite coolly.

"Top off!" cried the mouse, "that is a very odd and uncommon name, is it a usual one in your family?"

"What does that matter," said the cat, "it is no worse than Crumb-stealer, as your godchildren are called."

Before long the cat was seized by another fit of yearning. She said to the mouse: "You must do me a favor, and once more manage the house for a day alone. I am again asked to be godmother, and, as the child has a white ring round its neck, I cannot refuse."

The good mouse consented, but the cat crept behind the town walls to the church, and devoured half the pot of fat. "Nothing ever seems so good as what one keeps to oneself," said she, and was quite satisfied with her day's work.

When she went home the mouse inquired: "And what was the child christened?"

"Half-done," answered the cat.

"Half-done! What are you saying? I never heard the name in my life, I'll wager anything it is not in the calendar!"

The cat's mouth soon began to water for some more licking. "All good things go in threes," said she, "I am asked to stand god-mother again. The child is quite black, only it has white paws, but with that exception, it has not a single white hair on its whole body; this only happens once every few years, you will let me go, won't you?"

"Top-off! Half-done!" answered the mouse, "they are such odd names, they make me very thoughtful."

"You sit at home," said the cat, "in your dark-grey fur coat and long tail, and are filled with fancies, that's because you do not go out in the daytime."

During the cat's absence the mouse cleaned the house, and put it in order, but the greedy cat entirely emptied the pot of fat. "When everything is eaten up one has some peace," said she to herself, and well filled and fat she did not return home till night.

The mouse at once asked what name had been given to the third child.

"It will not please you more than the others," said the cat. "He is called All-gone."

"All-gone," cried the mouse. "That is the most suspicious name of all! I have never seen it in print. All-gone; what can that mean?" and she shook her head, curled herself up, and lay down to sleep.

From this time forth no one invited the cat to be godmother, but when the winter had come and there was no longer anything to be found outside, the mouse thought of their provision, and said: "Come, cat, we will go to our pot of fat which we have stored up for ourselves—we shall enjoy that."

"Yes," answered the cat, "you will enjoy it as much as you would enjoy sticking that dainty tongue of yours out of the window."

They set out on their way, but when they arrived, the pot of fat certainly was still in its place, but it was empty. "Alas!" said the mouse, "now I see what has happened, now it comes to light! You are a true friend! You have devoured all when you were standing godmother. First top off, then half-done, then—"

"Will you hold your tongue," cried the cat, "one word more, and I will eat you too."

"All-gone" was already on the poor mouse's lips; scarcely had she spoken it before the cat sprang on her, seized her, and swallowed her down. Verily, that is the way of the world.

(*The Brothers Grimm*)

The Tale of Samuel Whiskers
This famous Beatrix Potter children's story offers a timely lesson about disobedience.

✳ ✳ ✳ ✳

ONCE UPON A time there was an old cat, called Mrs. Tabitha Twitchit, who was an anxious parent. She used to lose her kittens continually, and whenever they were lost they were always in mischief!

On baking day she determined to shut them up in a cupboard.

Mrs. Tabitha went up and down all over the house, mewing for Tom Kitten. She caught Moppet and Mittens, but she could not find Tom for Tom Kitten. She looked in the pantry under the staircase, and she searched the best spare bedroom that was all covered up with dust sheets. She went right upstairs and looked into the attics, but she could not find him anywhere.

It was an old, old house, full of cupboards and passages. Some of the walls were four feet thick, and there used to be odd noises inside them, as if there might be a little secret staircase. Certainly there were odd little jagged doorways in the wainscot, and things disappeared at night—especially cheese and bacon.

Mrs. Tabitha became more and more distracted, and mewed dreadfully.

While their mother was searching the house, Moppet and Mittens had got into mischief. The cupboard door was not locked, so they pushed it open and came out.

They went straight to the dough which was set to rise in a pan before the fire.

They patted it with their little soft paws—"Shall we make dear little muffins?" said Mittens to Moppet.

But just at that moment somebody knocked at the front door, and Moppet jumped into the flour barrel in a fright. Mittens ran away to the dairy, and hid in an empty jar on the stone shelf where the milk pans stand.

The visitor was a neighbour, Mrs. Ribby; she had called to borrow some yeast.

Mrs. Tabitha came downstairs mewing dreadfully—"Come in, Cousin Ribby, come in, and sit ye down! I'm in sad trouble, Cousin Ribby," said Tabitha, shedding tears. "I've lost my dear son Thomas; I'm afraid the rats have got him." She wiped her eyes with her apron.

"He's a bad kitten, Cousin Tabitha; he made a cat's cradle of my best bonnet last time I came to tea. Where have you looked for him?"

"All over the house! The rats are too many for me. What a thing it is to have an unruly family!" said Mrs. Tabitha Twitchit.

"I'm not afraid of rats; I will help you to find him; and whip him too! What is all that soot in the fender?"

"The chimney wants sweeping—Oh, dear me, Cousin Ribby—now Moppet and Mittens are gone!"

"They have both got out of the cupboard!"

Ribby and Tabitha set to work to search the house thoroughly again. They poked under the beds with Ribby's umbrella, and they rummaged in cupboards. They even fetched a candle, and looked inside a clothes chest in one of the attics. They could not find anything, but once they heard a door bang and somebody scuttered downstairs.

"Yes, it is infested with rats," said Tabitha tearfully. "I caught seven young ones out of one hole in the back kitchen, and we had them for dinner last Saturday. And once I saw the old father rat—an enormous old rat, Cousin Ribby. I was just going to jump upon him, when he showed his yellow teeth at me and whisked down the hole."

"The rats get upon my nerves, Cousin Ribby," said Tabitha.

Ribby and Tabitha searched and searched. They both heard a curious roly-poly noise under the attic floor. But there was nothing to be seen.

They returned to the kitchen. "Here's one of your kittens at least," said Ribby, dragging Moppet out of the flour barrel.

They shook the flour off her and set her down on the kitchen floor. She seemed to be in a terrible fright.

"Oh! Mother, Mother," said Moppet, "there's been an old woman rat in the kitchen, and she's stolen some of the dough!"

The two cats ran to look at the dough pan. Sure enough there were marks of little scratching fingers, and a lump of dough was gone!

"Which way did she go, Moppet?"

But Moppet had been too much frightened to peep out of the barrel again.

Ribby and Tabitha took her with them to keep her safely in sight, while they went on with their search.

They went into the dairy. The first thing they found was Mittens, hiding in an empty jar. They tipped up the jar, and she scrambled out.

"Oh, Mother, Mother!" said Mittens—

"Oh! Mother, Mother, there has been an old man rat in the dairy—a dreadful 'normous big rat, mother; and he's stolen a pat of butter and the rolling-pin."

Ribby and Tabitha looked at one another.

"A rolling-pin and butter! Oh, my poor son Thomas!" exclaimed Tabitha, wringing her paws.

"A rolling-pin?" said Ribby. "Did we not hear a roly-poly noise in the attic when we were looking into that chest?"

Ribby and Tabitha rushed upstairs again. Sure enough the roly-poly noise was still going on quite distinctly under the attic floor.

"This is serious, Cousin Tabitha," said Ribby. "We must send for John Joiner at once, with a saw."

Now this is what had been happening to Tom Kitten, and it shows how very unwise it is to go up a chimney in a very old house, where a person does not know his way, and where there are enormous rats.

Tom Kitten did not want to be shut up in a cupboard. When he saw that his mother was going to bake, he determined to hide. He looked about for a nice convenient place, and he fixed upon the chimney.

The fire had only just been lighted, and it was not hot; but there was a white choky smoke from the green sticks. Tom Kitten got upon the fender and looked up. It was a big old-fashioned fireplace.

The chimney itself was wide enough inside for a man to stand up and walk about. So there was plenty of room for a little Tom Cat.

He jumped right up into the fireplace, balancing himself upon the iron bar where the kettle hangs.

Tom Kitten took another big jump off the bar, and landed on a ledge high up inside the chimney, knocking down some soot into the fender.

Tom Kitten coughed and choked with the smoke; and he could hear the sticks beginning to crackle and burn in the fireplace down below. He made up his mind to climb right to the top, and get out on the slates, and try to catch sparrows.

"I cannot go back. If I slipped I might fall in the fire and singe my beautiful tail and my little blue jacket."

The chimney was a very big old-fashioned one. It was built in the days when people burnt logs of wood upon the hearth.

The chimney stack stood up above the roof like a little stone tower, and the daylight shone down from the top, under the slanting slates that kept out the rain.

Tom Kitten was getting very frightened! He climbed up, and up, and up.

Then he waded sideways through inches of soot. He was like a little sweep himself.

It was most confusing in the dark. One flue seemed to lead into another. There was less smoke, but Tom Kitten felt quite lost.

He scrambled up and up; but before he reached the chimney top he came to a place where somebody had loosened a stone in the wall. There were some mutton bones lying about—

"This seems funny," said Tom Kitten. "Who has been gnawing bones up here in the chimney? I wish I had never come! And what a funny smell? It is something like mouse; only dreadfully strong. It makes me sneeze," said Tom Kitten.

He squeezed through the hole in the wall, and dragged himself along a most uncomfortably tight passage where there was scarcely any light.

He groped his way carefully for several yards; he was at the back of the skirting-board in the attic.

All at once he fell head over heels in the dark, down a hole, and landed on a heap of very dirty rags.

When Tom Kitten picked himself up and looked about him— he found himself in a place that he had never seen before, although he had lived all his life in the house.

It was a very small stuffy fusty room, with boards, and rafters, and cobwebs, and lath and plaster.

Opposite to him—as far away as he could sit—was an enormous rat.

"What do you mean by tumbling into my bed all covered with smuts?" said the rat, chattering his teeth.

"Please sir, the chimney wants sweeping," said poor Tom Kitten.

"Anna Maria! Anna Maria!" squeaked the rat. There was a pattering noise and an old woman rat poked her head round a rafter.

All in a minute she rushed upon Tom Kitten, and before he knew what was happening—

His coat was pulled off, and he was rolled up in a bundle, and tied with string in very hard knots.

Anna Maria did the tying. The old rat watched her and took snuff. When she had finished, they both sat staring at him with their mouths open.

"Anna Maria," said the old man rat (whose name was Samuel Whiskers),—"Anna Maria, make me a kitten dumpling roly-poly pudding for my dinner."

"It requires dough and a pat of butter, and a rolling-pin," said Anna Maria, considering Tom Kitten with her head on one side.

"No," said Samuel Whiskers, "make it properly, Anna Maria, with breadcrumbs."

"Nonsense! Butter and dough," replied Anna Maria.

The two rats consulted together for a few minutes and then went away.

Samuel Whiskers got through a hole in the wainscot, and went boldly down the front staircase to the dairy to get the butter. He did not meet anybody.

He made a second journey for the rolling-pin. He pushed it in front of him with his paws, like a brewer's man trundling a barrel.

He could hear Ribby and Tabitha talking, but they were busy lighting the candle to look into the chest. They did not see him.

Anna Maria went down by way of the skirting-board and a window shutter to the kitchen to steal the dough. She borrowed a small saucer, and scooped up the dough with her paws. She did not observe Moppet.

While Tom Kitten was left alone under the floor of the attic, he wriggled about and tried to mew for help.

But his mouth was full of soot and cobwebs, and he was tied up in such very tight knots, he could not make anybody hear him.

Except a spider, which came out of a crack in the ceiling and examined the knots critically, from a safe distance.

It was a judge of knots because it had a habit of tying up unfortunate blue-bottles. It did not offer to assist him.

Tom Kitten wriggled and squirmed until he was quite exhausted.

Presently the rats came back and set to work to make him into a dumpling. First they smeared him with butter, and then they rolled him in the dough.

"Will not the string be very indigestible, Anna Maria?" inquired Samuel Whiskers.

Anna Maria said she thought that it was of no consequence; but she wished that Tom Kitten would hold his head still, as it disarranged the pastry. She laid hold of his ears.

Tom Kitten bit and spat, and mewed and wriggled; and the rolling-pin went roly-poly, roly; roly, poly, roly. The rats each held an end.

"His tail is sticking out! You did not fetch enough dough, Anna Maria."

"I fetched as much as I could carry," replied Anna Maria.

"I do not think"—said Samuel Whiskers, pausing to take look at Tom Kitten—"I do not think it will be a good pudding. It smells sooty."

Anna Maria was about to argue the point, when all at once there began to be other sounds up above—the rasping noise of a saw; and the noise of a little dog, scratching and yelping!

The rats dropped the rolling-pin, and listened attentively.

"We are discovered and interrupted, Anna Maria; let us collect our property—and other people's,—and depart at once."

"I fear that we shall be obliged to leave this pudding."

"But I am persuaded that the knots would have proved indigestible, whatever you may urge to the contrary."

"Come away at once and help me to tie up some mutton bones in a counterpane," said Anna Maria. "I have got half a smoked ham hidden in the chimney."

So it happened that by the time John Joiner had got the plank up—there was nobody under the floor except the rolling-pin and Tom Kitten in a very dirty dumpling!

But there was a strong smell of rats; and John Joiner spent the rest of the morning sniffing and whining, and wagging his tail, and going round and round with his head in the hole like a gimlet.

Then he nailed the plank down again and put his tools in his bag, and came downstairs.

The cat family had quite recovered. They invited him to stay to dinner.

The dumpling had been peeled off Tom Kitten, and made separately into a bag pudding, with currants in it to hide the smuts.

They had been obliged to put Tom Kitten into a hot bath to get the butter off.

John Joiner smelt the pudding; but he regretted that he had not time to stay to dinner, because he had just finished making a wheelbarrow for Miss Potter, and she had ordered two hen-coops.

And when I was going to the post late in the afternoon—I looked up the lane from the corner, and I saw Mr. Samuel Whiskers and his wife on the run, with big bundles on a little wheelbarrow, which looked very like mine.

They were just turning in at the gate to the barn of Farmer Potatoes.

Samuel Whiskers was puffing and out of breath. Anna Maria was still arguing in shrill tones.

She seemed to know her way, and she seemed to have a quantity of luggage.

I am sure I never gave her leave to borrow my wheelbarrow!

They went into the barn, and hauled their parcels with a bit of string to the top of the hay mow.

After that, there were no more rats for a long time at Tabitha Twitchit's.

As for Farmer Potatoes, he has been driven nearly distracted. There are rats, and rats, and rats in his barn! They eat up the chicken food, and steal the oats and bran, and make holes in the meal bags.

And they are all descended from Mr. and Mrs. Samuel Whiskers—children and grandchildren and great great grandchildren. There is no end to them!

Moppet and Mittens have grown up into very good rat-catchers. They go out rat-catching in the village, and they find plenty of employment. They charge so much a dozen, and earn their living very comfortably. They hang up the rats' tails in a row on the barn door, to show how many they have caught—dozens and dozens of them.

But Tom Kitten has always been afraid of a rat; he never durst face anything that is bigger than—

A Mouse.

(Beatrix Potter)

Chapter 13

Miscellaneous Cat Facts

Things I Have Learned From My Cats

✳ Make the world your playground.

✳ Whenever you miss the sandbox, cover it up. Dragging a sock over it helps.

✳ If you can't get your way, lie across the keyboard till you do.

✳ When you are hungry, meow loudly so they feed you just to shut you up.

✳ Always find a good patch of sun to nap in.

✳ Nap often.

✳ When in trouble, just purr and look cute.

✳ Life is hard, and then you nap.

✳ Curiosity never killed anything except maybe a few hours.

✳ When in doubt, cop an attitude.

* Variety is the spice of life. One day, ignore people; the next day annoy them, and play with them when they're busy.

* Climb your way to the top, that's why the curtains are there.

* Make your mark in the world, or at least spray in each corner.

* Always give generously; a bird or rodent left on the bed tells them, "I care."

The "Cat's Pajamas"

"Hey Daddy-O, you're the cat's pajamas!" Meaning, "great" or "way cool," the saying originated in the 1920s when pajamas were still something of a novelty. The cat's pajamas kept good company along with "the bee's knees," "the duck's quack," "the tiger's stripes," and "the leopard's spots."

Catnip Facts

* It's estimated that only about 60 to 70 percent of cats respond to catnip.

* Baby kittens don't respond to catnip. They start to respond when they're a couple months old.

* It's not just households that are affected! Many big cats like leopards, lynx, and tigers also love catnip!

* You can keep catnip fresh and strong by storing it in the freezer in an airtight container.

Cats on Record

✳ **World's Smallest Cat:** Mr. Peebles, named after a ventriloquist's dummy on an episode of *Seinfeld*, is a fully grown cat weighing a meager three pounds.

✳ **World's Longest Cat:** Verismo's Leonetti Reserve Red (also known as Leo), a Maine Coon owned by a Chicago couple, measured 48 inches from nose to tail in March 2002.

✳ **World's Shortest Cat:** Tinker Toy, a male Himalayan-Persian cat from the United States, measured 2.7 inches high and 7.5 inches long.

✳ **Longest Cat Whiskers:** Another Maine Coon, this one named Mingo from Turku, Finland, set the record for the longest single cat whisker on July 30, 2004. Mingo's whisker measured 6.8 inches.

✳ **Feline with Most Toes:** Many cats are *polydactyl*, meaning they have extra toes, typically one or two on the front or back paws. However, an orange Tabby from Canada named Jake left all other polydactyl cats in the dust after his tootsies were counted—all 28 of them!

✳ **Longest Time Spent in a Tree:** A female feline named Mincho may win the award for weirdest cat. Mincho climbed a tree in Argentina and didn't come down until she died six years later. She did not, however, allow the height to interfere with her social life. Mincho had three litters of kittens while up in the tree.

* **Longest Cat Name:** English poet Robert Southey (1884–1843) named his cat The Most Noble the Archduke Rumpelstizchen, Marquis Macbum, Earle Tomemange, Baron Raticide, Waowler, and Skaratchi. However, when calling the cat, Southey settled for the shortened Rumpel.

* **Smartest Cat:** Cuty boy, a Persian living in Bur Dubai, is no ordinary cat. In fact, some believe he may be the smartest cat in the world. According to his owners, Cuty boy can count to 20 (he "counts" by touching his nose to his owner's face), understands eight different languages, and can identify colors. Independent experts have confirmed that Cuty boy is indeed one talented feline.

* **Oldest Cat to Give Birth:** In 1987, a feline named Kitty gave birth at the ripe old age of 30.

* **Oldest Cat:** Claims abound of cats having lived well beyond their prime years. However, the oldest documented cat is Creme Puff, who lives in Austin, Texas. She was born on August 3, 1967, and turned 38 in 2005.

* **Largest Collection of Cat Memorabilia:** Florence Groff of France began collecting cat memorabilia after buying her first cat, Ulysses, in 1979. Since then, Florence has amassed 11,717 cat-related items including more than 2,000 cat figurines, 86 decorative plates, 140 metallic boxes, 9 lamps, 36 stuffed toys, 41 painted eggs, and close to 3,000 postcards.

* **Most Mice Caught:** Towser, a tortoise-shell domestic cat kept as a pet in a Scottish distillery, owns the record for best mouser. Between April 21, 1963, and March 20, 1987, Towser caught an astounding 28,899 mice! The distillery erected a statue on the grounds to honor Towser and his devotion to duty.

Top Ten Ways Humans Resemble Cats

1. We're convinced the world revolves around us.

2. We'll never turn down a back massage.

3. We sometimes hide when people come to the door.

4. We like to stare at ourselves in the mirror.

5. We can nap anytime, anywhere, regardless of appropriateness or noise levels.

6. All our toys bore us after the first five minutes.

7. We believe in the value of snuggling.

8. We're not so sure about the intelligence level of dogs.

9. Sometimes we run around for no apparent reason.

10. We'd rather torture people by making them guess what we want versus just telling them outright.

What's in a Phrase?

* **In the catbird seat:** a high, commanding position; a position of power.

* **Cat burglar:** a stealthy intruder able to enter premises undetected.

* **Catcall:** shout, whistle, hiss, boo.

* **Catty:** malicious, spiteful, mean, vicious, back-biting.

* **Fat cat:** an important person; a wealthy person.

* **"Has the cat got your tongue?"** Children were asked this during the mid-nineteenth century by parents trying to figure out if their child had been into mischief.

Western Zodiac: Leo

Does your birthday fall between July 23 and August 22?
Congratulations—you're a Leo!

❋   ❋   ❋   ❋

Lᴉᴋᴇ ᴛʜᴇ ᴄᴀᴛs we love, Leos are ruled by the sun. People born under this sign exude warmth and caring. Known for being generous and warmhearted, Leos strive to be individuals in their own right. Their natural magnetism and gravity draw them to positions of leadership, though at times they can be bossy, dogmatic, and quick to judge. Overall, an expansive and creative spirit guides those fortunate enough to be born under this sign.

Famous Leos:

LEO
ZODIAC SIGN

❋ Andy Warhol

❋ Amelia Earhart

❋ Mick Jagger

❋ Dorothy Hamill

❋ Lucille Ball

❋ Napoleon Bonaparte

❋ Magic Johnson

❋ Robert Redford

❋ Henry Ford

❋ Jacqueline Kennedy Onassis

❋ Robert De Niro

❋ Dustin Hoffman

Chinese Zodiac: Year of the Tiger

You're a tiger if you were born in any of the following years: 1938, 1950, 1962, 1974, 1986, 1998, 2010.

* * * *

PEOPLE BORN IN the Year of the Tiger are courageous and adventurous. They easily earn the respect of others but are prone to conflict with those in authority. Playful and powerful, they like to take risks and seek new adventures. Although sometimes short-tempered, people born under this sign are also known to be sensitive, generous, and contemplative. Tigers are compatible with horses, dragons, and dogs

Famous people born in the Year of the Tiger:

* Marilyn Monroe

* Natalie Wood

* Hilary Swank

* Jay Leno

* Stevie Wonder

* Leonardo DiCaprio

* Mel Brooks

* Tom Cruise

* Usain Bolt

* Penelope Cruz

* Mahershala Ali

* Harper Lee

* Kofi Annan

Fortunate Feline

If you've ever dined in a Chinese or Japanese restaurant, chances are good that you've seen a Maneki-neko, *a cat figurine, usually made of ceramic or plastic, depicted with a raised paw. But what are these feline figurines, and what do they mean?*

✳ ✳ ✳ ✳

W E'VE ALL SEEN them at least once or twice in our lives: a cat figurine with a raised paw, sometimes even mechanized so it moves back and forth in a hypnotic gesture. These are *Maneki-neko*—Japanese for "beckoning cat—and while the term may not sound familiar, no doubt the ubiquitous cat figurine is immediately recognizable. They're found in shops, restaurants, hotels, nightclubs, and other businesses, often at the entrance or lurking near the cash register, and are believed to bring good luck to whoever owns them.

While many Westerners, including Americans, may misinterpret the raised paw of the *Maneki-neko* as a waving gesture, it actually mimics the gesture used in Japan to beckon. But the *Maneki-neko* doesn't just randomly beckon—it is beckoning good luck, inviting it to visit its owner. The "luck" bestowed by the figurine is said to change depending on which paw the cat figure is raising. A raised left paw is said to bring in more customers; a raised right paw results in more wealth. While many believe that a *Maneki-neko* with a raised left paw is best for business while a figurine with a raised right paw is best for home, the cat can occasionally also be found with both paws raised, offering the best of both lucky worlds.

Maneki-neko are sometimes depicted holding different objects, including coins, fish, and hammers, all of which represent wealth or good fortune. The figurines are also found in different colors, which all have different meanings. A red *Maneki-neko* signifies good luck in love and relationships, while a green one is said to bring good health. Black wards off evil spirits, white symbolizes happiness, and gold, of course, represents wealth.

Legendary Lifesaver

The origins of the "fortune cat," as it is sometimes called, are not entirely clear, with some believing it began in Tokyo and others claiming Kyoto as its birthplace. But most historians believe that *Maneki-neko* first appeared sometime during the Edo period in Japan, a time that spanned between 1603 and 1868. The earliest records of the figurine date back to 1852, and by the turn of the century, advertisements for *Maneki-neko* began showing up in newspapers.

While the history is murky, there are several legends surrounding the first *Maneki-neko*. The most popular concerns the Gotoku-ji temple in Tokyo, where, the legend tells, a poor monk lived with a stray cat in the year 1620. The temple was in disarray and the monk had little money for food, but whatever he was able to scrounge up, he shared with his feline friend. One day, a wealthy samurai lord was passing by the meager temple when a rainstorm caught him unawares. He took shelter under a nearby tree, but as he waited there, he noticed the cat in the temple, who appeared to be making a beckoning motion. Intrigued, the samurai followed the cat into the temple, and as he did so, the tree he had been standing under was struck by lightning. Grateful for the shelter of the temple and to the cat for saving his life, the samurai paid to restore the temple and became its lifelong benefactor. When the cat died, a statue was created in its honor, its beckoning paw a reminder of the life it once saved.

Regardless of how *Maneki-neko* began, the figurines have become popular not only in Japan, but also in China and Vietnam, as well as in Chinatown districts in the United States. Perhaps the next time you see a *Maneki-neko*, you can follow its beckoning paw to good fortune.

Feline Forecasters

Over the ages, cats have been used as seers to predict the weather, good fortune, and tragedy. The Egyptian word for cat is mau, *meaning to see, or seer. Cats' eyes, which glow in the moonlight, were thought to hold second sight.*

The Irish believed if kitty lay with her paws stretched out in front of her, a storm was on the way. Sailors believed a cat carried "a gale in its tail" that could be released at will. A cat on a ship playing with her tail or even a dangling rope was believed to be stirring up winds.

According to folklore, calico cats have the gift of second sight. Burmese cats were housed as oracles in Burmese temples. Tricolor cats were believed to protect the house where they lived from being destroyed by fire.

From Friend to Foe: The Persecuted Cat

The early Middle Ages brought an end to the cat's truce with Christianity. Threatened by symbols of pagan religions, the church denounced cats as profane. By the thirteenth century, cats were associated with devil worship, sorcery, and every evil imaginable—they became scapegoats at every turn. Satan was said to roam the earth in the guise of a black cat. Witches, it was reported, rode their cats to meet with the devil. Although some people superstitiously kept and protected black cats, believing this courtesy to Satan's favored animal would keep him off their back and help them prosper, thousands of cats were tortured and killed in the name of religion.

Nature, perhaps, evened the score by sending the Black Plague through Europe. Carried by fleas on rats, the disease ran rampant; the elimination of cats had enabled rats to populate the streets unchecked. More than one quarter of Europe's population fell to the plague before it was over. However, the epidemic was the beginning of the end of the cat's suffering, as people recognized cats were needed to control the rat population. By the end of the seventeenth century, cats were restored to their rightful place as popular pets in the home.

Vampire Cats

Today, when we think of vampires, our minds turn immediately to bats. However, it wasn't until Bram Stoker's Dracula, published in 1897, that there was any association between vampires and bats. According to tradition in sixteenth- and seventeenth-century Europe, vampires were either wolves or cats.

Tales of cats as vampires date back to Adam. The ancient belief that cats steal breath from babies arose from Hebrew mythology. According to legend, Adam's first wife, Lilith, fled Eden and became a vampire who could assume the form of a huge black cat called El Broosha. Human newborns were supposedly El Broosha's favorite prey.

A Bridge Between Worlds

Cats were thought to serve as a bridge between this world and the next. When members of the royal house of Siam were buried, a favorite cat was entombed alive with them. The roof of the tomb contained small holes, and if the cat managed to escape, the priests believed the human soul had passed into the cat's body. These venerated cats were then cared for in the temple. When the cats finally died, they conducted the human soul into paradise.

When King Prajadhipok of Siam (now Thailand) was crowned in 1925, a cat took its rightful place in the coronation procession to represent the prior ruler, King Rama VI.

Ten Ways to Worship Your Cat

❋ Ring the scared jingle bell every morning.

❋ Scatter kibble offerings throughout the home.

❋ Announce to the dog that it has come to your attention that canines are an inferior species.

❋ Relinquish control of your bed.

❋ Remove warm towels from the dryer. Leave on the bed. Walk away.

❋ Offer the off-limits guest chair as a scratching post.

❋ Catnip always says, "I love you."

❋ Release live mice in the house.

❋ A 20-minute back scratch (ears included) never hurts.

❋ Bow and declare your eternal loyalty and servitude (as if this hasn't already occurred).

Cat's Paw

❋ If someone calls you a "cat's paw," beware! "Cat's paw" refers to a person easily duped. The phrase originates with a not-so-flattering feline story. An ancient fable tells of a monkey who longed for chestnuts roasting in a nearby open fire. The devious monkey convinced a not-so-smart cat to reach in and grab the chestnuts for him. The monkey got his food, the cat nursed a hotfoot, and a phrase that's the equivalent of calling someone a "chump" was born.

* We might not be ready to send cats into space (who would clean the litter box?) but that hasn't stopped them from leaving their mark there. The Cat's Paw Nebula, approximately 5,500 light years away, is shaped like a kitty's paw and glows red due to an abundance of hydrogen atoms. This nebula has birthed stars almost ten times as big as Earth's sun. Catnap at the Nebula, anyone?

Black Cat Crossing

* People in Britain and Japan believe a black cat crossing their path is a harbinger of good fortune.

* Scottish folks think a black kitten on the porch indicates happiness to come.

* Even better, according to Latvian farmers, is to find a black cat in your silo. This means Rungis, the god of harvests, has smiled upon you.

* Germans have to pay attention to direction to know whether they've been blessed or cursed. A black cat crossing their path from left to right is cause for celebration. Right to left, they might want to go in search of a four-leaf clover.

* Worse than a black cat crossing your path is you crossing its path. It is said that luck of the worst sort is sure to follow.

* *Crossing* the path of a black cat may be bad, but petting is always a good thing. Stroking a black cat is said to bring anyone health and prosperity.

* The Chinese believe black cats foretell times of famine and poverty.

* According to Italians, if a black cat curls up on the bed of a sick person, death will soon follow.

* Don't be anxious to rid your house of black felines. Chasing away a black cat is thought to seal the deal on bringing bad luck your way.

The First Cat Show

The First Cat Show in America took place on March 6, 1881, at a museum on Broadway in New York City. However, this was merely a follow-up to the first modern cat show held at the Crystal Palace in south London in 1871. There, cat lover, writer, and artist Harrison Weir not only staged a successful show at London's leading public venue, attracting thousands, he also went on to write the definitive work Our Cats, which for a time would become the bible for cat show organizers.

Weir was named President of the first National Cat Club, founded in London in 1887, but resigned in disgust over members being more interested in collecting ribbons than in promoting the welfare of the feline.

How Can It Rain Cats and Dogs?

It can't. Many of us are familiar with strange-but-true stories that describe fish, frogs, or bugs raining from the sky. Indeed, waterspouts and odd, windy weather patterns can suck up small animals, carry them a few miles, and drop them from the sky. But nowhere on record are confirmed reports of it raining felines and canines.

✳ ✳ ✳ ✳

IT'S A FIGURE of speech, and its origins are unknown. However, that hasn't prevented etymologists from speculating. One unlikely theory claims that in days of yore, dogs and cats that were sleeping in the straw of thatched roofs would sometimes slip off the roof and fall to the ground during a rainstorm.

Almost as unlikely is the belief that the phrase was cobbled together from superstitions and mythology. Some cultures have associated cats with rain, and the Norse god Odin often was portrayed as being surrounded by dogs and wolves, which were associated with wind. (Anybody who's had an aging dog around the house can vouch for it being an occasional source of ill wind, but that's hardly the stuff of legend.) The components seem right with this one, but it's hard to imagine someone stitching everything together to coin a catchy phrase.

A couple of simpler theories seem more plausible. Some folks think that "cats and dogs" stems from the Greek word *catadupe* or the archaic French *catadoupe*, both meaning "waterfall." Others point to the Latin *cata doxas* ("contrary to experience").

The most believable explanation, however, is the least pleasant. The earliest uses of the term occur in English literature of the seventeenth and eighteenth centuries. Around that time in London, dead animals, including cats and dogs, were thrown out with the trash. Rains would sweep up the carcasses and wash them through the streets. Jonathan Swift used the phrase "rain cats and dogs" in his book *A Complete Collection of Polite and Ingenious Conversation* in 1738. Twenty-eight years earlier, Swift had published a poem, "A Description of a City Shower," that included the lines: "Drown'd Puppies, stinking Sprats, all drench'd in Mud/Dead Cats and Turnip-Tops come tumbling down the Flood."

Hardly a love sonnet, but perhaps it answers our question.

No Cats Were Harmed

What's the story with so-called "catgut," the material used in tennis and musical-instrument strings? It is really made of guts, but the guts don't come from cats.

✳   ✳   ✳   ✳

Intestinal Fortitude

THE INTESTINES OF cattle and other livestock are cleaned, stripped of fat, and prepared with chemicals before they can be made into catgut string. Historically, preparation of string from animal tissue dates back thousands of years in recorded history and likely much longer ago in reality. Intestines are uniquely suited because of their combination of strength and elasticity, even in comparison to other pretty robust naturally occurring strings like horse hair or silk. This makes sense intuitively because of the role our intestines play in our bodies, but let's not think too hard about that. One downside is that the prepared gut fibers are still very absorbent— enough so that even atmospheric humidity can warp them out of shape.

In Stitches

Historical humans realized surprisingly early that gut string was a good way to sew up wounds, and in this case the absorbency is a bonus. These humans weren't aware of issues like infection, so their ingenuity with gut string was a matter of simple craftsmanship: you should sew with the strongest material you can find, whether for clothing or shelter or for a wound. Thousands of years later, scientists experimented and realized that gut string could dissolve in the human body. With the eventual rise of germ theory, doctors were able to create and use sterilized dissolving sutures that would be recognizable to the ancient Egyptians who first documented their sewing of wounds. In fact, most dissolvable stitches are still made with prepared animal fibers or with synthetics that were designed to mimic animal fibers in the body.

High Strung

For musical instruments, gut strings also date back thousands of years. In both Latin and Greek, the terms for strings and bowstrings (and our modern words chord and cord) were from the original Greek term meaning guts. Musicians found that gut strings made the best sound, but the strings warped, frayed, and broke quite quickly because of the effects of moisture in the air and from musicians' touch. Modern musicians can use strings with a core of gut that's surrounded by a snug winding of very fine metal. In a fine example of art imitating nature, this structure mimics the way our flexible gut fibers are arranged in our intestines, with both lengthwise fibers and circular bands.

The Gut Racket

Gut strings are still considered the gold standard by many high-level tennis players and manufacturers. In tennis, the absorbency of gut strings is counteracted with topical wax that seals the strings. Choosing and making gut strings for tennis rackets is still an artisan craft, and some cattle—most if not all tennis gut strings come from cattle—apparently produce finer quality gut strings than others, creating a Wagyu-beef-like hierarchy among cattle ranchers.

Digesting the Information

Humans have shown remarkable ingenuity since we first diverged from our most recent ancestor, but even by human standards, it's unusual to have a found material that works as both a durable tool and a nourishing food—depending on how you prepare it. Whether you're preparing for your Wimbledon debut or a period-correct Baroque chamber orchestra, consider the millennia-old tradition of the gut string.

The Amount of Space Needed to Swing a Cat

If you were to put this well-worn phrase to the test—theoretically, of course—exactly how much room would be required?

✳ ✳ ✳ ✳

The Murky Origins of an Odd Phrase

QUARTERS ARE TIGHT here in the war room. Towers of folders that are overflowing with archival research teeter dangerously over our postage-stamp-size desks, where we slave away amongst a heady blend of ink, paper, and each other. It's not pleasant. Anyway, in our cramped office, the following phrase is frequently muttered with dismay: "There's not enough room in here to swing a cat." And that got us wondering: Just how much room might one need to accomplish the task?

To answer this question, we need to trace the phrase's origin. There are multiple theories, and, no, they have nothing to do with the Jazz Age and all of its swingin' cats. Furthermore, according to the first explanation, the phrase might not even have anything to do with felines.

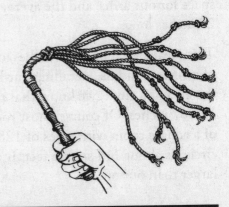

It seems that back in seventeenth and eighteenth centuries, any sailor in the British navy who misbehaved was rewarded with a flogging with a whip that featured nine knotted lashes. This menacing little device was known as a "cat o' nine tails." Because a great deal of open space was required for the whip to be used effectively—and because floggings were frequently done in view of other sailors as a lesson—the old cat o' nine tails was only broken out in a spacious area, such as the poop deck.

A second camp argues that the phrase originated with a medieval archery game in which a cat was put into a leather bag and swung from the nearest tree or rafter and used for target practice. This theory has some weaknesses, not the least of which is determining a conceivable reason for archers to practice so cruelly. There is also little historical evidence to back up this claim, though in Shakespeare's *Much Ado About Nothing*, the cantankerous Benedick says, "If I do, hang me in a bottle like a cat and shoot at me; and he that hits me, let him be clapped on the shoulder, and called Adam."

The Measurements

Neither of these theories seems to indicate that there was ever a time when people were swinging actual felines by the tail. But what if you wanted to? It seems clear that swinging a cat requires space, but just how much? Fortunately, we remember our geometry. Let's say that the average cat is about 24 inches long and that its tail is about 12 inches long. We also need space for our arms, and the average human male's arms are 28 inches long.

This means we'll need 64 inches, or more than five feet of swinging radius. Recalling our handy little formula for the area of a circle, we know that the total area required is 12,867 inches. Of course, most rooms aren't circular. The area of a square room with sides of 128 inches (the diameter of our circle) is about 114 square feet. In other words, a space far, far larger than our office.

When Pets Marry

Does your pet have a best friend in the neighborhood or at doggy day care? Does he always sniff around the same pooch at the dog park? Well, maybe it's time to think about having a pet wedding.

✳ ✳ ✳ ✳

Do You, Rover . . .

DON'T LAUGH. WELL, okay laugh. But pet weddings are more common than you might think. And for those companies who have already jumped on the gravy train, pet weddings are a big business.

If the idea of a pet wedding makes you think of two little girls dressing up their rabbits and singing, "Here Comes the Bride," you don't know the half of it. Sixty-three percent of Americans own pets—and a surprising number are buying into the pet wedding industry.

The Maltese Millennium Marriage

Shelley Johnson and Bunny Heller—and their husbands—actually became friends because of their dogs. The foursome met when each showed up at a Florida Safari Club rally driving the same motor home—and carrying nearly identical Maltese dogs in their arms. Shayna and Dusty hit it off right away. And so did the humans. Two years later, the moms decided it was time to make it official.

It all began with a diamond collar for Shayna at Labor Day. And then the moms had to hurry to get a wedding ready by

New Year's Eve. They sent out 60 invitations, and 25 people showed up for the festivities—one guest even came all the way from Texas.

There were bridal clothes, flowers, vows, a maid of honor, and even a blessing by an ordained minister. The canine couple exchanged gold dog tags shaped like hearts. The Maltese Millennium Marriage, as the moms call it, was a big hit. Although the dogs have a long-distance relationship, they were reunited the following summer for a honeymoon when their parents took the motor homes to Maine.

For As Long As You Both Shall Bark (or Purr)

Not too many doggy weddings can top that, but they're still taking place on a smaller scale. Two young girls in California talked their parents into having a wedding for the family's two Jack Russell Terriers. The girls felt sure that if the dogs were married, then puppies would soon be on the way. The girls dressed the dogs up and had a brief ceremony attended by the family. The girls thought it was fun; their mom thought it was a good teaching moment. And the dogs? Well, they tolerated it.

One not-so-tolerant animal was Comfrey the cat. When the Baltimore Humane Society planned a feline wedding to celebrate Valentine's Day, they shouldn't have had the bridal shower on the same day. After a whirlwind shower in the morning, Comfrey had had enough. She hid under a cabinet and refused to come out. So the staff pulled a switcheroo, substituting another black cat as the bride. Winslow, the groom, had never met Luna, but he didn't seem to mind. The pair was united in front of a crowd of well-wishers. They were given new collars and a slice of special wedding cake.

The Humane Society in Naples, Florida, celebrated Valentine's Day with pet nuptials as well, but this one was open to the public. A Pet Minister was on hand from 4:00 P.M. until 7:00 P.M. to unite pet couples in marriage. Dogs and cats, dressed in their bridal finery, arrived with their owners in tow.

Two shelter animals got the ball rolling with the first ceremony, and then the other eager brides and grooms were married a pair at a time for a $35 donation. In addition to the minister, there was music, photographs, and wedding cake.

Pet Wedding Planning

So if you're thinking of a wedding for your pet, there are numerous Web sites that offer bridal attire for prospective brides and grooms, big and small. You can even register the little critters at Pet Smart. My Best Friend Pet Bakery in San Diego will ship a pet-friendly cake anywhere in the country, with prices starting at $99. And if you're having an open bar, don't forget to order enough Bowser Beer and Pinot Leasheo for all the thirsty guests!

Newton's Genius

Although best known for his principles of gravity, Sir Issac Newton (1642–1727) is also credited with inventing the first cat flap. As the story goes, Newton was in his attic conducting light experiments but was disturbed when his cat nudged open the door and let in the light. To accommodate his beloved cat's comings and goings, Newton cut a flap in the door. His cat was then able to enter and exit the room without disturbing his work.

The story doesn't end there. It seems even the most brilliant of minds can be blindsided by love for their cats. Once his cat had kittens, Newton cut a second, smaller hole alongside the first for the kittens to use. Apparently it didn't occur to Newton that all the cats could use the same hole.

Chapter 14

More Cat Stories

The Lady, or the Tiger?

Did the tiger come out of the door, or did the lady?

✳ ✳ ✳ ✳

IN THE VERY olden time there lived a semi-barbaric king, whose ideas, though somewhat polished and sharpened by the progressiveness of distant Latin neighbors, were still large, florid, and untrammeled, as became the half of him which was barbaric. He was a man of exuberant fancy, and, withal, of an authority so irresistible that, at his will, he turned his varied fancies into facts. He was greatly given to self-communing, and, when he and himself agreed upon anything, the thing was done. When every member of his domestic and political systems moved smoothly in its appointed course, his nature was bland and genial; but, whenever there was a little hitch, and some of his orbs got out of their orbits, he was blander and more genial still, for nothing pleased him so much as to make the crooked straight and crush down uneven places.

Among the borrowed notions by which his barbarism had become semified was that of the public arena, in which, by exhibitions of manly and beastly valor, the minds of his subjects were refined and cultured.

But even here the exuberant and barbaric fancy asserted itself. The arena of the king was built, not to give the people an opportunity of hearing the rhapsodies of dying gladiators, nor to enable them to view the inevitable conclusion of a conflict between religious opinions and hungry jaws, but for purposes far better adapted to widen and develop the mental energies of the people. This vast amphitheater, with its encircling galleries, its mysterious vaults, and its unseen passages, was an agent of poetic justice, in which crime was punished, or virtue rewarded, by the decrees of an impartial and incorruptible chance.

When a subject was accused of a crime of sufficient importance to interest the king, public notice was given that on an appointed day the fate of the accused person would be decided in the king's arena, a structure which well deserved its name, for, although its form and plan were borrowed from afar, its purpose emanated solely from the brain of this man, who, every barleycorn a king, knew no tradition to which he owed more allegiance than pleased his fancy, and who ingrafted on every adopted form of human thought and action the rich growth of his barbaric idealism.

When all the people had assembled in the galleries, and the king, surrounded by his court, sat high up on his throne of royal state on one side of the arena, he gave a signal, a door beneath him opened, and the accused subject stepped out into the amphitheater. Directly opposite him, on the other side of the inclosed space, were two doors, exactly alike and side by side. It was the duty and the privilege of the person on trial to walk directly to these doors and open one of them. He could open either door he pleased; he was subject to no guidance or influence but that of the aforementioned impartial and incorruptible chance. If he opened the one, there came out of it a hungry tiger, the fiercest and most cruel that could be procured, which immediately sprang upon him and tore him to pieces as a punishment for his guilt. The moment that the case of the criminal was thus decided, doleful iron bells were clanged, great wails went up from the hired mourners posted on the outer rim of the arena, and the vast audience, with bowed heads and downcast hearts, wended slowly their homeward way, mourning greatly that one so young and fair, or so old and respected, should have merited so dire a fate.

But, if the accused person opened the other door, there came forth from it a lady, the most suitable to his years and station that his majesty could select among his fair subjects, and to this lady he was immediately married, as a reward of his innocence. It mattered not that he might already possess a wife and family, or that his affections might be engaged upon an object of his own selection; the king allowed no such subordinate arrangements to interfere with his great scheme of retribution and reward. The exercises, as in the other instance, took place immediately, and in the arena. Another door opened beneath the king, and a priest, followed by a band of choristers, and dancing maidens blowing joyous airs on golden horns and treading an epithalamic measure, advanced to where the pair stood, side by side, and the wedding was promptly and cheerily solemnized. Then the gay brass bells rang forth their merry peals, the people shouted glad hurrahs, and the innocent man, preceded by children strewing flowers on his path, led his bride to his home.

This was the king's semi-barbaric method of administering justice. Its perfect fairness is obvious. The criminal could not know out of which door would come the lady; he opened either he pleased, without having the slightest idea whether, in the next instant, he was to be devoured or married. On some occasions the tiger came out of one door, and on some out of the other. The decisions of this tribunal were not only fair, they were positively determinate: the accused person was instantly punished if he found himself guilty, and, if innocent, he was rewarded on the spot, whether he liked it or not. There was no escape from the judgments of the king's arena.

The institution was a very popular one. When the people gathered together on one of the great trial days, they never knew whether they were to witness a bloody slaughter or a hilarious wedding. This element of uncertainty lent an interest to the occasion which it could not otherwise have attained. Thus, the masses were entertained and pleased, and the thinking part of the community could bring no charge of unfairness against this plan, for did not the accused person have the whole matter in his own hands?

This semi-barbaric king had a daughter as blooming as his most florid fancies, and with a soul as fervent and imperious as his own. As is usual in such cases, she was the apple of his eye, and was loved by him above all humanity. Among his courtiers was a young man of that fineness of blood and lowness of station common to the conventional heroes of romance who love royal maidens. This royal maiden was well satisfied with her lover, for he was handsome and brave to a degree unsurpassed in all this kingdom, and she loved him with an ardor that had enough of barbarism in it to make it exceedingly warm and strong. This love affair moved on happily for many months, until one day the king happened to discover its existence. He did not hesitate nor waver in regard to his duty in the premises. The youth was immediately cast into prison, and a day was appointed for his trial in the king's arena. This, of course, was an especially important occasion, and his majesty, as well as all the people, was greatly interested in the workings and development of this trial. Never before had such a case occurred; never before had a subject dared to love the daughter of the king. In after years such things became commonplace enough, but then they were in no slight degree novel and startling.

The tiger-cages of the kingdom were searched for the most savage and relentless beasts, from which the fiercest monster might be selected for the arena; and the ranks of maiden youth and beauty throughout the land were carefully surveyed by competent judges in order that the young man might have a fitting bride in case fate did not determine for him a different destiny. Of course, everybody knew that the deed with which the accused was charged had been done. He had loved the princess, and neither he, she, nor any one else, thought of denying the fact; but the king would not think of allowing any fact of this kind to interfere with the workings of the tribunal, in which he took such great delight and satisfaction. No matter how the affair turned out, the youth would be disposed of, and the king would take an aesthetic pleasure in watching the course of events, which would determine whether or not the young man had done wrong in allowing himself to love the princess.

The appointed day arrived. From far and near the people gathered, and thronged the great galleries of the arena, and crowds, unable to gain admittance, massed themselves against its outside walls. The king and his court were in their places, opposite the twin doors, those fateful portals, so terrible in their similarity.

All was ready. The signal was given. A door beneath the royal party opened, and the lover of the princess walked into the arena. Tall, beautiful, fair, his appearance was greeted with a low hum of admiration and anxiety. Half the audience had not known so grand a youth had lived among them. No wonder the princess loved him! What a terrible thing for him to be there!

As the youth advanced into the arena he turned, as the custom was, to bow to the king, but he did not think at all of that royal personage. His eyes were fixed upon the princess, who sat to the right of her father. Had it not been for the moiety of barbarism in her nature it is probable that lady would not have been there, but her intense and fervid soul would not allow her to be absent on an occasion in which she was so terribly interested. From the moment that the decree had gone forth that her lover should decide his fate in the king's arena, she had thought of nothing, night or day, but this great event and the various subjects connected with it. Possessed of more power, influence, and force of character than any one who had ever before been interested in such a case, she had done what no other person had done—she had possessed herself of the secret of the doors. She knew in which of the two rooms, that lay behind those doors, stood the cage of the tiger, with its open front, and in which waited the lady. Through these thick doors, heavily curtained with skins on the inside, it was impossible that any noise or suggestion should come from within to the person who should approach to raise the latch of one of them. But gold, and the power of a woman's will, had brought the secret to the princess.

And not only did she know in which room stood the lady ready to emerge, all blushing and radiant, should her door be opened, but she knew who the lady was. It was one of the fairest and loveliest of the damsels of the court who had been selected as the reward of the accused youth, should he be proved innocent of the crime of aspiring to one so far above him; and the princess hated her. Often had she seen, or imagined that she had seen, this fair creature throwing glances of admiration upon the person of her lover, and sometimes she thought these glances were perceived, and even returned. Now and then she had seen them talking together; it was but for a moment or two, but much can be said in a brief space; it may have been on most unimportant topics, but how could she know that? The girl was lovely, but she had dared to raise her eyes to the loved one of the princess; and, with all the intensity of the savage blood transmitted to her through long lines of wholly barbaric ancestors, she hated the woman who blushed and trembled behind that silent door.

When her lover turned and looked at her, and his eye met hers as she sat there, paler and whiter than any one in the vast ocean of anxious faces about her, he saw, by that power of quick perception which is given to those whose souls are one, that she knew behind which door crouched the tiger, and behind which stood the lady. He had expected her to know it. He understood her nature, and his soul was assured that she would never rest until she had made plain to herself this thing, hidden to all other lookers-on, even to the king. The only hope for the youth in which there was any element of certainty was based upon the success of the princess in discovering this mystery; and the moment he looked upon her, he saw she had succeeded, as in his soul he knew she would succeed.

Then it was that his quick and anxious glance asked the question: "Which?" It was as plain to her as if he shouted it from where he stood. There was not an instant to be lost. The question was asked in a flash; it must be answered in another.

Her right arm lay on the cushioned parapet before her. She raised her hand, and made a slight, quick movement toward the right. No one but her lover saw her. Every eye but his was fixed on the man in the arena.

He turned, and with a firm and rapid step he walked across the empty space. Every heart stopped beating, every breath was held, every eye was fixed immovably upon that man. Without the slightest hesitation, he went to the door on the right, and opened it.

Now, the point of the story is this: Did the tiger come out of that door, or did the lady?

The more we reflect upon this question, the harder it is to answer. It involves a study of the human heart which leads us through devious mazes of passion, out of which it is difficult to find our way. Think of it, fair reader, not as if the decision of the question depended upon yourself, but upon that hot-blooded, semi-barbaric princess, her soul at a white heat beneath the combined fires of despair and jealousy. She had lost him, but who should have him?

How often, in her waking hours and in her dreams, had she started in wild horror, and covered her face with her hands as she thought of her lover opening the door on the other side of which waited the cruel fangs of the tiger!

But how much oftener had she seen him at the other door! How in her grievous reveries had she gnashed her teeth, and torn her hair, when she saw his start of rapturous delight as he opened the door of the lady! How her soul had burned in agony when she had seen him rush to meet that woman, with her flushing cheek and sparkling eye of triumph; when she had seen him lead her forth, his whole frame kindled with the joy of recovered life; when she had heard the glad shouts from the multitude, and the wild ringing of the happy bells; when she had seen the priest, with his joyous followers, advance to the couple, and make them man and wife before her very eyes; and when she had seen them walk away together upon their path of flowers, followed by the tremendous shouts of the hilarious multitude, in which her one despairing shriek was lost and drowned!

Would it not be better for him to die at once, and go to wait for her in the blessed regions of semi-barbaric futurity?

And yet, that awful tiger, those shrieks, that blood!

Her decision had been indicated in an instant, but it had been made after days and nights of anguished deliberation. She had known she would be asked, she had decided what she would answer, and, without the slightest hesitation, she had moved her hand to the right.

The question of her decision is one not to be lightly considered, and it is not for me to presume to set myself up as the one person able to answer it. And so I leave it with all of you: Which came out of the opened door—the lady, or the tiger?

(Frank R. Stockton)

The White Cat

Here's a tale of an extraordinary cat.

* * * *

ONCE UPON A time there was a king who had three sons,
who were all so clever and brave that he began to be afraid
that they would want to reign over the kingdom before he was
dead. Now the King, though he felt that he was growing old,
did not at all wish to give up the government of his kingdom
while he could still manage it very well, so he thought the best
way to live in peace would be to divert the minds of his sons by
promises which he could always get out of when the time came
for keeping them.

So he sent for them all, and, after speaking to them kindly,
he added:

"You will quite agree with me, my dear children, that my great
age makes it impossible for me to look after my affairs of state
as carefully as I once did. I begin to fear that this may affect the
welfare of my subjects, therefore I wish that one of you should
succeed to my crown; but in return for such a gift as this it
is only right that you should do something for me. Now, as I
think of retiring into the country, it seems to me that a pretty,
lively, faithful little dog would be very good company for me; so,
without any regard for your ages, I promise that the one who
brings me the most beautiful little dog shall succeed me
at once."

The three Princes were greatly surprised by their father's sudden fancy for a little dog, but as it gave the two younger ones a
chance they would not otherwise have had of being king, and as
the eldest was too polite to make any objection, they accepted
the commission with pleasure. They bade farewell to the King,
who gave them presents of silver and precious stones, and
appointed to meet them at the same hour, in the same place,

after a year had passed, to see the little dogs they had brought for him.

Then they went together to a castle which was about a league from the city, accompanied by all their particular friends, to whom they gave a grand banquet, and the three brothers promised to be friends always, to share whatever good fortune befell them, and not to be parted by any envy or jealousy; and so they set out, agreeing to meet at the same castle at the appointed time, to present themselves before the King together. Each one took a different road, and the two eldest met with many adventures; but it is about the youngest that you are going to hear. He was young, and gay, and handsome, and knew everything that a prince ought to know; and as for his courage, there was simply no end to it.

Hardly a day passed without his buying several dogs—big and little, greyhounds, mastiffs, spaniels, and lapdogs. As soon as he had bought a pretty one he was sure to see a still prettier, and then he had to get rid of all the others and buy that one, as, being alone, he found it impossible to take thirty or forty thousand dogs about with him. He journeyed from day to day, not knowing where he was going, until at last, just at nightfall, he reached a great, gloomy forest. He did not know his way, and, to make matters worse, it began to thunder, and the rain poured down. He took the first path he could find, and after walking for a long time he fancied he saw a faint light, and began to hope that he was coming to some cottage where he might find shelter for the night. At length, guided by the light, he reached the door of the most splendid castle he could have imagined. This door was of gold covered with carbuncles, and it was the pure red light which shone from them that had shown him the way through the forest. The walls were of the finest porcelain in all the most delicate colors, and the Prince saw that all the stories he had ever read were pictured upon them; but as he was terribly wet, and the rain still fell in torrents, he could not stay to look about any more, but came back to the golden door. There he saw a deer's foot hanging by a chain of diamonds, and he began to wonder who could live in this magnificent castle.

"They must feel very secure against robbers," he said to himself. "What is to hinder anyone from cutting off that chain and digging out those carbuncles, and making himself rich for life?"

He pulled the deer's foot, and immediately a silver bell sounded and the door flew open, but the Prince could see nothing but numbers of hands in the air, each holding a torch. He was so much surprised that he stood quite still, until he felt himself pushed forward by other hands, so that, though he was somewhat uneasy, he could not help going on. With his hand on his sword, to be prepared for whatever might happen, he entered a hall paved with lapis-lazuli, while two lovely voices sang:

"The hands you see floating above

Will swiftly your bidding obey;

If your heart dreads not conquering Love,

In this place you may fearlessly stay."

The Prince could not believe that any danger threatened him when he was welcomed in this way, so, guided by the mysterious hands, he went toward a door of coral, which opened of its own accord, and he found himself in a vast hall of mother-of-pearl, out of which opened a number of other rooms, glittering with thousands of lights, and full of such beautiful pictures and precious things that the Prince felt quite bewildered. After passing through sixty rooms the hands that conducted him stopped, and the Prince saw a most comfortable-looking arm-chair drawn up close to the chimney-corner; at the same moment the fire lighted itself, and the pretty, soft, clever hands took off the Prince's wet, muddy clothes, and presented him with fresh ones made of the richest stuffs, all embroidered with gold and emeralds. He could not help admiring everything he saw, and the deft way in which the hands waited on him, though they sometimes appeared so suddenly that they made him jump.

When he was quite ready—and I can assure you that he looked very different from the wet and weary Prince who had stood outside in the rain, and pulled the deer's foot—the hands led him to a splendid room, upon the walls of which were painted the histories of Puss in Boots and a number of other famous cats. The table was laid for supper with two golden plates, and golden spoons and forks, and the sideboard was covered with dishes and glasses of crystal set with precious stones. The Prince was wondering who the second place could be for, when suddenly in came about a dozen cats carrying guitars and rolls of music, who took their places at one end of the room, and under the direction of a cat who beat time with a roll of paper began to mew in every imaginable key, and to draw their claws across the strings of the guitars, making the strangest kind of music that could be heard. The Prince hastily stopped up his ears, but even then the sight of these comical musicians sent him into fits of laughter.

"What funny thing shall I see next?" he said to himself, and instantly the door opened, and in came a tiny figure covered by a long black veil. It was conducted by two cats wearing black mantles and carrying swords, and a large party of cats followed, who brought in cages full of rats and mice.

The Prince was so much astonished that he thought he must be dreaming, but the little figure came up to him and threw back its veil, and he saw that it was the loveliest little white cat it is possible to imagine. She looked young and sad, and in a sweet little voice that went straight to his heart she said to the Prince:

"King's son, you are welcome; the Queen of the Cats is glad to see you."

"Lady Cat," replied the Prince, "I thank you for receiving me so kindly, but surely you are no ordinary pussy-cat? Indeed, the way you speak and the magnificence of your castle prove it plainly."

"King's son," said the White Cat, "I beg you to spare me these compliments, for I am not used to them. But now," she added, "let supper be served, and let the musicians be silent, as the Prince does not understand what they are saying."

So the mysterious hands began to bring in the supper, and first they put on the table two dishes, one containing stewed pigeons and the other a fricassee of fat mice. The sight of the latter made the Prince feel as if he could not enjoy his supper at all; but the White Cat, seeing this, assured him that the dishes intended for him were prepared in a separate kitchen, and he might be quite certain that they contained neither rats nor mice; and the Prince felt so sure that she would not deceive him that he had no more hesitation in beginning. Presently he noticed that on the little paw that was next him the White Cat wore a bracelet containing a portrait, and he begged to be allowed to look at it. To his great surprise he found it represented an extremely handsome young man, who was so like himself that it might have been his own portrait! The White Cat sighed as he looked at it, and seemed sadder than ever, and the Prince dared not ask any questions for fear of displeasing her; so he began to talk about other things, and found that she was interested in all the subjects he cared for himself, and seemed to know quite well what was going on in the world. After supper they went into another room, which was fitted up as a theatre, and the cats acted and danced for their amusement, and then the White Cat said good-night to him, and the hands conducted him into a room he had not seen before, hung with tapestry worked with butterflies' wings of every color; there were mirrors that reached from the ceiling to the floor, and a little white bed with curtains of gauze tied up with ribbons. The Prince went to bed in silence, as he did not quite know how to begin a conversation with the hands that waited on him, and in the morning he was awakened by a noise and confusion outside of his window, and the hands came and quickly dressed him in hunting costume. When he looked out all the cats were assembled in the courtyard, some leading greyhounds, some blowing horns, for the White Cat was going out hunting. The hands led a wooden horse up to the Prince, and seemed to expect him to mount it, at which he was very indignant; but it was no use for him to object, for he speedily found himself upon its back, and it pranced gaily off with him.

The White Cat herself was riding a monkey, which climbed even up to the eagles' nests when she had a fancy for the young eaglets. Never was there a pleasanter hunting party, and when they returned to the castle the Prince and the White Cat supped together as before, but when they had finished she offered him a crystal goblet, which must have contained a magic draught, for, as soon as he had swallowed its contents, he forgot everything, even the little dog that he was seeking for the King, and only thought how happy he was to be with the White Cat! And so the days passed, in every kind of amusement, until the year was nearly gone. The Prince had forgotten all about meeting his brothers: he did not even know what country he belonged to; but the White Cat knew when he ought to go back, and one day she said to him:

"Do you know that you have only three days left to look for the little dog for your father, and your brothers have found lovely ones?"

Then the Prince suddenly recovered his memory, and cried:

"What can have made me forget such an important thing? My whole fortune depends upon it; and even if I could in such a short time find a dog pretty enough to gain me a kingdom, where should I find a horse who would carry me all that way in three days?" And he began to be very vexed. But the White Cat said to him: "King's son, do not trouble yourself; I am your friend, and will make everything easy for you. You can still stay here for a day, as the good wooden horse can take you to your country in twelve hours."

"I thank you, beautiful Cat," said the Prince; "but what good will it do me to get back if I have not a dog to take to my father?"

"See here," answered the White Cat, holding up an acorn; "there is a prettier one in this than in the Dogstar!"

"Oh! White Cat dear," said the Prince, "how unkind you are to laugh at me now!"

"Only listen," she said, holding the acorn to his ear.

And inside it he distinctly heard a tiny voice say: "Bow-wow!"

The Prince was delighted, for a dog that can be shut up in an acorn must be very small indeed. He wanted to take it out and look at it, but the White Cat said it would be better not to open the acorn till he was before the King, in case the tiny dog should be cold on the journey. He thanked her a thousand times, and said good-bye quite sadly when the time came for him to set out.

"The days have passed so quickly with you," he said, "I only wish I could take you with me now."

But the White Cat shook her head and sighed deeply in answer.

After all the Prince was the first to arrive at the castle where he had agreed to meet his brothers, but they came soon after, and stared in amazement when they saw the wooden horse in the courtyard jumping like a hunter.

The Prince met them joyfully, and they began to tell him all their adventures; but he managed to hide from them what he had been doing, and even led them to think that a turnspit dog which he had with him was the one he was bringing for the King. Fond as they all were of one another, the two eldest could not help being glad to think that their dogs certainly had a better chance. The next morning they started in the same chariot. The elder brothers carried in baskets two such tiny, fragile dogs that they hardly dared to touch them. As for the turnspit, he ran after the chariot, and got so covered with mud that one could hardly see what he was like at all. When they reached the palace everyone crowded round to welcome them as they went into the King's great hall; and when the two brothers presented their little dogs nobody could decide which was the prettier. They were already arranging between themselves to share the kingdom equally, when the youngest stepped forward, drawing from his pocket the acorn the White Cat had given him. He opened it quickly, and there upon a white cushion they saw a dog so small that it could easily have been put through a ring. The Prince laid it upon the ground, and it got up at once and began to dance. The King did not know what to say, for it was impossible that anything could be prettier than this little creature. Nevertheless, as he was in no hurry to part with his crown, he told his sons that, as they had been so successful the first time, he would ask them to go once again, and seek by land and sea for a piece of muslin so fine that it could be drawn through the eye of a needle. The brothers were not very willing to set out again, but the two eldest consented because it gave them another chance, and they started as before. The youngest again mounted the wooden horse, and rode back at full speed to his beloved White Cat. Every door of the castle stood wide open, and every window and turret was illuminated, so it looked more wonderful than before. The hands hastened to meet him, and led the wooden horse off to the stable, while he hurried in to find the White Cat. She was asleep in a little basket on a white satin cushion, but she very soon started up when she heard the Prince, and was overjoyed at seeing him once more.

"How could I hope that you would come back to me King's son?" she said. And then he stroked and petted her, and told her of his successful journey, and how he had come back to ask her help, as he believed that it was impossible to find what the King demanded. The White Cat looked serious, and said she must think what was to be done, but that, luckily, there were some cats in the castle who could spin very well, and if anybody could manage it they could, and she would set them the task herself.

And then the hands appeared carrying torches, and conducted the Prince and the White Cat to a long gallery which over-looked the river, from the windows of which they saw a magnificent display of fireworks of all sorts; after which they had supper, which the Prince liked even better than the fireworks, for it was very late, and he was hungry after his long ride. And so the days passed quickly as before; it was impossible to feel dull with the White Cat, and she had quite a talent for inventing new amusements—indeed, she was cleverer than a cat has any right to be. But when the Prince asked her how it was that she was so wise, she only said:

"King's son, do not ask me; guess what you please. I may not tell you anything."

The Prince was so happy that he did not trouble himself at all about the time, but presently the White Cat told him that the year was gone, and that he need not be at all anxious about the piece of muslin, as they had made it very well.

"This time," she added, "I can give you a suitable escort"; and on looking out into the courtyard the Prince saw a superb chariot of burnished gold, enameled in flame color with a thousand different devices. It was drawn by twelve snow-white horses, harnessed four abreast; their trappings were flame-colored velvet, embroidered with diamonds. A hundred chariots followed, each drawn by eight horses, and filled with officers in splendid uniforms, and a thousand guards surrounded the procession. "Go!" said the White Cat, "and when you appear before the King in such state he surely will not refuse you the crown which you deserve. Take this walnut, but do not open it until you are before him, then you will find in it the piece of stuff you asked me for."

"Lovely Blanchette," said the Prince, "how can I thank you properly for all your kindness to me? Only tell me that you wish it, and I will give up for ever all thought of being king, and will stay here with you always."

"King's son," she replied, "it shows the goodness of your heart that you should care so much for a little white cat, who is good for nothing but to catch mice; but you must not stay."

So the Prince kissed her little paw and set out. You can imagine how fast he traveled when I tell you that they reached the King's palace in just half the time it had taken the wooden horse to get there. This time the Prince was so late that he did not try to meet his brothers at their castle, so they thought he could not be coming, and were rather glad of it, and displayed their pieces of muslin to the King proudly, feeling sure of success. And indeed the stuff was very fine, and would go through the eye of a very large needle; but the King, who was only too glad to make a difficulty, sent for a particular needle, which was kept among the Crown jewels, and had such a small eye that everybody saw at once that it was impossible that the muslin should pass through it. The Princes were angry, and were beginning to complain that it was a trick, when suddenly the trumpets sounded and the youngest Prince came in. His father and brothers were quite astonished at his magnificence, and after he had greeted them he took the walnut from his pocket and opened it, fully expecting to find the piece of muslin, but instead there was only a hazel-nut. He cracked it, and there lay a cherry-stone. Everybody was looking on, and the King was chuckling to himself at the idea of finding the piece of muslin in a nutshell.

However, the Prince cracked the cherry-stone, but everyone laughed when he saw it contained only its own kernel. He opened that and found a grain of wheat, and in that was a millet seed. Then he himself began to wonder, and muttered softly:

"White Cat, White Cat, are you making fun of me?"

In an instant he felt a cat's claw give his hand quite a sharp scratch, and hoping that it was meant as an encouragement he opened the millet seed, and drew out of it a piece of muslin four hundred ells long, woven with the loveliest colors and most wonderful patterns; and when the needle was brought it went through the eye six times with the greatest ease! The King turned pale, and the other Princes stood silent and sorrowful, for nobody could deny that this was the most marvelous piece of muslin that was to be found in the world.

Presently the King turned to his sons, and said, with a deep sigh:

"Nothing could console me more in my old age than to realize your willingness to gratify my wishes. Go then once more, and whoever at the end of a year can bring back the loveliest princess shall be married to her, and shall, without further delay, receive the crown, for my successor must certainly be married."

The Prince considered that he had earned the kingdom fairly twice over but still he was too well bred to argue about it, so he just went back to his gorgeous chariot, and, surrounded by his escort, returned to the White Cat faster than he had come. This time she was expecting him, the path was strewn with flowers, and a thousand braziers were burning scented woods which perfumed the air. Seated in a gallery from which she could see his arrival, the White Cat waited for him. "Well, King's son," she said, "here you are once more, without a crown." "Madam," said he, "thanks to your generosity I have earned one twice over; but the fact is that my father is so loth to part with it that it would be no pleasure to me to take it."

"Never mind," she answered. "It's just as well to try and deserve it. As you must take back a lovely princess with you next time

I will be on the lookout for one for you. In the meantime let us enjoy ourselves; tonight I have ordered a battle between my cats and the river rats on purpose to amuse you." So this year slipped away even more pleasantly than the preceding ones. Sometimes the Prince could not help asking the White Cat how it was she could talk.

"Perhaps you are a fairy," he said. "Or has some enchanter changed you into a cat?

But she only gave him answers that told him nothing. Days go by so quickly when one is very happy that it is certain the Prince would never have thought of its being time to go back, when one evening as they sat together the White Cat said to him that if he wanted to take a lovely princess home with him the next day he must be prepared to do what she told him.

"Take this sword," she said, "and cut off my head!"

"I!" cried the Prince. "I cut off your head! Blanchette darling, how could I do it?"

"I entreat you to do as I tell you, King's son," she replied.

The tears came into the Prince's eyes as he begged her to ask him anything but that—to set him any task she pleased as a proof of his devotion, but to spare him the grief of killing his dear Pussy.

But nothing he could say altered her determination, and at last he drew his sword, and desperately, with a trembling hand, cut off the little white head. But imagine his astonishment and delight when suddenly a lovely princess stood before him, and, while he was still speechless with amazement, the door opened and a goodly company of knights and ladies entered, each carrying a cat's skin! They hastened with every sign of joy to the Princess, kissing her hand and congratulating her on being once more restored to her natural shape. She received them graciously, but after a few minutes begged that they would leave her alone with the Prince, to whom she said:

"You see, Prince, that you were right in supposing me to be no ordinary cat. My father reigned over six kingdoms. The Queen, my mother, whom he loved dearly, had a passion for traveling and exploring, and when I was only a few weeks old she obtained his permission to visit a certain mountain of which she had heard many marvelous tales, and set out, taking with her a number of her attendants. On the way they had to pass near an old castle belonging to the fairies. Nobody had ever been into it, but it was reported to be full of the most wonderful things, and my mother remembered to have heard that the fairies had in their garden such fruits as were to be seen and tasted nowhere else. She began to wish to try them for herself, and turned her steps in the direction of the garden. On arriving at the door, which blazed with gold and jewels, she ordered her servants to knock loudly, but it was useless; it seemed as if all the inhabitants of the castle must be asleep or dead. Now the more difficult it became to obtain the fruit, the more the Queen was determined that have it she would. So she ordered that they should bring ladders, and get over the wall into the garden; but though the wall did not look very high, and they tied the ladders together to make them very long, it was quite impossible to get to the top.

"The Queen was in despair, but as night was coming on she ordered that they should encamp just where they were, and went to bed herself, feeling quite ill, she was so disappointed. In the middle of the night she was suddenly awakened, and saw to her surprise a tiny, ugly old woman seated by her bedside, who said to her:

"'I must say that we consider it somewhat troublesome of your Majesty to insist upon tasting our fruit; but to save you annoyance, my sisters and I will consent to give you as much as you can carry away, on one condition—that is, that you shall give us your little daughter to bring up as our own.'

"'Ah! my dear madam,' cried the Queen, 'is there nothing else that you will take for the fruit? I will give you my kingdoms willingly.'

"'No,' replied the old fairy, 'we will have nothing but your little daughter. She shall be as happy as the day is long, and we will give her everything that is worth having in fairy-land, but you must not see her again until she is married.'

"'Though it is a hard condition,' said the Queen, 'I consent, for I shall certainly die if I do not taste the fruit, and so I should lose my little daughter either way.'

"So the old fairy led her into the castle, and, though it was still the middle of the night, the Queen could see plainly that it was far more beautiful than she had been told, which you can easily believe, Prince," said the White Cat, "when I tell you that it was this castle that we are now in. 'Will you gather the fruit yourself, Queen?' said the old fairy, 'or shall I call it to come to you?'

"'I beg you to let me see it come when it is called,' cried the Queen; 'that will be something quite new.' The old fairy whistled twice, then she cried:

"'Apricots, peaches, nectarines, cherries, plums, pears, melons, grapes, apples, oranges, lemons, gooseberries, strawberries, raspberries, come!'

"And in an instant they came tumbling in one over another, and yet they were neither dusty nor spoilt, and the Queen found them quite as good as she had fancied them. You see they grew upon fairy trees.

"The old fairy gave her golden baskets in which to take the fruit away, and it was as much as four hundred mules could carry. Then she reminded the Queen of her agreement, and led her back to the camp, and next morning she went back to her kingdom, but before she had gone very far she began to repent of her bargain, and when the King came out to meet her she looked so sad that he guessed that something had happened, and asked what was the matter. At first the Queen was afraid to tell him, but when, as soon as they reached the palace, five frightful little dwarfs were sent by the fairies to fetch me, she was obliged to confess what she had promised. The King was very angry, and had the Queen and myself shut up in a great tower and safely guarded, and drove the little dwarfs out of his kingdom; but the fairies sent a great dragon who ate up all the people he met, and whose breath burnt up everything as he passed through the country; and at last, after trying in vain to rid himself of this monster, the King, to save his subjects, was obliged to consent that I should be given up to the fairies. This time they came themselves to fetch me, in a chariot of pearl drawn by sea-horses, followed by the dragon, who was led with chains of diamonds. My cradle was placed between the old fairies, who loaded me with caresses, and away we whirled through the air to a tower which they had built on purpose for me. There I grew up surrounded with everything that was beautiful and rare, and learning everything that is ever taught to a princess, but without any companions but a parrot and a little dog, who could both talk; and receiving every day a visit from one of the old fairies, who came mounted upon the dragon. One day, however, as I sat at my window I saw a handsome young prince, who seemed to have been hunting in the forest which surrounded my prison, and who was standing and looking up at me. When he saw that I observed him he saluted me with great deference. You can imagine that I was delighted to have some one new to talk to, and in spite of the height of my window our conversation was prolonged till night fell, then my prince reluctantly bade me farewell. But after that he came again many times and at last I consented to marry him, but the question was how was I to escape from my tower. The fairies always supplied me with flax for my spinning, and by great diligence I made enough cord for a ladder that would reach to the foot of the tower; but, alas! just as my prince was helping me to descend it, the crossest and ugliest of the old fairies flew in. Before he had time to defend himself my unhappy lover was swallowed up by the dragon. As for me, the fairies, furious at having their plans defeated, for they intended me to marry the king of the dwarfs, and I utterly refused, changed me into a white cat. When they brought me here I found all the lords and ladies of my father's court awaiting me under the same enchantment, while the people of lesser rank had been made invisible, all but their hands.

"As they laid me under the enchantment the fairies told me all my history, for until then I had quite believed that I was their child, and warned me that my only chance of regaining my natural form was to win the love of a prince who resembled in every way my unfortunate lover.

"And you have won it, lovely Princess," interrupted the Prince.

"You are indeed wonderfully like him," resumed the Princess— "in voice, in features, and everything; and if you really love me all my troubles will be at an end."

"And mine too," cried the Prince, throwing himself at her feet, "if you will consent to marry me."

"I love you already better than anyone in the world," she said. "But now it is time to go back to your father, and we shall hear what he says about it."

So the Prince gave her his hand and led her out, and they mounted the chariot together; it was even more splendid than before, and so was the whole company. Even the horses' shoes were of rubies with diamond nails, and I suppose that is the first time such a thing was ever seen.

As the Princess was as kind and clever as she was beautiful, you may imagine what a delightful journey the Prince found it, for everything the Princess said seemed to him quite charming.

When they came near the castle where the brothers were to meet, the Princess got into a chair carried by four of the guards; it was hewn out of one splendid crystal, and had silken curtains, which she drew round her that she might not be seen.

The Prince saw his brothers walking upon the terrace, each with a lovely princess, and they came to meet him, asking if he had also found a wife. He said that he had found something much rarer—a white cat! At which they laughed very much, and asked him if he was afraid of being eaten up by mice in the palace. And then they set out together for the town. Each prince and princess rode in a splendid carriage; the horses were decked with plumes of feathers, and glittered with gold. After them came the youngest prince, and last of all the crystal chair, at which everybody looked with admiration and curiosity. When the courtiers saw them coming they hastened to tell the King.

"Are the ladies beautiful?" he asked anxiously.

And when they answered that nobody had ever before seen such lovely princesses he seemed quite annoyed.

However, he received them graciously, but found it impossible to choose between them.

Then turning to his youngest son he said:

"Have you come back alone, after all?"

"Your Majesty," replied the Prince, "will find in that crystal chair a little white cat, which has such soft paws, and mews so prettily, that I am sure you will be charmed with it."

The King smiled, and went to draw back the curtains himself, but at a touch from the Princess the crystal shivered into a thousand splinters, and there she stood in all her beauty; her fair hair floated over her shoulders and was crowned with flowers, and her softly falling robe was of the purest white. She saluted the King gracefully, while a murmur of admiration rose from all around.

"Sire," she said, "I am not come to deprive you of the throne you fill so worthily. I have already six kingdoms, permit me to bestow one upon you, and upon each of your sons. I ask nothing but your friendship, and your consent to my marriage with your youngest son; we shall still have three kingdoms left for ourselves."

The King and all the courtiers could not conceal their joy and astonishment, and the marriage of the three Princes was celebrated at once. The festivities lasted several months, and then each king and queen departed to their own kingdom and lived happily ever after.

(*Madame d'Aulnoy*)

The Master Cat, or Puss in Boots

How does this cat become a great lord? Read on to find out.

✳ ✳ ✳ ✳

THERE WAS A miller who left no more estate to the three sons he had than his mill, his ass, and his cat. The partition was soon made. Neither scrivener nor attorney was sent for. They would soon have eaten up all the poor patrimony. The eldest had the mill, the second the ass, and the youngest nothing but the cat. The poor young fellow was quite comfortless at having so poor a lot.

"My brothers," said he, "may get their living handsomely enough by joining their stocks together; but for my part, when I have eaten up my cat, and made me a muff of his skin, I must die of hunger."

The Cat, who heard all this, but made as if he did not, said to him with a grave and serious air:

"Do not thus afflict your-self, my good master. You have nothing else to do but to give me a bag and get a pair of boots made for me that I may scamper through the dirt and the brambles, and you shall see that you have not so bad a portion in me as you imagine."

The Cat's master did not build very much upon what he said. He had often seen him play a great many cunning tricks to catch rats and mice, as when he used to hang by the heels, or hide himself in the meal, and make as if he were dead; so that he did not altogether despair of his affording him some help in his miserable condition. When the Cat had what he asked for he booted himself very gallantly, and putting his bag about his neck, he held the strings of it in his two forepaws and went into a warren where was great abundance of rabbits. He put bran and sow-thistle into his bag, and stretching out at length, as if he had been dead, he waited for some young rabbits, not yet acquainted with the deceits of the world, to come and rummage his bag for what he had put into it.

Scarce was he lain down but he had what he wanted. A rash and foolish young rabbit jumped into his bag, and Monsieur Puss, immediately drawing close the strings, took and killed him without pity. Proud of his prey, he went with it to the palace and asked to speak with his majesty. He was shown upstairs into the King's apartment, and, making a low reverence, said to him:

"I have brought you, sir, a rabbit of the warren, which my noble lord the Marquis of Carabas" (for that was the title which puss was pleased to give his master) "has commanded me to present to your majesty from him."

"Tell thy master," said the king, "that I thank him and that he does me a great deal of pleasure."

Another time he went and hid himself among some standing corn, holding still his bag open, and when a brace of partridges ran into it he drew the strings and so caught them both. He went and made a present of these to the king, as he had done before of the rabbit which he took in the warren. The king, in like manner, received the partridges with great pleasure, and ordered him some money for drink.

The Cat continued for two or three months thus to carry his Majesty, from time to time, game of his master's taking. One day in particular, when he knew for certain that he was to take the air along the riverside, with his daughter, the most beautiful princess in the world, he said to his master:

"If you will follow my advice your fortune is made. You have nothing else to do but go and wash yourself in the river, in that part I shall show you, and leave the rest to me."

The Marquis of Carabas did what the Cat advised him to, without knowing why or wherefore. While he was washing the King passed by, and the Cat began to cry out:

"Help! help! My Lord Marquis of Carabas is going to be drowned."

At this noise the King put his head out of the coach-window, and, finding it was the Cat who had so often brought him such good game, he commanded his guards to run immediately to the assistance of his Lordship the Marquis of Carabas. While they were drawing the poor Marquis out of the river, the Cat came up to the coach and told the King that, while his master was washing, there came by some rogues, who went off with his clothes, though he had cried out: "Thieves! thieves!" several times, as loud as he could.

This cunning Cat had hidden them under a great stone. The King immediately commanded the officers of his wardrobe to run and fetch one of his best suits for the Lord Marquis of Carabas.

The King caressed him after a very extraordinary manner, and as the fine clothes he had given him extremely set off his good mien (for he was well made and very handsome in his person), the King's daughter took a secret inclination to him, and the Marquis of Carabas had no sooner cast two or three respectful and somewhat tender glances but she fell in love with him to distraction. The King would need have him come into the coach and take part of the airing. The Cat, quite overjoyed to see his project begin to succeed, marched on before, and, meeting with some countrymen, who were mowing a meadow, he said to them:

"Good people, you who are mowing, if you do not tell the King that the meadow you mow belongs to my Lord Marquis of Carabas, you shall be chopped as small as herbs for the pot."

The King did not fail asking of the mowers to whom the meadow they were mowing belonged.

"To my Lord Marquis of Carabas," answered they altogether, for the Cat's threats had made them terribly afraid.

"You see, sir," said the Marquis, "this is a meadow which never fails to yield a plentiful harvest every year."

The Master Cat, who went still on before, met with some reapers, and said to them:

"Good people, you who are reaping, if you do not tell the King that all this corn belongs to the Marquis of Carabas, you shall be chopped as small as herbs for the pot."

The King, who passed by a moment after, would needs know to whom all that corn, which he then saw, did belong.

"To my Lord Marquis of Carabas," replied the reapers, and the King was very well pleased with it, as well as the Marquis, whom he congratulated thereupon. The Master Cat, who went always before, said the same words to all he met, and the King was astonished at the vast estates of my Lord Marquis of Carabas.

Monsieur Puss came at last to a stately castle, the master of which was an ogre, the richest had ever been known; for all the lands which the King had then gone over belonged to this castle. The Cat, who had taken care to inform himself who this ogre was and what he could do, asked to speak with him, saying he could not pass so near his castle without having the honor of paying his respects to him.

The ogre received him as civilly as an ogre could do, and made him sit down.

"I have been assured," said the Cat, "that you have the gift of being able to change yourself into all sorts of creatures you have a mind to; you can, for example, transform yourself into a lion, or elephant, and the like."

"That is true," answered the ogre very briskly; "and to convince you, you shall see me now become a lion."

Puss was so sadly terrified at the sight of a lion so near him that he immediately got into the gutter, not without abundance of trouble and danger, because of his boots, which were of no use at all to him in walking upon the tiles. A little while after, when Puss saw that the ogre had resumed his natural form, he came down, and owned he had been very much frightened.

"I have been, moreover, informed," said the Cat, "but I know not how to believe it, that you have also the power to take on you the shape of the smallest animals; for example, to change yourself into a rat or a mouse; but I must own to you I take this to be impossible."

"Impossible!" cried the ogre. "You shall see that presently."

And at the same time he changed himself into a mouse, and began to run about the floor. Puss no sooner perceived this but he fell upon him and ate him up.

Meanwhile the King, who saw, as he passed, this fine castle of the ogre's, had a mind to go into it. Puss, who heard the noise of his Majesty's coach running over the drawbridge, ran out, and said to the King:

"Your Majesty is welcome to this castle of my Lord Marquis of Carabas."

"What! my Lord Marquis," cried the King, "and does this castle also belong to you? There can be nothing finer than this court and all the stately buildings which surround it; let us go into it, if you please."

The Marquis gave his hand to the Princess, and followed the King, who went first. They passed into a spacious hall, where they found a magnificent collation, which the ogre had prepared for his friends, who were that very day to visit him, but dared not to enter, knowing the King was there. His Majesty was perfectly charmed with the good qualities of my Lord Marquis of Carabas, as was his daughter, who had fallen violently in love with him, and, seeing the vast estate he possessed, said to him, after having drunk five or six glasses:

"It will be owing to yourself only, my Lord Marquis, if you are not my son-in-law."

The Marquis, making several low bows, accepted the honor which his Majesty conferred upon him, and forthwith, that very same day, married the Princess.

Puss became a great lord, and never ran after mice any more but only for his diversion.

(Charles Perrault)

The Cat's Elopement

Once upon a time there lived a cat of marvelous beauty, with a skin as soft and shining as silk, and wise green eyes, that could see even in the dark.

✳ ✳ ✳ ✳

HIS NAME WAS Gon, and he belonged to a music teacher, who was so fond and proud of him that he would not have parted with him for anything in the world.

Now not far from the music master's house there dwelt a lady who possessed a most lovely little pussy cat called Koma. She was such a little dear altogether, and blinked her eyes so daintily, and ate her supper so tidily, and when she had finished she licked her pink nose so delicately with her little tongue, that her mistress was never tired of saying, "Koma, Koma, what should I do without you?"

Well, it happened one day that these two, when out for an evening stroll, met under a cherry tree, and in one moment fell madly in love with each other. Gon had long felt that it was time for him to find a wife, for all the ladies in the neighborhood paid him so much attention that it made him quite shy; but he was not easy to please, and did not care about any of them.

Now, before he had time to think, Cupid had entangled him in his net, and he was filled with love towards Koma. She fully returned his passion, but, like a woman, she saw the difficulties in the way, and consulted sadly with Gon as to the means of overcoming them. Gon entreated his master to set matters right by buying Koma, but her mistress would not part from her. Then the music master was asked to sell Gon to the lady, but he declined to listen to any such suggestion, so everything remained as before.

At length the love of the couple grew to such a pitch that they determined to please themselves, and to seek their fortunes together. So one moonlight night they stole away, and ventured out into an unknown world. All day long they marched bravely on through the sunshine, till they had left their homes far behind them, and towards evening they found themselves in a large park. The wanderers by this time were very hot and tired, and the grass looked very soft and inviting, and the trees cast cool deep shadows, when suddenly an ogre appeared in this Paradise, in the shape of a big, big dog! He came springing towards them showing all his teeth, and Koma shrieked, and rushed up a cherry tree.

Gon, however, stood his ground boldly, and prepared to give battle, for he felt that Koma's eyes were upon him, and that he must not run away. But, alas! his courage would have availed him nothing had his enemy once touched him, for he was large and powerful, and very fierce. From her perch in the tree Koma saw it all, and screamed with all her might, hoping that someone would hear, and come to help. Luckily a servant of the princess to whom the park belonged was walking by, and he drove off the dog, and picking up the trembling Gon in his arms, carried him to his mistress.

So poor little Koma was left alone, while Gon was borne away full of trouble, not in the least knowing what to do. Even the attention paid him by the princess, who was delighted with his beauty and pretty ways, did not console him, but there was no use in fighting against fate, and he could only wait and see what would turn up.

The princess, Gon's new mistress, was so good and kind that everybody loved her, and she would have led a happy life, had it not been for a serpent who had fallen in love with her, and was constantly annoying her by his presence. Her servants had orders to drive him away as often as he appeared; but as they were careless, and the serpent very sly, it sometimes happened that he was able to slip past them, and to frighten the princess by appearing before her. One day she was seated in her room, playing on her favorite musical instrument, when she felt something gliding up her sash, and saw her enemy making his way to kiss her cheek. She shrieked and threw herself backwards, and Gon, who had been curled up on a stool at her feet, understood her terror, and with one bound seized the snake by his neck. He gave him one bite and one shake, and flung him on the ground, where he lay, never to worry the princess any more. Then she took Gon in her arms, and praised and caressed him, and saw that he had the nicest bits to eat, and the softest mats to lie on; and he would have had nothing in the world to wish for if only he could have seen Koma again.

Time passed on, and one morning Gon lay before the house door, basking in the sun. He looked lazily at the world stretched out before him, and saw in the distance a big ruffian of a cat teasing and ill-treating quite a little one. He jumped up, full of rage, and chased away the big cat, and then he turned to comfort the little one, when his heart nearly burst with joy to find that it was Koma. At first Koma did not know him again, he had grown so large and stately; but when it dawned upon her who it was, her happiness knew no bounds. And they rubbed their heads and their noses again and again, while their purring might have been heard a mile off.

Paw in paw they appeared before the princess, and told her the story of their life and its sorrows. The princess wept for sympathy, and promised that they should never more be parted, but should live with her to the end of their days. By-and-bye the princess herself got married, and brought a prince to dwell in the palace in the park. And she told him all about her two cats, and how brave Gon had been, and how he had delivered her from her enemy the serpent.

And when the prince heard, he swore they should never leave them, but should go with the princess wherever she went. So it all fell out as the princess wished; and Gon and Koma had many children, and so had the princess, and they all played together, and were friends to the end of their lives.

(folk tale collected by Andrew Lang)

The Philanthropist and the Happy Cat

An ode to the content cat.

❋   ❋   ❋   ❋

JOCANTHA BESSBURY WAS in the mood to be serenely and graciously happy. Her world was a pleasant place, and it was wearing one of its pleasantest aspects. Gregory had managed to get home for a hurried lunch and a smoke afterwards in the little snuggery; the lunch had been a good one, and there was just time to do justice to the coffee and cigarettes. Both were excellent in their way, and Gregory was, in his way, an excellent husband. Jocantha rather suspected herself of making him a very charming wife, and more than suspected herself of having a first-rate dressmaker.

"I don't suppose a more thoroughly contented personality is to be found in all Chelsea," observed Jocantha in allusion to herself; "except perhaps Attab," she continued, glancing towards the large tabby-marked cat that lay in considerable ease in a corner of the divan. "He lies there, purring and dreaming, shifting his limbs now and then in an ecstasy of cushioned comfort. He seems the incarnation of everything soft and silky and velvety, without a sharp edge in his composition, a dreamer whose philosophy is sleep and let sleep; and then, as evening draws on, he goes out into the garden with a red glint in his eyes and slays a drowsy sparrow."

"As every pair of sparrows hatches out ten or more young ones in the year, while their food supply remains stationary, it is just as well that the Attabs of the community should have that idea of how to pass an amusing afternoon," said Gregory. Having delivered himself of this sage comment he lit another cigarette, bade Jocantha a playfully affectionate good-bye, and departed into the outer world.

"Remember, dinner's a wee bit earlier tonight, as we're going to the Haymarket," she called after him.

Left to herself, Jocantha continued the process of looking at her life with placid, introspective eyes. If she had not everything she wanted in this world, at least she was very well pleased with what she had got. She was very well pleased, for instance, with the snuggery, which contrived somehow to be cosy and dainty and expensive all at once. The porcelain was rare and beautiful, the Chinese enamels took on wonderful tints in the firelight, the rugs and hangings led the eye through sumptuous harmonies of colouring. It was a room in which one might have suitably entertained an ambassador or an archbishop, but it was also a room in which one could cut out pictures for a scrap-book without feeling that one was scandalising the deities of the place with one's litter. And as with the snuggery, so with the rest of the house, and as with the house, so with the other departments of Jocantha's life; she really had good reason for being one of the most contented women in Chelsea.

From being in a mood of simmering satisfaction with her lot she passed to the phase of being generously commiserating for those thousands around her whose lives and circumstances were dull, cheap, pleasureless, and empty. Work girls, shop assistants and so forth, the class that have neither the happy-go-lucky freedom of the poor nor the leisured freedom of the rich, came specially within the range of her sympathy. It was sad to think that there were young people who, after a long day's work, had to sit alone in chill, dreary bedrooms because they could not afford the price of a cup of coffee and a sandwich in a restaurant, still less a shilling for a theatre gallery.

Jocantha's mind was still dwelling on this theme when she started forth on an afternoon campaign of desultory shopping; it would be rather a comforting thing, she told herself, if she could do something, on the spur of the moment, to bring a gleam of pleasure and interest into the life of even one or two wistful-hearted, empty-pocketed workers; it would add a good deal to her sense of enjoyment at the theatre that night. She would get two upper circle tickets for a popular play, make her way into some cheap tea-shop, and present the tickets to the first couple of interesting work girls with whom she could casually drop into conversation. She could explain matters by saying that she was unable to use the tickets herself and did not want them to be wasted, and, on the other hand, did not want the trouble of sending them back. On further reflection she decided that it might be better to get only one ticket and give it to some lonely-looking girl sitting eating her frugal meal by herself; the girl might scrape acquaintance with her next-seat neighbour at the theatre and lay the foundations of a lasting friendship.

With the Fairy Godmother impulse strong upon her, Jocantha marched into a ticket agency and selected with immense care an upper circle seat for the "Yellow Peacock," a play that was attracting a considerable amount of discussion and criticism. Then she went forth in search of a tea-shop and philanthropic adventure, at about the same time that Attab sauntered into the garden with a mind attuned to sparrow stalking. In a corner of an A.B.C. shop she found an unoccupied table, whereat she promptly installed herself, impelled by the fact that at the next table was sitting a young girl, rather plain of feature, with tired, listless eyes, and a general air of uncomplaining forlorn-ness. Her dress was of poor material, but aimed at being in the fashion, her hair was pretty, and her complexion bad; she was finishing a modest meal of tea and scone, and she was not very different in her way from thousands of other girls who were finishing, or beginning, or continuing their teas in London tea-shops at that exact moment. The odds were enormously in favour of the supposition that she had never seen the "Yellow Peacock"; obviously she supplied excellent material for Jocantha's first experiment in haphazard benefaction.

Jocantha ordered some tea and a muffin, and then turned a friendly scrutiny on her neighbour with a view to catching her eye. At that precise moment the girl's face lit up with sudden pleasure, her eyes sparkled, a flush came into her cheeks, and she looked almost pretty. A young man, whom she greeted with an affectionate "Hullo, Bertie," came up to her table and took his seat in a chair facing her. Jocantha looked hard at the new-comer; he was in appearance a few years younger than herself, very much better looking than Gregory, rather better looking, in fact, than any of the young men of her set. She guessed him to be a well-mannered young clerk in some wholesale ware-house, existing and amusing himself as best he might on a tiny salary, and commanding a holiday of about two weeks in the year... He was obviously on terms of friendly intimacy with the girl he was talking to, probably they were drifting towards

a formal engagement. Jocantha pictured the boy's home, in
a rather narrow circle, with a tiresome mother who always
wanted to know how and where he spent his evenings. He
would exchange that humdrum thraldom in due course for a
home of his own, dominated by a chronic scarcity of pounds,
shillings, and pence, and a dearth of most of the things that
made life attractive or comfortable. Jocantha felt extremely
sorry for him. She wondered if he had seen the "Yellow
Peacock"; the odds were enormously in favour of the supposition that he had not. The girl had finished her tea and would
shortly be going back to her work; when the boy was alone
it would be quite easy for Jocantha to say: "My husband has
made other arrangements for me this evening; would you care
to make use of this ticket, which would otherwise be wasted?"
Then she could come there again one afternoon for tea, and,
if she saw him, ask him how he liked the play. If he was a nice
boy and improved on acquaintance he could be given more
theatre tickets, and perhaps asked to come one Sunday to tea
at Chelsea. Jocantha made up her mind that he would improve
on acquaintance, and that Gregory would like him, and that
the Fairy Godmother business would prove far more entertaining than she had originally anticipated. The boy was distinctly
presentable; he knew how to brush his hair, which was possibly
an imitative faculty; he knew what colour of tie suited him,
which might be intuition; he was exactly the type that Jocantha
admired, which of course was accident. Altogether she was
rather pleased when the girl looked at the clock and bade a
friendly but hurried farewell to her companion. Bertie nodded
"good-bye," gulped down a mouthful of tea, and then produced
from his overcoat pocket a paper-covered book . . .

The laws of tea-shop etiquette forbid that you should offer
theatre tickets to a stranger without having first caught the
stranger's eye. It is even better if you can ask to have a sugar
basin passed to you, having previously concealed the fact that
you have a large and well-filled sugar basin on your own table;

this is not difficult to manage, as the printed menu is generally nearly as large as the table, and can be made to stand on end. Jocantha set to work hopefully; she had a long and rather high-pitched discussion with the waitress concerning alleged defects in an altogether blameless muffin, she made loud and plaintive inquiries about the tube service to some impossibly remote suburb, she talked with brilliant insincerity to the tea-shop kitten, and as a last resort she upset a milk-jug and swore at it daintily. Altogether she attracted a good deal of attention, but never for a moment did she attract the attention of the boy with the beautifully-brushed hair, who was some thousands of miles away . . .

Jocantha went back to her house in Chelsea, which struck her for the first time as looking dull and over-furnished. She had a resentful conviction that Gregory would be uninteresting at dinner, and that the play would be stupid after dinner. On the whole her frame of mind showed a marked divergence from the purring complacency of Attab, who was again curled up in his corner of the divan with a great peace radiating from every curve of his body.

But then he had killed his sparrow.

(H.H. Munro, aka "Saki")

The Tale of Tom Kitten

Once upon a time there were three little kittens, and their names were Mittens, Tom Kitten, and Moppet.

❋   ❋   ❋   ❋

THEY HAD DEAR little fur coats of their own; and they tumbled about the doorstep and played in the dust.

But one day their mother—Mrs. Tabitha Twitchit—expected friends to tea; so she fetched the kittens indoors, to wash and dress them, before the fine company arrived.

First she scrubbed their faces (this one is Moppet).

Then she brushed their fur, (this one is Mittens).

Then she combed their tails and whiskers (this is Tom Kitten).

Tom was very naughty, and he scratched.

Mrs. Tabitha dressed Moppet and Mittens in clean pinafores and tuckers; and then she took all sorts of elegant uncomfortable clothes out of a chest of drawers, in order to dress up her son Thomas.

Tom Kitten was very fat, and he had grown; several buttons burst off. His mother sewed them on again.

When the three kittens were ready, Mrs. Tabitha unwisely turned them out into the garden, to be out of the way while she made hot buttered toast.

"Now keep your frocks clean, children! You must walk on your hind legs. Keep away from the dirty ash-pit, and from Sally Henny Penny, and from the pig-stye and the Puddle-Ducks."

Moppet and Mittens walked down the garden path unsteadily. Presently they trod upon their pinafores and fell on their noses.

When they stood up there were several green smears!

"Let us climb up the rockery, and sit on the garden wall," said Moppet.

They turned their pinafores back to front, and went up with a skip and a jump; Moppet's white tucker fell down into the road.

Tom Kitten was quite unable to jump when walking upon

his hind legs in trousers. He came up the rockery by degrees, breaking the ferns, and shedding buttons right and left.

He was all in pieces when he reached the top of the wall.

Moppet and Mittens tried to pull him together; his hat fell off, and the rest of his buttons burst.

While they were in difficulties, there was a pit pat paddle pat! and the three Puddle-Ducks came along the hard high road, marching one behind the other and doing the goose step—pit pat paddle pat! pit pat waddle pat!

They stopped and stood in a row, and stared up at the kittens. They had very small eyes and looked surprised.

Then the two duck-birds, Rebeccah and Jemima Puddle-Duck, picked up the hat and tucker and put them on.

Mittens laughed so that she fell off the wall. Moppet and Tom descended after her; the pinafores and all the rest of Tom's clothes came off on the way down.

"Come! Mr. Drake Puddle-Duck," said Moppet—"Come and help us to dress him! Come and button up Tom!"

Mr. Drake Puddle-Duck advanced in a slow sideways manner, and picked up the various articles.

But he put them on himself! They fitted him even worse than Tom Kitten.

"It's a very fine morning!" said Mr. Drake Puddle-Duck.

And he and Jemima and Rebeccah Puddle-Duck set off up the road, keeping step—pit pat, paddle pat! pit pat, waddle pat!

Then Tabitha Twitchit came down the garden and found her kittens on the wall with no clothes on.

She pulled them off the wall, smacked them, and took them back to the house.

"My friends will arrive in a minute, and you are not fit to be seen; I am affronted," said Mrs. Tabitha Twitchit.

She sent them upstairs; and I am sorry to say she told her friends that they were in bed with the measles; which was not true.

Quite the contrary; they were not in bed: not in the least.

Somehow there were very extraordinary noises overhead, which disturbed the dignity and repose of the tea party.

And I think that some day I shall have to make another, larger, book, to tell you more about Tom Kitten!

As for the Puddle-Ducks—they went into a pond.

The clothes all came off directly, because there were no buttons.

And Mr. Drake Puddle-Duck, and Jemima and Rebeccah, have been looking for them ever since.

(Beatrix Potter)

The Story of Androcles and the Lion

Many hundred years ago, there lived in the north of Africa a poor Roman slave called Androcles.

✳ ✳ ✳ ✳

HIS MASTER HELD great power and authority in the country, but he was a hard, cruel man, and his slaves led a very unhappy life. They had little to eat, had to work hard, and were often punished and tortured if they failed to satisfy their master's caprices. For long Androcles had borne with the hardships of his life, but at last he could bear it no longer, and he made up his mind to run away. He knew that it was a great risk, for he had no friends in that foreign country with whom he could seek safety and protection; and he was aware that if he was overtaken and caught he would be put to a cruel death. But even death, he thought, would not be so hard as the life he now led, and it was possible that he might escape to the sea-coast, and somehow some day get back to Rome and find a kinder master.

So he waited till the old moon had waned to a tiny gold thread in the skies, and then, one dark night, he slipped out of his master's house, and, creeping through the deserted forum and along the silent town, he passed out of the city into the vineyards and corn-fields lying outside the walls. In the cool night air he walked rapidly. From time to time he was startled by the sudden barking of a dog, or the sound of voices coming from some late revellers in the villas which stood beside the road along which he hurried. But as he got further into the country these sounds ceased, and there was silence and darkness all round him. When the sun rose he had already gone many miles away from the town in which he had been so miserable. But now a new terror oppressed him—the terror of great loneliness. He had got into a wild, barren country, where there was no sign of human habitation. A thick growth of low trees and thorny mimosa bushes spread out before him, and as he tried to thread his way through them he was severely scratched, and his scant garments torn by the long thorns. Besides the sun was very hot, and the trees were not high enough to afford him any shade. He was worn out with hunger and fatigue, and he longed to lie down and rest. But to lie down in that fierce sun would have meant death, and he struggled on, hoping to find some wild berries to eat, and some water to quench his thirst. But when he came out of the scrub-wood, he found he was as badly off as before. A long, low line of rocky cliffs rose before him, but there were no houses, and he saw no hope of finding food. He was so tired that he could not wander further, and seeing a cave which looked cool and dark in the side of the cliffs, he crept into it, and, stretching his tired limbs on the sandy floor, fell fast asleep.

Suddenly he was awakened by a noise that made his blood run cold. The roar of a wild beast sounded in his ears, and as he started trembling and in terror to his feet, he beheld a huge, tawny lion, with great glistening white teeth, standing in the entrance of the cave. It was impossible to fly, for the lion barred the way. Immovable with fear, Androcles stood rooted to the spot, waiting for the lion to spring on him and tear him limb from limb.

But the lion did not move. Making a low moan as if in great pain, it stood licking its huge paw, from which Androcles now saw that blood was flowing freely. Seeing the poor animal in such pain, and noticing how gentle it seemed, Androcles forgot his own terror, and slowly approached the lion, who held up its paw as if asking the man to help it. Then Androcles saw that a monster thorn had entered the paw, making a deep cut, and causing great pain and swelling. Swiftly but firmly he drew the thorn out, and pressed the swelling to try to stop the flowing of the blood. Relieved of the pain, the lion quietly lay down at

Androcles' feet, slowly moving his great bushy tail from side to side as a dog does when it feels happy and comfortable.

From that moment Androcles and the lion became devoted friends. After lying for a little while at his feet, licking the poor wounded paw, the lion got up and limped out of the cave. A few minutes later it returned with a little dead rabbit in its mouth, which it put down on the floor of the cave beside Androcles. The poor man, who was starving with hunger, cooked the rabbit somehow, and ate it. In the evening, led by the lion, he found a place where there was a spring, at which he quenched his dreadful thirst.

And so for three years Androcles and the lion lived together in the cave; wandering about the woods together by day, sleeping together at night. For in summer the cave was cooler than the woods, and in winter it was warmer.

At last the longing in Androcles' heart to live once more with his fellow-men became so great that he felt he could remain in the woods no longer, but that he must return to a town, and take his chance of being caught and killed as a runaway slave. And so one morning he left the cave, and wandered away in the direction where he thought the sea and the large towns lay. But in a few days he was captured by a band of soldiers who were patrolling the country in search of fugitive slaves, and he was put in chains and sent as a prisoner to Rome.

Here he was cast into prison and tried for the crime of having run away from his master. He was condemned as a punishment to be torn to pieces by wild beasts on the first public holiday, in the great circus at Rome.

When the day arrived Androcles was brought out of his prison, dressed in a simple, short tunic, and with a scarf round his right arm. He was given a lance with which to defend himself—a forlorn hope, as he knew that he had to fight with a powerful lion which had been kept without food for some days to make it more savage and bloodthirsty. As he stepped into the arena of the huge circus, above the sound of the voices of thousands on thousands of spectators he could hear the savage roar of the wild beasts from their cages below the floor on which he stood.

Of a sudden the silence of expectation fell on the spectators, for a signal had been given, and the cage containing the lion with which Androcles had to fight had been shot up into the arena from the floor below. A moment later, with a fierce spring and a savage roar, the great animal had sprung out of its cage into the arena, and with a bound had rushed at the spot where Androcles stood trembling. But suddenly, as he saw Androcles, the lion stood still, wondering. Then quickly but quietly it approached him, and gently moved its tail and licked the man's hands, and fawned upon him like a great dog. And Androcles patted the lion's head, and gave a sob of recognition, for he knew that it was his own lion, with whom he had lived and lodged all those months and years.

And, seeing this strange and wonder-ful meeting between the man and the wild beast, all the people marvelled, and the emperor, from his high seat above the arena, sent for Androcles, and bade him tell his story and explain this mystery. And the emperor was so delighted with the story that he said Androcles was to be released and to be made a free man from

that hour. And he rewarded him with money, and ordered that the lion was to belong to him, and to accompany him wherever he went.

And when the people in Rome met Androcles walking, followed by his faithful lion, they used to point at them and say,

"That is the lion, the guest of the man, and that is the man, the doctor of the lion."

(Aesop)

Lion's Share

This tale follows the adventures of a lion and a jackal.

❊   ❊   ❊   ❊

LION AND JACKAL went together a-hunting. They shot with arrows. Lion shot first, but his arrow fell short of its aim; but Jackal hit the game, and joyfully cried out, "It has hit."

Lion looked at him with his two large eyes; Jackal, however, did not lose his countenance, but said, "No, uncle, I mean to say that you have hit." Then they followed the game, and Jackal passed the arrow of Lion without drawing the latter's attention to it. When they arrived at a crossway, Jackal said: "Dear uncle, you are old and tired; stay here." Jackal went then on a wrong track, beat his nose, and, in returning, let the blood drop from it like traces of game. "I could not find anything," he said, "but I met with traces of blood. You had better go yourself to look for it. In the meantime I shall go this other way."

Jackal soon found the killed animal, crept inside of it, and devoured the best portion; but his tail remained outside, and when Lion arrived, he got hold of it, pulled Jackal out, and threw him on the ground with these words: "You rascal!"

Jackal rose quickly again, complained of the rough handling, and asked, "What have I now done, dear uncle? I was busy cutting out the best part.

"Now let us go and fetch our wives," said Lion, but Jackal entreated his dear uncle to remain at the place because he was old. Jackal then went away, taking with him two portions of the flesh, one for his own wife, but the best part for the wife of Lion. When Jackal arrived with the flesh, the children of Lion, seeing him, began to jump, and clapping their hands, cried out: "There comes cousin with flesh!" Jackal threw, grumbling, the worst portion to them, and said, "There, you brood of the big-eyed one!" Then he went to his own house and told his wife immediately to break up the house, and to go where the killed game was. Lioness wished to do the same, but he forbade her, and said that Lion would himself come to fetch her.

When Jackal, with his wife and children, arrived in the neighborhood of the killed animal, he ran into a thorn bush, scratched his face so that it bled, and thus made his appearance before Lion, to whom he said, "Ah! what a wife you have got. Look here, how she scratched my face when I told her that she should come with us. You must fetch her yourself; I cannot bring her." Lion went home very angry. Then Jackal said, "Quick, let us build a tower." They heaped stone upon stone, stone upon stone, stone upon stone; and when it was high enough, everything was carried to the top of it. When Jackal saw Lion approaching with his wife and children, he cried out to him:

"Uncle, whilst you were away we have built a tower, in order to be better able to see game."

"All right," said Lion. "But let me come up to you."

"Certainly, dear uncle; but how will you manage to come up? We must let down a thong for you."

Lion tied the thong around his body and Jackal began drawing him up, but when nearly to the top Jackal cried to Lion, "My, uncle, how heavy you are!" Then, unseen by Lion, he cut the thong. Lion fell to the ground, while Jackal began loudly and angrily to scold his wife, and then said, "Go, wife, fetch me a new thong"—"an old one," he said aside to her.

Lion again tied himself to the thong, and, just as he was near the top, Jackal cut the thong as before; Lion fell heavily to the bottom, groaning aloud, as he had been seriously hurt.

"No," said Jackal. "That will never do: you must, however, manage to come up high enough so that you may get a mouthful at least." Then aloud he ordered his wife to prepare a good piece, but aside he told her to make a stone hot, and to cover it with fat. Then he drew Lion up once more, and complaining how heavy he was to hold, told him to open his mouth, and thereupon threw the hot stone down his throat. Lion fell to the ground and lay there pleading for water, while Jackal climbed down and made his escape.

(*James A. Honey*)

The Tiger and Ulta's Mother

What happens when a tiger cub befriends a crane? Read on to find out.

✳   ✳   ✳   ✳

A TIGER CUB WAS in the habit of playing under the shade of a certain tree, in which was a crane's nest with a young one in it. The parent cranes brought frogs and lizards to their young one, and what it could not eat it used to throw down to the young tiger, and in this way the two became greatly attached to each other. After a time the tigress died, and left the cub alone in the world. The young crane felt much pity for its afflicted friend, and could not bear the thought of itself being in a better position. So one day it said to the tiger, "Let us kill my mother." The tiger replied, "Just as you please. I cannot say do it, nor can I say do not do it." When the mother crane came to give its young one food, the latter set upon her and killed her. The friendship between the two increased so that they could not be separated from each other. Day and night they spent in each other's society.

After a time the two said, "Come let us make a garden, and plant in it turmeric." So they prepared a piece of ground, and the crane brought roots of turmeric from a distance. They then discussed the matter as to which part of the crop each would take. The crane said to the tiger, "You, my brother, choose first." The tiger said, "If I must speak first, I will take the leaves." Then, said the crane, "I will take the roots." Having settled this point to their satisfaction, they began to plant. The tiger dug holes, and the crane put in the roots, and covered them over with earth.

A year passed, and they again said to each other, "Which of us will take the roots, and which the leaves?" The tiger said, "I will take the leaves." The crane replied, "I will take the roots." So they began to dig up the plants, and cutting the leaves from the roots, placed each by themselves. The tiger collected an immense bulk of leaves, and the crane a large heap of roots. This done each surveyed the other's portion. That of the crane was of a beautiful, reddish tinge, and excited the envy of the tiger, who said to the crane, "Give me half of yours, and I will give you half of mine." The crane refused, saying, "I will not share with you. Why did you at first chose the leaves? I gave you your choice." The tiger insisted, but the crane was obdurate, and before long they were quarrelling as if they had been lifelong enemies. The crane seeing it was being worsted in the wrangle, flew in the face of the tiger, and pecked its eyes, so that it became blind. It then flew away, and left the tiger lamenting its sad fate. Having lost its sight it could not find its way about, so remained there weeping.

One day, hearing the voice of a man near by, the tiger called out, "Oh! man, are you a doctor?" The man stupefied with fear stared at the tiger, and gave no reply. The tiger again said, "Oh! man, why do you not reply to my question? Although you are a human being, have you no pity?" The man then said, "Oh! renowned hero, what did you ask me? I am terror stricken, so did not reply. You may devour me." The tiger replied, "If I had wished to kill you, I could have done so, but I mean you no harm." The tiger again asked the man if he possessed a knowledge of medicine, but he replied, "I do not." The tiger then asked, "Is there one amongst you who does know?" The man replied, "Yes." The tiger enquired, "Who is he?" The man said, "There is a certain widow with two sons, the name of one of whom is Ulta, who possesses a knowledge of medicine, she will be able to cure you." Having given the tiger this information the man went away.

The tiger went to the house of Ulta's mother, and hid himself behind a hedge. He said within himself, "When I hear any one call Ulta then I will go forward." Shortly after the tiger arrived Ulta's mother called Ulta, "Ulta, come to your supper." Then the tiger ran hastily forward, and cried, "Oh! Ulta's mother, Oh! Ulta's mother." But she was afraid, and exclaimed, "This tiger has done for us today." The tiger said to the woman, "Do you know medicine?" She replied, "Yes, Wait till I bring it." So hastily running out she said to her neighbors, "A tiger has come to my house. He is blind, and wishes me to cure his blindness." The neighbors said to her, "Give him some of the juice of the Akauna tree. It will increase his blindness." So she quickly brought Akauna juice, and giving it to the tiger, said, "Go to some dense jungle and apply it to your eyes. Do not apply it here, or it will have no effect. Take it away. We are about to sit down to supper, and then my children will go to sleep. The medicine will cause you pain at first, but it will effect a complete cure."

The tiger hurried away to the jungle, and poured the Akauna juice into his eyes. The pain it caused was as if his eyeballs were being torn out. He tossed himself about in agony, and at last struck his head against a tree. In a short time, his blindness was gone. He could see everything plainly, and was delighted beyond expression.

One day several traders were passing along a pathway through the jungle in which the tiger hunted. He was lying concealed watching for prey, and when the traders were passing he jumped out upon them. Seeing the tiger they fled, and left behind them their silver, and gold, and brass vessels. The tiger collected all and carried them to Ulta's mother's house, and presenting them to her said, "All this I give to you, for through you I have again seen the earth. Had it not been for you, who knows whether I should ever have been cured or not." Ulta's mother was delighted with the generosity of the tiger. He had made her rich at once. But she was anxious to get rid of him, and said "Go away. May you always find a living somewhere." So the tiger returned to the jungle again.

Sometime afterwards the tiger was minded to take a wife, and sought his old friend Ulta's mother. On arriving at her house he called out, "Oh! Ulta's mother, where are you? Are you in your house?" She replied, "Who are you?" The tiger answered, "It is I, the forest hero. You cured my blindness." So Ulta's mother came out of her house, and said, "Wherefore, Sir, have you come here?"

"I wish you," replied the tiger, "to find a bride for me." Ulta's mother said, "Come tomorrow and I will tell you. Do not stay today." So the tiger left.

Ulta's mother then went to her neighbors and said, "The tiger has put me in a great difficulty. He wishes me to find a bride for him." They said to her, "Is he not blind?" She replied, "No. He sees now, and it is that, which distresses me. What can I do?" They said, "Get a bag, and order him to go into it, and then tie up the mouth tightly, and tell him to remain still. Say to him, 'If you move, or make a noise, I will not seek a bride for you.' An when you have him tied securely in the bag, call us." The next day the tiger appeared, and Ulta's mother told him to get into the bag, and allow her to tie it. So he went in, and she tied the bag's mouth, and said, "You must not move, lie still, or I shall not be your go-between." Having secured him, Ulta's mother called her neighbors, who came armed with clubs, and began to beat the helpless animal. He called out, "Oh! Ulta's mother, what are you doing?" She said, "Keep quiet. They are beating the marriage drums. Lie still a little longer." The tiger remained motionless, while they continued to beat him. At length they said, "He must be dead now, let us throw him out." So they carried him to a river, and having thrown him in, returned home.

The current bore the tiger far down the river, but at length he stranded in a cove. A short time afterwards a tigress came down to the river to drink and seeing the bag, and thinking it might contain something edible she seized it and dragged it up on to the bank. The tigress then cut the bag open with her teeth, and the tiger sprang out, exclaiming, "Of a truth she has given me a bride. Ulta's mother has done me a good turn, and I shall remember her as long as I live." The tiger and the tigress being of one mind on the subject agreed never to separate.

One day the two tigers said, "Come let us go and pay a visit to Ulta's mother, who has proved so helpful to us. As we cannot go empty handed, let us rob some one to get money to take with us." So they went and lay in wait near a path which passed through the forest in which they lived. Presently a party of merchants came up, and the tigers with a loud roar sprang from their ambush on to the road. The merchants seeing them, fled, and left behind them all their property in money and cloth. Those they carried to Ulta's mother. When she saw the tigers approaching her throat became dry through terror.

Before entering the courtyard they called out to Ulta's mother announcing their approach. Ulta's mother addressed the tiger thus, "Why do you come here frightening one in this way?" The tiger replied, "There is no fear. It is I who am afraid of you. Why should you dread my coming? It was you who found this partner for me. Do you not yet know me?" Ulta's mother replied, "What can you do Sir? Do you not remember that we give and receive gifts on the Karam festival day? On the days for giving and receiving, we give and receive. Now, that you are happily wedded, may you live in peace and comfort; but do not come here again."

The tiger then gave Ulta's mother a large amount of money and much cloth, after which the two tigers took their leave, and Ulta's mother entered her house loaded with rupees and clothing.

(A. Campbell)

The Discontent Cat

This curious tale begins with an old woman and her gray cat.

✳   ✳   ✳   ✳

O NCE UPON A time—I can't say exactly when it was—there stood a neat, tidy little hut on the borders of a wild forest. A poor old woman dwelt in this hut. She lived on the whole pretty comfortably; for, though she was poor, she was able to keep a few goats, that supplied her with milk, and a flock of chickens, that gave her fresh eggs every morning: and then she had a small garden, which she cultivated with her own hands, and that supplied her with cabbages and other vegetables, besides gooseberries and apples for dumplings. Her goats browsed upon the short grass just outside the garden, and her chickens ran about everywhere, and picked up everything they could find. There were some fine old trees which defended the cottage on three sides from the cold winds, and the front was to the south; so it was very snug and sheltered. The forest afforded her sticks and young logs for fuel, so that she never was in want of a fire; and, altogether, she managed to make out a pretty comfortable life of it, as times went.

The only friend and companion the old woman had, was her gray cat. Now, the cat was a middle-aged cat: she had arrived at a time of life when people grow reflective; and she sat by the hearth and reflected very often. What did she reflect about? That is rather a long story. You must know, then, that a few leagues from the old woman's hut, on the other side of the forest, there rose a grand castle, belonging to a very great baron. And sometimes, on fine summer mornings, as the old woman and the cat were sitting in the sunshine, by the door, the old woman at her spinning-wheel, and puss curled up for a nap after her breakfast, the forest would suddenly ring with the sound of hunting-horns, shouts and laughter; and a train of gay ladies and richly dressed gentlemen would sweep by on horseback, with hawk and hound, and followed by servants in splendid liveries; for the baron was fond of hawking and hunting, and frequently took those diversions in the neighboring forests. Now, it so happened, that in one of the tall trees behind the cottage, there lived a magpie: not by any means an ordinary magpie, but a bird that had seen a good deal of the world; indeed, at one time of her life, she had, as she took care to inform everybody, lived in the service of the Countess Von Rustenfustenmustencrustenberg. How she happened to leave such a grand situation, the magpie never explained: to be sure, some ill-natured people did say that there had been an awkward story about the loss of one of the countess's diamond bracelets, which was found one fine morning, in the inside of a hollow tree in the garden; and that Mag was turned away in disgrace directly. But how the matter really was, I cannot say: all that I know is, that she took up her abode half-way up one of the large oaks, behind the old woman's hut, a long time before our story begins; and that, being of a particularly sociable and chatty disposition, she soon established an ardent friendship with the cat, and they became the greatest cronies in the world. So when, as I said just now, the baron's grand hunting parties swept past, they afforded the magpie a fine opportunity for displaying her knowledge of life and the world.

And sometimes, too, she would dwell at great length on the splendor and happiness she had enjoyed while she lived with the countess in her palace, till the cat's fur almost stood on end to hear the wonders she related.

Now, these conversations with the magpie sadly unsetled the mind of the cat; more particularly when the mapie related to her how daintily the Countess Von Rustenfustenmustencrustenberg's cat always lived—what nice bits of chicken she dined upon, what delicious morsels of buttered crumpet she often had for breakfast, what soft cushions she lay upon, and a great deal more to the same purpose: all which made a powerful impression upon our humble friend. So she sate and reflected by the fire, while the good old woman, her mistress, went on spinning the wool which she sold afterwards at the nearest town, to buy food and clothes.

The more the cat talked to the magpie, the more dissatisfied she became with her present condition; till, at last, I am sadly afraid that when, in a morning, the old woman gave her her breakfast of goats' milk with some nice brown bread broken into it, she began rather to despise it, instead of taking it thankfully, as she ought to have done, for she was really very comfortably off in the cottage—having bread and milk every morning and night, and something for dinner too; besides what mice she could catch, to say nothing of a stray robin or sparrow now and then. But, as I said just now, the magpie's chattering stories unsettled her; she thought it would be so charming to dine upon bits of roast chicken, and have buttered crumpets for breakfast, and fine cushions to lie upon, like the countess's cat. All this was very silly, no doubt; but she wanted experience: she knew nothing of the thousands and thousands of poor cats who would have thought her life quite luxurious. It is a very bad thing to get unsettled; it sets people wishing and doing many foolish things.

One fine bright evening, the magpie was perched upon a projecting bough of her oak, and the cat, who thought the cottage particularly dull that day, had come out for a little gossip.

"Good evening!" screamed the magpie, as soon as she saw her. "Do come up here and let us talk politics a little." So the cat climbed up, and seated herself on another bough a little below.

"You look out of spirits to-day," began the magpie, bending down a very inquisitive eye to her friend's face. "I am afraid you are not well; but I'm not surprised: that old sparrow I saw you eating for dinner must have been as tough as leather; it is no wonder you are ill after it! You should really be more careful, and only catch the nice tender young ones."

"Thank you," replied the cat, in a rather melancholy tone. "I am perfectly well."

"Then what in the world ails you, my dear friend?"

"I don't know," answered the cat; "but I believe I am getting rather tired of staying here all my life."

"Ah!" exclaimed the magpie. "I know what that is—I feel for you, puss! You may well be moped, living in that stupid cottage all day. You are not like myself, now; I have had such advantages! I declare to you I can amuse myself the whole day with the recollection of the wonderful things I have seen when I lived in the great world."

"There it is!" interrupted the cat. "To think of the difference in people's situations! Just compare my condition, in this wretched hole of a hut, with the life that you say the countess's cat lives. I'm sure I can hardly eat my sop in the morning for thinking of her buttered crumpets—dear! dear! it's a fine thing to be born in a palace!"

"Indeed," replied the magpie, "there is a great deal of truth in what you say; and sometimes I half repent of having retired from her service myself; but there's a great charm in liberty—

it is pleasant to feel able to fly about wherever one likes, and have no impertinent questions asked."

"Does the countess's cat ever do any work?" inquired puss.

"Not a bit," answered the magpie. "I don't suppose she ever caught a mouse in her life; why should she? She has plenty to eat and drink, and nothing to do but to sleep or play all day long."

"What a life!" said the cat; "and here am I, obliged to take the trouble to catch birds or anything I can, if I want to make out my dinner,—what a world it is!"

"Your most obedient servant, ladies!" Just at that moment hooted an old owl from a neighboring fir-tree; "a fine evening to you!"

"Dear me, Mr. Owl! how you made me jump!" cried the magpie, rather pettishly. "I had nearly toppled down from the bough—"

To say the truth, the magpie did not particularly fancy the owl's company—he was apt to come out with very rude things sometimes; besides, he was reckoned a very sensible bird, and Mag always declared she hated sensible birds—they were so dreadfully dull, and thought themselves so much wiser than other people.

"I beg pardon—I am afraid I have interrupted an interesting discourse," began the owl, observing that his salutation had rather discomposed the magpie.

The cat, however, was not sorry to have the opportunity of imparting her griefs and perplexities to a bird who was so generally respected for his wisdom; so she replied:

"Why, indeed, my dear sir, we were conversing upon the lamentable differences there are in the world."

"You may well say that," answered the owl, giving a blink with his left eye. "I suppose, now, ma'am," he added, rather dryly, turning to the magpie, "your ladyship finds a good deal of difference between your present abode, and the countess's grand palace-garden? I only wonder how you could bring yourself to make such a change—at your time of life, especially."

What an abominable uncivil speech, thought the magpie; she fidgeted upon the branch, drew herself up, and muttered something between her beak about the propriety of people attending to their own concerns.

"But you, my dear cat," continued the owl, "you have every reason, I should think, to be perfectly satisfied with your lot in life?"

"I am not so sure of that," said the cat. "I think I have a good many reasons for being quite the contrary; the countess's cat has buttered crumpets and cream for breakfast, and sleeps on a beautiful soft cushion all night, and all day too, if she likes it: and just look what a dull life of it I lead here! and I have nothing but the hearth to lie upon, and nothing for breakfast but milk and brown bread!"

"And you ought to be thankful you can get that!" cried the owl, quite angrily. "I tell you what, Mrs. Puss, I have seen more of the world than you have, and I just say this for your comfort— if you could see how some poor cats live, you would be glad enough of your present condition."

"Humph!" muttered the cat. "I really don't know how you have contrived to see so much of the world, sitting as you do in a tree all day, blinking your eyes as if you couldn't bear a ray of sunshine: now, with all due submission to your superior wisdom, I should think the magpie ought to know something of life, after the high society she has lived in,—and I do say it is a shame that one cat should have buttered crumpets and cream for breakfast, just because she happens to live in a palace, while another has only brown sop, because she happens to live in a cottage!"

"But suppose," replied the owl, "that some other cat, who lives in a cellar, and never gets anything to eat, except what she can pick up in the gutters, should take it into her head to say, 'What a shame it is that some cats should have nice snug cottages over their heads, and warm hearths to sit by, and bread and milk for breakfast, while I am obliged to live in this horrid cold cellar, and never know how to get a mouthful?'"

The cat was rather disconcerted by this observation at first; but presently answered:

"My dear Mr. Owl, don't let us exaggerate,—you can't seriously mean to say there are any cats in the world in such a condition as you speak of? I am sure the magpie, with all her experience of life, would have told me about it, if it were really so—you must be mistaken."

The magpie, by this time, had become exceedingly tired of such a long silence, and was beginning to think that she had stood upon her dignity quite long enough.

"You will excuse me, my worthy friend," she said, turning to the owl, "but really you do sit there so, day after day, blinking in the sun, without a soul to speak to, that I don't wonder at your taking very strange fancies into your head. I can only say, that during the whole of my residence in the palace of the Countess Von Rustenfustenmustencrustenberg, my late respected mistress, I never came in contact with any cat in the condition you are pleased to imagine; and I should know something of the world, I think."

"Well," replied the owl, quietly, "I will not dispute your lady-ship's knowledge of the world, but I strongly advise our friend Mrs. Puss to remain contented at home, and not try to improve her fortune by going into the town: people should learn to know when they are well off."

Just then, patter, patter, patter, came a few large drops through the leaves; the magpie making a prodigious chattering, and declaring that a tremendous storm was coming on, flew down from the bough; and, whispering the cat not to mind what the owl said—"a stupid old bird!"—she presently hid herself, very snug, in a hollow place in the trunk: not very sorry, to say the truth, to break up the conversation. The owl very deliberately nestled himself in a thick bush of ivy that grew near, and the cat ran into the cottage, to sit by the fire and reflect; for between her two friends, her mind was a little perplexed.

The old woman shut the cottage door, heaped some dry fir-logs on the fire, and sate down to her spinning-wheel. The rain pelted against the shutters, the wind howled in the tree-tops, and roared loudly in the forest behind the hut; it was a terrible night out of doors, but within the cottage it was snug enough,—the fire was blazing merrily, the old woman's wheel turned briskly round, the kettle was singing a low quiet song to itself beside the crackling logs, and the cat was sitting on the hearth, looking warm and comfortable. But I am afraid she was not at all comfortable—in her mind; for discontented people seldom are. It never entered her head to consider whether there were any poor cats abroad that night, without a shelter over them; for grumblers are always selfish, and never think of the wants of others. In fact, she could think of nothing, just at that time, but the luxuries enjoyed by the fortunate cats who might happen to be born in grand palaces; so, curled up in the warmest corner of the hearth, she sat watching the little spouts of flame that kept flashing up from the pine logs, and wishing, for the hundredth time that day, that she had had the good luck to be a palace cat. Presently a very strange thing happened to her.

All of a sudden she felt something very lightly touch her coat; and looking round, there stood, close by her, the most beautiful little thing that anybody ever dreamt of. She was not many inches high; her robe seemed made of gold and silver threads, fine as gossamer, woven together: on her head she wore a circlet of diamonds, so small and bright, that they looked like sparks of fire, and in her tiny hand she bore a long and very slight silver wand—it was more like a very, very fine knitting-pin than anything else.

The cat looked at her with unutterable astonishment: it was very odd that the old woman did not seem to see her at all.

The beautiful little lady looked at the cat for a minute or two very steadily, and then said, "You are wishing for something; what is it?"

By this time the cat had sufficiently recovered from her consternation to be able to speak: so she answered, "Please your majesty, whoever you are, you have guessed right for once—I am wishing for something: I wish to live in the palace of the magpie's grand countess!"

Wonderful to relate—the words were no sooner spoken, then the Fairy struck her wand upon the floor three times, and lo! and behold! instantly there appeared—though how it got there, I can't imagine—a car made of four large scallop shells joined together, and lined with rich velvet; the wheels were studded with the whitest pearls, and it was drawn by eight silver pheasants. The Fairy seated herself inside, and told the cat to jump in after her. Puss obeyed, and in an instant the hut, the old woman, the little garden, all had vanished! and she and the Fairy were sailing through the air as fast as the eight pheasants could fly.

"Where in the world are we going, please your majesty?" said poor puss, in a dreadfully frightened tone, clinging to the sides of the car with her claws, that she might not be tossed out. "Hush!" said the Fairy, in a voice so solemn, that the cat did not venture to ask another question.

On—on—on they flew, till the gloomy forest was left far behind; the storm had subsided; and, as the moon came out from behind the clouds, the cat perceived they were passing over a wild moorland country. On—on, the birds flew, and the wild heath swelled into mountains, and sank again into plain and valley; and they heard beneath them, like the distant sea, the rustling of the wind among clumps of pine-trees. On—on, the birds flew, till, at length there appeared, far before them, the glimmering lights and dim outlines of a stately city. On—on, the birds flew, and the city grew nearer and nearer; turrets and spires and ancient gables rose in the bright moonlight, and the houses grew thicker and thicker together.

At length the pheasants flew more slowly, and the cat saw that they were approaching a very magnificent palace. How her heart beat, partly with fright, partly with the rapid motion, partly with expectation! Yes, they were evidently drawing near to a magnificent palace. It had high towers and curiously carved gateways, that threw strange deep shadows upon the walls, and the panes of the lattices glittered like diamonds in the moonbeams, and the smoke from the chimneys curled up into the cat's face, and got down her throat, and made her sneeze dreadfully—she wondered how the Fairy could bear it. But now, slowly, slowly, slowly, the wonderful car began to descend, till it was just on a level with one of the windows, which happened, very conveniently, to have been left wide open: so in flew the pheasants, car and all, and alighted on the hearth-rug.

"Jump out—be quick!" cried the Fairy. The cat did not wait to be told twice—she was out in a twinkling; but before she could turn her head round, car, Fairy, and pheasants had vanished, and she was left alone in the strange room. "To be sure," she exclaimed to herself, "was there ever anything so extraordinary?"

What an adventure! And what a room it was! It was so large, that three or four huts, like her old mistress's, would have stood in it. The floor was covered with something so thick, so warm, and so beautiful, all over flowers in bright colors, that she had never seen anything like it before: in short, everything in the room was so fine, or so soft, or so large, or so bright, that the cat could not conceive what such strange things could be meant for.

However, she soon decided that the hearth-rug was the most delightful bed she had ever reposed upon; and, stretching out her limbs upon it, before the huge fire that was burning in the grate, she strove to collect her bewildered ideas ere she proceeded any further to investigate these unknown regions. Suddenly the door opened.

"Dear! What a pretty cat!" exclaimed a waiting-maid, entering the room, "and just as we were wanting another, too: my lady, the countess, will be quite pleased." Then, coming up to the cat, she took her in her arms, and began stroking her most affectionately. "Pretty pussy! how could you ever get into the room? O I see they have left the window open, so you have wandered in out of the street, poor little cat! It's really quite lucky, just as the old one is dead." So saying, she again stroked the cat, and carried her away with her into an inner room, where there sat an old lady in an easy chair by the fire, apparently employed in eating her supper.

"Please your ladyship," said the waiting-woman. "Here's a poor cat come into the house to-night, just as we were wanting one—will your ladyship be pleased to let it remain here?"

"To be sure," said the old Countess Von Rustenfustenmustencrustenberg (for it was she). "It has just come in to supply the place of poor old Finette: put it into Finette's bed to-night, Ermengarde, and give it a good meal first, for I dare say it is hungry enough, poor creature! But, first, bring it here, and let me stroke it."

You may imagine how puss purred her very loudest as the countess patted her, and called her a pretty cat. She thought herself now the luckiest cat in the world: how she wished that spiteful old owl could but know about it! Ermengarde, the waiting-woman, now took her back into the room she had first entered, and setting her down on the hearth-rug, went out. Presently she returned, and placed before the cat a dish,

containing such a supper, as had never entered her imagination till the magpie enlightened her on these subjects: it
was some minutes before she could believe it; was it real?
However, she did it full justice in time; and then, after a
great deal more patting and petting, the maid again took her
up, and deposited her by the side of the fire, in a very pretty
basket lined with soft cushions. And could she go to sleep?
Not for some time, in spite of her long ride. It all seemed
so strange—so wonderful! that she, who had been longing
for months to belong to the household of the Countess Von
Rustenfustenmustencrustenberg, should now be actually in her
palace! It was extraordinary indeed. But she fell asleep at last.

The next morning the cat was awake early, and the sun was
shining through the satin curtains of the splendid room, and
everything in it looked so very beautiful! How different from
the old woman's hut! So the cat sat up in the basket, and looked
about her. After she had thus amused herself in this way for
some time, Ermengarde opened the door.

"Well, Pussy," she said, "so you are wide awake, and ready, I dare
say, for your breakfast."

Now for the buttered crumpets! thought the cat. The maid
went out, and quickly returned with a large saucer full of rich
milk, with some roll crumbled into it. No buttered crumpets.

The cat felt a sort of blank feeling of disappointment; it was
very odd: but perhaps she should have some another morning.
However, she made an exceedingly good breakfast, as it was;
but it must be confessed she was a little cross all day. Soon after
breakfast, the old countess came in, followed by a lap-dog—a
fat, spoilt, disagreeable looking animal, and the cat took a dislike to him at first sight. And as for the dog, he almost growled
out aloud when the countess stooped down to stroke the cat. It
was evident that the hatred was quite mutual.

"Now, Viper," said the old lady. "Be good! You know you are my own darling, that you are; but you must not quarrel with poor pussy: no fighting you know, Viper!"

Whereupon Viper struggled down out of his mistress's arms, for she had taken him up to bestow a kiss upon him, and giving a short snarl, by way of showing his perfect contempt for her admonition, he mounted upon a stool before the fire, and sat eyeing his new acquaintance with such a fierce pair of eyes, that the poor cat really shook all over, and wished herself safe out of the palace again. However, whenever the countess left the room, she always called Viper away too; so they were not left together at all the first day. On the following, the cat began to get used to Viper's cross looks, and did not mind him so much: and the old lady petted and made so much of her, that she thought no cat had ever been so fortunate before. As to that, we shall see.

Dinner-time came: and as Viper was to dine with the cat, Ermengarde brought in two plates this time, and to work they fell with all their might. Viper had nearly eaten up all his own dinner, and the cat was saving a beautiful merrythought for her last tit-bit, when, as ill luck would have it, the countess was suddenly called out of the room.

Instantly, with a growl that sounded in the cat's ears like thunder, Viper darted full at the merrythought, exclaiming:

"You vile little wretch of a stray cat, do you suppose I shall suffer you to come in here, and rob me of my bones?"

"Indeed, my lord," said the cat, dreadfully frightened. "I did not mean to take more than my share!"

"And pray, madam," screamed Viper. "What do you mean by that? Do you intend to insinuate that I have taken more than mine? Now, Mrs. Puss, just listen to me once for all,—if you give me any more of your impertinence, I'll worry you to death in two minutes!"

Poor puss! She trembled so from head to tail, that she could hardly stand. But just as she was going to beseech him not to be offended, the countess came in again; and as she soon afterwards took Viper out an airing with her, the cat saw no more of him for that afternoon. Poor puss! She had a great deal of sorrowful reflection all that evening. The result of it was, that she very seriously asked herself what she had gained by leaving her mistress's cottage? To be sure, she had cream for breakfast, and chicken for dinner, but what was that, if, every mouthful she ate, she was in fear of that savage brute of a dog snatching away her meal, or even attacking and worrying her?

Fifty times did she wish herself a hundred leagues off. How careful she resolved to be to do nothing that could possibly offend the dog. And so, for the next three or four days, by dint of giving up to him all her best bones, and always jumping down from her cushion whenever he wanted to lie upon it, and looking the picture of humility whenever he was in the room, she contrived to get on in tolerable peace with him. But unluckily, one morning, puss, finding herself all alone in the drawing-room, and everything quiet, and feeling very sleepy (for she had had very little repose the night before, from distress of mind), thought she might as well take the opportunity of getting a nap; so she jumped upon a high footstool, beside the fire, and was soon fast asleep. How long she had napped she could not tell, when she was awakened by a furious barking; and opening her eyes, she saw Viper standing at a little distance, looking as if he was going into fits with passion.

Poor puss! She recollected, all in a moment, that she had got upon Viper's own footstool! She jumped down before you could count one.

"You audacious little upstart!" cried the dog, as soon as his rage allowed him to speak. "Do you think I shall submit to such impertinent liberties?"

"Indeed, indeed," stammered the poor cat. "I humbly beg your lordship's pardon, but I really quite forgot—"

"Forgot, indeed!" roared Viper. "I'll teach you to forget, Mrs. Puss!" Making a tremendous dash at her, he would doubtless have demolished her in no time, had not, fortunately, the window been open a little, just enough for the cat to get through.

She was on the window-seat in an instant, and had scrambled out of the window before Viper, who was very fat, could come up to her. It was with some difficulty that he got up upon the window-seat, and quite in vain that he tried to squeeze his fat body through the opening of the window. How he growled with disappointed passion, as he stood on his hind-legs on the window-seat, stretching his head, as far as his little short neck would allow, through the opening, to see what had become of puss.

What had become of her? She had dropt down into the street, and had crept into the shade of one of the heavy broad stone-carvings beneath the window, knowing that there she was safe enough for the present; and she lay down, panting with the fright, to recover her breath a little, and consider what was to be done. To go back to the palace was clearly out of the question. But then where could she go? Poor cat! What a perplexity she was in! She lay snug for the best part of an hour before she durst venture out of her hiding-place. At last, cautiously peeping about her, she crept out, and ran, with all her speed, down the street, not knowing in the least whither she was flying. She had not gone far before she attracted the attention of a group of children, who were playing in the street. Shouting, whooping, and laughing, they pursued her. She redoubled her speed, and darting suddenly down a little side alley, was soon out of sight of her pursuers. She heard their screams and yellings, growing fainter and fainter, in the distance; and feeling that the immediate danger had past, she relaxed her pace, and looked to see where she was. She found that she was in a little, dirty, miserable court, open at the end, through which she saw trees and green fields. But she thought it would be very hazardous to loiter; so she ran on, and in a short time found that she had left the town behind her, and was once more in the open country. Dreading lest she might encounter any more dogs, she carefully avoided approaching any human habitation; so she glided along among the grass, till she came to a small clump of trees, which put her in mind of the forest near her old mistress's hut. Seeing no better prospect of shelter for the night, she climbed up into the largest of the trees, knowing that, at least, she should be out of the way of dogs there; and finding a snug place among the branches in the middle of the tree (for, though it was autumn, yet the leaves were still pretty thick), she made up her mind to pass the night there.

But it wanted some hours yet of night: and what was she to do for supper? It was not at all a pleasant consideration. Moreover, her squabble with Viper had taken place before dinner; and now there was no prospect of any supper but such as she could earn by her own exertions. Perhaps she might, with good luck, catch a robin before night; but that could very ill supply the place of the nice bits of fowl, and saucers of rich milk, that Ermengarde gave her every night. However, she was too glad to be safe and snug up in the tree, to be very particular. So she made up her mind to lie there till it grew towards roosting-time, and then see what she could find for supper. She peeped out as well as she could between the branches to see what the surrounding country was like; it all looked quite wild and lonely, and she saw but few dwellings anywhere near the clump of trees.

Her place of refuge seemed at a considerable distance from the high-road; so she hoped she was tolerably safe from both men and dogs.

At length the cold dews of the evening began to fall, and the little birds began to return home to their trees: so the cat ventured to descend and look about for her supper. I am sorry to say, that being by this time exceedingly hungry, she obeyed the dictates of nature, and in a very few minutes had attacked and devoured a dear little robin, that might have sung merrily all through the autumn, if puss had only been contented, and staid quietly at home in the cottage. Be that as it may, poor little Redbreast fell a victim to her hunger, and yet she considered him but a very poor supper, after all. He was the best she could get that night, however; for the other birds proved too nimble for her: so, weary and hungry, puss climbed up her tree again, and was soon asleep—for she was very tired indeed, with all she had done that day. The next morning, when she awoke, her limbs felt quite stiff; for the night had been frosty, and she was very cold. But there was no fire in the tree; so she had nothing for it but to crawl down, and try to warm herself with catching a bird for her breakfast. She was so benumbed, that she could hardly get down, and her bones ached as if she had got the rheumatism all over her: however, jumping about after the birds revived her by degrees, and she began to feel in a little better spirits; till, spying, at a distance on the high-road, a carriage with a large dog running after it, all her panic returned, and she climbed up into her tree again with all expedition. But the carriage rolled along, and took no notice of puss; and the rumbling of the wheels soon died away, and all was quiet again.

What a melancholy long day it seemed! And, moreover, she could hardly catch a bird—they all seemed to fly away from the trees, instead of settling upon them; and puss had really hard work to get any dinner at all that day. And then the night was so cold again. Many a time when she awoke, and felt the frosty wind whistling round the trees, stripping away more and more of the leaves at every gust, did the poor cat, in her cold and hunger, think of the nice bright fire on her old mistress's hearth, and her brown bread and milk, till she was ready to cry her eyes out with vexation at her own folly—and what was still worse, her own ingratitude—in being willing to leave the good old woman, her best friend, who had taken care of her all her life long, merely because she fancied it would be very grand to live in a palace. People sometimes find out their mistakes when it is too late.

But, to make a long story short—three or four more days and nights—melancholy days, and cold wretched nights—passed over in much the same miserable way, or, rather, things grew worse: for the weather became stormy, the trees were almost stripped of their leaves, so that they scarcely afforded her any shelter from the wind, and the cat was so dreadfully cold!

It became still more difficult, too, to procure any food; and the birds became very shy of venturing within her reach: the poor cat did not know what to do—she was really half dead with cold and hunger!

"Oh!" groaned she, stretching herself out upon some of the fallen leaves at the foot of the tree—"Oh, that I had never listened to that deceitful, mischievous magpie!"

And, indeed, she had good cause to say so.

It was drawing towards sunset; there had been several storms during the day, but, as the evening came on, the weather had a little cleared up; and a gleam of sunshine just then shot out from among the black clouds, and fell upon something glittering beside her.

She lifted her eyes languidly, for she had no strength to be alert now, and saw the bright and beautiful Fairy, with her car drawn by the silver pheasants.

"Have you learnt yet to be contented with plain fare at home?" said the Fairy to the cat, with an expression in her countenance that the cat could hardly make out: she did not know whether her strange visitor meant to be kind or not to her.

"Oh! If you would but take me back to my old mistress again!" cried the poor cat, clasping her paws in an agony of entreaty. "I would never be discontented any more!"

The Fairy smiled, and touching her lightly with her silver wand, bade her close her eyes—another moment, and she bade her open them; and, most wonderful of all the wonderful things that had happened to her, the trees, the country, the distant city, all were gone! There was a charming log-fire on the hearth, sparkling and crackling; whirr, whirr, whirr, went the old woman's wheel, and there she sate in her chair just as usual; and the wind was blowing, and the rain was pelting against the shutters, exactly as it did the very night puss had left the cottage in such a mysterious way. In fact, everything looked precisely the same. The cat rubbed her eyes, but nothing could she see of the Fairy, or the car, or the silver pheasants.

However, had she got back, and so quick too? And the old woman did not seem at all surprised to see her—it was very odd. She could not make it out anyhow: at last it struck her that, perhaps, she might have been dreaming, and never have been out of the hut at all. Yet those terrible growls of Viper's, and those dismal days and nights in the trees—no, they must have been real! Still, it was very strange that the old woman should take no more notice of her, if she had been lost—how could it be? It was really unaccountable.

But her perplexities were interrupted by the cheerful voice of her old mistress calling out,

"Come, my pussy! It is supper-time!" and as she spoke, she rose up from her spinning-wheel, and taking down some eggs and a cake of brown bread, with a large jug, from her corner cupboard, she broke the eggs into the frying-pan, and they were soon hissing and sputtering over the fire. Then she placed a large saucer on the table, and broke some bread into it; and returning to the fire, she took off the frying-pan, and emptied the eggs into a dish on the table, and sat down to her supper. But before she tasted a bit herself, she poured some nice goat's milk over the bread in a saucer, and set it down on the hearth before the cat.

Now I will venture to say, puss never ate a meal in her life half so thankfully before. She made a resolution, between every mouthful, never to say one word to that silly chattering magpie again; and never to indulge in any more foolish wishes, but to stay at home, do her duty in catching her mistress's mice, and be contented, and thankful for the brown bread and milk, without troubling her head about countesses and buttered crumpets any more.

And I am happy to be able to tell you that she faithfully kept her resolution. She never spoke to the magpie afterwards; but contracted a steady friendship with the owl, which lasted to the day of his death; and when he did die, which was not till he had attained a venerable old age, he bequeathed to her his share of the mice that infested the neighborhood of the cottage.

As to the magpie, finding that her company was no longer desired in that part of the world, she very wisely took her flight far away to the other side of the wood.

Whether she still lives there, and goes on chattering about the grand things she used to see in the palace of the Countess Von Rustenfustenmustencrustenberg, is more than I can inform you. If you want to ascertain that fact, you must go to the northern part of the Duchy of Kittencorkenstringen, and then you must walk seventeen leagues and three quarters still further north, and then you must turn off to your right, just where you see the old fir-stump with the rook's nest in it; and then you must walk eleven leagues and a quarter more, and then turn to your left, and after you have kept straight on for about fifteen leagues more, you will see the wood where the magpie lives;— and then, if you walk quite through it to the other side, you will see the old woman's cottage; and if it should happen to be a fine day, I dare say you will see her sitting in the sunshine spinning, and, curled round beside her, the contented cat.

(Tabitha Grimalkin)

Raggedy Ann and the Kittens

What happens when dolls encounter kittens?

✳   ✳   ✳   ✳

Raggedy Ann had been away all day.

Marcella had come early in the morning and dressed all the dolls and placed them about the nursery.

Some of the dolls had been put in the little red chairs around the little doll table. There was nothing to eat upon the table except a turkey, a fried egg and an apple, all made of plaster of paris and painted in natural colors. The little teapot and other doll dishes were empty, but Marcella had told them to enjoy their dinner while she was away.

The French dolly had been given a seat upon the doll sofa and Uncle Clem had been placed at the piano.

Marcella picked up Raggedy Ann and carried her out of the nursery when she left, telling the dolls to "be real good children, while Mamma is away!"

When the door closed, the tin soldier winked at the Dutch-boy doll and handed the imitation turkey to the penny dolls. "Have some nice turkey?" he asked.

"No thank you!" the penny dolls said in little penny-doll, squeaky voices. "We have had all we can eat!"

"Shall I play you a tune?" asked Uncle Clem of the French doll.

At this all the dolls laughed, for Uncle Clem could not begin to play any tune. Raggedy Ann was the only doll who had ever taken lessons, and she could play Peter-Peter-Pumpkin-Eater with one hand.

In fact, Marcella had almost worn out Raggedy Ann's right hand teaching it to her.

"Play something lively!" said the French doll, as she giggled behind her hand, so Uncle Clem began hammering the eight keys on the toy piano with all his might until a noise was heard upon the stairs.

Quick as a wink, all the dolls took the same positions in which they had been placed by Marcella, for they did not wish really truly people to know that they could move about.

But it was only Fido. He put his nose in the door and looked around.

All the dolls at the table looked steadily at the painted food, and Uncle Clem leaned upon the piano keys looking just as unconcerned as when he had been placed there.

Then Fido pushed the door open and came into the nursery wagging his tail.

He walked over to the table and sniffed, in hopes Marcella had given the dolls real food and that some would still be left.

"Where's Raggedy Ann?" Fido asked, when he had satisfied himself that there was no food.

"Mistress took Raggedy Ann and went somewhere!" all the dolls answered in chorus.

"I've found something I must tell Raggedy Ann about!" said Fido, as he scratched his ear.

"Is it a secret?" asked the penny dolls.

"Secret nothing," replied Fido. "It's kittens!"

"How lovely!" cried all the dolls. "Really live kittens?"

"Really live kittens!" replied Fido. "Three little tiny ones, out in the barn!"

"Oh, I wish Raggedy Ann was here!" cried the French doll. "She would know what to do about it!"

"That's why I wanted to see her," said Fido, as he thumped his tail on the floor. "I did not know there were any kittens and I went into the barn to hunt for mice and the first thing I knew Mamma Cat came bouncing right at me with her eyes looking green! I tell you I hurried out of there!"

"How did you know there were any kittens then?" asked Uncle Clem.

"I waited around the barn until Mamma Cat went up to the house and then I slipped into the barn again, for I knew there must be something inside or she would not have jumped at me that way! We are always very friendly, you know." Fido continued. "And what was my surprise to find three tiny little kittens in an old basket, 'way back in a dark corner!"

"Go get them, Fido, and bring them up so we can see them!" said the tin soldier.

"Not me!" said Fido, "If I had a suit of tin clothes on like you have I might do it, but you know cats can scratch very hard if they want to!"

"We will tell Raggedy when she comes in!" said the French doll, and then Fido went out to play with a neighbor dog.

So when Raggedy Ann had been returned to the nursery the dolls could hardly wait until Marcella had put on their nighties and left them for the night.

Then they told Raggedy Ann all about the kittens.

Raggedy Ann jumped from her bed and ran over to Fido's basket; he wasn't there.

Then Raggedy suggested that all the dolls go out to the barn and see the kittens. This they did easily, for the window was open and it was but a short jump to the ground.

They found Fido out near the barn watching a hole.

"I was afraid something might disturb them," he said, "for Mamma Cat went away about an hour ago."

All the dolls, with Raggedy Ann in the lead, crawled through the hole and ran to the basket.

Just as Raggedy Ann started to pick up one of the kittens there was a lot of howling and yelping and Fido came bounding through the hole with Mamma Cat behind him. When Mamma Cat caught up with Fido he would yelp.

When Fido and Mamma Cat had circled the barn two- or three-times Fido managed to find the hole and escape to the yard; then Mamma Cat came over to the basket and saw all the dolls.

"I'm s'prised at you, Mamma Cat!" said Raggedy Ann. "Fido has been watching your kittens for an hour while you were away. He wouldn't hurt them for anything!"

"I'm sorry, then," said Mamma Cat.

"You must trust Fido, Mamma Cat!" said Raggedy Ann, "because he loves you and anyone who loves you can be trusted!"

"That's so!" replied Mamma Cat. "Cats love mice, too, and I wish the mice trusted us more!"

The dolls all laughed at this joke.

"Have you told the folks up at the house about your dear little kittens?" Raggedy Ann asked.

"Oh, my, no!" exclaimed Mamma Cat. "At the last place I lived the people found out about my kittens and do you know, all the kittens disappeared! I intend keeping this a secret!"

"But all the folks at this house are very kindly people and would dearly love your kittens!" cried all the dolls.

"Let's take them right up to the nursery!" said Raggedy Ann. "And Mistress can find them there in the morning!"

"How lovely!" said all the dolls in chorus. "Do, Mamma Cat! Raggedy Ann knows, for she is stuffed with nice clean white cotton and is very wise!"

So after a great deal of persuasion, Mamma Cat finally consented. Raggedy Ann took two of the kittens and carried them to the house while Mamma Cat carried the other.

Raggedy Ann wanted to give the kittens her bed, but Fido, who was anxious to prove his affection, insisted that Mamma Cat and the kittens should have his nice soft basket.

(*Johnny Gruelle*)